Heirs to Dionysus

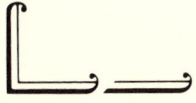

HEIRS TO DIONYSUS

A Nietzschean Current in Literary Modernism

John Burt Foster, Jr.

PRINCETON UNIVERSITY PRESS

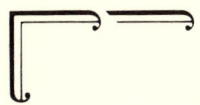

Copyright © 1981 by Princeton University Press
Published by Princeton University Press, Princeton, New Jersey
In the United Kingdom: Princeton University Press, Guildford, Surrey

All Rights Reserved
Library of Congress Cataloging in Publication Data will be
found on the last printed page of this book

This book has been composed in Linotron Bembo

Clothbound editions of Princeton University Press books
are printed on acid-free paper, and binding materials are
chosen for strength and durability

Printed in the United States of America by
Princeton University Press, Princeton, New Jersey

To Andrea Dimino

Contents

Acknowledgments

I should like to thank some of the many people who have helped this book along its way. At Yale University, where I first sensed the possibilities of the subject, I am especially grateful to Charles Feidelson, Jr., whose seminar on modernism was my finest experience in a classroom, and to Geoffrey Hartman, who patiently directed the dissertation in the course of which I discovered this topic. I also received valuable encouragement and advice from Franklin Baumer, Victor Erlich, Thomas Greene, R.W.B. Lewis, Lowry Nelson, Jr., and Edward and Elizabeth Zlotkowski.

At Stanford, where I conceived and wrote *Heirs to Dionysus*, I am indebted to Ian Watt for his judicious comments and suggestions at several stages of this project. Herbert Lindenberger shared his wide knowledge of recent developments in comparative literature, and was generous with his warm support. I must also thank Albert Guerard, founder of Stanford's program in Modern Thought and Literature, for the intellectual stimulus provided by the program and by two memorable conferences on myth, symbol, and culture and on the creative process. During my years at Stanford I was greatly heartened by the friendly interest and assistance of Bill Todd, George Dekker, John Bender, and Rob Polhemus. I would also like to thank J. G. Bell, Bill Chace, David Halliburton, Anne Mellor, Ron Rebholz, and Will Stone, who read all or parts of some version of the manuscript and gave me their candid reactions.

During the initial stages of the project, a fellowship from the German Academic Exchange Service made possible a year of research in the congenial surroundings of Konstanz and the Bodensee. I began a final draft with the aid of a Mellon Fellowship for junior faculty at Stanford. Both the

Gift Fund and the Research Fund of the English Department helped to cover the costs of preparing the manuscript, which were partly defrayed also by the Joseph Drown Research Fund of the Graduate School. I wish to thank John Loftis, Richard Scowcroft, and George Dekker, chairmen of the English Department, and W. Bliss Carnochan, Dean of the Graduate School, for making these funds available.

Many libraries have been helpful in the course of my research: in the first stages, the Sterling Library at Yale University and the fledgling library of the University of Konstanz; and later on, the libraries of the British Council, the Centre Culturel Français, and the Goethe Institut in Rome. I am also grateful to Andrea Schulman of the Widener Library, Harvard University, for clearing up a point about French translations of Nietzsche. Over the years the Stanford University Libraries have provided assistance of all kinds, and by giving me a study in the new Green Library made the last phase of the project much easier.

I am grateful to Princeton University Press, and especially to Margot Cutter, for assistance at all stages in the process of publication. I also wish to thank Josephine Guttadauro and Pauline Tooker for their skill in typing the manuscript and their willingness to work at short notice.

The dedication acknowledges my debts to a person who set high standards for my writing and whose Mediterranean spirit, as flavored by Brooklyn, gave zest to the years spent on the project. I only hope that I can contribute as much to her work.

Note on Translation, Annotation, and Abbreviation

In writing this book, I based my discussions of works written in foreign languages on a detailed knowledge of the original texts. However, because I am addressing an English-speaking audience, I give all quotations in English. I have consulted the readily available translations whenever they exist, and have profited especially from Walter Kaufmann's excellent renditions of Nietzsche. But often I have preferred to use my own wording, especially for difficult or ambiguous passages. On occasion I have had to supply omissions or rectify misconstructions. Attention is drawn to major corrections of this nature by a dagger following the page reference for the quotation.

For books that are cited many times, annotation has been simplified by placing references in parentheses immediately after the quotations. Page numbers follow the best widely accessible editions, as specified in the list below. With Nietzsche, whose books come in such a variety of formats that page references are useless, citations are limited to unit and/or aphorism numbers, designated by Roman and Arabic numerals respectively. Thus the parenthetical note for a quotation from "On Self-Overcoming," which is the twelfth chapter of the second part of *Thus Spoke Zarathustra*, would read Z:II, 12.

The list that follows provides a key to the system of abbreviations used for titles. The abbreviations are arranged in alphabetical order. For Nietzsche, prefaces or prologues, forewords, postscripts, and epilogues are indicated with the abbreviations Pr, F, Po, and E; while the sections in *Ecce Homo* in which Nietzsche reviews his own books are designated by the corresponding abbreviated titles. Thus a reference to the second section of Nietzsche's preface to *On the Genealogy of Morals* would be G:Pr, 2; the third section of his discussion of *Zarathustra* in *Ecce Homo* would be E:Z, 3.

The entries below include all the information needed for bibliographical purposes. The works by Nietzsche come from *Friedrich Nietzsche: Werke in drei Bänden*. Edited by Karl Schlechta. Munich: Carl Hanser Verlag, 1966.

A   Malraux, André. *Les Noyers de l'Altenburg (The Walnut Trees of the Altenburg)*. 1943; 1st French ed., Paris: Gallimard, 1948.

AC   Nietzsche, Friedrich. *Der Antichrist (The Antichrist)*.

AR   Lawrence, D. H. *Aaron's Rod*. 1922; rpt. New York: Viking Press, 1961.

B   Nietzsche, Friedrich. *Die Geburt der Tragödie (The Birth of Tragedy)*.

C   Nietzsche, Friedrich. *Der Fall Wagner (The Case of Wagner)*.

CL   Lawrence, D. H. *The Collected Letters of D. H. Lawrence*, in two volumes. Edited by Harry T. Moore. New York: Viking Press, 1962.

E   Nietzsche, Friedrich. *Ecce Homo*.

F   Mann, Thomas. *Doktor Faustus* in *Gesammelte Werke in zwölf Bänden*, vol. VI. n.p.: S. Fischer Verlag, 1960.

G   Nietzsche, Friedrich. *Zur Genealogie der Moral (On the Genealogy of Morals)*.

GE   Nietzsche, Friedrich. *Jenseits von Gut und Böse (Beyond Good and Evil)*.

GS   Nietzsche, Friedrich. *Die fröhliche Wissenschaft (The Gay Science)*.

H   Nietzsche, Friedrich. *Menschliches, Allzumenschliches (Human, All-Too-Human)*.

I   Gide, André. *L'Immoraliste (The Immoralist)* in *Romans*, pp. 365–472. Introduction by Maurice Nadeau and editorial apparatus by Yvonne Davet and

Jean-Jacques Thierry. Paris: Bibliothèque de la Pléiade.

J   Malraux, André. "D'Une Jeunesse Européenne" ("Concerning a European Youth"). A. Chamson, A. Malraux, J. Grenier, H. Petit, P. J. Jouve. *Écrits* ("Les Cahiers Verts." 70). Paris: Bernard Grasset, 1927, pp. 129-153.

K   Lawrence, D. H. *Kangaroo.* With an Introduction by Richard Aldington. 1923; rpt. New York: Viking Press, 1960.

L   Lawrence, D. H. *Women in Love.* With a Foreword by the Author. 1920; rpt. New York: Modern Library, n.d. (follows the first New York edition).

M   Malraux, André. *La Condition Humaine (Man's Fate)* in *Romans*, pp. 179-432. Paris: Bibliothèque de la Pléiade, 1964.

P   Lawrence, D. H. *Phoenix: The Posthumous Papers of D. H. Lawrence.* Edited and with an Introduction by Edward D. McDonald. 1936; rpt. New York: Viking Press, 1968. (Contains "German Books: Thomas Mann," pp. 308-313; "Study of Thomas Hardy," pp. 398-516; and "Surgery for the Novel—or a Bomb," pp. 517-520.)

PR   Gide, André. *Prétextes, suivi de Nouveaux prétextes.* 1903, 1911; rpt. Paris: Mercure de France, 1963.

S   Lawrence, D. H. *The Plumed Serpent (Quetzalcoatl).* With an Introduction by William York Tindall. 1926; rpt. New York: Vintage, n.d.

T   Nietzsche, Friedrich. *Götzendämmerung (Twilight of the Idols).*

TW   Malraux, André. *La Tentation de l'Occident (Temptation of the West).* Paris: Bernard Grasset, 1926.

V   Mann, Thomas. *Der Tod in Venedig (Death in Venice)* in *Gesammelte Werke in zwölf Bänden*, vol. VIII, pp. 444-525. n.p.: S. Fischer Verlag, 1960.

W:IX   Mann, Thomas. *Gesammelte Werke in zwölf Bänden*, vol. IX. n.p.: S. Fischer Verlag, 1960. (Contains

"Goethe as Representative of the Bourgeois Age," pp. 297-332; "Sufferings and Greatness of Richard Wagner," pp. 363-426; "Freud and the Future," pp. 478-501; "Dostoevsky—with Measure," pp. 656-674; and "Nietzsche's Philosophy in the Light of Our Experience," pp. 675-712.

W:X   Mann, Thomas. *Gesammelte Werke in zwölf Bänden*, vol. X. n.p.: S. Fischer Verlag, 1960. (Contains "On Spengler's Doctrine," pp. 172-180; "*Si le grain ne meurt . . .*," pp. 711-721; and " 'André Gide' by Albert J. Guerard," pp. 802-810.)

W:XI   Mann, Thomas. *Die Entstehung des Doktor Faustus (The Story of a Novel)* in *Gesammelte Werke in zwölf Bänden*, vol. XI, pp. 145-301. n.p.: S. Fischer Verlag, 1960.

W:XII   Mann, Thomas. *Gesammelte Werke in zwölf Bänden*, vol. XII. n.p.: S. Fischer Verlag, 1960. (Contains *Betrachtungen eines Unpolitischen* [*Reflections of an Apolitical Man*], pp. 9-589).

WP   Nietzsche, Friedrich. *Der Wille zur Macht (The Will to Power)*.

Z   Nietzsche, Friedrich. *Also sprach Zarathustra (Thus Spoke Zarathustra)*.

Heirs to Dionysus

Introduction

Shortly after he went insane in 1889, Friedrich Nietzsche became an international celebrity. His writings, which had previously gained the attention of only a few intellectuals, became the object of scandalized disgust, of passionate admiration, and—more rarely—of thoughtful scrutiny. Anyone who came to intellectual maturity in Europe and much of the Americas between the 1890s and the 1930s would have had trouble avoiding contact, either direct or indirect, with his work. This widespread interest in Nietzsche has had important repercussions outside his chosen field of philosophy. In literature it coincides with the rise and full development of a distinctive kind of writing now usually known as modernism.

Like all names for literary movements, this term has a tendency to dissolve when an unambiguous, univocal definition is called for; it is easy to imagine another Lovejoy demanding a discrimination of modernisms.[1] But perhaps the term will prove fruitful if we take as its irreducible core of meaning an exacerbated feeling of being modern. The modernist has a sense of having made a break with the traditions of the recent past that is more drastic than would have occurred in a continuous process of growth and development. This sense of a break, in turn, has two aspects which individual writers can emphasize in varying ways. In their creation of forms modernists are radically experimental, whereas in their thinking or values they are radically questioning of accepted orthodoxies. This attitude has not, of course, been limited to any particular epoch, so that it would be quite proper to speak of the "modernism" of Petronius or Villon, to see it as a perennial quality that crops up throughout literary history. But modernism in this sense does appear with increasing frequency during the nineteenth century and culminates in novelists like Joyce, Proust, Kafka, and Faulkner and in poets like Rilke, Valéry, Eliot, and Pound. According to this view, the movement is a Continental phenomenon as well as simply an Anglo-American one, and the term "modernist" becomes a period concept referring primarily to the early twentieth century. The important but vexing problem of how or whether to distinguish it from late nineteenth-century symbolism need not concern us here.

That Nietzsche's writings should have an affinity with this movement is not surprising. He was, after all, a philosopher with strong artistic and literary interests. His lifelong involvement with Wagner and his occasional attempts at composing music come to mind first. But he was also a brilliant literary scholar and became a professor of classical philology at the unheard-of age of twenty-four. Even after turning to philosophy he remained acutely sensitive to style and form; he had hopes of making his writings a landmark of German prose, and he wrote poems that regularly appear in collections of German poetry. Nietzsche's marked concern with expression has led twentieth-century philosophers of the austere analytic school to dismiss him as "merely literary."

But a far more suggestive and deeply ingrained affinity with the modernists emerges from the dominant mood of his writings. It would be hard to imagine a more intense and uncompromising modernism in either form or content. His stylistic experiments, which range from the tightly packed phrases and abrupt shifts of perspective in his aphoristic books to the use of image and story to convey his ideas in *Thus Spoke Zarathustra* break sharply with what he saw as the plodding tradition of German philosophical writing. His thinking is nothing if not radically distrustful of continuity, since he envisions a total revaluation of values and looks on almost all of recorded history with suspicion.

Nietzsche's sense of modernity is especially strong in the period just before his collapse, when he remarks of his most recent work that "The newness, the *courage* of innovation is really of the first rank."[2] He can make the following claim for the importance of his accomplishments as a stylist: "That the Germans have even been able to bear their philosophers . . . gives no small idea of German notions of elegance. . . . One must learn to *write*—but at this point I would become a complete riddle for German readers" (T:VIII, 7). He considers the tendencies of his thought to be equally unprecedented: "One day my name will be associated with the memory of something tremendous—a crisis without equal on earth, the most profound collision of conscience, a decision that was conjured up *against* everything that had been believed, demanded, hallowed so far" (E:IV, 1). Nietzsche was to become a commanding presence for the modernists because he had expressed some of their deepest impulses so fully and so pointedly.

But to analyze this impact by invoking a general mood of modernity does not take us very far. The concept of the modern has a troubling relativity: with the passage of time, the excitingly new can lose its novelty and become accepted, even obvious. As long as we argue on this level, we find ourselves dealing with little more than a highly fugitive cultural mystique. Hence, though Nietzsche has kept most of his power to astonish and disturb, we must look for more specific and more substantial definitions, both of his contribution to modernism and of modernism itself. Such, in the very broadest terms, was the impetus for this study. But in taking a fresh and more searching look at this philosopher's relevance to early twentieth-century literature, I discovered a narrower and less diffuse phenomenon. Nietzsche's impact on some of the best work by a loosely knit group of writers throughout Europe had been surprisingly extensive and deep. Eventually I learned to see him as the fountainhead for an explicitly Nietzschean current within the modernist movement. The consequences of this perception, for understanding both Nietzsche and the writers, were so far-reaching that I abandoned my original project of trying to determine Nietzsche's general significance. And this new way of seeing things had a further advantage: it opened up areas of inquiry that promised to have precisely that substance and specificity that I had sought from the beginning. Such are the final dimensions of this study, though I do intend to return to the question of Nietzsche and modernism as a whole in my conclusion.

My approach differs in three important respects from previous attempts to consider Nietzsche's relation to literature. First, as my recent remarks have begun to suggest, I shall be stressing cases of direct contact. The numerous general discussions of how Nietzsche typifies various tendencies in the sensibility of our age certainly have their place. They do serve to stimulate debate about the significance of his work. But broad analogies and intuitive overviews can distort the meaning of any writer; and with Nietzsche especially, it is all too easy to separate some dramatic or suggestive turn of phrase from the ideas and values it originally expressed. There is a built-in danger of becoming loosely emblematic in criticizing him. In *Dionysus and the City*, when Monroe Spears begins the description of one of his two "symbols" for modernism with Nietzsche's concept of the Dionysian, he sacrifices most of the fascinating nuances and complexity that this concept was to have in the actual development of modernism.[3] Similarly, when Conor Cruise O'Brien chooses a Nietzschean phrase as his title in *The Suspecting Glance*, and then turns it against its inventor, his critique of the philosopher's political attitudes rests on some notorious aphorisms publicized by the Nazis.[4] He neglects the possibility of broader responses from more careful readers who were not committed to a fixed ideology. My focus in this study on cases of direct contact will restore precision to a subject that has too often invited overly broad generalizations.

In addition, direct contact brings out one distinctive feature of Nietzsche's effect on literature. His role contrasts markedly with that of figures like Kierkegaard and Freud, both often mentioned as spokesmen for modernist concerns, yet neither of them as intimately involved in the careers of writers from 1890 to the 1930s. Only around 1910 did psychoanalysis begin to excite widespread interest, and though Kierkegaard became a force in central Europe around the same time, he had to wait until 1940 in the English-speaking countries. A striking confirmation of this point would be Thomas Mann's belated shocks of recognition on discovering Freud and then Kierkegaard; by contrast, Nietzsche had been a central intellectual experience for him since before the turn of the century.[5] Among modern thinkers, then, the German philosopher was in an especially good position to affect writers directly. The vogue for his work ran through the whole period, increasing the likelihood of his becoming an active presence for them from their formative years onward. This drama of direct contact needs to be part of any account of how Nietzsche contributed to literature during the heyday of modernism.

As a second difference from previous studies, I have been careful to do justice to the international dimensions of Nietzsche's impact. Some years ago, when Crane Brinton reviewed the scholarship on the subject, he remarked on the tendency for single-author, single-culture titles like "Nietzsche and X," or "Nietzsche in Y."[6] This tendency distorts the true scope both of interest in Nietzsche and of the modernist movement. The topic demands the broader perspective provided by the methods of comparative literature. More specifically, I have in mind the willingness of comparatists to explore cultural affiliations that go beyond narrow conceptions of "the" national literary tradition. I also admire their insistence on confronting writers and texts in their native language; translation falsifies essential data, and so I have worked with original editions throughout this study. And, finally, comparatists have often carried their cross-cultural studies beyond exclusively literary relationships into the area that will be our main concern, the interplay between literature and issues from the history of ideas, philosophy, and intellectual history. I have had three great models for this kind of scholarship—Erich Auerbach's *Mimesis*, with its broad international scope and philological precision; René Wellek's *A History of Modern Criticism*, which is equally wide-ranging and rigorous as it relates literary criticism to the history of ideas in the later eighteenth and the nineteenth centuries; and Richard Ellmann and Charles Feidelson's *The Modern Tradition*, which emphasizes the international scope of modernism and places it among a great variety of recent intellectual developments.

Of course, it must be admitted that as we move into the eighties even these generous conceptions of comparative literature might seem a bit limited. Some people are now seeking, not a Western, but a world-wide sense of the international; and others are engaged in ambitious reassessments of the intellectual foundations for literary study. In this latter effort, in particular, Nietzsche has a role by virtue of his impact on figures like Heidegger, Derrida, and their followers. But my investigation of his significance for the modernists has taught me that the comparative methods I have outlined are the most suitable. My subject is largely a Western phenomenon, though we shall see that it includes attempts at portraying cultures like the East Asian, the Islamic, or the pre-Columbian. Nor, for the most part, do the writers I examine draw on the Nietzsche who has helped raise questions about the very nature of language and writing.

Since many of these questions originate with recent French thinkers, it will clarify my aims if I refer to one of them in more detail. Throughout *The Order of Things*, Michel Foucault draws on Nietzsche for crucial insights into the problems and prospects of modern intellectual life.[7] Yet these insights mesh only in the most general way, if at all, with the issues I shall be discussing. This discrepancy occurs because Nietzsche is a remarkably Protean thinker; his impact changes continually, and I am dealing with one particular phase in its development. Foucault comes from another phase—I am very reluctant to call it "postmodernist," and it may best be seen as a more philosophical, less literary phase—yet in commenting on Nietzsche he shows little awareness of the major shift in *modes* of interpretation that separates him from some of his predecessors. This is ironic, since in other contexts he has analyzed these shifts so impressively. In fact, should some readers see parallels between my conception of intellectual history and Foucault's notion of an "archeology," I would not be displeased. Just as *The Order of Things* uncovers the characteristic but profoundly different conceptions of economics, biology, and language study that prevailed in the classical period and on into the nineteenth century, so I shall be describing the Nietzsche of the literary modernists, who is not the Nietzsche of recent French vintage. But whereas the earlier stages of Foucault's disciplines may now seem quaint, the modernists developed a detailed and reasonably consistent interpretation of the philosopher that often reached further into the concerns and motives of his work than the post-structuralists do.

But even when I adopt comparative methods by drawing on several major literatures and weighing intellectual factors, I have neglected the most important feature of Nietzsche's impact on early twentieth-century writers. This interaction of literature and ideas takes place *within* some of their best imaginative work. This is the different mode of interpretation overlooked by Foucault, and it is also the third and most serious deficiency of previous scholarship, which—when it discusses Nietzsche in relation to a group of writers—has tended to emphasize biographical questions and explicit recorded opinions.[8] Typically, the student learns the circumstances of a writer's first encounters with Nietzsche, and then gets a summary of how he referred to the philosopher throughout his career. Such information is useful as far as it goes, but it fails to address the most important issues. How do these facts illuminate the writer's creative work, or do they have any bearing on it at all? Could there have been a shift or a widening in the writer's interest in Nietzsche once he set out to write a novel or a poem? Is he necessarily aware of the full extent of the philosopher's impact on him? And, above all, shouldn't imaginative writings be given the first priority by the critic? It is pertinent at this point to recall T. S. Eliot's famous dictum on the value of attitudes expressed in art as compared with critical opinions: "In one's prose reflexions one may legitimately be occupied with ideals, whereas in the writing of verse one can only deal with actuality."[9] Or, to take a more pointed statement, we might turn again to Thomas Mann. Despite the many comments he made about Nietzsche in essays and letters, he felt that his response was so complex that it could never be adequately rendered by discursive means. The only proper vehicle would be art, with its far richer expressive resources. So he insists that his attitude toward Nietzsche "might speak out of the depths of a creative work; to write a critical essay about it seems to me an indiscretion, to put it mildly" (W:IX, 657). In such a case, no mere record of opinions could hope to do justice to the wealth of meanings that can be generated by imaginative literature.

Accordingly, the main task of this book will be to interpret major literary works. Such an emphasis does not conflict with my insistence on direct contact, but serves instead to bring out its most important features. To be sure, as I focus on the development of artistic careers in those periods when Nietzsche had become a powerful factor, I cannot ignore the expressed opinions and biographical data that help document a writer's involvement. But the climactic moments of direct contact occur when writers are pushing their capacities for expression to the limit. By and large these moments come in imaginative writings, and so our primary concern has to be the critical interpretation of literary works.[10]

Because high literary achievement has been my leading criterion, this study centers on three novels whose excellence has been widely recognized quite apart from their connection with Nietzsche. *Women in Love*, *Man's Fate*, and *Doctor Faustus* display a readiness for intellectual exploration and a technical resourcefulness that make it natural to mention their authors alongside the eight classic modernists I mentioned above. And yet, despite this high merit, the conception and meaning of these novels are heavily dependent on the keen interest their authors had in Nietzsche. So great was his stimulus, in fact, that when I set out to reinterpret the books in the light of Nietzsche's impact, I discovered that he had strongly affected them in several major aspects. As a result, I had to use a variety of approaches—and to write several separate, though interconnected essays—in order to do justice to the range of formal and thematic initiatives to which he had contributed. It is with these masterpieces that Lawrence, Malraux, and Mann demonstrate the breadth and force of a specifically Nietzschean current in modern literature.

In focusing on these three achievements, I do not separate them from the careers of their authors. With each writer, I have looked back to see how Nietzsche could have become such a massive presence in some of their best creative work. What were the conditions of their earliest contacts with the philosopher? How was it that he became not just an intellectual force, but a literary one? I answer these preliminary questions in the course of my introductory remarks on the writers. But I pay much more attention to how their interest in Nietzsche had repercussions elsewhere in their careers. The nature of the philosopher's impact is best appreciated in the context of other creative work, and at times the most explicit evidence on the character of an author's long-term preoccupation with him can only be found there.

The most instructive story takes different forms with different figures. In Lawrence's case, in Chapter IV, I follow the continuities in his art and the growing willingness to confront Nietzsche directly, along with the fresh departures and mounting difficulties that mark his novels after *Women in Love* and which come to a head with his Mexican novel *The Plumed Serpent*. With Malraux, in Chapter V, I consider the transitions from Nietzschean ideas to fictive presentation that make *The Temptation of the West* a sketchy anticipation of the world depicted in *Man's Fate*. But I give more emphasis to the major changes in attitude toward Nietzsche that help make his unfinished last novel, *The Walnut Trees of the Altenburg*, such an interesting new departure. With Mann, the crucial moment comes with his classic short novel *Death in Venice*, which resolves a major dilemma in his early career—the problem of how to exploit Nietzschean material in fiction. I take up this story in its proper chronological place, in Chapter III; but it is also important because it points ahead to that major work of Mann's old age, *Doctor Faustus*, which I discuss in Chapter VI not merely because it comes after Lawrence and Malraux in time but because it represents the culmination of the Nietzschean current in literary modernism.

By including additional works by Lawrence, Malraux, and Mann, I have been able to examine an important topic for comparatists—the various shocks of recognition that pull these writers together in spite of their differing literary traditions and their unique ways of handling Nietzsche. Shortly before Lawrence started the first draft of *Women in Love*, he read *Death in Venice* and responded to it in a revealing way; Malraux, in turn, made some telling remarks about *The Plumed Serpent* in the midst of writing *Man's Fate*. No such direct relations join Mann and Malraux, but they did share several significant cultural experiences. Both of them encountered the work of Oswald Spengler, the cultural historian and self-proclaimed Nietzschean, to whom they referred pointedly in *The Temptation of the West* and *Doctor Faustus* as they developed their own very different versions of the philosopher. Mann and Malraux also shared an interest in Gide's fine short novel *The Immoralist*, itself a product—and a very early one—of Nietzsche's literary impact. This book alerted Malraux to the very possibility of using fiction to explore the implications of Nietzsche's philosophy, and it had a decisive role in reinforcing basic tendencies in Mann's imagination in the period between *Death in Venice* and *Doctor Faustus*. Indeed, so striking are the similarities in structure between *The Immoralist* and *Death in Venice*, similarities that testify to their authors' close involvement with Nietzsche, that in Chapter III I have supplemented my discussion of Mann's story with a stage-by-stage comparison to Gide's. These two works are enlightening examples of an early, pre-war phase in the literary appropriation of the philosopher. The masterpieces on which I focus in the following three chapters illustrate a later, more complicated development that falls between the two world wars.

For further insight into Nietzsche's impact, I shall at times be looking beyond this circle of works and writers. In the Anglo-Irish poet William Butler Yeats and in the poet and novelist Andrei Bely, one of the leading figures in twentieth-century Russian literature before the advent of socialist realism, I found several interesting parallels and fresh perspectives that put my subject in sharper relief. It seemed better to mention these points in passing since detailed treatment of Yeats and Bely would have brought needless complications or repetitions to my argument. Yeats's response to Nietzsche by way of Blake introduces a "layering effect" of the kind I discuss in Chapter VI, where Mann's prior interest in Nietzsche guides his appropriation of other figures; to do justice to Yeats and Nietzsche would, therefore, have required an unwieldy digression on Blake. Much of Bely involved an unnecessary recapitulation of issues I had already addressed in the young Gide and Mann.

Undoubtedly my sweep could have been even wider. In omitting the entire genre of drama, or poets other than Yeats, or a leading novelist like the Austrian Robert Musil, I am far from thinking them unsuitable topics. But as I proceeded with this study, I discovered that the writers I have chosen—for all the differences among them—formed a coherent group in one important respect. From their separate perspectives, their works converge on a set of important problems in Nietzsche and do a great deal to illuminate them. It is this coherence, much more than the interconnections between the individual writers, that brings them together as an identifiable group within modernism. I am not denying that other aspects of Nietzsche might also have been fruitful for other writers; I therefore emphasize that I am working with *a* Nietzschean current. But if we view modernism as both Anglo-American and Continental, this current was undoubtedly the most important: not only do the writers reinforce each other, but Lawrence, Gide, Malraux, and Mann have also been preeminent figures in their own literatures and have had significant international reputations, notably in the United States.

Since Nietzsche is the point of origin for the developments to be traced in the writers, he has a crucial role to play in this book. He is, as I indicated in my remarks on Foucault, a peculiarly elusive figure, one who can be interpreted in a great, even bewildering variety of ways. As a result, it soon became apparent that I would have to provide a connected, close analysis of what he looked like from the perspective of this group of writers. How the modernists read Nietzsche has never received adequate attention. When philosophers or historians discuss his significance, they view him in terms of their own disciplines, and the Nietzsche I have come to know shows up on the periphery, if at all. Literary critics tend to focus on isolated points or broad analogies. This kind of commentary reduces Nietzsche's work to a hodge-podge of suggestive insights and striking phrases—to thinking that is a stimulating but confused medley of fresh approaches, daring concepts, and controversial issues; to writing that loosely joins vivid images, pointed character sketches, and obscurely fascinating myths. In all this I could see some elements of the coherent and sharply contoured image of Nietzsche that fascinated the writers, but the connections and articulations and nuances were missing. And, of course, the evidence provided by outstanding literary works had been largely disregarded. Therefore, in my second chapter, I will make up for this omission by describing the themes and methods that formed Nietzsche's legacy to this part of the modernist movement.

Concerning these themes and methods, I should stress that

the title of this book does not reflect a narrow interest in what Nietzsche meant by the Dionysian. I have singled out Dionysus because this mythic figure best captures all aspects of the fascination writers felt for him. In its very broadest implications, it can be identified with Nietzsche himself, who signed several letters with the name Dionysus shortly after his collapse into insanity. Throughout his career, it was one of the most richly suggestive of the key words he used to guide his thinking and to tie its various concerns together. Dionysus contributes to each of the four topics that make up the Nietzschean current among literary modernists: at first the polarized counterpart to Apollo in *The Birth of Tragedy*, it then expands to take in his basic outlook as a psychologist, his sense of approaching a cultural turning point of millennial dimensions, and his proclamation of the will to power.

Before we can turn to these topics, however, we need to consider yet another implication of this mythic figure. Above all, Dionysus epitomized the open-ended spirit in which Nietzsche hoped to be read. He wanted his teachings to be dynamic in their effect, free to be developed and refined, or even to be contradicted. So it is that the hero of his personal favorite among his own books tells his disciples not to become blind followers—"Go away from me and resist Zarathustra"—and Nietzsche underscores the point by repeating the passage in his autobiography (Z:I, 22; E:Pr, 4). And in the same spirit he calls on Dionysus twice, addressing him as "the genius of the heart from whose touch everyone walks away richer . . . not as blessed and oppressed by alien goods, but richer in himself, newer to himself than ever before" (GE, 295; E:III, 6). With these appeals from Nietzsche for independent readers, we have come to an important problem I have so far avoided even naming, since it is so easily misconceived and misunderstood. That is the problem of influence, to which we shall turn in the first chapter. This problem deserves careful scrutiny if we are to understand the full significance of being an heir to Dionysus.

I

Influence as Transformation, Nietzsche as Influence

Influence has played a key conceptual role in many treatments of direct contact or close relationship between writers. One thinks immediately of the collections of sources for medieval and Renaissance authors that appeared in the later nineteenth and early twentieth centuries. In such cases, influence usually becomes a relatively simple, immediate response in which a later writer imitates or elaborates on something characteristic or original in the work of an earlier writer. In a well-known essay on Nietzsche's importance for twentieth-century German writers and thinkers, Erich Heller has proposed a similar relationship: "He is to them all—whether or not they know and acknowledge it (and most of them do)—what St. Thomas Aquinas was to Dante: the categorical interpreter of a world which they contemplate poetically or philosophically without ever radically upsetting its Nietzschean structure."[1] I disagree with this statement, perhaps because Nietzsche's influence looks very different from an international perspective. I shall comment on the analogy with Aquinas later on; for the moment we should notice another point of Heller's. Although he allows for situations where an author might not know that he is drawing on Nietzschean ideas, he insists that the author never seriously disturbs the basic tendency of those ideas. Nietzsche has become a source, and the critic is invited to consider instances of imitation, or at most of elaboration.

This categorical version of influence clashes sharply with Nietzsche's own aspirations, with their emphasis on dynamic processes of transformation and revision. And, in fact, without a recognition of these factors, it is impossible to see the full dimensions of his impact. Here several twentieth-century attempts to rethink the problem of influence become relevant. As part of his theoretical program in *Literature as System*, Claudio Guillén has made an effective critique of source studies and what he calls the "concept of transfer."[2] Unfortunately, he has little to offer beyond this valuable negative warning. He does touch on the importance of situations where "no one-to-one relationship exists," on the need for assessing the "textual function" of an influence once it enters a literary work, on the frequency of misreading and reinterpretation in one author's response to another.[3] But Guillén's main purpose is to restrict the problem of influence to the writer's biography or to the origins of a work, and thus to separate it from the aesthetic appreciation of the completed work. This disjunction is no doubt useful and important in many cases, but it does not do justice to Nietzsche's direct contact with his literary heirs, where impact and art are so thoroughly implicated with each other that I have had to treat them as a single process.

The issue of transformation comes to the fore in the work of Harold Bloom and the Russian formalists, who have buttressed their somewhat divergent theoretical insights with detailed studies of specific cases. Concentrating on English and American romantic poetry and its modern aftermath, Bloom has developed a doctrine that emphatically questions the subordination of the follower to the predecessor: "Poetic Influence—when it involves two strong, authentic poets—always proceeds by a misreading of the prior poet, an act of creative correction that is actually and necessarily a misinterpretation."[4] I have found no basis for Bloom's special categories for separate stages of influence in a poet's life history. But his general position does conform with Nietzsche's insistence on an open-ended dynamism, and Bloom has in fact acknowledged an intellectual debt to Nietzsche.[5] Moreover, in highlighting the problem of misreading, Bloom brings up an issue I shall consider later in this chapter, when I turn from general theories of influence to the main features of Nietzsche's impact in itself. Psychological pressures are an important factor in influence as transformation: it may indeed be impossible for someone committed to a creative project to take a balanced view of a previous writer's distinctive achievement.

A more pointedly relevant theory of transformation may be found among the Russian formalists of the 1920s. Since the advent of structuralism, their work has become widely known in the English-speaking world, and yet their view of influence remains insufficiently appreciated. Translators have naturally selected short, rather sketchy programmatic statements, and so have popularized their doctrines of polemical interaction, the struggle between styles, parody, or literary evolution—where this last term means drastic modification and deformation more than gradual change. But the real accomplishments of the formalists came when they took up specific cases of influence. Here even the essays available in English, such as Tynyanov's work on how the young Dostoevsky struggled to supplant a predecessor like Gogol or Eichenbaum's on the young Tolstoy's similar relationship to Rousseau and Sterne, are misleading. Much more decisive for my own thinking are currently untranslated books like Eichenbaum's *Lev Tolstoy*, when it investigates Tolstoy's complicated path through the fast-moving intellectual world of Russia in the late 1850s and the 1860s, or Tynyanov's *Arkhaisty i Novatory* with its detailed presentation of conflicting literary groups in the age of Pushkin.[6] Their remarkable precision and thoroughness have shown how far one can go with notions of influence that stress reworking rather than continuity. I would fault them only for paying too much attention to discursive statements by the writers and not enough to their imaginative works. Meanwhile, as they focus on quarrels and disagreements, they emphasize deliberate reinterpretation instead of misreading; they therefore highlight the role of intellectual and ideological factors, factors that are especially valuable for understanding Nietzsche's impact on writers. Since Nietzsche was, after all, a thinker, Bloom's category of "authentic poet" is not fully applicable, as Bloom himself notes when he prefaces his book on Yeats with the remark that Nietzsche's influence presents "critical problems of another kind."[7]

But both Bloom and the formalists have succeeded in showing that influence necessarily involves innovation. They ask that a critic consider how a writer transformed Nietzsche in any number of ways, such as revision or critique, the expansion or contraction of leading concepts, the absorption of motifs into new structures, and inspired misreadings or willful failures of understanding. Hence my emphasis on metaphors of inheritance, which help to highlight these dynamic possibilities: if some people seek piously to preserve a legacy, others take possession of what a previous generation gives them and exploit it for their own purposes. Among those of Nietzsche's heirs who understood him best, this second attitude was to be almost mandatory.

And yet, despite the great value of allowing for influence as transformation, there is one major problem with Bloom and the Russian formalists. In discussing the affiliations between writers, they rely on overly rigid schemes of cause and effect, schemes which are better suited to the simpler imitative notion of influence. Dynamism brings with it an inherent uncertainty, for how is the critic to prove that a character, image, or thought in a given work is the product of a specific influence? The cases where very little transformation has taken place will be obvious, but could just as easily be viewed as imitative. Elsewhere one faces a number of awkward possibilities. First, the data provided by the text itself will be treacherous: in a major work that has successfully gone beyond its sources, all conclusive evidence of a starting point will have vanished. At most the critic will find suggestive traces, but often only silence. Second, even if the writer has discussed how he arrived at the finished text, his testimony is open to question. For example, as I shall show in Chapter VI, Mann's account of his work on *Doctor Faustus* is exceptionally detailed, yet it is often ambiguous or even misleading about influences and basic motives. Finally, there is the problem of multiple determination. If one accepts Coleridge's analysis of the creative imagination as an "esemplastic power" that fuses diverse elements into a new unity, one must be prepared to find several different sources behind any character, image, or thought.[8] To insist on some single factor might well seem arbitrary, but to locate all the factors and assess their relative importance would be impossible.

Because the model of unambiguous cause and effect leads to difficulties like these, I prefer a somewhat more flexible concept for dealing with literary relationships where transformation has a leading role. The works and authors discussed in this book are best seen in terms of a cluster-effect or constellation; one discovers a network of problems, themes, and attitudes emanating from Nietzsche which makes it natural to consider all these figures together. But composing this picture necessarily involves informed conjecture, probability, illuminating comparison, and interpretation. Such methods depend on the perspective of the person using them and will fail to give full objective certainty in all cases. The outline of the Big Dipper, the creation of observers with one set of expectations, does not exist in itself. But few skywatchers through the ages have resisted placing constellations in the heavens.

This approach is far from authorizing total relativism. Instead, it takes account once again of a major tenet of Nietzsche's, whose careful scrutiny of cause-and-effect reasoning offers useful guidance to the critic. On the one hand, Nietzsche warns that such reasoning is simply a habit of mind projected onto phenomena, that it often serves to reduce the disquietingly strange and original to the more familiar. But he also acknowledges that cause and effect does at least give an order and coherence to data. Like other ways of explaining a highly varied world, it is essentially fictive and provisional. These reflections are doubly relevant to my more specialized concerns. They suggest that we should not overvalue cause-and-effect reasoning, since it is itself not objective. At the same time, however, Nietzsche has justified the broader human need to place things in relationship and find coherence 'without authorizing an arbitrary and overly subjective approach: his insistence on the great diversity of phenomena makes it impossible to be satisfied with free associations and fuzzy conclusions. The critic who wishes to do justice to this variety must be certain that he is dealing with firm relationships, ones that will support detailed and precise comparisons and analyses. Therefore, as I charted this constellation of writers, I have aimed to be very specific in showing connections even when it has been impossible to prove cause and effect.

These remarks have set forth my general approach to the uncertainties that are the result of transformed sources and inadequate authorial testimony. But more needs to be said about the Coleridgean issue of multiple determination. In large measure, I have been able to avoid this problem because this book concentrates on multiple consequences. Unlike Bloom, who must distinguish several strands of influence in one writer when he studies Yeats's affiliations with the romantic movement, I am charting a number of trajectories away from Nietzsche.[9] Normally, therefore, I must focus on varied interpretations of the philosopher and not on the confluence of sources in any given writer.

But I should add immediately that these concerns do not mean that I reject the possibility of other constellations within modernist literature. Frederick J. Hoffman and John Vickery have done as much in their studies of English-language authors in relation to Freud and Frazer,[10] and it would be possible to do the same with Dostoevsky, Baudelaire, and others. Nor, more narrowly, do I deny the presence of factors other than Nietzsche in the works of the authors I discuss. But the story I have to tell would become entirely too complicated if I were to analyze such factors at any length. I assume that sympathetic readers can make allowances for my brief references to other thinkers like Marx, Freud, and

Plato, to other writers like Dostoevsky and Oscar Wilde, to
historical events like World War I and the rise of Fascism,
and to biographical issues like Malraux's trip to Indochina,
and the premature death of Mann's two sisters. All of these
varied kinds of additional connections are relevant in specific
cases, and in general I shall identify them as contributing
factors when the occasion arises. My main concern, of
course, will be to assess the Nietzschean impetus.

I have had to be equally brief with another, and especially
ticklish, aspect of multiple determination. There are writers
and thinkers who had an active part in Nietzsche's intellectual life, and then went on to affect his literary heirs. As a
result, it can be hard to distinguish the philosopher as influence from the philosopher as intermediary. This problem is
most acute with Mann, who shared many of Nietzsche's en-
thusiasms, but it also arises with Malraux's debt to Hegel,
with Gide's to Goethe, and with Lawrence's to Wagner or
Schopenhauer. It would be difficult to decide how much
Hegel's views on Asia as a cultural entity collaborate with
Nietzsche's in coloring Malraux's presentation of the East
after his youthful work. Similarly, the "Dionysian titanic"
images of oceanic immensity in *Death in Venice* could just as
easily come from Mann's response to visions of nature in
Schopenhauer. In these and other instances, I have chosen to
isolate the Nietzschean element, a simplification imposed by
my project of following one current through several exemplary modernist careers in place of showing the convergence
of many currents in one work. When I do mention Goethe,
Hegel, Schopenhauer, or Wagner, these references will serve
mainly to indicate Nietzsche's special attitude toward these
predecessors as he develops the aspects of his thought that
would later fascinate his literary heirs.

But what has happened to the notion of influence, now
that we have moved from traditional source studies to the
Russian formalists, weighed the contributions of Heller,
Guillén, and Bloom, and developed the insights of Coleridge
and Nietzsche himself? Clearly the term has acquired a new

breadth and complexity. It must mean a great deal more than imitation and strict causality, though later we shall see how these narrower concepts do account for one part of even Nietzsche's influence. But to understand this topic in its entirety requires an eye for dynamic transformations and a sophisticated acceptance of uncertainty and multiple determination. Even as the critic traces a single pattern in one area of the literary firmament, he cannot help being aware of how many other patterns crisscross his field of vision. Not that the pattern he has fixed on is arbitrary. I am simply insisting that, with the exception of a few clear and sometimes thuddingly obvious examples, any writer's influence will be joined with many other elements that shift from case to case. To isolate one line of development, therefore, involves more than cause-and-effect reasoning; it requires critical finesse and a sense for accumulating significance.

□

My candor about the uncertainties of influence in no way qualifies Nietzsche's overwhelming importance for a group of writers in the early twentieth century. The quick sketch that follows will establish the extraordinary intensity of their interest in him, an interest that is equally notable because it directly nourishes their developing literary vocations. It was my discovery of these strong responses that led me to shift from the rather diffuse question of Nietzsche and modernism to the story of how direct contact inspired ambitious artistic projects. But my sketch will do more than confirm Nietzsche's major importance, and so set a limit to the ambiguities of transformative influence. It will also provide revealing information on several special features of his influence in itself which I shall be discussing in the rest of this chapter—the problem of idea and image, and the shift in attitudes that changes Nietzsche from a model to a rival.

Direct contact begins with the immediate excitement of discovery, which speaks out most strikingly in comments by writers outside the inner circle treated in this book. In Moscow around the turn of the century, as Andrei Bely tells it in his autobiography, he experienced "a simply crazed enthusiasm for Nietzsche" that went to such lengths that he turned to *The Birth of Tragedy* for help in understanding his parents' unhappy marriage. But Nietzsche also encouraged his literary ambitions: he was "the creator of the most vivid images, the theoretic or esthetic meaning of which was revealed only through creative emulation and not simply by following his thought. . . . I saw in him . . . an artist of genius."[11] Bely's "creative emulation" of Nietzsche resulted in a career that produced *Petersburg*, perhaps the most hauntingly original novel in twentieth-century Russian literature. In 1902, when Yeats first read Nietzsche at the urging of his American friend John Quinn, he found him to be "a strong enchanter" who was so fascinating that he injured his eyes in reading him. Soon he began to criticize his own most recent work for being "too lyrical, too full of aspirations after remote things, too full of desires"; in looking forward to becoming more creative, he appealed to Nietzsche's example.[12] Two decades later, when Yeats had reached the height of his powers as a poet, he would assign to Nietzsche the role of "The Forerunner" in the system of thought that he expounds in *A Vision*.[13]

Gide's and Mann's discoveries of the philosopher had occurred some years earlier and were somewhat more reserved in tone. To be sure, when Gide first reacted publicly to early translations of Nietzsche into French, he hailed his "splendid vigor which brings enthusiasm" (PR, 81). But he went on to remark that the philosopher's main value was to have settled certain preliminary theoretical issues so that writers could concentrate on their proper activity, the concrete problems of their art: "It is from this point of departure that we must create and that the work of art is possible" (PR, 85). Despite the sharp distinction between philosophy and literature, indicating an effort to keep Nietzsche at a distance, Gide's use of the first person is noteworthy; it suggests the importance of these remarks for his own activity as a writer, which at the time meant his work on *The Immoralist*. Thomas Mann was even younger than Gide when he first read Nietzsche. When he looked back to this period just before the turn of the century, he could sum it up by saying that "it owed an infinite amount to him" (W:IX, 712). Later on, the history of the composition of two of Mann's most famous novels suggests the intimate connection between his art and Nietzsche. Having begun *The Magic Mountain* before the outbreak of World War I, he interrupted work at an early stage to write *Reflections of an Apolitical Man*, a wartime searching of conscience that was greatly to enrich the novel when he finally returned to it. So saturated are these essays with Nietzsche that Mann shows a certain uneasiness and apologizes for seeing him "everywhere and only him" (W:XII, 497). But a quarter of a century later, when he sought to determine the first stirrings for what had later grown into *Doctor Faustus*, his verdict on its roots in personal experience was terse and unabashed: "Music, then, and Nietzsche" (W:XI, 151).

Neither Lawrence nor Malraux has been as open about his response to Nietzsche, which began a good bit later. But a similarly deep involvement can be inferred. Indeed, though both writers have little to say in discursive statements, they take the extraordinary step of explicitly calling on the philosopher in their fiction. Concerning the young Lawrence, a memoir by a close friend reports that around 1908 she "began to hear about the 'Will to Power,' and perceived that he had come upon something new and engrossing."[14] Like Mann, Lawrence reacted to World War I with intense self-searching; the earliest outcome was a personal philosophy that is permeated with Nietzschean motifs. These speculative concerns affected his subsequent fiction, with the most obvious but hardly exclusive result being the polemic against Nietzsche and the will to power that concludes *Aaron's Rod*. As for Malraux, he has admitted, in spite of his notorious reluctance to speak unequivocally about himself, that Nietzsche was one of his primary intellectual experiences as he came of age in the years after the war. Such was the centrality and persistence of this interest that he placed an imagined episode involving Nietzsche in his last novel, *The Walnut Trees of the Altenburg*. And it surely points to his underlying priorities that when he finally came to write an autobiography, the unconventional *Anti-Memoirs*, he reprinted this episode right after the preface so that it became the first narrative section of the book.

One special feature of Nietzsche's influence emerges from the comments by Gide and Bely. As a philosopher with strong literary interests, he could affect writers in various ways; the result is a more complicated situation than the one assumed by Heller when he calls Nietzsche the Aquinas of twentieth-century German literature. Heller is relying on a sharp dichotomy between philosophy and literature, in which writers learn from a thinker the definitive intellectual framework for their age. But this simple scheme is inadequate to the nature of Nietzsche's achievement and the aspirations of his heirs. One must think instead of an interlocking network of possibilities that allows for literary factors in Nietzsche, intellectual concerns in the writers, and a full gamut of mixed modes where thought and literature interact. I shall be referring to this whole network as the problem of idea and image.

For example, a writer might see Nietzsche as a philosopher without deferring to him as a grand intellectual authority. Thus Gide, who condescendingly views him as a "point of departure," as someone who had advanced intriguing theoretical points for which he failed to find a satisfactory literary form. In discussing Nietzsche, he can go so far as to complain of the fatal monotony of philosophy as compared with art and to reject what he calls the "formless movements of thought" (PR, 83, 85). Gide's attitude overturns Heller's position, according to which some philosopher's idea provides the interpretation for literary images, and takes instead a characteristically modernist stance that radically elevates image over idea. Image becomes constitutive of an entire conception of art, somewhat as in Pound's manifestoes for imagism. Because art should be thoroughly concrete, it must be purged of explicit ideas, though there is often an intellectual fruitfulness to images that have become sufficiently intense in their rendition of individual particularity. Such images evoke ideas with an energy and complexity denied to the abstract or discursive.

For a novelist like Gide, of course—and this point will be crucial when I discuss fiction later on—image would have more meanings than would immediately occur to a poet like Pound. Along with imagery or metaphor, it would include such resources of the concrete as the portrayal of character, the description of setting, the sense of pace or structure in a story and so on. So the writer who acknowledges Nietzsche's power as a thinker need not assume the distinctly subordinate role of a translator of philosophy into art. On the contrary, because of the great prestige of the image among modernists, he might feel that he was bringing ideas to life, even expressing intellectual nuances, in ways impossible in merely theoretical language. For an attitude that closely parallels Gide's distrust of ideas, but with more emphasis on the need for producing intellectual images, one may turn to one of Lawrence's manifestoes for the novel, which he wrote in the early twenties shortly after his polemic with Nietzsche in *Aaron's Rod*: "it was the greatest pity in the world when philosophy and fiction got split. They used to be one, right from the days of myth. . . . So the novel went sloppy, and philosophy went abstract-dry. The two should come together again—in the novel" (P, 520). For Lawrence, fiction is a better vehicle for speculative concerns precisely because it is concrete, because it is an image in the extended sense discussed above.

Bely's comment on Nietzsche's vivid images suggests yet another possibility. Once the literary side of his achievement was recognized, Nietzsche became a formidable figure who had appealed successfully to both the artistic sensibilities and the intellectual capacities of his readers. No longer just a point of departure, he became the direct predecessor for aspiring young writers who sought to fuse idea and image in their art. This attitude contains a great deal of truth: Nietzsche admired the energy and concreteness of imagery, for which he often used the suggestive term of *Gleichnis*.[15] This German word combines the broadly fictive and the more narrow, poetic sense of image; its primary meaning is "parable" and so suggests narrative, but it can also signify "figure of speech." In Nietzsche's usage *Gleichnis* is also closely bound up with image in the sense of a concrete visual impression (*Bild*) or even a particularly direct experience of things. As early as *The Birth of Tragedy*, in an interesting comment which joins the poetic and fictive concerns often subsumed by *Gleichnis*, he outlines these possibilities and indicates as well that the image can serve as a powerful equivalent for thought: "Metaphor for the true poet is not a rhetorical figure, but a substitute image (*Bild*), which actually appears before him in the place of a concept. Character is for him . . . a person who is insistently alive before his eyes" (B, 8).

But Nietzsche's crucial statement on this subject is his explanation in his autobiography for why he preferred *Thus Spoke Zarathustra* over all his other books. In writing *Zarathustra*, he had done nothing less than realize the imagistic imperative in his style; he had found *Gleichnisse* for his thought. According to Nietzsche, this book had surpassed even "the most powerful capacity of *Gleichnis*" by virtue of its extraordinary concreteness, its unprecedented "return of language to the nature of imagery (*Bildlichkeit*)" (E:Z, 6). Associated with this "involuntariness of *Bild*, of *Gleichnis*" was a peculiar transparency of language that tended to abolish the distinction between words and objects. As he wrote *Zarathustra*, "everything offer[ed] itself as the nearest, most obvious, simplest expression"; it was as if "things themselves approached and offered themselves as *Gleichnisse*." In short, the concrete qualities of the image had become so expressive that "on every *Gleichnis* you ride to every truth" (E:Z, 3). Images in themselves had become the best vehicle for ideas.

Nowhere is this reliance on imagery so striking as in "On

the Vision and the Riddle," Zarathustra's surrealistic account of the dwarf and gate that first shadows forth what Nietzsche saw as "the fundamental conception" of his work, the doctrine of the eternal return (E:Z, 1). The title of the episode captures the strategy he followed in writing it, for it does consist of a vision ending in a riddle, of vivid and disturbing concrete visual impressions that precede the idea which they render in an obscurely suggestive manner, and which in fact never receives a full discursive explanation in the rest of the book. Moreover, near the end of this account Zarathustra refers to his vision as a *Gleichnis*, thus making some allowance for the passage's narrative movement as well as for its concrete descriptions. In singling out this term, of course, Nietzsche is already anticipating his celebration of the distinctive qualities of *Thus Spoke Zarathustra* in his autobiography.* In actual practice as well as in his claims, therefore, he could be a daunting exemplar of how image could be mobilized to express idea, so daunting that Bely could see him as "an artist of genius" for his capacity to produce both theoretic and esthetic meanings.

This vision of dwarf and gate might well be Nietzsche's most striking experiment with a more direct and concrete language. He was not always so successful. Even Bely, it will be noticed, realizes that there is room for efforts of his

---

* The Kaufmann translation, normally so admirable, muddies this confluence of the narrative and poetic senses of image by rendering *Gleichnis* as "metaphor" in the autobiography, but as "parable" in the passage describing Zarathustra's vision. Kaufmann also misunderstands a suggestive phrase for the imagistic imperative in Nietzsche's writing. In his autobiography Nietzsche speaks of having embodied the concept of the superman in Zarathustra, and then goes on to say that given this character one should refrain "from seeking his *Gleichnis*" (E:Z, 6). Kaufmann remarks that this phrase makes little sense,[16] but actually Nietzsche is saying that *this* image for his idea is so satisfactory that no further images need be generated with Zarathustra as a starting point: a *Gleichnis* for *him* is unnecessary since he is such a splendidly concrete presence. The judgment is debatable, and we shall see in Chapter II that Nietzsche does go on to link Zarathustra with images of dancer and fountain; but at least it is clear that the phrase refers to Nietzsche's interest in fusing image and idea.

own, for "creative emulation." Writers like Joyce or Lawrence would go further, for they highlighted the loose or
abstract rhetoric in some of Nietzsche's poetic images, and
then demonstrated how to handle them more effectively. In
Ulysses, the strained, bombastic qualities of Zarathustra's
style become apparent when it is placed among the parodies
of English prose in the "Oxen of the Sun": "You milked
your cow, affliction, now you drink the sweet milk of her
udder."[17] When Joyce rephrases Nietzsche a few lines later,
he is far more concrete, for he avoids abstract nouns and uses
an exuberant vocabulary that is sensuous in itself and in the
details it evokes: "Thy cow's dug was tough, what? Ay, but
her milk is hot and sweet and fattening. No dollop this but
thick rich bonnyclaber." At the same time Joyce has made
cattle imagery one of the organizing principles of the chapter
so that the metaphor acquires a structural function missing
in *Thus Spoke Zarathustra*.

   In *The Plumed Serpent*—as I shall argue with the necessary
qualifications in Chapter IV—Lawrence transforms Zarathustra's animals, the eagle and the serpent, so that they become the presiding symbols of his book. Separate or combined, they take on different shades of meaning in different
contexts so as to comment on and integrate the actions of
the novel; they are complex and suggestive, for they generate
ideas out of their concrete presence. In Lawrence's hands, the
animals serve to realize his program for a novel with intellectual images. They are more than the simple emblems that
they seem to be in Zarathustra's eyes when he quickly identifies eagle and serpent as "the proudest animal under the sun
and the wisest animal under the sun" (Z:I, 10). But in this
case Nietzsche's images have some of the richer nuances that
he claimed in his comments on *Zarathustra*. As Heidegger
has pointed out, the circling flight of the eagle and the winding coils of the snake prefigure the ring of recurrence.[18] In
other words, this image involves more than the direct translation into idea with which Lawrence quarrels; it also has an
unexplained concrete element whose intellectual significance

emerges slowly in the course of *Zarathustra*. Zarathustra's animals may therefore serve as a convenient emblem for Nietzsche's mixed success in giving poetic imagery a decisive role in furthering his thought.

If we turn to the broader, novelistic sense of image, Nietzsche's attempts at making philosophy more concrete remain problematic. His claims for himself in this area were not as grandiose: he had a low opinion of the novel as a genre, and his enthusiastic praise for Stendhal and Dostoevsky applied to their skill as psychological observers and not as novelists.[19] In his own writing he is more given to succinct parables or pointillist overviews of historical developments than to detailed and consecutive fictional narrative. Even in *Zarathustra*, story in this last sense (as distinguished from the intellectual drama of gradually revealing the idea of eternal recurrence) plays a minor role, except in the fourth part, which is hardly a high point in Nietzsche; the account of Zarathustra overcoming pity seems surprisingly sketchy if we remember Nietzsche's acute eye for suppressed motives and mixed feelings.

Yet elsewhere he could be brilliant in drawing on aspects of the novelist's art in his philosophical writing. He never lost the touch that, as he remembers it, attracted attention in graduate school: "My old teacher . . . claimed that I planned even my philological essays like a Parisian *romancier*—absurdly exciting" (E:III, 2). Most striking is the vivid communication of concepts through personification (perhaps mythical transfiguration would be the better phrase) in *The Birth of Tragedy*; it is a measure of his success that everyone knows about his interpretation of Apollo and Dionysus, though we shall find in Chapter II that modernist writers pursued the implications of this contrast much further than is usually the case. Nietzsche often used his descriptive powers to good effect in creating appropriate landscapes, as in Zarathustra's mountain world or in the contrast between the cloudy northland of gloomy transcendental philosophies and the sun-flooded Mediterranean of his this-worldly gay science. And when Nietzsche works with actual people, he can often round off intellectual themes with a pointed character study. Consider how he draws on his life story to develop his philosophy in his autobiography, or how much of his thinking about cultural crisis centers on Socrates and Wagner.

It has become clear that Nietzsche's accomplishments on the boundary between philosophy and literature were less startling than they seemed to Nietzsche himself or to the young Bely. Gide, after all, could contrive to minimize the philosopher's reliance on images; and if Joyce notices the images, he does so only to bring extraordinary new sophistications to them. Meanwhile, Lawrence attacks Nietzsche's schematism in generating ideas from images. These responses suggest how much Heller's paradigm leaves out in supposing that the Nietzschean idea guides the writer's image. In Gide, the role of images is to transcend or enrich the idea; but Joyce focuses on a Nietzschean image and transforms it, and Lawrence takes Nietzsche's imagery as the basis for a new and more literary presentation of ideas. Bely's remarks bring out the fourth and remaining possibility, not with his program for an art fusing idea and image but rather in his admiration for Nietzsche's "thought" and "theoretic" meanings. He is making room for a kind of writing that would draw on Nietzsche's ideas without, as Bely is careful to stress, merely following them; such writing would be speculative rather than narrowly literary, and would include such productions as Bely's "symbolist" philosophy and "metaphysical," "systematic," or "meditative" works by Lawrence, Yeats, and Mann.[20] Here idea generates idea, instead of idea inspiring image, image another image, or images suggesting ideas—four possibilities that exhaust a writer's options in the network of idea and image. It is, of course, a consequence of influence as transformation that in each case Nietzsche is subject to revision and change.

In drawing on these examples, I am not making critical generalizations about the writers named, nor am I asserting that this kind of influence is unique to Nietzsche. There is no absolute separation of idea and image: thinkers will use images, poets will draw on ideas, and in any case images have intellectual possibilities of their own. So in theory any writer's impact could exhibit all of these alternatives. But figures who straddle the line between these two modes of expression represent a special case because then each option can have a leading role. Though it is important to recognize the limitations in Nietzsche's achievement, in the end he resembles Plato or Kierkegaard in the thoroughness with which he exploits both idea and image.[21] And this special quality in his work has had a decisive effect on the ways he could influence other writers.

□

For the second of my two points about this influence, I need to consider some more material from my survey of writers and responses. Notice, for example, how Yeats's extraordinary fascination on first reading Nietzsche changed in time to a more coolly distanced attitude that placed the philosopher in the definite but limited position of a forerunner. In Lawrence's case, a more dramatic shift took place, for his initial discovery of something "new and engrossing" in Nietzsche eventually gave way to direct attack. Similarly, Bely's emphasis on creative emulation came after a period of "crazed enthusiasm" for Nietzsche, and his insistence on intellectual independence led him in the end to be contemptuous of people he called Nietzscheans, who took the philosopher's thought as a rigid ideology.[22] There is a pattern here that adds depth to the notion of influence as transformation, and complicates the tendency I mentioned a moment ago for writers to take an independent approach toward problems of idea and image in Nietzsche. Despite the individual flavor of every literary career, it is evident that writers did not automatically detach themselves from the philosopher's authority but first underwent an often lengthy period of subordination. I shall be referring to this pattern as the shift from taking Nietzsche as a model to considering him a rival. Writers begin by feeling an intense identification with Nietzsche but later discover that it threatens their sense of artistic integrity and originality. The philosopher has become a rival, and they must struggle to disengage themselves from him in a process that involves both the psychological pressures emphasized by Bloom and the intellectual quarrels analyzed by the Russian formalists.

This process stands out in fuller relief in Thomas Mann's eventual choice of deliberate resistance to Nietzsche. At one point in *Reflections of an Apolitical Man*, while he is reviewing his early work, he describes how he dealt with his youthful admiration for Nietzsche. According to this account, the decisive experience occurred when he wrote the historical play *Fiorenza* (1905). Such was his admiration for the essay on ascetic ideals in *On the Genealogy of Morals* that it overwhelmed his conception of the characters, his outlook on history, even his choice of setting: his Savonarola was simply a dramatized version of the ascetic priest, and he depicted Renaissance Florence in Nietzschean terms as noble, life-affirming, and magnificently artistic. The reader of *Fiorenza* may feel Mann is being overly modest, but in any case he decided that he had lost his freedom of invention, that he needed to be less doctrinaire in drawing on Nietzsche. He had to make room for "something further, more my own, less theoretical" that would (in the case of characters) "give more intimacy to their psychological typology and connect it with more burning problems" (W:XII, 94-95). These phrases neatly crystallize the two main factors in the shift from model to rival, a revision of thought that aims to go further than Nietzsche by taking up more immediately relevant issues, and an urge for self-assertion which looks for something more intimately one's own. Meanwhile, Mann's impatience with mere theory or typology shows how writers could turn to the problem of idea and image for ammunition in their revolt against the philosopher.

This last item brings out the lurking ironies in the shift from model to rival. By failing to do justice to Nietzsche's own artistry, Mann's statement neglects the underlying continuities that can soften any break with a predecessor. With other writers who are less self-conscious about problems of influence, Nietzsche's role as an unacknowledged model can be equally important but less visible. On closer inspection, for example, Gide's one-sided view that contrasts the philosopher's ideas with literary images might be a willful inaccuracy protecting his fragile sense of originality as a writer. Thus Wolfgang Holdheim, after studying Gide's guarded remarks about Nietzsche throughout his career, has concluded that the novelist was defending himself against a predecessor he felt was "frighteningly similar" to him.[23] Along the same lines, Lawrence's partially mistaken polemic against Zarathustra's animals, as discussed above, could have been a strategy for making his own creative project seem more original than it actually was. In short, a writer who casts himself as Nietzsche's rival might nonetheless be still following him as a model. At any point, therefore, the process of transformation might have to be questioned by the critic. It could include important elements of imitation, even though the writer vehemently denies their presence, or—like Malraux—is simply silent about them.

As we know, Nietzsche himself welcomed the prospect of rivals, for he wanted followers only if they were capable of resisting him. But throughout the modernist period, readers who went beyond direct statements to consider the kind of appeal implicit in his work as a whole could get ambiguous and confusing messages on this issue. Certainly the aphoristic style Nietzsche developed for many of his later books, a style in which a great deal depended on amplifying suggestive phrases and supplying missing connections, acted to encourage creative collaboration rather than blind discipleship. For sophisticated readers these books were often more satisfactory as literary works than *Thus Spoke Zarathustra*. Nietzsche's sudden insanity accentuated this deliberate openendedness; at the very moment his work began to excite widespread interest, the only sure authority fell silent. His

work also appeared before the world missing that final systematization of his thought which Nietzsche had announced
under the titles of *The Will to Power* or *The Revaluation of All
Values*, and compared with which he saw all his books from
Zarathustra on as simple prologues or diversions. The career
was not only enigmatic; it was also unresolved.

Yet alongside this play of multiple possibilities, now so
often stressed in readings of Nietzsche, there were aspects of
his work that gave him the appearance of an authority or
model. Throughout the period of the modernists he had
many readers who responded to him in a spirit that was far
from open-ended. We have already encountered doctrinaire
Nietzscheans by way of Bely's contemptuous dismissal of
them; the story of these ideologues often belongs to the prehistory of Fascism.[24] Especially important was the role of
Nietzsche's sister, who had a strong sense of political mission
but no philosophical interests. She gained control of his manuscripts after his collapse, gave out an "official" interpretation of his ideas based on a pretended intimacy that she doc-
umented with forgeries, and survived his insanity by almost
fifty years—on into the period of Hitler, whom she welcomed. It was under her sponsorship that editors put together a collection of Nietzsche's unpublished notes and
fragments, arranging them under headings so as to imply an
argument and giving them the title of the missing master-
work, *The Will to Power*.[25] Of course, the writers to be studied in this book were no more ready than Bely to accept the
interpretations offered by dogmatic Nietzscheans; their response would be far more discriminating and valuable.
Nonetheless, it was difficult to avoid being caught up in
some way by the headlong rush toward synthesis that underlies the books from *Zarathustra* onward. The doctrines of
superman and eternal recurrence, the diagnosis of contemporary culture, and the philosophy of power all seemed to
demand some form of assent. And so the problem of the
hidden or suppressed model could extend to values and
ideas, and not simply involve the matters of expression illus-

trated by Gide's and Lawrence's refusal to acknowledge the full significance of Nietzsche's images for their own writing.

The shift from model to rival is therefore best viewed as taking place along a continuous spectrum. In general, this study emphasizes the independence of writers from Nietzsche. After all, I have chosen to focus on works widely accepted as great on their own terms; and such works, which emerged from some of the most intense and sustained periods of creativity known by their authors, are clearly not derivative in any simple way. At times, in fact, as may have been the case with Mann when commenting on *Fiorenza*, the writer can be overly humble in acknowledging Nietzsche's authority. But if the emphasis falls on fruitful rivalry, there are also many situations where the philosopher reasserts himself as a model, though the precise extent to which he dominates over the writer's revisionary impulses can only be determined by the critical analysis of specific instances. As a result, imitation still has a role alongside transformation in assessments of Nietzsche's influence, but it is an imitation that is often unconscious or strenuously rejected.

□

This analysis of the special nature of Nietzsche's influence has separated the two main factors at work. But actually the problem of idea and image and the shift from model to rival operate together in practically all cases: a writer who sets out to criticize a Nietzschean idea or rework one of his images may nonetheless absorb something from his outlook. As a result, the distinction between independence and subordination will rarely be as sharp as it appeared when I discussed the four ways of resolving the problem of idea and image in Gide, Joyce, Lawrence, and Bely.

Now that we have illuminated the notion of influence as transformation, and have found a convenient, flexible shorthand for discussing the intricacies of a writer's direct contact with Nietzsche, we are ready to take up the main business before us. To understand the substance of what happened when modernist writers became involved with Nietzsche, it will be necessary to begin with their point of departure. Who was the Nietzsche whose achievement, like an unstable atom throwing off fragments in all directions, had so great an impact on the creative work of Lawrence, Malraux, and Mann, and on Gide, Bely, and Yeats as well? What are the issues, problems, and methods, and what are the images, character types, and settings that pull together this constellation of works and writers?

II

Nietzsche's Legacy to the Modernists

My approach to Nietzsche in this chapter must be distinguished from a rigorous philosophic analysis. Since I am describing his legacy to writers, I have had to take a more general, flexible attitude toward his ideas than if I were interested in them for themselves or even for their place in the philosophic tradition. I have had to allow for the shift from model to rival, to bear in mind the variations, reversals, and hidden continuities that link him with his heirs. I have also had to give special prominence to the place that image, in the broad sense outlined in Chapter I, holds in his thought. This concern will put the emphasis on areas of his work that are usually passed over by commentators.

The reader should be warned against the notion that an inquiry into a literary legacy means nothing more than a demonstration of how writers misunderstood a philosopher. Nietzsche's significance is far from being settled, and philosophers themselves have disagreed markedly. They can identify him as an existentialist, as a pragmatist, as a neo-Kantian; they sometimes place him on a level with Aristotle or Hegel and sometimes dismiss him as a charlatan or a villain.[1] With so many opinions to choose from and with their own riveting experience of reading Nietzsche to reckon with, writers cannot be blamed for going their own way. It will become clear that their interest in Nietzsche could be partial and limited; nonetheless, they were careful and sensitive readers who at the very least were better prepared than philosophers to understand the nature of his experiments with image. They often cast a searching light on specific areas of his thought.

The writers largely avoid one of the major issues confronting any interpreter of Nietzsche. Are the canonical works the ones that he published, as Walter Kaufmann insists, or are they rather the unpublished notes, collected after his death, as Heidegger assumes? As far as I can tell, writers moved back and forth without making sharp distinctions. The arresting insights they discovered in books like *On the Genealogy of Morals* and *Twilight of the Idols* were also to be found in *The Will to Power*; it is therefore usually irrelevant to ask whether writers turned to the books or to the notes. Of course, none of them could have had the kind of detailed insight into the development of Nietzsche's thinking and the nature of his creative process that has only recently become possible. I refer to the new edition of his works which for the first time is making all of his notes available in the order that he wrote them.[2] It will be a surprise if this material doesn't produce further substantial changes in Nietzsche's fluctuating reputation, but it obviously has no bearing on what the modernists found in him.

The four topics I have identified as Nietzsche's legacy to the modernists generally correspond to the course of his development as a thinker. Among writers his first book had a special place, and so *The Birth of Tragedy* dominates the opening section of this chapter, which deals with polaristic thinking in the context of Nietzsche's entire career. In the next section, attention begins to shift to the mature work; I study Nietzsche's central concern as a psychological observer, his analysis of states of inadequacy and creativity. This concern is apparent even in his first book, but Nietzsche greatly expands on it and offers ambitious new generalizations in his last writings. I limit myself in this section to the two crucial examples of *ressentiment* and the response to tragedy, since so much of Nietzsche's psychology spills over into broader cultural and philosophical issues. The third section will follow up the first of these alternatives by exploring how inadequacy converges with problems of cultural crisis, and especially with its two distinct phases of decadence and nihilism. Again, this topic was with Nietzsche from the beginning, but in his mature work it widens in scope and takes on an extraordinary force of expression. Finally, in the fourth section, I turn to the second alternative: the philosophical doctrines of power and life which became the main focus for his interest in creativity. Nietzsche grasped the importance of these doctrines only in the last six years of his career, after the aphorisms in *The Gay Science* that prefigure the breakthroughs in *Thus Spoke Zarathustra*. But actually, when I refer to the mature Nietzsche, I mean especially the two books mentioned above—*On the Genealogy of Morals* and *Twilight of the Idols*. They are Nietzsche's most pointed and suggestive works, and they bring together insights often expressed less cogently elsewhere. In addition, writers absorbed a great deal from his more literary productions, not only from the inevitable *Zarathustra* but also from the polemical essay *The Case of Wagner* and the autobiographical *Ecce Homo*.

As I interpret Nietzsche's career, I have tried to remain faithful to his way of presenting the various issues. As a result, some of my initial comments will go over material that may seem familiar. But these comments are essential for understanding how the various areas in his literary legacy fit together; they should demonstrate one of the most impressive features in Nietzsche's influence—the meaningful context that draws together what might at first seem a host of random echoes. In any case, as I move further into the specific issues and methods that interested the writers, I shall be bringing fresh perspectives and new information to bear on the interpretation of Nietzsche. In some cases, this approach will lead to problems and possibilities in his work that have never been discussed before.

Then, at the end of these probes into Nietzsche's thought, I will briefly indicate the lines of development that point ahead to the writers. At times, and especially in the section on polaristic thinking, I shall draw on some of their speculative writings; but the main emphasis will fall on imaginative literature. These issues and questions will be considered at greater length in Chapters III through VI, which will analyze the integration of this literary legacy into the new and independent systems represented by complex and ambitious novels and stories. In other words, my discussion of Nietzsche will include a quick survey of many of the problems to be treated from a different perspective in the rest of the book. Of course, the elaborations or combinations of Nietzschean topics in the imaginative works are sometimes so extensive that they can only be discussed in later chapters.

On most questions I have given Nietzsche a chance to speak for himself, often because the passages I cite had an immediate impact on writers. But I also wanted to show the reader where my points were coming from; one of the banes of Nietzsche studies has been a vagueness about sources. These quotations will serve as well to illustrate that vividness of image, that capacity for suggestive turns of phrase, and that sudden acceleration of thought which make reading this philosopher so powerful an experience. Without these essentially literary qualities, the Nietzschean current among modernist writers could hardly have come into being.

POLARISTIC THINKING

Dualisms have a prominent place in Nietzsche's writings. The first and most celebrated example is the pairing of Apollo and Dionysus in *The Birth of Tragedy*, but there are other important specimens in his very last works: the contrast between master and slave moralities in *On the Genealogy of Morals*, and the discussion of sickness and health as complementary perspectives in *Ecce Homo*. Nietzsche once coined an epigram that neatly captures his preference for sharp oppositions: "I am a *Doppelgänger*, I have a 'second' face in addition to the first" (E:I, 3).

No obvious continuity of meaning joins the early and the late dualisms. In *The Birth of Tragedy* Nietzsche tends to favor the Dionysian, though he would later identify its qualities of mass religious enthusiasm with slave morality, which he distrusts. The important continuity is one of method. Nietzsche did reread his first book just before the period of the late works, for in 1886 he wrote the "Attempt at a Self-Critique" which now appears at the beginning of *Birth*. Though he sharply criticizes the book for showing "German dialectical ill-humor" (B:Pr, 3), the contrast of Apollo and Dionysus returned to haunt him. He repeatedly brought up the topic in aphorisms published in the fifth book of *The Gay Science* (1887) and in *Twilight of the Idols* (1889), and in notes eventually printed in *The Will to Power*. Despite the great changes in his philosophic position since his early work, this renewed interest in *Birth* perhaps lay behind his exploration of other dramatic contrasts in these final years. Certainly writers tended to see some such continuity. The special prestige of *The Birth of Tragedy* in literary circles meant that they used the contrast between Apollo and Dionysus as the model for understanding his use of dualistic arguments.

Apollo and Dionysus

The Birth of Tragedy is, however, a highly ambiguous work. In it, a young classical scholar discovers his philosophical vocation; the result is the intellectual ferment described in one of Nietzsche's letters: "Science, art, and philosophy are now growing into one another so much in me that I shall give birth to a centaur someday."[3] This centaur-effect, this sense of dealing with categories that suddenly turn into something quite different, is only too familiar to the critic who seeks to determine what kind of dualism is represented by Apollo and Dionysus. *Birth* is a churning sea of dualisms. We have seen that in the "Self-Critique" Nietzsche refers to his reliance on dialectic, a view he outlines at more length when he gives a quick review of *Birth* in *Ecce Homo*: "it smells offensively Hegelian. . . . An 'idea'—the antithesis of the Dionysian and the Apollinian. . . . In tragedy this antithesis is sublimated [*aufgehoben*, a Hegelian term] into a unity" (E:B, 1).[4] This observation stands at the basis of many accounts of Nietzsche's intellectual development. Recently, however, one of Derrida's students has usefully asked whether Nietzsche's conception of the Hegelian dialectic may not be "abridged and limited" and, further, whether this description of the relationship of Apollo and Dionysus might not have been achieved "at the cost of fastening down and reducing the two terms."[5] It should certainly be recalled that Nietzsche also criticizes his use of "Schopenhauerian and Kantian formulas" (B:Pr, 6), thus highlighting the very different dualisms of will and idea or of phenomenon and noumenon, which propose a split between appearance and ultimate reality. Key passages in *Birth* also suggest that he drew on Schiller's distinction between the naive and the sentimental.

None of these various dualisms does justice to the response of the writers. Though just as critical of dialectic as Nietzsche later became, they nonetheless admired the contrast between Apollo and Dionysus because they saw it as a polarity. At issue were two kinds of dualism, to be distinguished by the role that they assign to negation. In a dialectic the second term, the antithesis, is derived by negating the first term or thesis and is thus dependent on a prior affirmation. In a polarity—as the underlying image of a magnet might suggest—the two terms, though contradictory, exist each in their own right and are thus both affirmative. Neither presupposes the other. Yeats confronts this issue in *A Vision* when he censures Hegel for thinking that "the two ends of the see-saw are one another's negation." Though he turns to Blake for the alternative view that "Contraries are positive . . . contraries are equally true," he might equally have named Nietzsche.[6] During his first encounter with the philosopher he had remarked that "Nietzsche completes Blake and has the same roots,"[7] and *A Vision* itself contains an admirable allusion to this later source of inspiration. On completing his book, Yeats remarks that "the mountain road from Rapallo to Zoagli seems like something in my own mind," thus recalling Nietzsche's account in *Ecce Homo* of one of the most creative periods in his life.[8]

And yet Paul de Man's recent close study of *Birth* has led him to speak of "the pseudo-polarity of the Apollo/Dionysus dialectic."[9] How is it that writers could come to the opposite conclusion? One answer is to look at *Birth* itself, where Nietzsche does proclaim the polaristic position in some strategically placed passages, ones in which he cuts loose from other thinkers and tries to sum up his arguments. For example, he begins the book with a simile which presents Apollo and Dionysus not as thesis and antithesis but as independent powers: "the duality of the sexes, involving perpetual strife with only periodically intervening reconciliations" (B, 1). Then, at the end of an obviously labored exposition in which he himself seems puzzled by "the intricate relation of the Apollinian and the Dionysian," he stresses symmetry by describing their interaction as a "fraternal union" (B, 21). The conclusion of *Birth* returns to the inherent self-assertiveness in both halves of the duality: "these two art drives must unfold their powers in a strict proportion, according to the law of eternal justice. Where the Dionysian powers rise up as impetuously as we experience them now, Apollo too must already have descended among us . . ." (B, 25). And at the very end of *Birth*, after depicting a Greek scene with such vividness that Mann would later elaborate on it during Hans Castorp's haunting dream in *The Magic Mountain*,[10] Nietzsche takes the voice of an aged and pious Athenian so as to affirm both Apollo and Dionysus: "But now follow me to witness a tragedy, and sacrifice with me in the temple of both deities" (B, 25).

Looking beyond *Birth* to Nietzsche's whole career, we find the position of the writers even more understandable. Like most of his audience they got to know him only after he went insane, and so were unlikely to follow his development from work to work. From this perspective the polaristic qualities of Apollo and Dionysus would be all the more evident. For the later Nietzsche repeatedly stresses the inherent positivity of opposing qualities, as when he advances the credo, "We do not readily deny, we seek our honor in *affirm-*

ing" (T:IV, 6). For Gilles Deleuze, in fact, this attitude defines the basic tenor of his entire philosophy, which is an "absolute anti-dialectic" replacing "negation of the other" with "affirmation of the self."[11] Our writers, therefore, have chosen to focus on that aspect of *Birth* which is most akin to later developments. Polarity is simply a dualistic version of what would later become an advocacy of multiple perspectives.

Polarities have another feature besides independent dualistic affirmation. The passages from *Birth* that were quoted above include phrases like "intervening reconciliations" and "strict proportion"; they suggest that polarities interact in a variety of ways. In order to describe these possibilities, Nietzsche uses a speculative historical sketch which does double duty as a conceptual model; he develops his thought by exploiting the narrative sequence underlying his pointillist treatment of history. Thus, when he divides Greek culture into six periods—the Titanic, the Homeric, the age of Archilochus, the Doric, the tragic, and the age of "theoretical man"—and identifies the Dionysian Greek as a persistent seventh factor, he is also delineating the ways that Apollo and Dionysus can relate with each other. The most important form of interaction occurs at the midpoint where the forces are in balance, where Apollo stands in exact proportion to Dionysus. The result is a new unity possessing greater energy and complexity than either pole; in order to distinguish it from a dialectical synthesis, I shall call it a point of bipolar unity. For Nietzsche, of course, Greek tragedy is the supreme example of such a unity; the tragic age represents "the common goal of both these drives whose mysterious marriage, after many and long precursory struggles, found glorious consummation in this child" (B, 4). The age of Archilochus, when the forces of Dionysus returned to Greece following the Apollinian achievement of Homer, was also a period of bipolar unity, though Nietzsche sees its significance less as a fulfillment in itself than as a prelude to the tragic age. Nietzsche's description of this age shows how highly dynamic bipolar unity can be. It forms, falls apart, and reforms continuously so that to describe its presence in even a single lyric or play calls for expressions like "several successive discharges," or "scattering image sparks all around" (B, 6).

Other kinds of polarized relationships occur at varying distances from the midpoint and thus involve at least the partial dominance of either Apollo or Dionysus. The degree of dominance can range from a situation in which there is still considerable interaction to one in which the existence of the other pole is completely ignored. Nietzsche strongly favors interaction; in the absence of strict proportion he at least looks for some form of reconciliation. The Homeric age is a splendid achievement because the Apollinian, though triumphant, is still closely linked to the Dionysian by virtue of its origins in the Titanic culture which preceded it: "we should recognize the highest effect of Apollinian culture—which always must first overthrow an empire of Titans and slay monsters, and which must have triumphed over an abysmal and terrifying view of the world and the keenest susceptibility to suffering through recourse to the most forceful and pleasureable illusions" (B, 3). The connection of the Doric to the Dionysian is looser; rather than being entangled with a force it has just overcome, it stubbornly maintains an already established position: ". . . the *Doric* state and Doric art are explicable only as a permanent military encampment of the Apollinian. Only incessant resistance to the titanic-barbaric nature of the Dionysian could account for the long survival of an art so defiantly prim and so encompassed with bulwarks . . ." (B, 4).

In the other direction from the midpoint Nietzsche favors the Dionysian Greek whose response to Dionysus has been strongly colored by the heritage of Apollinian culture from the Homeric age and who is separated by an "immense gap" from the barbarian. Though it stops short of balance, this figure does express an interaction of two forces: "The two antagonists were reconciled; the boundary lines to be observed henceforth by each were sharply defined, and there was to be a periodical exchange of gifts of esteem. At bottom, however, the chasm was not bridged over" (B, 2). The forms of reconciliation represented by the Homeric and Doric ages and by the Dionysian Greek can be grouped together as examples of polarized interaction. Though Apollo and Dionysus are at odds with each other, there remains an undercurrent of energy flowing between the two poles so that some of the complex relatedness of bipolar unity is preserved.

If polarization breaks down, if one pole asserts itself to the full exclusion of the other so that it is unable to contribute its force to a larger whole, the situation of polar nullities arises. I have borrowed this term from Lawrence, who wrestled with polaristic ways of thinking through several volumes in the wartime statements of principle mentioned in the first chapter. The particular drive invested in one pole, when no longer polarized, turns upon itself and nullifies its own energies. In a late note which found its way into *The Will to Power*, Nietzsche discussed this situation from a perspective different from the polaristic one: "Retreat from the high-point of becoming . . . to be represented as a consequence of this highest force, which, turning against itself when it no longer has anything left to organize, spends its force on disorganization" (WP, 712). The same kind of dissolution of energy is shown in *Birth*. I have already mentioned Nietzsche's distrust for the unalloyed Dionysian, whether Titanic or barbaric. He views it as a return to the state of nature, which he defines in terms starkly opposed to the idyllic or pastoral. The earliest Dionysian festivals exhibit basic aggressive and sexual drives in their most brutal, degraded forms: "the most savage natural instincts were unleashed, including even that horrible mixture of sensuality and cruelty which has always seemed to me to be the real 'witches' brew' " (B, 2). The same mixture appears in the "glance into the abyss" that Nietzsche finds in the story of Oedipus; anticipating Freud, he sees great significance in the

way Oedipus breaks "the most sacred natural orders by mur-
dering his father and marrying his mother" (B, 9). Such a
chaotic overflow of energies is inherently unstable. The final
result of these "intoxicated" excesses is a state of lethargy or
nausea that denies the instincts and leads to "an ascetic will-
negating mood" or even to the "wisdom of Silenus" with its
yearning after death (B, 7).

The corresponding state on the side of Apollo is the condition of "theoretical man," in which loss of polarity again
results in the negation of the isolated drive. In Nietzsche's
account, the theoretical originates with the death of Greek
tragedy at the hands of Euripides and Socrates with his "one
great Cyclops eye" (B, 14). These men outdid Doric culture
in their efforts to exclude the Dionysian. But to subtract one
drive does not leave the other: ". . . because you had abandoned Dionysus, Apollo abandoned you" (B, 10). Now
Apollinian lucidity does not necessarily conflict with the scientific rationalism of "theoretical man"; if, as Nietzsche
holds, the essence of the Apollinian lies in a serenely distanced perspective on reality, for which his analogy is
dreams, then it could easily be seen as a symbol for the sci-
entist's mode of representing the world. Latent in his argument, therefore, are his frequent celebrations of science later
on in an almost positivistic vein, and even in *Birth* he is ready
to say that the theoretical offers the *"noblest opposition"* to the
tragic (B, 16). Nonetheless, the theoretical differs from the
Apollinian because it reverses the relation between mind and
instinct. Instead of flowing out of a self-critical intellectual
passion, ideas are normally generated in an existential void.
In someone like Socrates, impulse has become a rare exception: "in this utterly abnormal nature, instinctive wisdom
reveals itself only now and then in order to *hinder* conscious
knowledge. While in all productive men it is instinct that is
the creative-affirmative force and consciousness acts critically
and dissuasively" (B, 13). Nietzsche uses a vivid image to
evoke the polar nullity of theoretical man who, alienated
from his instincts, "no longer dares commit himself to the

fearsome icy current of existence; he runs anxiously up and down the bank" (B, 18). The shallow technological optimism which Nietzsche held to be a consequence of "theory" will occupy us later during our discussion of cultural crisis.

The polaristic method so vividly dramatized by the contrast between Apollo and Dionysus might well seem artificial to an outsider to the traditions of German thought. Why fix on such an elaborate way of generating multiple possibilities from paired concepts? There is a refreshing directness to the later Nietzsche when he talks about perspectivism, thus admitting the validity of a varying number of determining viewpoints and accepting multiplicity on its own terms. But writers could be attracted by its symmetries of categorization. One thinks of the elaborate schemes regulating the interaction of plexuses and ganglia in Lawrence's *Fantasia of the Unconscious*, or of the dark and light of the moon when Yeats classifies personality types in *A Vision*. More to the point, however, is the impact of the polaristic method on less speculative, more specifically imaginative writing, where writers tended to be more discriminating because they were dealing with their own art. Lawrence, for example, grafts the polarities onto a basic narrative situation of intense conflict in love. Having decided that art should have intellectual resonance, he holds that the novel cannot be "a mere record of emotion-adventures, floundering in feelings"; it must also be "a thought-adventure, if it is to be anything at all complete."[12] As a result, Nietzsche's opening analogy between Apollo and Dionysus and the battle of the sexes gains a startling prominence: the Laurentian love story develops a more precise structure and broader implications. Mann, in turn, has saluted Nietzsche for encouraging a new kind of art, "a most lofty, most erotically crafty *irony* playing between life and intellect" (W:XII, 84). In *Death in Venice*, at any rate, the terms of this irony are very close to Apollo and Dionysus; the story shows an awareness of degrees and levels of qualified assertion that is polaristic. And Gide, in *The Immoralist*, builds from the same polarities toward a similar ironic vision.

Of course, Nietzsche's method also implies a set of values. Dualistic affirmation conveys an impatience with absolutes as one-sided nullities ("monotonotheism" to the late Nietzsche), a preference for the rich scale of nuance arising out of the confrontation of one truth with an opposite. Polarized interaction suggests an exaltation of complex relationship, of creative tension and fruitful struggle, an idea which Nietzsche reinforces with many though not all of his glorifications of war. Bipolar unity—"only periodically intervening"—is central to an essentially dynamic outlook where no achievement is permanent but, lost almost as soon as gained, must always be striven for again. All of these attitudes will circulate among his literary heirs as they draw on the polaristic method.

Sociocultural Perspectives

Nietzsche's twin art deities held other fascinations for writers. Even as he used these mythic figures to dramatize dualistic modes of thought, he himself began to think mythically. As a result, Apollo and Dionysus can serve as vivid embodiments for a whole series of qualities that are joined by association rather than logic. In particular, they sometimes address problems of social and political atmosphere or of a broad geographical framework for cultural history. In these areas Nietzsche's thought is neither precise nor thorough: it registers possibilities and attitudes without becoming a political creed. It therefore leaves a great deal of room for elaboration, and its tendencies may surprise someone who comes to Nietzsche after reading the conventional historical judgments that he was the philosopher of Fascism or imperialism.

As a social force, the Apollinian represents a more complex array of possibilities than the obvious category of political rationality. It is the principle behind the state, identified in one of Nietzsche's late notes with "aristocratic legislation" (WP, 1049), and accordingly its greatest achievement lay in political structures which allowed for "an affirmation of the individual personality" (B, 21). The best concrete example Nietzsche can find in *Birth* doesn't quite measure up to this standard. He considers the Roman Empire to be magnificent yet terrifying; he has reservations about its "extreme secularization" and, more in accord with the later development of his attitudes, finds some of its "national instincts" limiting (B, 21). These reservations become sharper when he examines the Doric, which, it will be recalled, was an extreme form of the Apollinian. Sparta's "cruel and relentless political structure" showed how the state could gain absolute supremacy and block the development of both the suppressed Dionysian and the Apollinian tendency to affirm the individual (B, 4). As it moves toward polar nullity, Apollinian politics degenerates into the imperial idea and the authoritarian state, both of which Nietzsche finds troubling.

The Dionysian, on the other hand, is fundamentally apolitical, expressing itself "in a diminution of, in indifference to, indeed in hostility to, the political instincts" (B, 21). This trait can lead to Buddhist mysticism or to the "witches' brew" of total social disintegration, but less extreme versions work to create a primitive sense of community. The hierarchical structure and specialization of roles in everyday society disappear, to be replaced by a fraternal feeling uniting people simply as people: "Now the slave is a free man; now all the rigid, hostile barriers that necessity, caprice, or 'impudent convention' have fixed between man and man are broken" (B, 1). Insofar as it negates all the Apollinian structures of the state, this condition must be called essentially anarchistic. Yet is it hardly a form of individualism, since it causes people to feel "as one with their neighbor" (B, 1); rather, it testifies to an elemental social sense in humanity that is prior to politics. The late Nietzsche will, of course, sharply reject this spirit of community.

The cultural and geographical implications of Apollo and Dionysus are already becoming visible. Apollo should not be equated with modern Europe or western civilization in general. After all, theoretical man is a deformation of the Apollinian, while *Birth* passes over so decisive a factor as Christianity with what Nietzsche was to call "hostile silence" (B:Pr, 5). But because of his important role in classical Greece and in the Roman Empire, Apollo is at least crucially implicated in the origins of Europe. Meanwhile, *Birth* presents the Dionysian as Asian. Not only does it develop into Buddhism, but its prehistory in primitive cults lay in "Asia Minor, as far back as Babylon and the orgiastic Sacaea" (B, 1). Hence Greece had a special geographical significance as a land of the middle, "placed between Rome and India," possessing a political will that enabled it to defeat the Persians yet open to cultural forces originating in Asia (B, 21). In a note published in *The Will to Power* Nietzsche restates this interpretation of the Greeks, but with an accent somewhat less sympathetic to the Dionysian: "The Dionysian Greek needed to become Apollinian. . . . The immoderate, disorderly Asiatic lies at his roots: the bravery of the Greek consists in his struggle with his Asiaticism" (WP, 1050).

Generally, however, the later Nietzsche abandons the contrast between Apollo and Dionysus, so that Dionysus is free to acquire a much broader meaning than it had in *Birth*.* I shall consider some larger implications of this shift when I discuss his myths of power in the section on power and life. But this new conception of Dionysus also expands on the topic of culture and geography, with the leading tendencies all appearing near the end of one of the most elaborate notes in *The Will to Power*. At one point, Dionysus points southward: "The Christian doctrine was the counterdoctrine to the Dionysian: to rediscover the South in one and to spread

* So far as I can tell, Walter Kaufmann was the first to make this simple but essential point. A great many readers of Nietzsche misunderstand the basic intentions of his later work because they assume that when he calls on Dionysus he means the same thing as in *The Birth of Tragedy*. Later in this section we shall see that Nietzsche's one-sided comments on *Birth* in his "Self-Critique" contributed to this error. For a possible English-language influence on this shift in Nietzsche's ideas, see Sander L. Gilman, "Nietzsche's Reading on the Dionysian," *Nietzsche-Studien* 6 (1977), pp. 292-294.

out above one a bright, glittering mysterious southern sky; to reconquer southern health and hidden powerfulness of soul . . ." (WP, 1051). Nietzsche is evoking the Mediterranean landscapes which had become so important to him; since *Birth* he had spent much of his time in Italy and the south of France, and had come to admire the Renaissance and the Provençal troubadors as additional examples of the cultural excellence he had discovered in the Greeks. He gives a Dionysian twist to the widespread enthusiasm felt by northern European writers in southern Europe. At times this southerly inclination reaches beyond the Mediterranean, as in his panegyric for the "African" cheerfulness of *Carmen* (C, 2) or in the picture of oasis and palms in the poem "Deserts Grow" from *Zarathustra*, later included among the *Dionysus Dithyrambs*.

Later in the note, the eastern component to Dionysus reappears, but now it is subordinated to a larger conception in which the Dionysian signifies a union of the originally distinct terms of Europe, Asia, and Greece: "step by step to become more comprehensive: more supranational, more European, more supra-European, more Oriental, finally more Greek—for the Greek was the first great binding and synthesis of everything Oriental and especially on that account the *inception* of the European soul, the discovery of our '*new world.*' " The puzzling switch whereby Europe is first surpassed only to emerge later as the final goal may be explained by the new inclusiveness of the Dionysian. Europe marks two separate levels of attainment. There is first the viewpoint of Nietzsche's good Europeans, who have overcome the divisiveness of nationalism but whose situation parallels that of Doric culture in that they hold back from the Asian. But once an inclusion of "everything Oriental" has taken place, a new Dionysian Europe becomes possible, a culture for which only the Greeks could provide a model. The "binding" of Asia that gives rise to this European "new world" corresponds to the balanced interaction of Dionysus with Apollo; only when one pole comes to its full expression can the other pole realize its full possibilities. But now the result is itself called Dionysian. So limited in fact is all previous European culture in Nietzsche's eyes, presumably because its assumptions were so largely Christian, that earlier in the note he denies the Dionysian status even to great artists like Goethe, Shakespeare, Beethoven, and Raphael.

So the new culture of Nietzsche's hopes goes beyond both the Asian and conventional definitions of the European. Of course, his persistent association of the Dionysian with the East cannot be accepted as a meaningful analysis of Asian culture. Nietzsche's exploration of the theme is simply too sketchy; and in any case—as we shall see later in this section—his cultural geography also functions as a projection of psychological interests: it maps the human faculties. Still, his interest in Asia does have meaning as an aspiration, as a sign of what is usually an openness and sympathetic responsiveness to another cultural tradition.[13]

At times in the later work these sympathies broaden to the point where Nietzsche considers the possibility of a truly worldwide culture. One memorable example is Zarathustra's speech on the thousand and one goals: "A thousand goals have there been so far, for there have been a thousand peoples. Only the yoke for the thousand necks is still lacking: the one goal is lacking. Humanity still has no goal" (Z:I, 15). This vision of a universal humanism has, however, moved decisively beyond oppositions of Europe and Asia. Nietzsche has learned to think about cultural multiplicity in terms of a multitude of perspectives, and so he no longer needs to draw on the polaristic method.

Among writers, Gide and Mann would respond selectively to the political atmospheres associated with Apollo and Dionysus; Gide and Lawrence were strongly affected by the Dionysus of the South. In *Petersburg* Bely hearkens back to *Birth* as he seeks to dramatize Russia's ambiguous position between Europe and Asia: the foremost representative of the European principle is an authoritarian defender of the Empire, and bears the name of Apollon—a common Russian name which also means Apollo. A poem like Yeats's "The Statues," with its disdain for "Asiatic vague immensities," derives from the Nietzsche who is occasionally less sympathetic with the Dionysian. But Malraux is Nietzsche's foremost heir when it comes to the sociocultural implications of the polarities. Apollo and Dionysus provided him with a point of departure for his own, much more detailed exploration of contrasts between Europe and Asia. He was also attentive to questions of political atmosphere and to Nietzsche's hopes of moving beyond a narrowly European consciousness and discovering the basis for a global culture.

Later Polarities

After *The Birth of Tragedy* Nietzsche never again relies so heavily on the thinking through polarities dramatized by Apollo and Dionysus. I have already pointed out passages from the late works where Dionysus is no longer coordinated with Apollo, though there are also passages that show that the method has not been abandoned entirely. The dualities of master and slave, and of sickness and health, which Nietzsche develops in the final two years of his career, testify to the same mixed attitude. With both of them, Nietzsche can decisively elevate one term over the other, a distinctly nonpolar procedure which parallels his strong preference for Dionysus over Christianity. But elsewhere he does make statements which suggest a polaristic conception of these dualities and which help explain how writers responded to them.

Nietzsche's typology of moral systems, provocatively identified with conflicts between masters and slaves but more accurately defined as a contrast between the psychological categories of nobility and *ressentiment*,[14] will concern us more fully in later sections. Pertinent here is the fact that although Nietzsche defines his task in *On the Genealogy of Morals* as that of finding "the *order of rank among values*" (G:I, 17), he does not always speak in terms of a hierarchy. Polaristic language appears in several passages, one of them being the remarks concluding the first essay, where the duality of master and slave has been especially prominent: "Today there is perhaps no more decisive mark of a 'higher nature,' a more spiritual nature, than that of being divided in this sense and a genuine battleground of these opposed values" (G:I, 16).

The concept of the sovereign individual, which appears in the second essay, elaborates on this polaristic insight. Here Nietzsche belatedly introduces an important new issue into his discussion of master and slave, the issue of self-mastery. Usually central to his vision of nobility,[15] it was notably absent from the first essay, where he relied on primitive masters, the lurid and notoriously Nietzschean "blond beasts," as the vehicle for his thinking. But now, in the second essay, he again turns to speculative history for a narrative structure that allows him to rank and relate his concepts. Because self-mastery represents a crucial new factor, it is presented as the outcome of a "tremendous process"; the spontaneously active, creative instincts of the "blond beasts" become fused with the reversal of the instincts upon the self which characterized the slave (G:II, 2). In most cases, this reversal leads to instinctual alienation, the self-torture of bad conscience or the compensatory "ideals" of envious impotence. But this internalization of the instincts could also prepare for a higher development of the instincts, since Nietzsche admits that the slaves coerced into the first societies by the "blond beasts" represented something essentially new: "the existence on earth of an animal soul turned against itself . . . was something so . . . *pregnant with a future* that the aspect of the earth was essentially altered" (G:II, 16). Nietzsche has already named this "future," or more important concept. The "social straitjacket" of these first societies had opened the way for "the extraordinary privilege of *responsibility* . . . this power over oneself" (G:II, 2).

In other words, internalization could lead to a regulation of the instincts that was no longer alienated from the self; responsible self-mastery could penetrate "to the profoundest depths and become instinct, the dominating instinct" (G:II,

2). This portrait of the sovereign individual, in turn, gives Nietzsche a vantage point from which to judge the primitive masters of the first essay, who spontaneously followed the overflow of less developed instincts. They were, quite simply, "slaves of momentary affect and desire" (G:II, 3). Through an argument that relies even more than usual on rather widely separated "nodes of meaning" and on shifting perspectives in dealing with a key word, Nietzsche grants that master and slave have both contributed to that more important figure, the sovereign individual. He has affirmed the value of polar interaction in a situation originally set up in sharply hierarchical terms.

One develops a respect for D. H. Lawrence's powers as a reader of Nietzsche when one discovers that he was capable of following this argument. In his free-wheeling Australian novel *Kangaroo*, written in the period following *Women in Love*, he sets up a system of polarities that draws on the contrast of master and slave. But Lawrence's hero eventually seeks to resolve the conflicting terms; when he does so, he paraphrases the ideal of sovereign individuality. However, Yeats exploits the polaristic possibilities of the *Genealogy* more fully. A central distinction in *A Vision* involves what he calls the primary and the antithetical, states of being which are closely related to the psychological conditions of *ressentiment* and nobility.[16] Yeats's famous image of the phases of the moon, touched on earlier in this section, is a symbol for this distinction. When he declares that "there's no human life at the full or the dark,"[17] he has admitted that both psychologies have a part in everyone; the varying mixtures of light and dark in the remaining twenty-six phases illustrate the wide range of possibilities for interaction. It should be noted, however, that the bipolar positions of equal dark and light have no special value. And even as Yeats affirms the necessary coexistence of both poles, he follows the late Nietzsche in adopting a hierarchical attitude as well. It is clear that he prefers those situations where his antithetical version of noble morality takes precedence over the passivity and bitterness that characterize the primary state.

The duality of sickness and health has a prominent place in *Ecce Homo*, the autobiography Nietzsche wrote in 1888, just months before his collapse. Referring to the chronic illness that had plagued him intermittently since early adulthood, he calls it the most important fact in his biography. It had given him an intense exposure to a double perspective on life, so that by now he was equally at home in the two worlds of sickness and health, both of them taken in the widest possible philosophical senses. Nietzsche's attitude toward this duality can often be hierarchical, as when he ranks the two terms in accord with the statement that "I turned my will to health, to *life*, into a philosophy" (E:I, 2). He makes a similarly unconditional assertion of health in *The Case of Wagner*, written earlier in the same year, where he says: "My greatest experience was a recovery" (C:Pr). And in the same pamphlet he makes one of his most explicit denials of bipolar unity: "Biologically modern man represents a *contradiction of terms*; he sits between two chairs . . ." (C:E). Nietzsche no longer seems to find valuable complexity and heightened energy at the midpoint between two opposing forces. Yet in other passages he can defend the polaristic method. *The Case of Wagner* argues for the validity of two poles just a few paragraphs before the one I have cited; thus the insistence that "these opposite forms in the optics of values are *both* necessary" (C:E). And in *Ecce Homo* Nietzsche sees no difficulty in stressing the advantages of "that neutrality, that freedom from all partiality in relation to the total problem of life" which his sickness-and-health had given him (E:I, 1).

This second way of stating the duality appealed to writers, and not simply because *The Birth of Tragedy* caused them to prefer polarities. They also knew the dramatic outcome of Nietzsche's illness, which cruelly undermined his confident pronouncements about the advent of a "great health." This irony could not fail to impress an artist of disease as talented as Thomas Mann. In *Reflections of an Apolitical Man* he speaks of the paired opposites surrounding the hero in his early novella *Tonio Kröger*, then likens this self-definition in terms of a "situation pathos" to the presentation of sickness in Nietzsche, "who derived the cognitive worth of his philosophy precisely from the fact that he was at home in *both* worlds, in decadence and in health" (W:XII, 91–92). Later on in the *Reflections*, Mann makes this particular contrast his own: "I belong intellectually to that generation of writers spread throughout Europe, who come out of decadence but at the same time bear in their hearts the emancipatory will to break with it" (W:XII, 201). But "emancipatory will" is too much of a concession to a Nietzschean "will to health," and Mann immediately softens the phrase: "Let us say pessimistically the velleity for making this break." Replacing recovery with a complex hesitation between sickness and health, he chooses the polaristic strand in Nietzsche's attitudes toward the subject. It is revealing that both in Mann's early story *Tristan* and in *The Magic Mountain* Zarathustra's Alpine landscape is transformed; no longer an appropriate setting for the philosophy of the future, it becomes a place where tuberculosis patients are sometimes cured and sometimes die.

The interplay of sickness and health becomes especially important when writers echo portions of Nietzsche's own life story. In *The Immoralist* there are curious, indirect parallels between Michel's recovery from illness and situations in *Ecce Homo*; in the end Gide reveals the complexities that underlie his hero's euphoric glorification of life. Malraux takes the opposite tack in *The Walnut Trees of the Altenburg*, where he presents Nietzsche after his breakdown and uses this imagined episode to suggest the possibility for affirmation in the midst of disease. And, of course, Mann has explained in *The Story of a Novel* how greatly Nietzsche's life affected his conception of Adrian Leverkühn, the composer-hero of *Doctor Faustus*. On this level, the novel may be seen as a fictive revision of *Ecce Homo*: in particular, by treating medical questions that Nietzsche left out or did not know, it provides a strong corrective to the autobiography's tendency to partiality in handling the theme of sickness and health.

From Art Drives to Aesthetic Naturalism and Psychology

However, Apollo and Dionysus were not just vivid emblems for polaristic thinking, nor did they simply anticipate the perspectivism and cultural pluralism of Nietzsche's later philosophy. Writers also found that they highlighted several other leading issues raised by his work as a whole.

When Nietzsche concludes *Birth* with a phrase like "these two art drives must unfold their powers," his reliance on words like "drive" and "power" shows the extent to which he sees Apollo and Dionysus as manifestations of energy. In part, of course, his vocabulary derives from Schiller, whose *Letters on the Aesthetic Education of Man* had discussed entities like a "form-drive" and a "material drive." But *Birth* is more explicitly biological, for Nietzsche explains his two art-gods from the very outset by referring to the physiological analogies of dream and intoxication. Indeed, once we deduct from *Birth* the transcendental element which Nietzsche attacks so vehemently in the "Self-Critique" when he disowns the doctrine of a "metaphysical comfort" in tragedy (B:Pr, 7), this language of art drives has important implications. Both Apollo and Dionysus lose their divine aura and become instincts, but instincts with the special quality of possessing enough energy to shape themselves into an aesthetically satisfactory form. They are characterized by an inherent capacity toward differentiation, refinement, and a complex interrelation of parts, yet maintain a formal coherence which comes from one originating impulse—or, in the case of tragedy, a unified set of impulses. This artistry of energy will become a key feature in Nietzsche's mature philosophy of the will to power.

Similar overtones accompany the celebrated remark which appears twice in *Birth* and which Nietzsche emphasizes in the "Self-Critique" (B:Pr, 5) that "it is only as an *aesthetic phe-*

nomenon that existence and the world are eternally justified"
(B, 5, 24). As often occurs with fundamental Nietzschean
doctrines, this insight first surfaces as a sudden movement of
thought that breaks through a discussion of more routine
and specialized concerns. In context it involves more than a
simple celebration of art. Because Nietzsche has been closely
analyzing Schopenhauer, terms like "existence" and "world"
must be understood against the background of that philosopher's conception of the will as a basic force suffusing man
and nature. The concern with justification would then suggest that this primal energy has real value only when it
undergoes a process of transformation whose unfolding of
complexity in unity is basically an "aesthetic phenomenon."
As a result, art provides the key for all significance in life. It
brings to fulfillment a core of energy which must be identified with the instincts if we are concerned with man rather
than nature and if we follow the later Nietzsche in rigorously
excluding all references to metaphysical comfort. As with
the physiological analogies for Apollo and Dionysus, Nietzsche
has begun to generalize the notion of an art drive so that it
explains the place and function of instinct.

The importance to writers of these emerging ideas is very
broad but nonetheless real. To use the catchwords of late
nineteenth-century literary movements, the underlying tendency of *Birth* is to unite aestheticism's cult of art with the
biological imperatives of naturalism. Outside the various
German literatures, this outlook might well seem surprising
and even paradoxical, for it cuts across the normal associations. We have let ourselves be conditioned by the contrast
in England between Oscar Wilde and T. H. Huxley or the
even sharper split separating Mallarmé and Zola in France.
Nietzsche is one major figure to suggest a way of bridging
these gaps, and so prepares for the ferment of literary modes
that comes with modernism. For his heirs, it would be impossible to view art as insulated or "pure."

Nietzsche's aesthetic naturalism has important consequences as a psychological doctrine, since it implies that a

person can no longer be defined in traditional terms as a point where higher and lower realms intersect. The emphasis shifts to continuity. The instincts are not simply a primitive substratum, the animal in man, to be guided or held in check by some superior entity such as intellect or spirit, both suggested by the German word *Geist*. Rather, they are the fundamental material of human nature, for they give rise to the higher faculties through their inherent capacity to transform themselves. Existence is at its richest and most significant after a person has passed beyond an original state where he is merely the creature of elemental instincts. But he shouldn't go too far, thus becoming a theoretical man who has severed all meaningful connection with the instincts.

But having established a general framework that sets an artistic self-heightening at the center of psychology, Nietzsche wavers. For if Apollo and Dionysus personify the workings of instinct, they differ not simply in the kind of instinct they represent but also in their openness to the process of transformation. As a result, it becomes possible to overlook their parallel status as art drives. Thus Nietzsche conceives of Apollo as the instinct of representation, as an essentially human instinct whose effect is to distance people from their world and to develop their sense of individuality. This is because Nietzsche stresses the element of illusion in representations, so that to become aware of them is to realize that one is a separate entity. It is significant that Nietzsche passes over the more spontaneous or automatic expressions of this instinct. He lacks Aristotle's interest in simple mimicry or anything like Freud's discussions of primitive representations, in spite of his references to Apollinian dreams.[18] Instead, he emphasizes the fullest realizations of the instinct, in the visual arts where he considers Greek statuary, in language where he focuses on Homeric epic, in political life as it provides for individuality. It is, of course, the excessive development of the Apollinian that is responsible for theoretical man.

Setting out from the tigers and panthers of traditional iconography, Nietzsche presents Dionysus as less specifically human. This group of instincts is related to an elemental force of change throughout the universe as a whole, a contradictory force closely related to Schopenhauer's Will and bringing both creation and destruction, triumph and pain. The creative side dominates when he associates Dionysus with "the potent coming of spring that penetrates all nature with joy" (B, 1). The human manifestations of this ambivalent force are the sexual and aggressive instincts. Nietzsche did pay attention to these basic forms of the Dionysian, as his remarks on the "witches' brew" and the crime of Oedipus indicate; and the physiological analogue of intoxication seems, in his treatment, to be far more elemental than dreams. But this drive can undergo an artistic self-heightening, as may be seen in the contrast between Greek Dionysian festivals and barbaric ones. Its fullest realization comes in music, and especially in "the *orgiastic flute tones of Olympus*" (B, 6) that transformed Homeric culture or in Beethoven's Ninth Symphony, which gives Nietzsche crucial insights into the Dionysian (B, 1). There is no Dionysian state beyond art that would correspond to theoretical man.

Thus, as art drives, Apollo and Dionysus both illustrate the self-transformation of instinct, even though the instincts in question differ sharply. But the differences in their susceptibility to development could give the impression of a basic asymmetry. In that case, Apollo and Dionysus might suggest a contrast between intellect and instinct, or between disembodied reason and vital energy. This contrast is even more evident in passages (as in sec. 16) where Nietzsche leans heavily on Schopenhauer, and presents Apollo not as a power equal to Dionysus but as secondary, as an idea masking an underlying and prior will. Further support for this view would come from the "Self-Critique" to *Birth*. By neglecting to mention Apollo at all, and emphasizing instead the opposition between Dionysus and theoretical man, Nietzsche heightens the impression of asymmetry. Readers who failed to understand that the Dionysus of this later period is a far more inclusive figure and that even the Dionysus of *Birth* is an art drive could easily interpret his praise here for the Dionysian as a glorification of raw instinct over the intellect. However, the partiality of this position becomes apparent when the "Self-Critique" is compared with the discussion of Dionysus and Apollo that takes place in *Twilight of the Idols*. There the two art gods represent complementary drives, for Nietzsche returns to the problem of physiological analogies and redefines the Apollinian in terms that strengthen the parallel with the Dionysian. Now he identifies it not with dreams but with an intoxication of the eye (T:IX, 10).

All of Nietzsche's heirs would draw on specific details from these comments on the two art drives. More broadly, Nietzsche's ambivalence meant that *Birth* could encourage two quite different psychologies of the instinctual and the irrational. One of them blunts the full force of Nietzsche's aesthetic naturalism by simply reversing the traditional dichotomy of higher and lower and exalting the lower term. Thomas Mann never fully disengages himself from this interpretation, which often underlies his reservations about Nietzschean psychology. Even when he says that Nietzsche's philosophy prepared the way for an art based on the interplay of life and intellect, this more sympathetic formulation stresses a contrast between vital energy and distanced theory. At times, however, Mann is ready to allow for a more radical psychology, one that replaces the traditional dichotomy with the single continuum of aesthetic naturalism. But it is Lawrence who is much more consistent in envisioning a transformation of lower forces into higher ones. Despite the baroque luxuriance with which polarities proliferate in his essays on the unconscious, they do point to one fundamental distinction. Rather than separating mind and instinct, Lawrence describes the interaction of two kinds of instinct which he locates in the upper and lower halves of the body. These instincts are capable of refinement, and can even account for the growth of knowledge along with the more subjective or impulsive aspects of the personality. As theory stands to

Apollo, so—for Lawrence—does reason stand to his upper center: it is a relatively late by-product whose proper role is to regulate the instincts rather than to control them.[19]

Nietzsche's ambivalence in *Birth* thus results in a major split among his literary heirs. These varied psychological doctrines also make their presence felt among the themes of culture and geography inspired by Apollo and Dionysus. Mann makes the basic connection in his speech honoring Freud, a speech which begins by paying tribute to Nietzsche as Mann's first master in psychology. The relationship between consciousness and instinct ("intellect" and "life") may be compared to Europe's position as "a small and lively province of a greater Asia" (W:IX, 486). This parallel is, of course, crucial for Malraux, who exploits it on a much larger scale. Insofar as he tries to relate Apollo and Dionysus to characteristically European and Asian modes of art, and to see them in terms of impulses that are specifically human or larger than humanity, he treats them as parallel art drives. But when he contrasts a Western reliance on reason to instinctual chaos, or the limited sphere of political action to an Eastern sense of awe before the cosmos, he is responding to the asymmetries in the two terms. As a result, Malraux's presentation of the two continents raises psychological issues in accord with both interpretations deriving from Apollo and Dionysus.

PSYCHOLOGIES OF INADEQUACY AND CREATIVITY

In his later career Nietzsche became very proud of his skill as a psychological analyst. Ranging far beyond the questions of the irrational and the instinctive that he had dramatized with Apollo and Dionysus, he claimed a special talent for ferreting out hidden motives. In *Ecce Homo* he calls this approach "that psychology of 'looking around the corner' " (E:I, 1), and in *On the Genealogy of Morals* he briefly presents a Mr. Rash and Curious whose "most perilous kind of inquisitiveness" consists of investigating mental activity hidden by the "false iridescent light" of immediate consciousness (G:I, 14). The most important psychological problems remain to be uncovered and articulated; or, as Nietzsche puts it in a late note on the Dionysian experience: "here is the great depth, the great silence" (WP, 1051).

Nietzsche's psychological observations can often be scattered and elusive, for in this area he is especially given to experimenting with varied perspectives or drawing out the implications of isolated bits of knowledge. At times, too, he will make grandiose claims for his insights, as in his remarkably obtuse declaration that he was "the foremost psychologist of the eternal feminine" (E:III, 5). This diversity and unevenness produced a great many admirations and disagreements of a minor order, and make it difficult to assess the full range of his impact. But there was one persistent and clearly defined set of topics that was a major source of interest for writers. As a psychologist of inadequacy, Nietzsche exposed and attacked those emotions and ideas that derive from a basic inability to accept oneself and the conditions of human existence. Then, in order to build up an alternative vision of humanity, he turned to creativity with its qualities of active power and an absorbed engagement with life. These two broad concerns underlie the more specialized psychological issues to be explored in this section, the problem of *ressentiment* and the nature of the tragic response.

An early and illuminating expression of Nietzsche's interest in psychologies of inadequacy and creativity appears in *The Birth of Tragedy*, in the course of a digression on why later societies resisted acknowledging the cultural preeminence of the Greeks. Nietzsche finds the reason to be a deepseated lack of self-confidence: "in their presence everything one has achieved oneself, though apparently quite original and admired with great sincerity, suddenly seemed to lose color and life and shriveled into a poor copy, even a caricature" (B, 15). This passage fails to indicate whether the cultural model became so awesome to the latecomers because of an inner sense of inadequacy, which took the Greeks as a convenient pretext for negating achievements in themselves valuable—they merely "seemed to lose color and life"—or whether the achievements were only "apparently quite original" so that the feelings of inadequacy came from a direct comparison with genuine excellence. In either case, whether innate or induced, the basic mood of self-denigration produces a number of hostile emotions directed against the outer object which is felt to be superior. Thus Nietzsche goes on to specify "all the poison that envy, calumny, and rancor created" (B, 15). For a counterweight to this psychological dynamic of self-distrust leading to resentment, he looks to the rewards of creativity, a major theme in *Birth* as a whole which surfaces in this passage as the "self-sufficient splendor" of the Greeks themselves and the "great sincerity" that the latecomers enjoyed before they felt themselves belittled. Possibly these glimpses of an adequate selfhood should also include the Greek ideal of *sophrosune*, which Nietzsche admiringly describes later in the same section as "that calm sea of the soul, so difficult to attain" (B, 15). As he moved onward from these early formulations, he would greatly extend his investigation of the hidden sources of inadequacy and creativity.

Ressentiment

Nietzsche liked to claim that the aphoristic books he wrote around 1880 represented an important new phase in his psychological thought. In his preface to *On the Genealogy of Morals*, he looked back at *Human, All-Too-Human* with its sequels and at *The Dawn*, and acknowledged their value in making his thought "riper, clearer, stronger, more perfect" (G:Pr, 2). In effect, he is providing a rationale for a certain repetitiveness in his work. His earlier books had allowed him to rehearse and refine his premises, to introduce new distinctions and explore their usefulness, to heighten the vigor and inventiveness of his style, to suggest more ambitious generalizations. Since the *Genealogy* is presented as the result of all this effort, it is no surprise that many philosophers consider it to be Nietzsche's most systematic book.[20] It is a culminating achievement in another sense too, since it is an extraordinary rhetorical performance, well calculated to appeal to the literary imagination. *Genealogy* epitomizes to an uncommon degree Nietzsche's power as a writer: the mastery of tempo, the vividness of phrase and image, and the audacity of tone—"unconcerned, mocking, violent" (Z:I, 7), as he characterizes it.

As an analysis of inadequacy, *Genealogy* is chiefly important because it introduces the concept of *ressentiment*. This concept is not exclusively psychological. When Nietzsche assumes the role of a "natural historian" of morality or criticizes the basic assumptions of Western philosophy, he discovers that *ressentiment* has broad cultural consequences. At such points his thinking parallels and complements his discussion of decadence and nihilism, both of them terms which describe cultural crisis through a psychology that analyzes declines in the intrinsic vitality of the self. But with these forms of inadequacy, cultural concerns have become sufficiently important to justify postponing them for a later section. For the moment, as our attention focuses on the self, we shall not be dealing with a fall in its inherent energies, but with how Nietzsche develops his sketch in *Birth* of a self poisoned by outer pressures.

Ressentiment is a French word which addresses this issue by its very construction. It pointedly suggests a loss of self-sufficiency: rather than having one's own sentiments, one responds to the circumstances of others and thus experiences only re-sentiments. Nietzsche prepares the scene for this psychological generalization in a characteristically dramatic way. In the foreground of the first essay of the *Genealogy* is a provocative revision of conventional views of the past; the origins of Christianity coalesce with the story of Spartacus to produce *"the slave revolt in morality"* (G:I, 7). The special emphasis that Nietzsche has given this phrase suggests a private twisting of language, a sudden dawning interest in the multiple resonances latent in the "historical" label. In particular, his iconoclasm here exemplifies a stylistic tendency he later refers to as "speaking crudely . . . , which does not mean that I want to be heard crudely or understood crudely" (G:III, 6). Soon the talk about slaves gives way to psychological doctrine: "The slave revolt in morality begins when *ressentiment* itself becomes creative and gives birth to values" (G:I, 10).

The paradoxical entrance of creativity into these introductory comments will occupy us shortly. So far as inadequacy is concerned, Nietzsche stresses the essential reactivity of *ressentiment*. He defines his new concept in terms of an excessive sensitivity to the outside world which he calls "this *need* to direct one's view outward instead of back to oneself" (G:I, 10). In *Ecce Homo*, where the review of *Genealogy* confirms the underlying priorities of his thought by singling out *ressentiment* to the exclusion of slave values, he describes this reactive trait of "pathological vulnerability" in vivid detail. The description is all the more compelling because he is summarizing his own experiences in life: "One cannot get rid of anything, one cannot get over anything, one cannot repel anything—everything hurts. Men and things obtrude too closely; experiences strike one too deeply; memory becomes a festering wound" (E:I, 6). This basic failure in maintaining one's identity against outside pressures leads, in turn, to strategies of denial. By saying "No to what is 'outside,' to what is 'different,' to what is 'not itself' " (G:I, 10), the self negates the forces pressing upon it and achieves a measure of independence.

Up to this point Nietzsche's concerns may recall Dostoevsky, and especially the lacerated characters who struggle obsessively to maintain their self-respect. It is, in fact, a matter of record that he discovered Dostoevsky and eagerly read some of his works shortly before starting the *Genealogy*.[21] But as the book proceeds, and Nietzsche explores the varied modes of denial in scattered passages, the distinctive features of his psychological thinking become apparent. He is ready to investigate a wide array of mental states which he then analyzes in terms of a single basic but flexible situation; this psychology also serves to buttress some of his characteristic judgments on the appeal of dogmas and systems. In its details, therefore, Nietzsche's sketch for a schematic analysis of inadequacy differs profoundly from Dostoevsky's efforts to dramatize the psychological need for Christianity.[22]

Ressentiment, it would appear, typically manifests itself in moods of impotent vengefulness. Nietzsche introduces the concept by mentioning "imaginary revenge" and "suppressed hatred," thus focusing on the powerful feelings generated by the self's incapacity to express in action its denial of the other. But in the second essay of the *Genealogy* he can associate *ressentiment* with more actively hostile states of mind like rancor and malice. Envy and suspiciousness, which get a certain prominence in the third essay, suggest another possibility: low self-esteem has not yet proceeded to an explicit negation of the other, and so the self remains in the initial stage of excessive sensitivity to the outside world.[23] And if *ressentiment* clearly cannot be limited to revenge, neither can it simply be identified as a mood or state of mind. It often provides the impetus for elaborate intellectual constructs which permit the mind to circumvent or banish the object with which it has become obsessed. The result is an ideological falsification that transforms such an object "into a real caricature and a monster" (G:I, 10).

Though Nietzsche's leading examples of ideological falsification are cultural, he insists in his autobiography on the basic psychological issues: thus, "the fight against Christianity is merely a special case" of a broad attack on vengeful and reactive feelings (closely related in Nietzsche's German, which is *Rach- und Nachgefühlen*; E:I, 6). In other words, Nietzsche contends that Christianity, along with other religions and moralities of good and evil, generates complex systems of thought with the ultimate purpose of condemning this world by comparison with higher values located in some metaphysical realm. These higher values serve to justify the self for having a persistent sense of inadequacy before life; they are therefore a product, a fabrication of *ressentiment*. When Mr. Rash and Curious in the *Genealogy* surveys the workshop where ideals are manufactured, he discovers how common it is to rationalize inadequacy: "Weakness is being lied into something *meritorious*" (G:I, 14). This analysis of intellectual systems and ideologies has the further consequence of introducing a concern for unconscious and suppressed motivation into the psychology of inadequacy. Doctrine can be so seductive in itself that it destroys all awareness of why certain ideas became attractive in the first place. Hence, when Nietzsche chooses a revealing emblem from the history of Christian sentiment, he turns not to Dante's inferno, with its inscription that it was created by eternal love, but to Tertullian's vision of heaven as a place where he could enjoy seeing the unending punishment of his enemies. The contrasting examples suggest that though Christian teachings stress that it is a religion of love, its inner spirit is best captured by another slogan: "I too was created by eternal *hate*" (G:I, 14–15).

At this point, Nietzsche is in a position to ask whether *ressentiment* is necessarily impotent, and so he comes back to the paradoxical question of how inadequacy can be creative. After all, ideology makes it possible for essentially passive or reactive states of mind to take an active role in shaping history. The success of Christianity is only one massive instance of a phenomenon that Nietzsche also discusses in referring to contemporary political movements like the anarchists or the anti-Semites (G:II, 11). But he also allows for pre-ideological forms of reactive action. The *Genealogy* can speak with admiration of early legal codes for "putting an end to the senseless raging of *ressentiment*" in such largely emotional outbreaks as vendettas or scapegoating (G:II, 11). Nietzsche's arresting slogan "slave revolt" makes a real contribution to his developing argument insofar as it serves to highlight these paradoxical conversions of passive into active.

What assumptions lie behind this wide-ranging analysis of *ressentiment*? One might see it as a polemical doctrine that

serves conservative or reactionary politics; discontent with
the established order is nothing more than a symptom of
unacknowledged envy for the privileged and successful. One
tenacious advocate of this view is the Marxist aesthetician
Georg Lukács, who must admit the abundance of "first-rate
observations" in Nietzsche's work but nonetheless concludes
that not only his psychology but his whole philosophy are
"an aggressive defensive action against the main enemy, the
working class and socialism."[24] Undoubtedly Nietzsche has
had many readers who take him in just this spirit, though a
good number diverge sharply from Lukács in their political
aims. But my discussion of *ressentiment* shows how seriously
these attitudes distort the development of Nietzsche's thought.
The main emphasis falls on psychological understanding, on
illuminating a great variety of emotional and intellectual
states by reference to a unifying yet flexible concept. Socialism enters the sketch as one among many possible ideological consequences of *ressentiment*, not as the point of departure
for the whole intellectual effort. Thus, when the *Genealogy*
touches on socialism, it does so in a parenthetical question
which stands at a far remove from the main topic Nietzsche
is pursuing, the comparison of types of moral systems (G:I,
5). For Nietzsche, the task of bringing reactive feelings under
control vastly outweighs the question of specific political arrangements. The concept of *ressentiment* is not a propaganda
tool but the diagnosis of a psychic malady.

A passage from *Ecce Homo* is useful in further clarifying
Nietzsche's assumptions: "Born of weakness, *ressentiment* is
most harmful for the weak themselves. Conversely, given a
rich nature, it is a *superfluous* feeling; mastering this feeling
is virtually what proves riches" (E:I, 6). In replacing economic definitions of wealth with psychic factors like declines
in creative energy and failures in the integrity of the self,
Nietzsche has taken *ressentiment* to be the most pressing form
of human poverty. He apparently sees no ambiguities in the
desire "to prove riches," and one wonders how he would
have analyzed modern consumer societies. So much of his

psychology of inadequacy seems applicable to economic issues he has largely excluded from consideration, issues like
how people respond to pressures to buy or how they perceive differences in income or possessions. The passage from
Ecce Homo also reveals the close connection between *ressentiment* and self-mastery. It implicitly concedes that even rich
natures experience reactive feelings, thus emphasizing the
necessity for a struggle within the self rather than political
doctrine. We have already encountered this attitude in the
previous section, in Nietzsche's polaristic description of
higher natures as a battleground of master and slave; in the
same spirit, the *Genealogy* states explicitly that reactive affects are part of "the entire biological problem" (G:II, 11)
and cannot be ignored in any account of human nature.

Evidently Nietzsche thinks of psychic life in terms of fluctuating energy levels: even the most actively inclined individual can occasionally slip back into reactive attitudes. Such
is the case with his portrayal of himself and his main hero.
In *Ecce Homo*, in the midst of celebrating his own triumph
over *ressentiment*, he turns back on himself and acknowledges, somewhat obliquely, that his chronic illnesses had ac-
quainted him with these variations of psychic intensity:
"sickness itself *is* a kind of *ressentiment*" (E:I, 6). Zarathustra
is more forthright when he discusses revenge in "On the
Tarantulas." This central problem in the psychology of inadequacy leads him to confess his own vulnerability: "Alas,
then the tarantula, my old enemy, bit me. . . . And alas,
now it will make my soul, too, whirl with revenge" (Z:II,
7). Because *ressentiment* is an ever-present possibility, Zarathustra's resolve to struggle against it has a special urgency.
He concludes his speech humorously—"if he is a dancer, he
will never dance the tarantella"—but the image of the dancer
suggests a cultivation of the self's best impulses that resembles the work of an artist. A creativity that is free from
reactive impulses is considered the best defense against inadequacy.

Responses to Nietzschean psychology were usually suc-

cessful at getting beyond the brash theses about slave morality so as to consider the scattered but ambitious remarks on
ressentiment. Thus Mann can show an episodic interest in specific insights into vengeance; but Lawrence is more recep-
tive, so that aspects of inadequacy can enter into major symbolic scenes, contribute to his critique of ideals, and have a
key role in his conception of characters. Malraux comes closest to the full range of Nietzsche's thinking. In his novels he
builds directly on the psychology of varying intensities and
insists on the importance of coming to terms with one's own
resentful feelings. He is so well attuned to the priority of
psychological understanding over political thought that he
ventures to speak of "Nietzschean socialism"[25] and can portray his revolutionary heroes in ways that make their struggles against inadequacy the key to their stature. Finally, Malraux is intrigued by the paradoxes of a Nietzschean "slave
revolt" and seeks to explore further the meaning of this conversion of inadequacy into creativity.

Guilt, Pity, Love

Loosely associated with Nietzsche's analysis of *ressentiment*
are some remarks on the origin of feelings of guilt and his
criticisms of love and pity as professed ideals. He discusses
guilt and bad consciousness in the most detail in the second
essay of the *Genealogy,* but does not draw on the psychology
of inadequacy in any meaningful way. Instead, as we saw
from his later uses of polarities, he preferred to account for
these states of mind by an internalization of instinct that was
one result of the relationship of master and slave. But in the
third essay, the one on the ascetic ideal, he advances another
explanation for self-lacerating internalization. Confronted
with feelings of inadequacy among his flock, the ascetic
priest comes up with an audacious new strategy for satisfy-
ing the need for a victim: "Quite so, my sheep! someone
must be to blame for it: but you yourself are this someone,
you alone are to blame for it—*you alone are to blame for yourself!*" (G:III, 15). Nietzsche is quick to point out the psycho-

logical consequences of this maneuver; it shifts the direction of *ressentiment* so that hostility turns inward from the outside world, embodying itself in "such paradoxical and paralogical concepts as 'guilt,' 'sin,' 'sinfulness,' 'depravity,' 'damnation' " (G:III, 16). As Mann portrays the guilt-saturated imagination of his artist-hero in *Doctor Faustus*, one of his purposes will be to test this psychological unmasking of venerable religious categories.

Nietzsche's attitudes toward love and pity are also connected with his distrust of Christian values. The remarks on Tertullian cited above suggest, for example, that traditional doctrines have little to do with the actual psychological condition of believers. But Nietzsche's critique involves larger questions than his polemic with a religion infected by *ressentiment*, since on occasion he interprets pity and love as devices chosen for themselves by an inadequate self. They become plausible excuses for losing oneself in others and thus evading one's own identity. Strictly speaking, Nietzsche is again expanding his original formulation of inadequacy; as with *ressentiment* an outside entity remains crucial, but its role has changed from a superior force that shatters one's sense of personal worth to a pretext for ignoring the very existence of selfhood. For Nietzsche's most forceful expressions of this position, we should turn to pithy maxims scattered through his late works and standing to the side of his effort at systematization in the *Genealogy*.

For Zarathustra, the last obstacle to attaining the "great noon" of vital selfhood is the temptation of pity. Most of the fourth part of his book is devoted to this problem, but his last speech settles the matter with a play on words which suggests that pity derives from a general sense of living inadequately: "my suffering and my pity [*Leid* and *Mitleiden*]— what of them!" (Z:IV, 20). Zarathustra resolves instead to dedicate himself to creative activity, using the word *Werke* which can be applied to artistic achievements: "I aspire after my *work!*" *The Antichrist* is more explicit, shifting from linguistic nuance to direct statement as it thunders against pity for being "more harmful than any vice" because "it stands opposed to the tonic emotions which heighten the energy of the feeling of life" (AC, 2, 7). But despite these revaluations of what had been a supreme value for Schopenhauer, Nietzsche continues to acknowledge the importance of some kind of sensitivity to others. Even in *The Antichrist* he insists that the exceptional person has a duty to treat the mediocre more tenderly (AC, 57), while he goes so far as to portray Zarathustra admitting the emotion if not the name: "if I must feel compassion, I still do not want to be called compassionate" (Z:II, 3). This problematic area where pity shades into more affirmative yet unnamed forms of fellow-feeling will be the subject of crucial scenes in Malraux's fiction.

In the case of love, it is Lawrence who builds most directly on Nietzsche. His work after *Women in Love* and culminating with *The Plumed Serpent* shows a heightened awareness for how the word can mask an avoidance of selfhood or a usurpation of otherness. Nietzschean maxims have pointed the way. In *Ecce Homo*, for example, the ideal of unegoistic love is condemned as a violation of the psychological facts of life: "One has to sit firmly on *oneself*, one must stand bravely on one's own two legs, otherwise one is simply *incapable* of loving" (E:III, 5). *The Case of Wagner* suggests that a ruthless possessiveness underlies the selfless attitudes of idealists, so that love becomes "a more refined form of nestling down in another soul, sometimes even in the flesh of another—alas, always decidedly at the expense of 'the host' " (C, 3). But love in nature, in Nietzsche's alternate vision to these distorted ideals, is "war in its means" (C, 2). This metaphor, we have seen, implies a different conception of relationship— the polaristic model that was to be even more important for Lawrence.

Tragic Affirmation

When the mature Nietzsche turns from inadequacy to the contrasting state of active creativity, he prefers to speak of power or life, terms whose relevant implications, philosophical as well as psychological, will be considered in a later section. But as early as *The Birth of Tragedy* he had already advanced a somewhat different analysis of the creative self, one whose presence continues to be felt in his later work and which was to become an important part of his literary legacy. Nietzsche's most pointed comments on this topic are only loosely related to his more general assertions about art, such as his comments on the self-assurance fostered by Greek culture or his contention that existence and the world could only be justified as an aesthetic phenomenon. Rather, they emerge from his discussions of the specific impact of tragedy, and outline a psychological process that might best be called tragic affirmation.

Nietzsche shows the greatest self-awareness about his ideas in one monstrous paragraph near the end of *Birth*, where he criticizes other theories of tragedy and particularly the notion of catharsis derived from Aristotle. He agrees that one should focus on the emotions of the audience, but maintains that the spectator feels a paradoxical pleasure which outweighs the famous purgation of pity and fear: "He shudders at the sufferings which will befall the hero, yet anticipates in them a higher, much more overpowering joy (*übermächtigere Lust*, where *mächtig* uses the same root as his later term for power; B, 22). Though Nietzsche relates this joy to the Dionysian pole of tragedy, he also pursues another line of thought when he emphasizes—as part of his critique of Aristotle—that there is "an aesthetic activity of the listener." He has identified a psychological process whereby the capacity for actively confronting tragedy, as shown by an aesthetic response to representations of disaster, has a bracing effect on the emotions that offsets the seemingly depressing content.

In the same sentence he includes an important corollary when he speaks of "artistic conditions" as an equivalent psychological state. Here he gathers up an earlier assertion that knowledge of "the experiences of the truly aesthetic listener" will suffice "to bring to mind the tragic artist himself," who is capable of feeling "the highest artistic primal joy" in the very act of creating the panorama of destruction that is his art. Both the aesthetic response to tragic drama and the artistic creativity that produced it testify, therefore, to the mind's ability to envisage everything that threatens the self, to attain a kind of mastery in the process, and—what is more—to delight in that mastery. With this insight Nietzsche realizes that he has answered in the affirmative a searching question asked by Goethe. The deepest pathos *can* be transformed into aesthetic play, and his swelling rhetoric conveys the excitement of breakthrough: one has reached the "primal phenomenon of the tragic" after "glorious experiences" that fill one with "astonishment."

Nietzsche might well feel a sense of revelation. Even as he looks around one of his first psychological corners and finds emotional strength instead of disarray, he has touched on the issues of power and activity that will be central to his later reflections on creativity. At this stage, of course, his interest in the subject is not as broad as it will become later on. He is outlining a psychology of art rather than analyzing human motives in general; and when he focuses on the joy felt by tragic artist and spectator, he is dealing with an extreme situation. In surmounting fate, death, and the essential absurdity of the human situation, tragic affirmation confronts some of the grander sources of inadequacy but neglects the more mundane and petty emotions that derive from *ressentiment*.

However, in some earlier passages in *Birth* Nietzsche has at least sketched out the transition from the realm of aesthetic play to broader psychological concerns. Tragic affirmation becomes an elemental psychic strength, an instinctive vitality, that springs up as humanity's best response to disaster. Nietzsche doesn't actually argue this point, but it does underlie some passages with memorable literary qualities; he anticipates advances in his thought by coming up with breakthroughs in expression. Thus the neat turn of phrase that suddenly opens up a whole new perspective on the importance of tragedy to the Greek: "Art saves him and

through art—life" (B, 7). *Birth* fails to exploit this shift from
an aesthetic to an existential attitude, but Nietzsche would
find these words so fertile at a later stage of his career that
he simply rephrases them when he needs a slogan to sum up
the development of his interests. In the "Self-Critique," he
credits his first book with having glimpsed a set of priorities
he now realizes is crucial: *"to view science in the perspective of
art, but art in that of life"* (B:Pr, 2).

A vivid image in *Birth* is even more effective in suggesting
how Nietzsche's attitudes toward tragic affirmation are widening. He compares works of tragic art to a basic physiological phenomenon, the dark spots one sees after looking directly at the sun; these works are "necessary effects of a
glance into the inside and terrors of nature; as it were, luminous spots to cure eyes damaged by gruesome night" (B,
9). Perhaps the awkward reversal of the underlying comparison with dazzled eyes helps explain why Nietzsche would
later censure *Birth* for being "image-mad and image-con-
fused" (B:Pr, 3). Still, the metaphor does open up new territory, since it manages to convey both a direct confrontation
with a threatening and inhuman challenge and a response
that, even though it is an illusion, testifies to human powers
of resistance and survival. The passage also provides a fuller
account of how Nietzsche relates his tragic psychology to
the polaristic argument of *Birth*. The "aesthetic activity" discussed above cannot be seen simply as a release of the Dionysian, for here it is presented as an Apollinian containment
of the Dionysian, with the "gruesome night" that marks the
strength of the latter arousing a corresponding intensity in
the "luminous spots" of the former.

These early maxims and images foreshadow the late
Nietzsche when he praises tragic art for expressing and com-
municating existential courage. Attacking the art for art's
sake movement because it insisted on the separation of art
from life, he points to the tragedian as a different kind of
artist whose aim was to heighten one's feeling of life. His
work is valuable because it epitomizes a state of mind that

extends far beyond art, one in which humanity manages to affirm itself in the presence of everything that seeks to negate it: "the condition of *fearlessness* in the face of the fearsome and questionable. . . . Courage and freedom of feeling before a powerful enemy, before a sublime calamity, before a problem that rouses dread—this triumphant state is what the tragic artist chooses, what he glorifies" (T:IX, 24). The shift of focus registered in this passage is taken further in famous slogans like "pessimism of strength" or *"amor fati"* or "what does not kill me makes me stronger."[26] In such phrases, the late Nietzsche has turned away from art entirely and celebrates the fullness of being that can result from any openeyed avowal of the negative aspects of life. Tragic affirmation has become a supremely desirable psychological state, one in which the most dramatic signs of human inadequacy are turned into further incitements to life.

This broader outlook is also Yeats's when he says that "we begin to live when we have conceived life as tragedy."[27] It is again Malraux who responds most fully to Nietzschean psychology. Though initially somewhat dubious about the life-enhancing or tonic effects of facing up to negativity—he asks in an essay on Gide's Nietzschean hero Ménalque whether there wasn't "a certain intellectual masochism" among his contemporaries—he is forced to admit that this attitude formed "the most interesting part" of the modern intellectual scene.[28] As this interest takes shape in his novels, it turns out to be both aesthetic and existential; tragic affirmation is an important theme in Malraux's meditations on art, and it is the state of being to which several of his heroes attain at critical moments. For other writers the issue is less central: Gide and Mann have some interest in tragic insight as a challenge to a character's innate strength, while Lawrence is chiefly important for comments that have little direct relation to the fabric of his fiction. Shortly before undertaking the project that eventually became *Women in Love*, he takes the affirmative stance that "tragedy ought really to be a great kick at misery"; but years later, when he says that "tragedy is lack of experience," he seems to chafe at the narrow spectrum of psychological possibilities that it offers.[29]

□

Lawrence's remarks parallel Nietzsche's own course, for if tragic affirmation enters his first book as an exhilarating discovery, it is far from being his central concern in later years. There is, after all, a telling discrepancy in the psychologies of inadequacy and creativity as they have been presented in this section. *Ressentiment* leads outward to a wide range of common, everyday emotional states, but tragedy remains confined to a limited number of exceptional situations. Inadequacy might well seem to be the norm, and so the later Nietzsche sets out to provide a more all-embracing and hence more satisfactory account of creativity. The result is his doctrine of the will to power, which introduces so many other important issues for writers that it needs to be taken up separately and on its own terms. It is not simply a psychological insight. But before we can consider these developments in the last few years of Nietzsche's career, we must discuss another major feature of his literary legacy. I am referring to the concern with cultural crisis which evolves through his entire work and which represents a vast prolongation of the theme of psychological inadequacy into the heady realm of historical speculation.

Cultural Crisis

Nietzsche's intense mood of cultural crisis caught our attention at the very beginning of this book, for it contributes to his modernist sense of having made a radical break with the immediate past. But when he links himself in his autobiography to a "crisis without equal on earth" (E:IV, 1), he is summing up a persistent tendency in his imagination. He is drawn to view history in units of vast dimensions that culminate with the present, which then becomes a turning point with epoch-making consequences. This point of view might be seen as an extreme version of what the Germans call the "world-historical," a grandiose outlook which has hardly been confined to Germany. Used speculatively this perspective can open up challenging though sometimes vague intellectual prospects; if it also acts to create a sense of historical mission, it is powerful but questionable, since it tends to submerge the individual in a cause and has at times degenerated into ruthless ideologies. In Nietzsche, however, the status of these historical overviews is a peculiar one. He rarely makes an effort to provide solid evidence for what he says, with the result that his insights have an ambiguous significance: they can be taken as provocative but highly controversial assertions about Western culture, or as a dramatization of personal values that colorfully draw on historical material. Nietzsche himself was eventually to recognize the presence of this enigmatic quality, at least in his early writings. In *Ecce Homo*, even as he congratulates himself on his "world-historical accents," he admits the crucial importance of subjective factors: "This is the strangest 'objectivity' possible: the absolute certainty about what I *am* was projected on some accidental reality" (E:B, 4).

Though it does not mention Nietzsche, Frank Kermode's study of "the sense of an ending" makes some penetrating comments about the mood of crisis.[30] Crisis, he argues, is a way of giving special importance against the backdrop of the ages to the piece of time in which we live. This intensification of the present ought to be analyzed as an almost instinctive response to an uneasy awareness of mortality. Of course, when Nietzsche—in his meditations on sickness and health—ascribed his philosophy to his will to live, he was himself admitting the key role of similar existential factors. More narrowly, Kermode's point accounts for the peculiar intertwining of historical theories with subjective values in Nietzsche's work; he shows how the analysis of cultural crisis depends on a sense of personal urgency. This personal element surfaces in several of Nietzsche's most searching and vivid presentations of crisis, when he moves from ineluctable world-historical laws to the individuals, with whom he strongly identifies, who experience these issues as problems in their own lives. In this area of Nietzsche's thought, we are never very far from writing that would look to a novelist like the preliminary sketch for a character study.

Kermode goes on to argue that "eschatological anxiety" is an inescapable part of the human situation, and that consequently it "is a peculiarity of the imagination that it is always at the end of an era." Such a sweeping statement would leave little room for definitions of modernism or for assessments of Nietzsche's role within it. But ultimately Kermode must admit that the sense of an ending can assume distinctive forms; having usefully reminded us that Nietzsche's general outlook was hardly unique or unprecedented, he opens the way for an inquiry into the special features of this version of crisis thinking. At the level of presuppositions and leading concerns, the imagination does make characteristic choices.

The basic assumption behind Nietzsche's sense of crisis is the idea of cultural form. Every society possesses a system of values, uniquely its own, which is held together by an overarching myth or—to use some less loaded terms he eventually preferred—a "fundamental idea" or a "conjecture."[31] In the absence of this original premise, the value-system would lose its coherence; human experience and perception would lose their unity and shape, and would present themselves as chaos. It is important to realize that Nietzsche was fully capable of regarding the great variety of cultures with the neutrality of the ideal anthropologist. The overarching cultural form could be any goal, any of the thousand goals that the thousand peoples have set for themselves, to revert to Zarathustra's parable. At this level, Nietzsche's notion of culture diverges sharply from the tendentiousness of the early twentieth-century distinction between culture and civilization, which was eventually used for propaganda during World War I. Mann's *Reflections of an Apolitical Man* relied heavily on this contrast, which seems to color his discussion of Nietzsche's thought when writing *Doctor Faustus*; for when Mann points out the central place of culture, he maintains that it is a specific positive goal, "the nobility of life" (W:IX, 685). Actually, as we shall see in a moment, cultures could wander very far from this happy state.

The fundamental choices that create a specific cultural form are prior to all other decisions about social organization. In particular, political issues must be interpreted as simply consequences of a cultural situation. This outlook becomes important for Nietzsche's heirs, who portray revolutions and historical crises directly or at least make them a major unspoken assumption behind their works. Thus Mann depicts the rise and fall of Hitlerism, Malraux chronicles events in the Chinese revolution, and World War I and its aftermath are ever-present in Lawrence's imagination. But these events, even for people who can be as political-minded as Mann and Malraux, are ultimately derivative, symptomatic. They turn out to be the expression of larger crises whose true nature they distort and which they are incapable of resolving. As a result, one characteristic strategy on the part of these writers is the attempt to get beyond the events in the foreground to the cultural framework which Nietzsche had taught them was more important.

Having adopted these general attitudes, Nietzsche goes on to identify two distinct cultural situations which also had a powerful hold on his imagination. Both are present from the time of his earliest writings, and yet he never devised a consistent terminology that would clarify the difference between them. Even in his last works, when he repeatedly warns against the decadence and nihilism of Western culture, he tends to use these words as if they were interchangeable. In what follows I propose to give these dramatic terms a precision of meaning that Nietzsche failed to provide, on the conceptual if not on the imaginative plane.

A culture is decadent so long as it offers a system of values that can shape experience to some extent, even though its capacity to affirm life fully and directly has slipped to a marked degree or has never existed. Of course, Nietzsche sees all cultures as victories over chaos and hence as arbitrary. But a decadent culture represents a new level of the arbitrary, since its form-giving impulse is capable of mastering only a part of the reality presented for assimilation; it operates only by virtue of a radical exclusion, and this exclusion is the measure of its decadence. The situation of nihilism arises when the shaping principle breaks down still further, to the point where no cultural form at all is produced. In that case people confront the essential chaos of the universe from which all cultural meaning has disappeared, and they experience a total loss of coherence. This situation corresponds to a total failure to affirm life that tends toward suicide and is intolerable over any long period of time.

If we use this more precise terminology, we see that Nietzsche's intense mood of crisis grows out of his conviction that nihilism was an immediate threat for the Europe of his day. Though he would obviously prefer not to live in a decadent culture, he is mainly concerned about those aspects of decadence that signal the approach of nihilism. Thus the curious occasions when he voices a certain resignation or even reconciliation: he can wonder, for example, whether humanity might not be decadent by nature (E:IV, 7), and he finds much to admire in Buddhism where decadence has been stabilized (AC, 21-23). But in the case of Western culture he makes the audacious assumption that its cultural principle is so constituted that it will consume itself as a result of its own inherent logic. Here the weakening of form necessarily foreshadows its imminent disappearance, and the recognition of decadence is in itself a prognosis of nihilism and crisis.

Decadence and nihilism are psychological concepts as well as cultural ones, and not simply as a result of Nietzsche's penchant for ambiguous conflations of the historical and the individual. Both terms are readily transferable to declines in the intrinsic vitality of the self, and in that sense make an important contribution to his analysis of inadequacy before the conditions of life. But they differ in one important way from *ressentiment*, which depended on comparative feelings of inadequacy; for now the problem centers on the individual in himself, prior to all comparison. In other words, Nietzsche is pursuing the other possibility that came up during his ambivalent reflections in *The Birth of Tragedy* on the cultural preeminence of the Greeks. With decadence and nihilism he has turned from induced to innate inadequacy.

Psychological decadence can suggest different issues at various times in Nietzsche's career: it can mean the deceptions of a theoretical mode of consciousness, the alienation from existence arising from a suppression of the instincts, or the problem of disintegration among the energies of the self. In discussing nihilism, Nietzsche seeks to uncover and identify the death-directed tendencies of the psyche. Meanwhile, the character sketches of "theoretical man," of Socrates and Wagner, and of the "ascetic priest" serve to flesh out these psychological doctrines even as they provide telling epitomes of different cultural moments.

As with the polaristic outlook, the concern with cultural crisis takes on different forms as Nietzsche's career moves forward. Again we shall have to allow for the disproportionate interest that writers had in *The Birth of Tragedy*. But this area is dominated by the late Nietzsche, the critic and analyst of Christian myths and values who foresees, in the death of God, the end of an entire cultural form. Not that this crisis of nihilism need be an unmitigated disaster, since it could clear the ground for the spread of a new culture based on more profound and inclusive principles. So it is that Nietzsche raises the slogan that hopefully proclaims a new dispensation: "Dionysus versus the Crucified." But his fuller visions of renewal, as personified by Zarathustra and the superman, are imaginatively feeble when placed alongside his stark sense of decline and fall.

Myth, Theory, and the Artistic Socrates

In *The Birth of Tragedy* Nietzsche's point of departure is cultural excellence. The historical example of the Greeks demonstrates the vital importance of possessing a characteristic, enduring, and wide-ranging set of principles for integrating experience, principles which aim at nothing less than constituting a culture in its entirety. At this stage Nietzsche identifies this cultural form with myth, defined as "a concentrated image of the world" or a "condensation of phenomena" which is associated with a "fixed and sacred primordial site" that "completes and unifies a whole cultural movement" (B, 23). Though there is much in this definition that might suggest extensiveness as well as unity, it does not do justice to the richness and complexity of the interaction between Apollo and Dionysus presented earlier in *Birth*. "Fixed" in particular implies an overly simple and static notion of unity and might represent a grafting of Wagner's project for Bayreuth onto Nietzsche's idea of the Greeks. "Sacred" raises another difficulty, which becomes more explicit later on when Nietzsche associates myth with "the true, that is metaphysical, significance of life" (B, 23). His occasional attempts in *Birth* to push culture toward a religious transcendence clash sharply with his later views, in which a culture was the more highly to be valued the more thoroughly it accepted this world in its totality. These attitudes may already be sensed in phrases like "image of the world" or "condensation of phenomena." And insofar as *Birth* tends to treat Apollo and Dionysus as expressions of the basic principles at work in the Greeks in their development from Homer to Socrates, Nietzsche views myth in purely immanent terms. He is interpreting the two gods as organizing forms projected out from the leading qualities of a people's life.

In taking up the problem of theoretical culture Nietzsche turns from his vision of excellence to the themes of decadence and nihilism central to his sense of crisis. These speculations were closely bound up with his personal situation. As he wrote *Birth*, and indeed until he gave up his position at the University of Basel, Nietzsche had very mixed feelings about being a scholarly specialist. He evaluates the theoretical outlook from the inside. In historical terms he treats it as a fall from the powerful and encompassing unity of the tragic age, tracing it back to "that Socratism which is bent on the destruction of myth" (B, 23). In particular, as our discussion of theoretical man in the first section has shown, he links this breakdown of myth to a radical exclusion of man's instinctual life. Because theory is reductive, it is decadent; Nietzsche admires Aristophanes for recognizing Socrates and Euripides as signs of "a degenerate culture" (B, 17).

Yet theory is far from being nihilistic since it still possesses a capacity to give meaning to experience which acts as a bulwark against total chaos. Nietzsche can speculate, perhaps thinking of the wisdom of Silenus and its yearning after death, that in the absence of the theoretical outlook there might have occurred a weakening of "the instinctive lust for life to such an extent that suicide would have become a general custom" (B, 15). In fact, theory has proven to be so strong a formative principle that it has been the dominant force in Western culture, the keystone on which all else depends, having the constitutive function though not the fullness of myth. It has been set "above all other capacities" so that other cultural values are to be "derived from the dialectic of knowledge"; it has made Socrates into the "one turning point and vortex of so-called world history" (B, 15). A startling and extreme example of how closely knit theoretical culture could appear to Nietzsche would be his discussion of the *deus ex machina*, for the stage device which had marked the original triumph of theory over myth in Euripidean drama still persists in new spheres of activity. The basic tendency of modern industrial society is to substitute "for a metaphysical comfort an earthly consonance, in fact, a *deus ex machina* of its own, the god of machines and crucibles" (B, 17). The result is a superficial technological optimism which expands theory's disavowal of instinct, the natural in man, into an attitude toward nature as a whole. Nature is no longer an elemental Dionysian realm of creation and destruction, but becomes "a limited sphere of solvable problems" (B, 17).

At present, however, the situation of theoretical culture is,

in Nietzsche's view, critical. An inherent logic to its formative principle is leading it to its own destruction; now that it
has reached its fullest extension, it "coils up at these boundaries and finally bites its own tail" (B, 15). Less picturesquely
Nietzsche alludes to the critical philosophies of Kant and
Schopenhauer which had used the very methods of theory to
"deny decisively the claim of science to universal validity
and universal aims" (B, 18). The keystone has been knocked
loose, confronting modern culture with two possibilities:
either the whole structure falls apart or a more adequate principle takes over. The present, as Nietzsche sees it, stands
between nihilism and a reawakened mythical sense based on
art.

The first possibility leads to a vision of modernity as increasingly shapeless. It rushes "longingly toward ever-new
forms" but is doomed because of its inability to find some
enduring central imperative "to exhaust all possibilities and
to nourish itself wretchedly on all other cultures" (B, 18,
23). Foremost in Nietzsche's mind is nineteenth-century historicism, which in his view had failed to produce a coherent
and sensitive interpretation of the past; it had resulted only
in a flood of fragmented facts and impressions. In Nietzsche's
imagination, this disorder is linked to a sharp decline in vital
force; he sees his age as a lifeless wasteland, "everywhere
dust, sand, rigidity, drought" (B, 20). This image of a
shapeless mass of particles anticipates his definition of nihilism as an "anarchy of atoms." But there is also a possibility
for renewal. Naive faith in theory could give way to a
broader outlook; Nietzsche suggests that it is the "necessary
consequence, indeed the purpose, of science" (B, 15) to take
its place in a culture whose leading principle will again be
mythical. It is, of course, in Wagner's operas that he finds
the strongest evidence for the new influx of tragic myth
needed to accomplish this cultural transformation.

However, Nietzsche sees not in Wagner but in Socrates
the individual who most strikingly personifies his cultural
concerns, a person who, as he remarks elsewhere, "stands so

close to me, that I almost always do battle with him."[32] Socrates is crucial, because he is a borderline character with access to both of the cultural worlds in *Birth*. The first theoretical man, he sees beyond theoretical culture at last and realizes the necessity for tragic myth. Plato's image of the dying Socrates had shown that theory had the capacity to provide cultural form; it had become a self-sufficient ethic that could conquer even the fear of death. Nietzsche describes this Socrates in terms of a "logical drive" so powerful that it equaled the "very greatest instinctive forces"; as a result, Dionysus vanished from his nature and even Apollo retired "into the cocoon of logical schematism"* (B, 13, 14). But his last days in prison furnish an alternative image, that of the artistic or music-practicing Socrates. Nietzsche breaks with Plato when he comes up with an interpretation for the dream vision that, in traditional accounts, told him to practice music. Though Socrates did not experience the turn of logic against itself which in modern times had decisively revealed the limits of theory, he had at least glimpsed the possibilities of myth; dream and music, after all, were under the care of Apollo and Dionysus. Thus the very image that founded theoretical culture also contained elements of a more satisfactory conception of humanity. This artistic Socrates embodies the hope that the crisis of theory will be resolved by the emergence of more comprehensive cultural principles and not by nihilism, that "the net of art, even if it is called religion or science" will be "woven ever more tightly and delicately" rather than being "torn to shreds in the restless, barbarous, chaotic whirl that now calls itself 'the present' " (B, 15).

This early version of cultural crisis already brings together

---

* There is a contradiction here, for Nietzsche has been presenting theory as alienated from instinct. How can it be a "logical drive" of great power? Nietzsche's naturalism, which impels him to derive higher faculties from instincts, clashes with a residual conviction that reason and instinct are essentially different. We shall see how he resolves this problem when he returns to the character of the dying Socrates in *Twilight of the Idols*.

Nietzsche's main assumptions and concerns. It relies on a notion of cultural form, which in turn provides the framework for analyzing situations that are distinctively decadent and nihilistic. Finally, these ideas all converge on one character, which in this case typifies not only the original crisis but also the possibilities of renewal. In responding, writers would at times focus on specific details from Nietzsche's argument. Thus Lawrence was struck by the peculiar prominence of the *deus ex machina* as a key for understanding the dynamics of theoretical culture in an industrial age. Malraux was deeply impressed by Nietzsche's analysis of modern nihilism as a proliferation of disparate and incompatible cultural artifacts. He also remembered the artistic Socrates, but this character comes decisively to the fore only when Mann presents the shift from theory to artistic creativity in the career of his composer-hero in *Doctor Faustus*. Even here, however, the psychological theme dominates over Nietzsche's concern with cultural epochs. The same is true with Gide, whose story of a dead end in the theoretical outlook restores the suppressed personal context of a distaste for scholarly specialism. It is undoubtedly Lawrence who is most willing to pursue the grand cultural contrast in *Birth* between myth and theory, at times to the point of overweighting or seriously interfering with the psychological foreground of his fiction.

Christian Decadence and the Dying Socrates

After *Birth*, and with growing insistence during the 1880s, Nietzsche's mood of crisis came to center on Christianity. The basic approach remains the same as in his discussion of theory; but what had once been comparatively diffuse, "stammered with difficulty" (B:Pr, 3), has now become vividly incisive argument. Nietzsche writes with a sureness of movement, a conceptual rigor, and an energy of epigrammatic expression that can be overpowering; he can seem even excessively confident in the historical truth of what he has to say. And, of course, his subject matter now has a new urgency as well. From having focused on the outlook of an intellectual elite, his analysis of culture has widened to deal with the religious faith of peoples.

Once again Nietzsche's cultural analysis closely parallels his personal experience; just as theoretical culture reflected his life in German universities, so his discussion of Christianity depends upon his having been the son and grandson of earnest clergymen. Dissatisfaction with his immediate environment helps provoke an historical vision of epochal dimensions, in which Christianity replaces theory as the formative principle which has shaped two millennia. Nietzsche argues that the assumptions on the basis of which Western man has constructed a coherent view of the world are Christian; without them, all the varied parts of a complex structure would cease to bear a meaningful relationship with each other, would cease therefore to form a culture: "Christianity is a system, a consistently thought out and *complete* view of things. If one breaks out of it a fundamental idea, the belief in God, one thereby breaks the whole thing to pieces: one has nothing of any consequence left in one's hands" (T:IX, 5). We recognize the threat of nihilism.

But even before the decline of Christianity led to the modern crisis of approaching nihilism, the culture had been a decadent one. The central assumptions on which it was based represented a drastic exclusion of reality; moreover, its very origins had also been decadent. For Nietzsche the essence of Christianity lies in such ideas as a transcendent God and a morality of good and evil, in doctrines like original sin and an existence after death, in the symbols of a God on the cross or of the virgin birth. This set of beliefs is equivalent to the enduring nucleus of myth that in *Birth* gave shape to a culture. Throughout his later writings Nietzsche is tireless in his efforts to demonstrate how these elements of Christian myth collaborate in a radical devaluation of man's life in this world. This attitude of negation, he goes on to argue, must be interpreted psychologically as the expression of an underlying hatred of life, as an inability to accept life on the terms that it presents itself to human perceptions. But it is precisely this failure of Christian myth to do justice to life in its knowable totality that defines its innermost character. It is, Nietzsche concludes, "the most convinced, the most painful affirmation of decadence in the form of sublime symbols and practices. The Christian wants to be rid of himself" (C:E).

To go back to the origins of Christianity confirms the judgment of decadence. Nietzsche's "genealogical" method depends on his notion of cultural form; the original myth that founds a culture and gives it unity throughout that culture's existence continues to express the attitudes toward life that created the myth. Only when it has been amalgamated into a new culture can these attitudes by transformed. In the case of Christianity, Nietzsche argues that the name of the religion is misleading since Christ had little to do with establishing the determining features of the myth. Though Christ was an extreme antirealist, Nietzsche finds much in him to admire, as a creator of metaphors, as a person incapable of dogma or negation, even as a freethinker of a sort. It was the early church that transformed him into the miracle worker, the redeemer, the God on the cross (hence Nietzsche's emphasis on "the Crucified") that it needed for its own purposes.

These purposes are best understood in the context of the Jewish and Greek cultures of the period. Christianity is the summation and intensification of their decadence, "one further conclusion of a fear-inspiring logic" (AC, 24). The chapter "How the 'Real World' at Last Became a Fable" in *Twilight of the Idols* is Nietzsche's most brilliantly condensed statement of this process (T:IV). Still convinced that the decline of Greek tragedy was a decisive cultural transition, Nietzsche begins by portraying Plato as the philosopher who established the distinctive attitudes of the decadent phase that followed. Platonism fashioned the "oldest form of the idea," by proclaiming a split between life in itself and a higher realm of value and truth; idea, of course, refers to Nietzsche's very broad conception of idealist philosophy, and not to each and every effort to make generalizations about reality. The next step would be the "progress of the idea" in Christianity. A similar fall into decadence had occurred in Jewish culture, where the loss of political independence eventually resulted in the transformation of Jahweh into a transcendent God, "no longer a nation's deepest instinct of life, but become abstract, become the antithesis of life" (AC, 25). Christianity took this decadent version of Judaism one step further by developing "an even more abstract form of existence, an even *more* unreal vision of the world" (AC, 27). The role of Christianity was thus to consolidate relatively recent tendencies in two long-established cultures, revealing them in retrospect to be the beginnings of a new cultural principle that was to spread far beyond its Greek and Jewish origins.

Although the central assumptions of Christianity are relatively static, Nietzsche insists that they are capable of generating a wide range of consequences that will account for the variety of Western culture. Seeming contradictions should be attributed to the differing conclusions that can be drawn from the same premises. Thus, in analyzing the origins of Christianity, he had in effect assumed an essential identity between it and Judaism under the Roman Empire. The same is true of Protestantism and the Reformation, which gave a new emphasis to Christian myth that also promoted a Catholic version of orthodoxy; this process of mutual reinforcement brought to nothing whatever promise the Renaissance held out for really new developments. As a result, Luther, whose hymns he had patriotically saluted in *Birth* as the "first Dionysian luring call(!)," is revalued as "this calamity of a monk" who should be honored in Rome as a restorer of the church (B, 23; E:C, 2).

Nietzsche's fullest demonstration of cultural continuity comes when he examines the persistence of Christian assumptions in modern Europe. Relying on suggestive insight rather than careful proofs and rarely showing much consistency in the kinds of connections he makes between myth and culture, Nietzsche nonetheless creates the sense of some general correspondence through an accumulation of details. "How the 'Real World' at Last Became a Fable," for example, advances one of his favorite theses, that German philosophy and positivistic science were to be understood as elaborations on Christian other-worldliness which finally strained the premise to the breaking point.[33] Much of politics is also fundamentally religious in origin, whether Nietzsche takes Rousseau and the French Revolution to be the continuation of Christian resentment, egalitarianism to be a consequence of the doctrine of the equality of souls before God, socialist rhetoric an appeal to Christian instincts, or the state a center of authority which fills the place of God.[34] A last, extreme example will show how completely Nietzsche believed that the old cultural principle continued to dominate modern life. Even atheism can be derived from a Christian passion for ultimate truth, making it "the awe-inspiring *catastrophe* of two thousand years of training in truthfulness that finally forbids itself the *lie involved in belief in God*" (G:III, 27).

Thus, when Nietzsche tells us that Zarathustra speaks with "a voice above millennia" and is capable of setting "the whole fact of man *beneath*" him "at a tremendous distance" (E:Pr, 4), this interpretation of his hero epitomizes his own basic outlook in analyzing Christianity as a cultural form. Direct experience, even of a lifetime, remains imprisoned within assumptions of a much longer duration; in order to perceive the immense units within which fundamental choices slowly generate and exhaust their implications, it is necessary to possess a far-reaching temporal perspective. Then the internal laws of cultural form will become evident. As Nietzsche's increasing fondness since *Birth* for words like consequence, deduction, or conclusion suggests, these laws consist essentially in an austere logical process. The organizing principle or mythical center of a culture comes into existence in a formative moment which may fuse several separate tendencies. Thereafter it will continue to group together all the seemingly hostile and contradictory modes in which a culture manifests itself throughout its development.

Since Christian decadence depends on tendencies in prior cultures, it is not surprising that the best personification of this phase in Nietzsche's cultural analysis should be Socrates. The portrait of the dying Socrates in *Twilight of the Idols* turns explicitly on the idea of decadence, which has now become a sharply focused concept. Nietzsche interprets Socrates as the most concentrated and influential manifestation of the basic downward movement of his society, the source of inspiration for Plato and the rest of Athenian youth at a time when "degeneration was everywhere silently preparing itself: the old Athens was coming to an end" (T:II, 9). This decline is ascribed to a loss of vitality and energy, which results in a growing anarchy among instincts no longer capable of ordering themselves. Soon a desperate faith in rationality emerges as the preferred strategy for combatting this inner chaos.

By taking this view of decadence, Nietzsche has resolved the latent contradiction in *Birth*, where he was forced to present the Socratic alienation from instinct as a drive more powerful than the complex instinctual unity achieved by the bipolar resolution of art drives in Greek tragedy. In *Twilight*, he no longer emphasizes the disappearance of tragedy. That has already occurred, at least as a psychological event, for the new term "anarchy" may be seen as a pluralistic successor to the polar nullities which conceptualized the breakdown in organization in dualistic terms; Nietzsche now can assume many instincts and not just two. In this account, therefore, the disembodied reason of "theoretical man" becomes preeminent only *after* the instincts have lost their inherent ordering power. To Socrates it can appear as a higher faculty descended from another realm to bind disorderly drives; actually, however, it can only be understood as an instinctual force at a lower ebb, since whatever is selected "as an expedient, as a deliverance, is itself only another expression of decadence" (T:II, 11). Reason reveals the weakened formative capacity of the instincts; the very need to place it in a higher realm is really a sign that it can give only an abstract and partial, rather than a full and direct, image of experience.

The function of Socrates is thus to give a stable form to decline, to establish the decadent culture that later developed into Christianity. He might be seen as the forerunner of the "ascetic priest," the character type Nietzsche portrays in the third essay of *On the Genealogy of Morals*, and whose cultural role consisted in holding back an accelerating process of disintegration. In this context the image of the dying Socrates becomes an early form of the myth that reached its maturity when the early church made Christ into a crucified and dying God. Nietzsche views this preferred image of Christ as a means of giving cultural expression to feelings that existence was *"worthless as such"*; it is thus a "paradoxical and horrifying expedient that afforded temporary relief for tormented humanity" (G:II, 21). Similarly, the deliberately open-ended sentences with which he lightly sketches the execution of Socrates reenact the hesitant emergence of a pregnant symbol for the loss of vitality that constitutes decadence. Socrates welcomes death, not as the natural end of life, but as the revelation of its inner meaning: "Socrates *wanted* to die . . . 'Socrates is no physician,' he said softly to himself: 'death alone is a physician here. . . . Socrates has only been a long time sick . . .' " (T:II, 12). Perhaps the self-awareness about his state suggested in this speech indicates that Nietzsche still felt that Socrates was something of a borderline character with some capacity to see beyond the presuppositions of the era he had inaugurated.

Taken at its narrowest and most specific, Nietzsche's examination of Christian decadence was not notably fruitful among writers. Lawrence, it is true, proved willing to criticize the symbolism of a dying god and to chart the hidden continuities that reveal the Christian background of modern culture. But when Malraux develops a post-Christian humanism, he carefully avoids Nietzsche's vehemence about religion; Gide's dramatization of Christian life-denial is finally highly problematic; and though Mann accepts some of his insights, he is repulsed by the extremities of *The Antichrist*. The real fascinations of Nietzsche's argument lay in its broader implications. First, it raised the issue of decadence in general, the question of identifying slow declines in vitality and showing how they declare themselves on either a cultural or a psychological level. A great host of possibilities opened up for writers, ranging from Mann's efforts to come to terms with twentieth-century German history to Malraux's concern with portraying states of partial life-denial in characters, and including many other initiatives as well. Nietzsche's analysis of Christianity also provided a compelling, definitive illustration of his assumptions about cultural form. In response, writers would become adept at presenting the long cultural backgrounds behind characters, ages, or societies. Emphases could vary: in famous poems like "Leda and the Swan" and "The Second Coming" Yeats shows a special interest in formative moments and the nucleus of myth, while Malraux focuses on what he calls the "gridwork" of characteristic features that continue through time. Such is the suggestiveness of Nietzsche's assumptions that they could readily be applied elsewhere to produce, with Mann's notion of bourgeois humanism or Malraux's meditations on the ancient civilizations of Asia, very different definitions of meaningful cultural epochs.

Nihilism at the Door: Wagner, Aesthetic Politics, and the Mood of Europe

In his analysis of Christianity, Nietzsche does more than uncover the logic of a cultural principle and demonstrate its inner decadence; he goes on to examine the breakdown of all cultural form, and to prophesy that Europe faces a crisis of nihilism. Nowhere have these latter ideas been stated more memorably than in the parable in *The Gay Science* of the madman who proclaims that God is dead. When a culture's central myth can no longer be believed, the resulting loss of structure and of any point of reference brings man to a confrontation with nothingness: "What did we do when we un-

chained this earth from its sun? Whither is it moving now?
. . . Are we not perpetually falling? Backward, sideward,
forward, in all directions? Is there any up or down left? Are
we not straying as through an infinite nothing?" (GS, 125).
There are some important later developments to this formulation of the issues. The madman ascribes the decline of
Christianity to human agency, but Nietzsche often explains
it by the inherent logic of the cultural form. Though all cultures are probably unstable, he argues that Christianity was
particularly so because its decadence was so extreme. Denying reality entirely, it was fated to fall apart as soon as even
a slight respect for reality reappeared: "*One* concept removed, a single reality substituted in its place—and the
whole of Christianity crumbles to nothing!" (AC, 39). Alternatively, as in the explanation for the origins of atheism
cited above, Christianity is itself seen to create the forces that
destroy it in the end. This situation corresponds to the turn
of logic against itself in *Birth*.

The prospect of nihilism places Christian decadence in a
new perspective. Though life-denying it is at least a culture,
creating a form within which a people's life can still go on.
Hence Nietzsche's critical attitude toward the ascetic priest,
for example, does not exclude recognition of his value: "You
will see my point: this ascetic priest, this apparent enemy of
life, this *denier*—precisely he is among the greatest *conserving*
and *yes-creating* forces of life" (G:III, 13). Much of the third
essay of *On the Genealogy of Morals* turns on an epigram that
catches the worth of decadence as compared with nihilism:
"Man would rather will *nothingness* than *not* will" (G:III, 1).
Christianity's life-denial was so extreme that it left literally
"nothing"; but this nothing was willed, elaborated into a
cultural form with its own system of ideas and symbols so
that life was implicated in it after all. A more intense nothing
arises from the absence of will, the incapacity to create any
cultural form, even one whose essence is nothingness. In this
situation man enters a "fearful *void*" where he feels himself
to be "a leaf in the wind, a plaything of nonsense"; this total

inability to give any form or interpretation to life is now seen as death-directed, opening the door to "suicidal nihilism" (G:III, 28). Earlier in *Genealogy* some doom-laden imagery had anticipated these remarks. Still seeing nineteenth-century historicism as nihilistic in tendency, Nietzsche envisioned it as an Arctic explorer in a symbolic landscape of death: "here is snow; here life has grown silent; the last crows whose cries are audible here are called 'wherefore?,' 'in vain!,' 'nada!' " (G:III, 26). At times medieval religious frenzy made the quick transition from Christian decadence into the nihilism of "those death-seeking mass deliria whose dreadful cry 'evviva la morte!' was heard all over Europe" (G:III, 21).

But Nietzsche's stark foreboding of a massive outbreak of suicidal tendencies regards the future. The present age has not yet confronted the full significance of what is happening to it; when the madman of his parable proclaims the advent of nihilism, he is laughed at. One of Nietzsche's responses to this situation is the coolly distanced attitude of a cultural diagnostician noting the signs of an intensifying decadence which show that nihilism, "this uncanniest of all guests," "stands at the door" (WP, 1). From this viewpoint the multitude of forms which nineteenth-century culture drew from a Christian gridwork was no longer to be interpreted as cultural continuity but as fragments flying randomly outward from an explosion which had not yet been heard. Nietzsche's other response is to give a push to the process of cultural disintegration; he directly attacks the central principle which still gives the West whatever form it has. Christianity becomes "the *one* immortal blemish of mankind" (AC, 62), a statement which seems to contradict all that he has said about the value of decadence when compared to nihilism.

But there is a positive side to nihilism best brought out by Zarathustra's words: "one must have chaos in one, to give birth to a dancing star" (Z:Pr, 5). Total formlessness is the greatest challenge to the creative instincts of the individual; nihilism may simply be the precondition for tragic affirmation, the disaster that calls forth a person's greatest powers. The same holding by extension for humanity as well, the clearing away of old myths can be a preparation for cultural renewal. Hence, though it signals approaching insanity, the late Nietzsche's identification with the Antichrist does have a certain logic. He has chosen a figure in which Christian mythology contemplates the possibility of its own disappearance, but shifts it from a religious vision of the end of the world and places it in a secular philosophy of cultural form. Thus he assumes a role in which he administers the *coup de grâce* to a dying myth in terms appropriate to that myth. But in so doing Nietzsche has narrowed his perspective to a particular point in the cultural process; after the real respect shown for Christianity in earlier works, *The Antichrist* is one-sided. He has taken on the "somewhat audacious, relentless, even shameless disposition" that he had said was necessary "in order to combat anything founded in reverence" (WP, 457).

Nietzsche's late portraits of Wagner gave him a chance to personify the catastrophic plunge into nihilism that awaited Western Europe. *The Case of Wagner* was especially important. If a parenthetical comment in the *Genealogy of Morals* may be trusted (G:III, 27), Nietzsche had turned his attention to the problem of European nihilism in the months between that book and this pamphlet. Even more than was the case with Socrates, his thought about this phase of cultural crisis has a tendency to fasten on a personality. Moreover, though *The Case of Wagner* is now often regarded as merely a squib, it once represented a major point of entry into Nietzsche's writings. It was buoyed up by Wagner's enormous reputation, both in Germany and elsewhere. On encountering it, the young Mann was forced to reassess everything connected with his enthusiasm for the composer; Bely pays careful attention to it in an ambitious essay on Nietzsche; it was one of the first of Nietzsche's books to be translated into French; and the discussion of the Life Force in the "Don Juan in Hell" episode of *Man and Superman* (1903) concludes with an account of the Nietzsche-Wagner dispute.[35] Finally, *The Case of Wagner* has a powerful autobiographical undercurrent that goes deeper even than Nietzsche's old friendship with Wagner. The medical allusion in the title points up the essay's reliance on a wide array of images connected with disease—epidemics and hidden illness, surgical intervention and self-cure, diagnosis and the experience of recovery. It is the clearest example in Nietzsche's work of how cultural issues of crisis and renewal are related to personal experiences with sickness and health. This link with the self is made explicit at the opening of the essay when Nietzsche identifies with Wagner to the point of calling him "one of my diseases" (C:Pr).

Nietzsche's choice of terminology in *The Case of Wagner* is misleading, since it stresses decadence at the expense of nihilism. And, indeed, his remarks about nihilistic instincts and "the nothing" are almost parenthetical, while decadence merits an explicit definition.[36] Nietzsche begins by describing its stylistic manifestations, the lack of unity in Wagner's art; it is here that he draws heavily on the theory of decadence that Bourget had outlined in an essay on Baudelaire.[37] But when he moves to a higher level of generalization, he starts voicing his own characteristic concerns. This lack of unity should be related to a decline in vital force and a corresponding anarchy among the instincts, which, somewhat like Dionysian polar nullity, can produce either lethargy or violence: "life no longer dwells in the whole . . . every time, the anarchy of atoms, disgregation of the will . . . everywhere paralysis, ardousness, torpidity *or* hostility and chaos" (C, 7). Offering a contrast to this state is the phrase that pops out during the somewhat ironic appreciation of *Carmen* with which the essay opens—"logic in passion" (C, 2). As this notion is developed elsewhere, strong instincts "give to things out of their own abundance" (C:E); they shape themselves into a tightly woven unity, the *"rigorous* logic" (C, 9) of classicism. In making these points, the late Nietzsche is assuming the aesthetic naturalism of his doctrines of power or life, an aesthetic naturalism already latent in his account of Greek tragedy in *The Birth of Tragedy*.

So Wagner's condition of decadence has many similarities with a Socratic decline in energy and alienation from instinct. But if we look more closely at this portrait, we will notice significant changes of emphasis that suggest a major conceptual shift. In the course of the essay, Nietzsche takes pains to point out Wagner's espousal of Schopenhauer's pessimism and Hegel's idealism.[38] These allegiances are important because they bear on a larger cultural argument; they testify to underlying Christian attitudes, the first to life-denial and the second to other-worldliness. At the very least, therefore, Wagner's art represents a terminal stage of decadence: "everything that ever grew on the soil of *impoverished* life, all of the counterfeiting of transcendence and the beyond has found its most sublime advocate in Wagner's art" (C:Po). Actually, however, this remarkable convergence of decadent values masks a dissolution of myth that must be seen as nihilistic. For one thing, Nietzsche concludes the essay by naming Wagner as the leading example of an important new phenomenon—the emergence of the actor as the typical artist. As a result, his relationship to the inner principles of Christianity has lost all authenticity and become mere posturing: "the need for *redemption*, the quintessence of all Christian needs, has nothing to do with such buffoons" (C:E). In addition, it should be noticed that the definition of a "decadent" style in *The Case of Wagner* assumes a far more drastic loss of organizing power than in the portraits of Socrates. By this point there is no longer a counteracting force capable of stabilizing growing anarchy in the manner of Greek rationality. Finally and probably most importantly, Nietzsche's imagination responds to Wagner as a portent of impending disaster; he has given a new tempo to history, seen repeatedly in terms of a rapidly accelerating fall. Wagner's influence "drives one yet faster into the abyss" (C, 5), and the spectator "stands horrified before this almost sudden motion, abyss-ward" (C:2Po). For Nietzsche, Wagner epitomizes the situation of modern Europe as decadence reaches its term and collapses into nihilism.

A more precise inquiry into the nature of this crisis will highlight some of Nietzsche's strengths and weaknesses as a critic of the modern world, and will also confirm the thesis that the real theme of *The Case of Wagner* is nihilism. In claiming that Wagner is the best guide to "the labyrinth of the modern soul" (C:Pr), Nietzsche is following an assumption that had already governed his earliest discussions of artists. The great artist resembles great philosophers, heroes, and religious leaders in standing particularly close to the inner principle or mythical heart of a culture. He may be a Homer, who crystallized the Apollinian phase of Greek culture; or he may, like Euripides, be the creator of forms which reveal the onset of disintegration in myth. As a youthful admirer of Wagner, Nietzsche (with some forcing) made him into the Homer of reawakening German myth; after discovering the inadequacy of this response to cultural crisis, he views him as the Euripides of European nihilism, the *"most instructive* case" (C:E) available for cultural diagnosis. Taken by itself, of course, this assumption could be worthless; it is one thing to study the Greeks through Homer, and quite another to locate the equivalent figure for one's own age. But due to the happy coincidence of Nietzsche's carefully meditated knowledge of Wagner, both as a man and an artist, with the development of Wagnerianism into a movement with a large and devoted following throughout Europe, the transition from artistic to social and political issues was not simply an arbitrary identification. The assumption had a solid empirical basis not always present in Nietzsche's cultural speculations; it led to some very suggestive historical results. It is not surprising to discover that *The Case of Wagner* has had its admirers among historians, with Jacques Barzun seeing it as a first attack on the nineteenth century by a twentieth-century mind, and Peter Viereck finding it to be an early and penetrating critique of the emerging Nazi mentality.[39]

Despite these warm endorsements, it must be admitted that the cultural analysis in the conceptual foreground of the essay seems questionable. In the course of defining decadence, Nietzsche argues that Wagner's stylistic anarchy should be seen as an emblem for the leading political tendencies of the age: " 'freedom of the individual,' to use moral terms—expanded into a political theory, *'equal rights for all'* " (C, 7). This type of analysis may be called aesthetic politics, since it assumes that categories of artistic form should apply directly to social questions. The artist's exemplary role within a culture becomes rigidly fixed: because he ought to pursue tightly organized form, liberal and egalitarian principles can only be decadent, the equivalent in the social sphere of sloppy art. Though Nietzsche rarely states his premises as clearly as in this passage, some such attitude guides him whenever he starts holding forth on political questions. Insofar as aesthetic politics leads him to doubt the value of democracy or freedom, it is undoubtedly a major factor behind the suspicion of Nietzsche that has often surfaced in the English-speaking world. Certainly it would appeal to Nietzscheans, once it had been detached from his work as a whole and hardened into a doctrine.[40]

But the cultural analysis in *The Case of Wagner* goes far beyond this extension of artistic decadence into social thought. Nietzsche also makes some cryptic but highly suggestive comments on social atmosphere, comments that show once again the greater interest of undercurrents in his thought as compared to hard-and-fast formulas. In Wagner Nietzsche claims to discern the three leading qualities of the modern world, which he baldly lists on two separate occasions—brutality, artificiality, and innocence (C, 1, 5). To this triad he later adds hysteria (C, 7). These terms, like so much else in this tightly compressed essay, can only be understood within the context of the whole. Once interpreted, they add up to a somber vision of Europe given over to the suicidal form of nihilism.

Nietzsche elsewhere uses "brutality" to describe the manner of the *Tannhäuser* overture, the prime example of the tyrannic Wagner who composes "to persuade the masses" (C, 7). On a broader scale, this domineering violence is characteristic of the whole age with its militarism and its nationalistic rivalries: "—Never has obedience been better, never commanding. Wagnerian conductors in particular are worthy of an age that posterity will call one day, with awed respect, *the classical age of war*" (C, 11). Artificiality evidently refers to the loss of wholeness and sustained power that marks a decadent style; Nietzsche's definition of decadence concludes with the remark: "The whole no longer lives at all: it is composite, calculated, artificial, and artifact" (C, 7). Thus Nietzsche finds Wagner's artistic inspiration to be essentially fragmentary; he is a miniaturist, "admirable and gracious only in the invention of what is smallest, in spinning out the details." This failure of wholeness stems from weakened instincts and a decline in organizing energy, symptoms of a fall away from life which would also explain the destructive potential implied by brutality.

Innocence in Nietzsche's vocabulary is often a favorable word, but here he sees it as the inability to understand the unhealthy elements in one's motives. Thus he speaks of "innocence among opposites, such a 'good conscience' in a lie" (C:E). Hysteria is a closely related phenomenon, responsible for an "overall change of art into histrionics" that finds expression in the actor's "talent to *lie*" (C, 7). Along the same lines, when Nietzsche reviews *The Case of Wagner* in *Ecce Homo*, he refers pointblank to "uncleanliness in relation to oneself . . .: one does not *want* to gain clarity about oneself" (E:C, 3). This innocent form of artificiality is distinct from the breakdown of instinctual unity portrayed in Socrates; all self-knowledge as to the death-directed nature of one's deepest impulses has now been excluded. For Nietzsche, Wagner has the "naïveté of decadence" (C:2Po); his is a personality for which authenticity is simply "a liability" (C, 11).

Nietzsche had already predicted a classic age of war the previous spring when he published book five of *The Gay*

Science (GS, 362), but at that time he rather welcomed the possibility. His attitude in *The Case of Wagner* is markedly different. Though voices prophesying war are a typical, even banal feature of crisis thinking, Nietzsche's account is arresting and carefully grounded in his developing thought. His deepening concern with nihilism was already apparent during the fall when he brought out the *Genealogy of Morals.* Now, during the following spring, as he uses Wagner to gauge the efforts of nation-states to perfect themselves as instruments of violence, he suggests that they do not realize that they are working out the consequences of a deep-seated hatred of life. Instead, they find ways to deceive themselves with mass ideologies or appeals to *raison d'état.* Thus Nietzsche can speak of Wagnerianism as "something made cruder, something twisted tendentiously, mendaciously, for the sake of the masses" (C:Po); thus he can insist that "it is full of profound significance that the arrival of Wagner coincides in time with the arrival of the 'Reich' " (C, 11). Beneath this veneer of rationalizations, however, the classical age of war will be an exercise in self-destruction, the latest and most dramatic embodiment of Nietzsche's persistent concern with suicidal nihilism as both a psychological and cultural threat. With this broader imagination of disaster, which so strikingly foresees that the twentieth century would not simply bring greater prosperity and progress over the nineteenth, Nietzsche transcends his great limitations as a political observer.

The reverberations of Nietzsche's reflections on nihilism were numerous and diverse, especially once World War I gave a new urgency to his prognosis for European culture. Malraux quickly fastened on the problem of "disgregation" that appears as one element in his nihilistic definition of decadence.[41] On this basis he will produce, in the character of Ch'en in *Man's Fate*, a vivid and closely worked out study of a suicidal psychology that draws on nihilistic tendencies not only in European but in Asian culture. Lawrence's response to this side of Nietzsche is even more complete. He accepts the war as a fulfillment of European nihilism, he insists still more emphatically on the role of death-directed rationality, he allows for the Christian roots of nihilism, he pays careful attention to Nietzsche's imagery of disaster. But above all he creates characters whose personalities, works, and modes of personal relationship are expressive of crisis, and in portraying them insists on the distinction between nihilism and decadence. Mann, as well, is interested in exploring this distinction, but his fascination with *The Case of Wagner* also leads him to test its assumptions about fragmentary inspiration and, on a much broader scale, about aesthetic politics. In *Doctor Faustus* he tells a story where the main issue is the possible linkage between rigorous form in art and antiliberal social movements, thus neatly reversing the terms of Nietzsche's facile thesis.

Visions of Renewal

So intense is Nietzsche's mood of cultural crisis that even this stern critic of wishful thinking voices hopes for renewal. His most searching comments on radical change occur in the second essay of *On the Genealogy of Morals* where he outlines his basic assumptions about the historical process and the modern situation (G:II, 12). Nietzsche again defines nihilism—with support from T. H. Huxley, as he makes a rare favorable reference to a Victorian thinker—in terms of a loss of form. As a result, perceptions of reality dissolve into a chaos of unrelated elements: "the absolute fortuitousness, even the mechanistic senselessness of all events." Nihilism can be overcome by a reestablishment of relationship through the will to power, "the spontaneous, aggressive, expansive, form-giving forces that give new interpretations and directions." Nietzsche's emphasis is thus on a process of metamorphosis, since individual elements from the past may well remain largely the same while their significance and ranking change by virtue of the new form which has arisen to include them: "whatever exists, having somehow come into being, is again and again reinterpreted to new ends, taken over, transformed, and redirected by some power superior to it." This process can take place within a culture, where it would involve readjustments in the consequences drawn from a stable set of presuppositions. Or—and here it becomes directly relevant to Nietzsche's sense of crisis—it could bring about a different cultural form by establishing new cultural presuppositions or myths.* Once again, the modern breakdown of form is a challenge to the creation of new forms.

As he becomes more specific about the possibility for some new culture, Nietzsche obviously would prefer one that was more life-affirming than Christianity had been. We have already touched on the features in his work that would encourage the first of the two important approaches to renewal associated with his name. Despite his disdain for Rousseau, his glorification of the tragic Greeks could encourage a version of primitivism; the Dionysian element lost to the modern world yet necessary for a fully integrated personality had descended to them from prehistoric times. Similarly, master morality might be seen as a suppressed but essential primeval component of human nature, though strictly speaking it was part of a typology of moral systems that could range over all levels of development (GE, 186).

Alongside primitivism is the approach to renewal pinpointed by another of Nietzsche's cultural personifications. In his autobiography, when he recalls the conception for Zarathustra, he shows that he thought of him as a new version of the borderline character. Like the artistic Socrates in *Birth*, Zarathustra is both the founder of the presuppositions of the modern world—here conceived in terms of moralities of good and evil—and a person capable of discovering in advance the inadequacies of this cultural framework: "Zarathustra created this most calamitous error, morality; consequently, he must also be the first to recognize it" (E:IV, 3).

---

* Malraux, in his histories of art, uses the concept of metamorphosis on both levels, as the achievement by a great artist of an individual style formed out of what he has learned from his predecessors, and as the originating moment of a new cultural tradition.

But if we compare the texture of *Thus Spoke Zarathustra* with
that of *Birth*, we notice that there has been a drastic shift
away from the historical personality of the borderline character. In portraying this seer of a new world, Nietzsche abandons interpretation for outright creation; little remains of the
Persian sage Zoroaster, not even the characteristic perspective of looking forward at an epoch which one has established and realizing its limitations. Zarathustra exists on a
different borderline, at the end of an inadequate epoch and
on the verge of unprecedented renovation. He suggests the
emergence of a more unconditionally utopian attitude on
Nietzsche's part.

Many of Zarathustra's pronouncements have little direct
bearing on cultural renovation, and are best discussed when
we turn to the will to power. But in the prologue, before
Zarathustra learns the error of preaching to crowds, he coins
Nietzsche's best-known formula for the new culture he
hoped would fill the void left by the death of God—the
superman. This figure might be seen as the attempt to invent
a myth capable of awakening the fullest intensity of life in
humanity. In Zarathustra's words he is a "conjecture" who
meets the condition of not reaching "beyond your creative
will" (Z:II, 2). He avoids encapsulation in the limited premises of the short-sighted and hedonistic "last men" who
claim to have succeeded Christianity and who perhaps represent technological optimism or utilitarianism. They have
found happiness and blink; the superman remains true to the
earth and gives birth to stars, accepting experience in its totality and asserting the power of human creativity to deal
with it. Beyond expressing this hope, he has few definite
traits; Zarathustra, as a borderline character, only glimpses
him from a distance. Indeed, a future so unprecedented and
so variously creative could not be the object of sober analysis
but only of a lyricism that too often takes the form of grandiose and vaporous rhetoric. Zarathustra's discovery of eternal recurrence, which forms the plot of *Thus Spoke Zara-*

thustra, results in a more powerful myth for intensifying life, one that is addressed to the solitary self.

Several modernist writers had little patience with Nietzsche's turn from problems of decadence and nihilism to prophecy of a better future. One reason for this attitude was their distaste for the Nietzscheans, whose will to believe disregarded nuance and clutched eagerly at slogans that promised renewal. Thomas Mann has sketched the coarsening that Nietzschean themes of cultural renovation had undergone when he came to maturity around the turn of the century: the formation of an "hysterical Renaissance" as a cultural model, based on an identification of Cesare Borgia with the superman; an exaltation of the "blond beast" of master morality that overrode complexities of historical and conceptual qualification; an extreme primitivism in interpreting the Dionysian which raised the barbarian form of the drive over the Greek.[42] Mann is emphatic as to where he feels the real value of Nietzsche's cultural thinking lies; Nietzsche was, he says, "for me not so much the prophet of some vivid 'superman,' as he was to most when he was the rage, but rather by far the greatest and most experienced psychologist of decadence" (W:XII, 79). In *Doctor Faustus* he will explore the historical repercussions of ideas of primitivistic and utopian renewal, of what he calls rebarbarization and breakthrough; but he will show that the same slogans have different meanings in the career of his composer-hero, an alter ego for Nietzsche. Gide's negative response to the visionary Nietzsche is close to Mann's. Of *Thus Spoke Zarathustra* he remarks with asperity that it is "IMPOSSIBLE," that it appeals to "the lowest classes of his readers, those still in need of a myth."[43] *The Immoralist* may be viewed as a polemic with the Nietzscheans, since it restores qualifications to Dionysian primitivism that they had neglected. Even Malraux, who greatly admired *Zarathustra*, portrays in Vincent Berger in *The Walnut Trees of the Altenburg* a man who must learn that the true value of Nietzsche lies elsewhere than in activist slogans or preaching (A, 95).

On the issue of renewal it is Lawrence who comes closest

to Nietzsche; as we have seen, the title of *The Plumed Serpent*
includes an allusion to Zarathustra's animals. But this presentation of a cultural rebirth relies on Dionysian primitivism rather than on utopian vision. In addition, as Lawrence
struggles to reconcile the best in Western consciousness with
what he most admires in pre-Columbian religion, he becomes meager and vague in his writing. His failure, one
might speculate, has something in common with Nietzsche's.
Both *Zarathustra* and *The Plumed Serpent* were books written
in periods of serious illness and depression by men who suffered from chronic diseases with phases of remission that
could be perceived as returns to relative health. It is tempting
to interpret these pictures of renewed humanity as projections of a personal longing for recovery, a longing that had
been fulfilled so many times in the past. Some such substi-
tution of prophetic generalizations for a self-conscious
awareness of their own situation would help explain their
indulgence in abstract and unconvincing rhetoric. But in a
novel like *Women in Love* even Lawrence conforms to the
more characteristic pattern among modernist writers. Visions of renewal exist only as remote and unclear possibilities
strongly qualified by a tragic present. The dominant mood
is one of cultural crisis.

□

In concluding, I should stress once more the peculiar nature
of Nietzsche's approach to this "world-historical" issue.
Countering faults he had criticized in the historical writing
of his day, his method replaces nihilism with coherence, objectivity with personality. His ideas on cultural form possess
a subjective unity which transcends the facts, often open to
question or obviously speculative, through which they are
expressed. I do not mean to deny that Nietzsche intended to
criticize science or Christianity. And certainly even specific
matters, like the historical Christ or the meaning of Luther,
are of direct interest to him, just as Oriental art or German
cultural history are important in novels by Malraux or
Mann. But for all their forcefulness and conceptual rigor,
which testify to an active and wide-ranging intellect, these

objective pronouncements grow out of, and remain closely implicated with, a personal situation.

Nietzsche's claim that he is not a dogmatic thinker deserves to be taken seriously; it implies an acceptance of the relativism of individual insight. On a less self-conscious level, this spirit pervades his presentation of history, which characteristically shifts from the observation of reality to the expression of self. Collective laws of cultural form find embodiment in portraits of individuals who in turn can be seen as aspects of Nietzsche himself. With varying degrees of self-awareness, the different phases of his cultural thinking emerge from his own situation.[44] Thus the broad sweep of history in the foreground masks a more abiding attitude: the sense of being born into a world based on inadequate assumptions; of living at a time when whatever stability tradition has provided is crumbling dangerously; of facing fundamental changes that will be painfully far-reaching, hard to identify (surely the innermost significance to Nietzsche's life-long fascination with Wagner), and exacting in the demands that they will place on human creativity. Undoubtedly Nietzsche could have been more explicit about the kind of validity he ascribed to his historical reflections. However, the continual tendency for his ideas on culture to have a strong psychological component—so that decadence and nihilism can be conditions of the self as well as of the group—must serve to confirm the subjective nature of his cultural analysis. For him the world-historical attitude, in its final implications, is an instrument for flexible insight; it thus runs counter to the rigidity of an ideological creed. This ultimately hypothetical spirit, so akin to the aesthetic distance of imaginative literature, will continue to characterize the handling of cultural crisis by modernist writers.

POWER AND LIFE

Modernist distaste for the Nietzsche who prophesied cultural renewal and the superman did not rule out keen interest in the concern for creativity that moved him to these prophesies. Nietzsche's heirs were able to make this distinction because, like him, they valued psychology more than history, and so left themselves open to the subjective undercurrents of his thought. This preference for the psychological fact also meant that they were sensitive to the actual tenor of his life, with its lack of any immediate impact and its growing isolation. The only real compensation was his tenacious commitment to his own intellectual and artistic gifts; this dedication to his writing in spite of all obstacles was far more impressive to his literary followers than any sketchy and dubious blueprints for a new age. Placed in this radically individualistic and existential setting, his reflections on the origin, meanings, and rewards of creativity had a profound impact.[45]

We have returned, therefore, to the question left hanging at the end of the second section. What happens to Nietzsche's broad concern for creativity as he moves into the 1880s and begins to develop his major philosophical doctrines? A comment from among the unpublished notes collected in *The Will to Power* will illustrate the arrival of a new vocabulary, which absorbs his old psychological discoveries. Tragic affirmation, with its tonic heightening of creative impulses in the face of disaster, becomes an aspect of the will to power. As so often in the late Nietzsche, this doctrine steps forward hesitantly, daring to speak only in veiled allusions and in strangely emphasized words and phrases: "I assess the *power* of a *will* by how much resistance, pain, torture it endures and knows how to turn to its advantage" (WP, 382).

Conversely, a short parable from *The Gay Science* reveals a great broadening of his psychological interests under the cover of the old vocabulary. This is the parable in which Zarathustra appears for the first time (GS, 342); its title is "Incipit tragoedia" or "The tragedy begins," but Nietzsche is already glimpsing the possibilities of the will to power through the character who will shortly proclaim it as an explicit doctrine. The nature of the sun imagery has shifted significantly since *The Birth of Tragedy*: instead of the momentary bright spot of affirmation offsetting an inhuman presence, we have the tradition of fire-worship in Zoroastrianism that causes Zarathustra to greet the sun. When he thanks it for shining every day during his ten years of solitude, he suggests a more continuous and unexceptional state of creative activity. Gone is the exclusive concern with mortality and ultimate meaning, for Zarathustra honors the sun's creative fullness as a bulwark against the day-to-day pettiness of one form of *ressentiment*: "Bless me then, you calm eye that can look without envy upon an all too great happiness." Different as well is the account of joy and pleasure. Zarathustra hopes to teach "the wise among men to enjoy their folly again and the poor their riches," thus replacing the artistic celebration of extreme situations with a wisdom that accepts the comic and ridiculous in existence, and insisting on a sense of identity based on intrinsic worth rather than comparative judgments of inferiority. Beneath the banner of tragedy, tragic affirmation is being converted into a larger notion of creativity that can combat *ressentiment*.

Before proceeding further with this issue, I should say that as a concept the will to power groups together an even wider array of phenomena than *ressentiment*. In his allusive way, Nietzsche connects it with all sorts of emotional and mental states, even with *ressentiment* itself, so that at times it seems to be the basic explanatory principle in his psychology. It can also provide the standard for judgments of psychological value, as in *The Antichrist* which answers the question "What is good?" with the famous formula: "Everything that heightens the feeling of power, the will to power, power itself in man" (AC, 2). Value implies cultural issues as well; and indeed, as we saw in the previous section, Nietzsche appealed to the will to power when he discussed cultural metamorphosis in the *Genealogy of Morals*. This set of meanings for the term can be traced back to Zarathustra's original proclamation of the will to power, in a speech dealing with the problem of cultural form: "A tablet of the good hangs over every people . . . behold, it is the voice of their will to power" (Z:I, 15). Often Nietzsche is even more ambitious in his generalizations. In a note chosen by his editors as the grand finale to *The Will to Power*, and admired by Mann as one of his three greatest triumphs as a stylist,[46] he places the concept at the center of his cosmology. "*This world is the will to power—and nothing besides!*" he concludes after describing "a sea of forces flowing and rushing together . . . out of the simplest forms striving toward the most complex, out of the stillest, most rigid, coldest forms toward the hottest, most turbulent, most self-contradictory, and then again returning home to the simple out of this abundance, out of the play of contradictions back to the joy of concord . . . this, my *Dionysian* world of the eternally self-creating, eternally self-destroying" (WP, 1067).

This sketch will have suggested why discussion of the will to power has such a large place in philosophic commentary on Nietzsche; it is obviously central to his thought, but much remains unclear because of the many different definitions he gives or implies and because his thought was still in process at the time of his breakdown. Fortunately, the issue of creativity imposes a certain order on this confused landscape. For Nietzsche, culture is entirely a human creation, and so Zarathustra's speech on cultural form can continue in the following vein: "Only man placed values in things to preserve himself—he alone created a meaning for things, a human meaning!" Even the cosmological finale to *The Will to Power* ends with the afterthought that "you yourselves are also this will to power—and nothing besides!" This panorama of interwoven energies is valid for an inner world as well, and recalls some of Nietzsche's earliest positions on creativity—the self-heightening and diversifying capacities of the art drives, and the inextricable union of creation and destruction (if only because production of the new depends upon passage of the old) that characterized the Dionysian in *Birth*. But now there exists "nothing besides" this exuberant creative flux, which has become emphatically immanent.

Creativity informs Nietzsche's conception of the will to power to such an extent that it colors his very choice of terminology. In one of the first passages where he speaks directly of the concept, in Zarathustra's speech on self-overcoming, he engages in a telling play on words. The speech begins with a polemic against the word "truth," and "thinkability" is proposed as a better description for how knowledge works; then Zarathustra enlarges on this notion by introducing the phrase "*make* thinkable." The point of this special emphasis becomes apparent a few lines later when the will to power is mentioned. Nietzsche's word for power is *Macht*, whose punning resemblance to the German word for "make" suggests that he intends power to mean an active capacity for construction and invention, an ability not simply to assimilate knowledge but to give it order and shape. Since Zarathustra specifies that he is analyzing "a will to power" that applies to "you who are wisest," he has clearly described only one, intellectual form of creativity. Nonetheless, Nietzsche has driven home the necessity for an active psychology that *makes* what it can of the material in its characteristic sphere. If creativity in this sense can be so important in the "objective" realm of knowledge, it will also be important in other areas, and especially in art.

The concern with creativity thus embedded in the word *Macht* does not, I repeat, represent the full sweep of Nietzsche's speculations about the will to power. But it is central to his literary legacy. From this point of departure, writers went on to confront several key issues in his thought, issues which converge on Nietzsche's basic stance of aesthetic naturalism but which also include several problems in psychology and value. We shall begin with some passages where Nietzsche speaks explicitly about the will to power; but because he so often becomes indirect or even secretive I shall also have to consider the memorable formulas and slogans that lead up to and accompany his first statement of the doctrine. Thereafter, he turns aside, especially in *Twilight of the Idols*, to argue the possibilities of an alternate term, that concept of "life" we have already encountered as the positive standard by which decadence and nihilism were to be measured.

Equally significant as a deviated expression of his ideas are a number of images of power, which naturally went on to have a major impact on writers. And when Nietzsche turns to myth to draw together the varied strands of his mature thought—and in the process goes back to his early work and calls forth a new embodiment of Dionysus—he tapped another important source of literary appeal.

The Will to Power and Aesthetic Naturalism

Since caution is advisable in dealing with a philosopher who plays hide-and-seek with his terms, let us approach the complex of problems surrounding the will to power by observing how Nietzsche actually uses the word *Macht* in discussions of creativity. A good point of entry would be the description of his experience in writing *Thus Spoke Zarathustra*. In another of the passages that Mann singled out for their remarkable style,[47] he compares his mood of exaltation to "what poets of strong ages have called *inspiration*" (E:Z, 3); the elemental force that seized on him was not the fragmented, overly deliberate, yet decaying creativity of a Wagner: "Everything happens involuntarily in the highest degree but as in a gale of a feeling of freedom, of absoluteness, of power (*Macht*), of divinity." He had known an access of power that was totally involuntary, thus refuting by personal example the psychologies of conscious effort or will-power so readily suggested by the phrase "will to power." But for Nietzsche in this passage, it is more important to do away with spiritual interpretations of creativity; in the next section, he goes on to reject the transcendental implications attaching to "inspiration," and offers a physiological explanation for artistic power: "The *body* is inspired; let us keep the 'soul' out of it" (E:Z, 4). In thus insisting on heightened bodily energies, Nietzsche has given ontological point to the naturalistic analogies in his discussion of art in *The Birth of Tragedy*.

In a series of aphorisms in *Twilight of the Idols* (T:IX, 8, 9) that typify the multiple levels of thought in his late work,

Nietzsche offers a fuller account of the artist's psychology. Beginning with the source of creativity, he again harks back to *Birth* since he assumes it may be found in physiological conditions of frenzy or intoxication (*Rausch*). The "most ancient and original form" is sexual excitement, but Nietzsche sketches in a process of transformation and differentiation when he describes a broad spectrum of other forms that range from strong emotions like desire and cruelty, to the stimulus provided by competition or the coming of spring, and ending up with the psycho-physiological pressure of "an overcharged and swollen will." Then, signaling with a dash the acceleration of his thought, Nietzsche leaps to the final outcome, the aspect of *Rausch* that carries over to the artist— "the feeling of increased strength or fullness" that is the precondition for creativity. When Nietzsche returns to this point in the next aphorism, he connects it explicitly with his conception of power: "A man in this state [i.e., of strength or fullness] transforms things until they mirror his power (*Macht*)—until they are reflections of his perfection." Thus creativity as described by his philosophy of the will to power is an intrinsically natural phenomenon rooted in the body and in instinctual energy.

It will be noticed that in the passage just quoted Nietzsche speaks of transformation in a way that fails to do justice to his previous sketch of physiological energies shifting along a scale of possibilities. Transformation now simply means the true relation of artists to the world, and thus serves to undermine late nineteenth-century realist theories of literature which argued that the work mirrored the world; the novelist-hero in Gide's *The Counterfeiters* admires this level of analysis when he quotes Nietzsche on the "formidable erosion of contours" that occurs in art.[48] But the next sentence in the aphorism moves suddenly to a more inclusive generalization: "This *having to* transform into perfection is— art." The special emphasis here allows Nietzsche to gather up the larger sense of transformation neglected in the first sentence; there is an inherent "must" in physiological energies with artistic potential that causes them to perfect themselves. This process needs no transcendent or spiritual or even intellectual sanctions. Art itself is enough, since—if we let this insight reflect back on the previous sentence—it is the nature of strong instincts to perfect themselves in direct proportion to their power. In effect, Nietzsche has taken a rather limited point and rapidly expanded its implications so that it expresses the full sweep of his doctrine of power, so that it includes not simply the physiological basis but also the artistic self-heightening that is integral to his aesthetic naturalism.

In pointing to feelings of strength and fullness, this discussion of the artist's psychology has touched as well on the rewards of creativity. But an inner sense of plenitude and force cannot be kept locked within the self, and despite his individualism Nietzsche raises the issue of its effect on others. In this passage he refers obliquely to one possibility, the communication of a new vitality and energy to one's surroundings: "Someone in this state enriches everything out of his own fullness." Here in germ is the attitude we noticed in Chapter I when discussing Nietzsche's hopes that his own creativity might be an incitement to others. It would become, to use the suggestive title of one of Zarathustra's speeches, a "gift-giving virtue" that shunned disciples and sought to set people on their own distinctive way. Power would be communicated in the form of awakened capacity.

But the late Nietzsche's forceful and even strident manner of expression can suggest a very different view of power that would appeal to Nietzscheans. A case in point would be a description of the elemental creative moment in the *Genealogy of Morals*. Here it is the notorious "blond beasts" who have the role of being "the most involuntary unconscious artists there are" (G:II, 17). Nietzsche portrays them as "triumphant monsters . . . not much better than uncaged beasts of prey," "a conqueror and master race which . . . unhesitatingly lays its claws upon a populace" (G:I, 11; II, 17). Such vivid language inevitably encouraged other interpretations of power than creative making. Yet Nietzsche is not simply glorifying violent constraint. His starting point had been, rather, the creation of values in what he called "a burning eruption of the highest rank-ordering, rank-defining value judgments" (G:I, 2). And he made an explicit appeal to power only when he reached a very sophisticated level in the self-heightening of domineering instincts: "one should allow oneself to conceive of the origin of language itself as an expression of power (*Machtäusserung*) on the part of rulers: they say 'this *is* this and this,' they seal every thing and event with a sound and, as it were, take possession of it." Nietzsche has been consistent in his aesthetic naturalism when he situates value judgments and linguistic invention on the same sliding-scale as barbaric violence. But his rhetoric has a tendency to overshadow the distinction between different intensities of power, to sweep away the crucial reservation that we noticed in the second section, that his "blond beast" is a slave in comparison to the "sovereign individual." The result is uncertainty over whether power in its relation to others means productive or coercive making, the capacity to give or simply the opportunity to compel.

In the passages just analyzed, Nietzsche has identified his philosophy of power with several distinct and characteristic positions on creativity. Arguing that instinct and the unconscious have the leading role in art, and that physiological explanations should replace spiritual ones, he nonetheless greatly expands the significance of the aesthetic. It comes to mean nothing else than the inherent disposition of these naturalistic energies to transform themselves, and thereby produce the higher manifestations of humanity. Then as he moves on to the impact of creativity, Nietzsche gets involved in ambivalences over whether it would be primarily generous or domineering. Of course, none of these positions was necessarily connected directly with his doctrine of power. Precisely because the will to power represented what Zarathustra called a "dominant thought" (Z:I, 22), each of the varied attitudes that it gathered under a single rubric could also appear elsewhere in Nietzsche's work, expressed

in different terms that were often equally striking and memorable. It may well be that writers learned of his characteristic positions on power and creativity in these more indirect
ways.

Thus, in the aphoristic books written around 1880,
Nietzsche has already begun to distance himself from the
"metaphysical comfort" he had sought in *Birth*, and starts
voicing some of the basic assumptions of his aesthetic naturalism. *Human, All-Too-Human* opens with a famous contrast
between the notion that higher qualities must have a miraculous origin and the naturalistic outlook conveyed by the
methods of history and science (H, 1). In the latter, Nietzsche
sees what he calls a "chemistry of concepts and sensations"
through which "the most magnificent colors are produced
from lowly, even despicable materials." He concludes by replacing the opposition of high and low with continuity; the
high arises as a transformation of the low so that "the basic
element appears almost volatilized and shows its presence
only to the most careful observation." Shifting from this
chemical account of transformation, Nietzsche develops an
aesthetic one in *The Gay Science*, whose title reflects his enthusiasm for the Provençal troubadors. Accordingly, he celebrates the ideal of giving style to one's character, of fitting
the strengths and weaknesses of nature into an artistic plan,
and of becoming "the poets of our life" (GS, 290, 299). With
the will to power still below the horizon, he has anticipated
several of its basic attitudes.

With Zarathustra, Nietzsche invented a spokesman whose
slogans on these issues were just as arresting (and probably
not as misleading) as "intoxication," "blond beast," or "let's
keep the 'soul' out of it." In the prologue, his hero coins
vivid metaphors for the central imperatives of aesthetic naturalism; there is the radical immanence of "Remain true to
the earth" and the impulse toward creative self-heightening
of "Give birth to a dancing star" (Z:Pr, 3, 5). Later speeches
develop these values and advance new formulas for them. In
"On the Despisers of the Body," despite its title, Zarathustra

argues for a positive state of acceptance where it is understood that "soul is only a word for something about the body" (Z:I, 4). A better term for this sense of identity based on physiological energies would be the self, "a multiplicity with a single meaning," "a powerful ruler, an unknown sage." In his next speech, "On Enjoying and Suffering the Passions" (Z:I, 5), Zarathustra returns to this naturalistic outlook when he stresses that virtues "grew out of your passions" and are earthly rather than a "signpost to overearths and paradises." By the time of "On the Way of the Creator," which comes after the first explicit appeal to the will to power, attention has shifted from physiological and instinctual origins to the process of transformation; Zarathustra proclaims his love for him "who wants to create over and beyond himself" (Z:I, 17). With "On Self-Overcoming," he becomes more specific about the inner necessity for self-heightening that guides the creative effort. Life is defined as *"that which must always overcome itself"* by virtue of its "will to procreate" or its "drive [*Trieb*, as in "art drives"] to an end, to something higher, farther, more manifold" (Z:II, 12). By now, of course, these attitudes have been closely associated with the will to power itself, though we shall return to the implicit contrast between procreation and power at a later point.

In accord with Nietzsche's experiences as he wrote the book, *Thus Spoke Zarathustra* presents creativity as essentially involuntary and unconscious, though necessarily prepared by careful effort. Zarathustra must spend ten years as a hermit before coming down to the marketplace; and in his first speech on the three metamorphoses of the spirit, he begins with the stage of the camel "that would bear much." But with the third stage, that of the child, he celebrates the final importance of creative spontaneity: "The child is innocence and forgetting, a new beginning, a game, a self-propelled wheel, a first movement, a sacred 'Yes.' For the game of creation, my brothers, a sacred 'Yes' is needed: the spirit now wills its own will . . ." (Z:I, 1). Along with having a "will" that simply trusts its own impulses, this authentic self exists as a creative unconscious. When Zarathustra speaks of the body and the instinctual self, he insists that they are "unknown" masters partly because Western thought has refused to recognize their importance, but also because they are inaccessible to the conscious mind. So great is the separation, in fact, that in "On Enjoying and Suffering the Passions" Zarathustra defines genuine manifestations of the self as "inexpressible and nameless," thus placing language itself under suspicion as a mere fabrication of consciousness.

The notions of creativity implied by these speeches have become psychological doctrine in the section of *Twilight of the Idols* called "The Four Great Errors." There Nietzsche undertakes to restore "the innocence of becoming" (T:VI, 8) by refuting what he calls "the entire old psychology, the psychology of the will" (VI,7). To this end he emphatically reduces categories like will, consciousness, and ego (the latter not yet a Freudian term, of course) to the status of "phantoms and will-o'-the-wisps," "mere surface" phenomena (VI, 3); and he advances the thesis that "all that is good is instinct—and hence easy, necessary, free" (VI, 2). This polemic makes it clearer than ever that the will to power has little to do with conventional notions of the will. Rather than deliberation and conscious effort, it implies an instinctive spontaneity whereby impulses shape themselves, often through a long period of incubation, according to the premise of aesthetic naturalism.

As for the conflict between generosity and constraint as modes of power, this problem emerges most memorably in the years after Zarathustra's praise of the gift-giving virtue. In *Beyond Good and Evil* Nietzsche's ambivalence is formulated in terms of nobility, though the will to power is never far in the background. At one extreme, he can emphasize generosity in an aphorism on master-morality (GE, 260) that sets out from the characteristic premise that "The noble type of man . . . is *value-creating*." He then describes the rewards of creativity, and shows how it can work to benefit others:

"In the foreground there is the feeling of fullness, of power that seeks to overflow, the happiness of high tension, the consciousness of wealth that would give and bestow." Generosity is sharply distinguished from one manifestation of the psychology of inadequacy, though Nietzsche admits here as he does elsewhere that fellow-feeling is a complex blend of elements: "the noble human being, too, helps the unfortunate, but not, or almost not, from pity, but prompted more by an urge begotten by excess of power."

But in the immediately preceding aphorism Nietzsche apparently speaks for the other extreme, for violent domination along the lines of the "blond beast." Resisting "sentimental weakness," he defines life as "*essentially* appropriation, injury, overpowering of what is alien and weaker; suppression, hardness, imposition of one's own forms, incorporation and at least, at its mildest, exploitation . . ." (GE, 259). For readers unfamiliar with Nietzsche's aesthetic naturalism, this passage might authorize some overall definition of power that would make exploitation a mild variant. But the special stress placed on "essentially" indicates that he is describing an untransformed instinctual core, what he later calls "a basic organic function." A fuller range of possibilities opens up only in the following aphorism where Nietzsche moves to a higher level. Coercive power now turns on the self and becomes self-control: "The noble human being honors himself as one who is powerful, also as one who has power over himself. . . ." Despite the drift of Nietzsche's more lurid account of nobility, it remains subordinated to an ideal of creative endeavor and the enrichment of others that is unrelated to any actual aristocracy.[49]

Nietzsche finds so many striking ways of phrasing his aesthetic naturalism, both as will to power and in numerous parallel lines of thought, that it necessarily had diverse repercussions among writers. Though Gide and Mann mention power as such infrequently, they do respond to Nietzsche's general premise. Their early masterpieces *The Immoralist* and *Death in Venice* raise questions about whether this way of viewing human nature—and especially the assumptions it makes about the inherent nature of instinct—is either tenable or desirable. Even in *Doctor Faustus*, near the end of Mann's career, the presentation of an aesthetic existence remains largely conditioned by Nietzschean categories, while a naturalistic vision of radical immanence transfixes his imagination even as it wakens intellectual and moral doubts.

With Lawrence and Malraux, attention shifts to the specific problems in psychology and value that are associated with aesthetic naturalism. Lawrence drastically misconstrues the will to power when he criticizes it for being a psychology of consciousness and deliberate effort; if anything, Nietzsche directly anticipated Lawrence's own campaigns against the will, the conscious mind, and the ego. Malraux as well as Lawrence was perplexed by Nietzsche's ambivalences about power and nobility, and both of them make the effort to distinguish more sharply between generosity and constraint by using two different terms for power. From generosity Malraux turns to new problems involving social feeling and human dignity. But Lawrence prefers to explore the significance of power in more depth: in his novels after *Women in Love*, as he dramatizes a diverse array of issues connected with this concept and others in Nietzsche's thought, he espouses a thoroughgoing naturalism that can be curiously tempered by an insistence on transcendence. However, not power but "life" was the crucial term for Lawrence before this phase, as it was at times for Gide and Mann. But above all it was Malraux who preferred to confront the basic outlook of aesthetic naturalism by way of this alternate formula.

The Instinct of Life

At one point in his remarks on nobility in *Beyond Good and Evil*, Nietzsche identifies the will to power with "life," stressing that "life simply *is* will to power" (GE,259). But though "life" could serve very well as an expression of naturalistic attitudes, it was less satisfactory in designating creativity; as a result, perhaps, Nietzsche could remark in a note in *The Will to Power* that the philosophy of power filled the need for "a new, more definite formulation of the concept 'life' " (WP, 254). Nonetheless, even as Zarathustra introduced the will to power, he spoke of it as "the unexhausted procreative will of life" (Z:II, 12). The inclusion of a biological analogue for creativity in this phrase undoubtedly made the concept more suitable for Nietzsche's philosophical vocabulary. It is in *Twilight of the Idols*—whose original title, *The Idleness of a Psychologist*, shows the extent to which it deals with psychological problems—that he provides his most searching discussion of "life."

Life, it turns out, is a concept whose special psychological status justifies its use as a first principle. Strictly speaking, it cannot be evaluated objectively, since all such judgments depend on the mental processes of living human beings. Nietzsche formulates this basic psychological paradox in a passage which shows the same excitement at reaching a fresh insight that marked his analysis of tragic affirmation: "Judgments, judgments of value, concerning life, for it or against it, can, in the end, never be true. . . . One must by all means stretch out one's fingers and make the attempt to grasp this amazing finesse, *that the value of life cannot be estimated.* Not by the living, for they are an interested party, even a bone of contention, and not judges; not by the dead, for a different reason" (T:II, 2). Lacking a standpoint outside life, thought has to conceive of it as immanent. So crucial is this point that Nietzsche argues it again, and then concludes that this immersion in life means that evaluations of it can only be taken as psychological symptoms: "life itself forces us to posit values; life itself values through us when we posit values" (T:V, 5). A person will reveal the nature of his commitment to life in the kind of judgments he makes about it.

On the basis of this "amazing finesse," Nietzsche has gained a standpoint from which to attack all nonnaturalistic world views, whether philosophic, religious, or ethical. For insofar as they lead to low evaluations of basic conditions for existence—as in the denial of becoming implied by static cat-

egories of reason, or in the extirpation of the passions ad-
vocated by early Christianity—they testify to a failure to
come to terms with life. Nietzsche's analysis of Socrates and
Wagner, and indeed of decadence and nihilism in general,
depends ultimately on this definition of life-denial. His contrasting thesis is that "every naturalism in morality—that is,
every healthy morality—is dominated by an instinct of life"
(T:V, 4). If evaluations of life cannot be verified, they at least
have meaning as signs of how affirmative one is capable of
being in one's attitude toward life.

Hence the importance to Nietzsche of formulas that accept
existence in its totality; unless he is an actor like Wagner,
these unconditional affirmations correspond to the fullness of
his own instinct of life. This aspiration lies behind several
myths of power we shall shortly be considering, but it also
colors the naturalistic views advanced in *Twilight*. Reality,
Nietzsche insists, "shows us an enchanting wealth of types,
the luxuriance of a prodigal play and change of forms" (T:V,
6). Such a conception of the world is necessary, at least in
part, because it testifies to the beholder's fullness of spirit.
Nietzsche will return to this language in his quarrel with the
"struggle for *life*" of Darwinian naturalism: "the total appearance of life is *not* hunger and distress, but rather wealth,
luxury, and even absurd prodigality—where there is struggle
it is a struggle for *power*" (T:IX, 14). The stressed words
reveal another facet of Nietzsche's hesitancy about terminology. *Macht*, he evidently feels, is more effective in conveying
an affirmative richness than Darwinian "life," which may be
too closely associated with what he elsewhere called "the
musty air of English over-population" (GS, 349).

Nietzsche's sweeping assertions in *Twilight* can be misleading. Though he accentuates the psychological foundations to definitions of reality, he is not denying the value of
science or advocating a simple biology of euphoria; rather,
he is drawing attention to the unspoken and usually unexamined assumptions that govern the framing of scientific hy-
potheses. The major difficulty with his naturalism in this

book lies elsewhere, in his failure to make it clear that by instinct he means a self-heightening drive whose model is to be found in aesthetic activity. Not that this position has been totally ignored: he does include the aphorisms on the artist's psychology, and he has stipulated that "life" is acting when we posit values. The aesthetic premise also makes itself felt when he attacks philosophic reason for confusing first and last, for this way of thinking makes it impossible to perceive processes of self-heightening: "This again is nothing but their way of showing reverence: the higher *may* not grow out of the lower, may not have grown at all" (T:III, 4). His characteristic attitude is again in evidence when he discusses the transformation of passions in "Morality as Anti-Nature" (T:V, 1). First he says that passions are transformed when "they wed the spirit" (*Geist*), a formula that expresses precisely that dichotomy of lower and higher he had criticized in philosophic reason. But then he corrects his phrasing: "they 'spiritualize' themselves (*sich 'vergeistigen'*)." Spirit is a problematic category, and therefore appears in quotation marks; while the reflexive verb brings out the inherent capacity of a passion to raise and shape itself. Indeed, it would not be excessive to say that Nietzsche's doctrine of the artistry of instinct rests on the possibilities registered by the reflexive verb form.

In the first of two passages that serve as codas in *Twilight*, the aesthetic and naturalistic currents come together to provide a broader and more satisfactory account of Nietzsche's concept of life. The tribute to Goethe (T:IX, 49) begins with a play on words that neatly evokes the transformative capacity of instinct: the old cliché of getting back to nature did not apply to him, for he sought instead a "going-*up* (*Hinauf* kommen) to nature."[50] The aphorism then establishes the broadly constitutive role of aesthetic activity, for although Nietzsche is discussing a poet and novelist, he is not concerned with his art but with his life—and yet there is a larger art at work in the midst of life: "He sought help from history, natural science, antiquity, and also Spinoza, but, above all, from practical activity . . . he did not retire from life but put himself into the midst of it. . . . What he wanted was *totality* . . . he disciplined himself to wholeness, he *created* himself." But if terms like life and totality show the extraordinary reach of Goethe's creativity, they also mark the affirmative fullness of his naturalism. To the extent that he dares "to afford the whole range and wealth of being natural," he accepts life as a whole; he "stands amid the cosmos with a joyous and trusting fatalism . . . *he does not negate any more.*" In contrast to *ressentiment* or to decadence and nihilism, he has attained a state of being that is fully adequate to existence.

Whether or not they paid attention to all the details of Nietzsche's argument, writers did notice this alternate approach to aesthetic naturalism. In *Women in Love*, before Lawrence turns more exclusively to power, one major value is the capacity to affirm life fully, in the manner of Nietzsche's Goethe; and even later on he can still appeal to "life." He also subordinates art to energies that may be found throughout existence and that are creative because they are vital. Malraux's reflections on art in *The Walnut Trees of the Altenburg*, which are closely related to an imagined anecdote about Nietzsche, are more specifically aesthetic; yet they take as their central theme the linkage between artistic creativity and the fundamental drives of "life." Basic for his fiction as a whole, however, is a method of characterization that parallels Nietzsche by focusing on underlying commitments to existence. Malraux's heroes are people whose actions are dominated by the instinct of life.

Images of Power: Tree and Star

Alongside the intellectual issues posed by Nietzsche's philosophies of power and life, there were literary challenges. We know from the problem of idea and image that he often turned to figurative language in developing his thought. Thus, though the discussion so far has concentrated on formulas and arguments, we have already noted Nietzsche's celebrations of creativity in terms of child and dancing star, of overflow and wheel. But these examples do not suggest the full importance for Nietzsche's later philosophical doctrines of a set of symbols that point up or even qualify their meaning. These symbols might be called images of power.

If Nietzsche's discussion of *Zarathustra* in *Ecce Homo* can be trusted, the most meaningful of these images were the dancer and the fountain. Even when he insisted that Zarathustra was a nonpareil among figurative representations of his thought, he went ahead almost immediately to link him with these privileged images (E:Z, 6, 7). But he does not linger over them; it is typical of Nietzsche's schematic way with symbols that he fails to seize these easy opportunities for evoking aspects of the will to power. The dancer could have pointed up the artistic elaboration of bodily energies, and the fountain such attributes of power as its continuous flux, its mysterious origins in a psychic underworld, or its close involvement with a larger natural whole. To be sure, Nietzsche does show a somewhat greater sense for the concrete possibilities of these images elsewhere. Just before one of Zarathustra's speeches on the will to power, he asserts that "only in the dance do I know how to tell the parable (*Gleichnis*) of highest things" (Z:II, 11); and in the prologue, some dramatic descriptions of the tightrope walker (*Seiltänzer* or rope dancer in German) had served as emblems of the superman. Zarathustra had also portrayed power as "a new deep murmur and the voice of a new fountain" (Z:I, 22), and even in *Ecce Homo* Nietzsche could make a start at adding detail to develop his doctrine: "The highest and lowest energies of human nature . . . well forth from *one* fountain with immortal assurance" (E:Z, 6). However, these experiments were less important among his literary heirs than two other images of power which got less attention in the autobiography, but which were both more concrete and more obviously evocative.

In *Thus Spoke Zarathustra* the image of the tree has an ambivalent role, as if Nietzsche were just discovering its possibilities. At first glance it seems merely illustrative of the narrow argument at hand, but some of the concrete details in the descriptions transcend this scheme and evoke the basic stance of aesthetic naturalism.[51] Thus the comparison of man to a tree in "On the Tree on the Mountainside" seems intended as a polemic against moral dualism: "The more he wants to rise into the height and light, the more strongly do his roots strive earthward, downward into the dark, the deep—into evil" (Z:I, 8). But the most vividly realized portion of the image is the picture of the roots forcing their way into the soil, a picture that suggests the naturalistic imperative of remaining true to the earth. The picture of the branches is more abstract, since the branches themselves remain unnamed; but their upward surge does capture the process of self-heightening, especially in the German where Nietzsche uses a vigorous verb construction.[52] Similarly, in "On the Flies of the Market-Place" when Nietzsche needs a contrasting emblem of proud solitude, he turns to the tree. But as he attends to the image, it becomes more concrete and begins to expand in meaning: "Be like the tree that you love with its wide boughs: silently listening, it hangs over the sea" (Z:I, 12). Here the branches have been named, with their broad spread suggesting the elaboration and refinement of basic drives that occur in art; and as the tree leans out over the ocean, it shows without explicit statement that it is responsive to nature and even oriented by it.

In the years following *Zarathustra*, Nietzsche would make good on the possibilities of this image, relating it in turn to his philosophies of power and life and to his underlying concern with creativity. Thus one of the most searching meditations on the will to power in *Beyond Good and Evil* leads up to a definition whose language echoes his descriptions of a growing tree rooted in the earth: "Suppose, finally, we succeeded in explaining our entire instinctual life as the coming to form and branching development of *one* basic ground of the will—namely of the will to power" (GE, 36).[53] Or, in an aphorism from book five of *The Gay Science*, he places this image in the foreground; it becomes a vehicle for his basic philosophic stance, phrased here in terms of life rather than power: "Like trees we grow—this is hard to understand, as is all of life—not in one place only but everywhere, not in one direction but equally upward and outward as inward and downward; our energy is at work simultaneously in the trunk, branches, and roots . . ." (GS, 371). Or, finally, in the autobiographical preface to the *Genealogy of Morals*, Nietzsche refers to a tree in describing his own philosophic creativity. His ideas, he insists, have risen "from a common root, from a *ground will* of knowledge, pointing imperiously into the depths" and have grown "with the necessity with which a tree bears fruit—related and with an affinity to each, and evidence of *one* will, *one* health, *one* soil, *one* sun" (G:Pr, 2). In all three versions, Nietzsche has found the tree to be a graphic image for showing how a radical and uncompromising naturalism meshes with aesthetic processes of self-heightening to produce a single, definite philosophic stance.

The star should be seen as a variant of an image that is much more important within *Thus Spoke Zarathustra* than the tree. As we saw at the beginning of this section, Nietzsche's original conception of the book drew on the sun as a symbol of creativity. The sun, in turn, relates back to the fountain, for it streams forth light instead of water; and in Zarathustra's opening words, when he speaks of the sun's overflow and then likens himself to a "cup that wants to overflow, that the water may flow from it golden" (Z:Pr, 1), his metaphors confirm the underlying connection between the two sets of images. As he addresses the sun, Zarathustra is also careful to emphasize the generosity of its creative outpouring: "what would be your happiness had you not those for whom you shine?" This pattern of images and values will eventually furnish an emblem for his philosophy, for at the end of the first book when his disciples give him a staff with a golden sun on the handle, he interprets the sun as power itself and the gold as the gift-giving virtue (Z:I, 22).

Against this background the star becomes a vehicle for

Nietzsche's ambivalences about the powerful person's relation to others. At one point in "On the Way of the Creator"
Zarathustra identifies the outpouring of light with self-dis-
ciplined creativity: "Free from what? As if that mattered to
Zarathustra. But brightly your eye (*Auge*) should tell me:
free for what?" (Z:I, 17). Should the connection between
shining eyes and stellar illumination seem tenuous, it should
be remembered that the German word for the pupil is *Au-
genstern*—eye-star. In any case, starlight becomes an explicit
symbol later in the speech, when Zarathustra teaches the
would-be creator not to be troubled if the crowd fails to
appreciate him: "my brother, if you would be a star, you
must not shine less for them because of that." Here the star
has evoked both the genuine creative state and the ideal of
generous overflow. But there has also been a second tendency in the imagery of this speech. Zarathustra made his first
appeal to the stars after describing the spontaneity and self-
generating energy of the creative state with images drawn
from the third metamorphosis of the spirit: "Are you a new
strength and a new light? A first movement? A self-propelled
wheel?" When he turned to the stars, however, he did not
continue this line of thought. Rather than stressing the ef-
fortless outpouring of light, he asked "Can you compel the
very stars to revolve around you?" By shifting from optics
to orbital dynamics, he had raised the issue of coercive
power.

But there is an even deeper level of ambivalence to the
image of the star, for through it Nietzsche expresses some of
his most intimate doubts about the personal costs of creativity. "On the Way of the Creator" refers to interstellar space
to describe the terrifying isolation of someone who goes his
own way: "Thus is a star thrown out into the void and into
the icy breath of solitude." This image has a detail and directness that surpass all the other star images in this speech.
And solitude is again the theme in "The Night Song" (Z:II,
9), a lyrical interlude in which Zarathustra reveals his own
feelings. To be a source of light can mean being cut off from

others, for a steady outpouring makes interchange impossible; creativity isolates: "Light am I; ah, that I were night! But this is my loneliness that I am girt with light. . . . Many suns revolve in the void: to all that is dark they speak with their light—to me they are silent." Not that Nietzsche consistently holds this position; Proust would criticize him for still having faith in friendship,[54] and Zarathustra tells his followers to become individuals because he expects to have a more balanced, mutual relationship with them. He prophesies the start of "another love" (Z:I, 22). Nevertheless, the star images in "The Night Song" have special weight in his work as a whole.

They are special both for intellectual and for personal reasons. The isolation of the stars undercuts their splendid overflow, and Zarathustra is forced to admit that his stellar mission conflicts with his "craving for love." In *Ecce Homo*, where Nietzsche praises "The Night Song" as a poetic masterpiece and quotes it in its entirety, he becomes even more explicit. It is Zarathustra's "immortal lament at being condemned by the overabundance of light and power (*Macht*), by his *sun*-nature, not to love" (E:Z, 7). In concept or argument Nietzsche will never show so much ambivalence about setting power over love in his philosophy as he does through the image of the star.

"The Night Song" may also be seen as a veiled confession of Nietzsche's actual experience with a prospective close relationship, an experience that belied his ideals of mutuality and "gift-giving" and was equally far from any display of coercive power. He first wrote it after his hapless association with Lou Salomé, whom he had regarded as one of his most promising students and perhaps as something more. Only later did he give it a place in *Thus Spoke Zarathustra*.[55] So when he quoted it in his autobiography, he was not simply exhibiting a piece of fine writing; in "The Night Song" he had captured the emotional tone of an episode he otherwise treated with great reticence. The star that shines alone in the midst of interstellar space suggests the deepening solitude of Nietzsche's own life.

Yeats shows how closely he is attuned to one of these images of power in *A Vision*, where he places Nietzsche among the personality types characterized by "a noble extravagance, an overflowing fountain of personal life."[56] And, though it would be hard to assess the extent to which Yeats's extraordinarily suggestive images are Nietzschean, all readers of his poetry know how often and how memorably he turns to dancer and tree. Even among the smaller circle of Nietzsche's heirs emphasized in this book, the repercussions were strikingly diverse. Malraux will bring his long fictional meditation on "life" to a close by building on one of Nietzsche's images of power; as the title indicates, the tree has a major place in *The Walnut Trees of the Altenburg*. Again Lawrence complements Malraux, for in *Women in Love* the image of the star serves to focus his brief but intense early response to the philosophy of power. In his hands, this image leads to a reconsideration of the issues of generosity, compulsion, and isolation as he places them in the context of a sharper concern for mutuality in relationship. Mann, in turn, was less interested in the imagery itself than in what it revealed of Nietzsche's deepest ambivalences about his main philosophical principle. In *Doctor Faustus* the composer-hero who bargains with the devil for artistic creativity receives assurances that echo Nietzsche on the will to power but in exchange must abandon the possibility of love.

Myths of Power: Eternal Recurrence and Dionysus

Since Nietzsche once defined myth as a concentrated image of the world, it may seem pointless to distinguish his myths of power from his images. But myths are concrete in a broader sense, for they do not simply consist of significantly vivid descriptions. Instead, they are figures or formulas which bring together, in a compelling embodiment or a graphic assertion, the most important values in an outlook or creed. Moreover, if the tendency of images is merely to illustrate some large meaning, myths make larger claims on their audience and can even excite belief. It is precisely because these figures and formulas are so impressive that Nietzsche makes the effort to create myths of power.

In *Thus Spoke Zarathustra*, as was already indicated in the previous section, this effort centers not on the figure of the superman but on the formula of eternal recurrence. For Nietzsche this idea involved more than myth: among his unpublished notes, in particular, he made numerous attempts to define and prove it and to explore its consequences, all of which has given rise to a large philosophical literature.[57] For our purposes, however, only the mythical element is important. Here *The Gay Science* again provides helpful guidance, for in the little parable called "The Greatest Weight" (GS, 341) it gives a preliminary sketch of eternal recurrence. Nietzsche imagines a demon who addresses the "loneliest loneliness," a level of the self where assertions can acquire a mythic force and "change you as you are or perhaps crush you." The demon proclaims one version of eternal recurrence: "This life as you live it and have lived it, you will have to live once more and innumerable times more." The main value conveyed by this formula is naturalistic, for it seeks to exclude all possibilities of transcendence; in place of an afterlife where the conditions of existence would be different, infinite repetition insists that "there would be nothing new."

But if you can only have the same life again, the result should be an extraordinary heightening in the importance of existence. Thus some of the other values that Nietzsche associates with his doctrine. It becomes a creative imperative, for it sets demanding standards for every action and promotes a new sense of responsibility, the "greatest weight" in the aphorism's title: "The question in each and every thing, 'Do you desire this once more and innumerable times more?' would lie on your actions as the greatest weight." Moreover, the fact that eternal recurrence affirms this life to an infinite degree should make it a suitable test of a person's psycholog-

ical capacity to accept existence in its totality. Nietzsche concludes the aphorism with an anticipation of his concern for
fullness of life: "Or how well disposed would you have to
become to yourself and to life *to crave nothing more fervently*
than this ultimate confirmation and seal?" Eternal recurrence
also becomes a formula for his increased sensitivity to the
complex texture of existence. Acquiescence in the doctrine
may depend on one "tremendous moment" of affirmation,
but it releases the perception "that everything unutterably
small or great in your life will have to return to you." Eternal recurrence has indeed assumed a mythic role, for it has
furnished a single graphic formula for Nietzsche's concerns
with creativity, "life," and fluctuating psychic energies.

Nietzsche expands on these themes throughout *Zarathustra*, and adds the elements of a philosophy of time. But writers were probably most interested in his method of exposition: he creates an intellectual drama turning on the excitement
of dawning insight and a simultaneous hesitancy in coming
to terms with the new ideas. By the beginning of part two,
Zarathustra is already implicitly turning away from his
hopeful prophecy of the superman; when he says that "it is
of time and becoming that the best parables should speak"
(Z:II, 2), a new line of thought has already begun. At the
end of this part, in "The Stillest Hour," his dissatisfaction
has grown, and the voiceless whisper warns him that he has
left the most important truth unspoken due to fear and
weakness. Soon afterward, he has overcome his reticence
and begun to outline the new truth, for early in part three,
in "On the Vision and the Riddle," he describes the mysterious images from his dream about eternal recurrence.
Thereafter, both Zarathustra and other characters will discuss
the doctrine and gradually define it more precisely, though
no complete definition has emerged even at the end of the
book. But Zarathustra has overcome his fear of his new ideas
and in a series of lyrical interludes celebrates his acceptance
of eternal recurrence, an acceptance that amounts to a joyful
affirmation of life.

Because in this case Nietzsche portrays both intellectual and psychological developments with care and even virtuosity, he preempted the best dramatic possibilities of eternal recurrence. Mann does draw on some motifs in depicting the inner life of his artist in *Doctor Faustus*, but otherwise *Zarathustra* could only have served as the most general model for getting literary excitement out of ideas. Nor do Nietzsche's heirs seem to appreciate the importance of eternal recurrence as a myth. The thought changed and crushed very few people besides its author, and therefore never attained the status it claimed for itself. As a result, it was only natural that writers failed to see how it provides a single formula for several leading themes in his philosophy of power; they tended to respond to eternal recurrence only in discursive writings, where they treated it coolly.[58] The one imaginative response would be Malraux's account of Berger's grandfather in *The Walnut Trees of the Altenburg*, but even there the doctrine is a very general affirmative credo that has nowhere near the central significance it had for Nietzsche. A fuller and more striking rendition of eternal recurrence may be found in Yeats's "A Dialogue of Self and Soul." When the self insists that he is "content to live it all again / And yet again" and speaks of a state where "We are blest by everything, / Everything we look upon is blest," he has joined the radical immanence of Nietzsche's doctrine with the ideal of being able to accept life totally. But though this statement is climactic within the poem, the poem has no special place within Yeats's whole career as a poet. He identifies for one moment with the myth of eternal recurrence and some of the most important values it crystallizes; but, like Malraux, he does not make it a central concern.

After completing *Zarathustra*, Nietzsche rediscovered the Dionysian. It will be recalled that in 1886 he reread *The Birth of Tragedy* and wrote his "Self-Critique"; in his following writings, Dionysus acquires an extraordinary mythic significance. But despite the alluring eloquence of his appeal to the "genius of the heart" in *Beyond Good and Evil*, and the numerous comments on Dionysus scattered through *The Will to Power*, the most suggestive discussion occurs in *Twilight of the Idols*. Here, in the book's second coda, which had been foreshadowed in the first by a fadeout linking Goethe's attitudes with Dionysus, Nietzsche creates another myth of power.

In a letter Nietzsche once referred to this climactic passage as his "Dionysus moral."[59] a phrase that draws attention to the way he handles Greek myth. He makes no real effort to join a number of important values by embodying them in one vivid figure; like eternal recurrence, Dionysus is impressive primarily as a formula. Above all else, it is designed to account for "the eternal joy of creating" (T:X, 4) and thereby to glorify creative power. But, though Nietzsche ends the coda by calling himself "the last disciple of the philosopher Dionysus . . . the teacher of eternal recurrence" (X, 5), the two myths of power are not identical. For if the Dionysian state is rooted in a basic desire for "*eternal* life, the eternal return of life" (X, 4), it does not lead to visions of endless repetition of the same events. That hypothesis had ingeniously combatted hopes of an afterlife, but Dionysian recurrence simply means the cycle of the generations and affirms the biological naturalism of *Twilight* by viewing "*true* life as the overall continuation of life through procreation." Moreover, whereas eternal recurrence sought to encourage creativity by placing extreme pressure on every act, the new procreative Dionysus makes creativity an outgrowth of sexual instincts, along the lines laid down in the aphorism relating the artist's psychology to sexual excitement. Thus Nietzsche admires the Greeks for making "the *sexual* symbol . . . the venerable symbol par excellence," and imagines their world as one where "Every single element in the act of procreation, of pregnancy, and of birth aroused the highest and most solemn feelings." Creativity has become part of a larger instinctive striving to maintain and enhance life.

Among the values and attitudes prominently associated with this myth is the inextricable union of creativity and destruction. This union, it will be remembered, was basic to Nietzsche's cosmology of the will to power, a cosmology he had also called "my *Dionysian* world." In *Twilight*, accordingly, he puts special emphasis on an aspect of procreation that can symbolize the anguish and effort of the creative process. At this point his handling of myth shifts momentarily toward personification, though Dionysus is not the figure in question: "the pangs of the woman giving birth hallow all pain; all becoming and growing—all that guarantees a future—involves pain. That there may be the eternal joy of creating . . . the agony of the woman giving birth *must* also be there eternally" (X, 4). Heightening the impact of this passage is its relationship with Nietzsche's image for the third metamorphosis of the spirit; for if the child represents the excitement and liberation and joyous innocence of creativity, then childbirth might properly suggest the negative side of the larger, indivisible process.

But elsewhere in the second coda to *Twilight*, myth is handled as a formula: Dionysus becomes the key word that ties together many of Nietzsche's most important doctrines. The coda closes by defining the Dionysian as a psychology of tragic affirmation, as "the will to life becoming joyous at its own inexhaustibility even when *sacrificing* its highest types" (X, 5). But earlier Nietzsche has described it as the antithesis of one major problem in his psychology of inadequacy, for its procreative symbolism reveals no trace of "*ressentiment* against life*" (X, 4). And Dionysus touches as well on the issues of decadence and nihilism, since the coda opens with a contrast that expresses—instead of the pressures of comparative judgment—the psychological and cultural consequences of a decline in inherent vitality. The failure of modern scholars to understand the Dionysian rituals of the Greeks testifies to their "poverty of instinct" as contrasted to "the still rich and overflowing Hellenic instinct." Finally, of course, Dionysus becomes the vehicle for Nietzsche's mature philosophy of power and especially of life. Not only does the myth symbolize "the deepest instinct of life" so fully that

Nietzsche can declare that he knows "no higher symbolism," but it is totally affirmative: it represents nothing less than "the triumphant Yes to life beyond death and change." But this procreative Dionysus also links up with the will to power itself. After all, Nietzsche had originally defined power as "the unexhausted procreative will to life" (Z:II, 12). There is, however, a certain divergence in that the Dionysus of *Twilight* stresses the sexual side in Nietzsche's account of instinctual energies, but power often brings out the aggressive elements.

Taken narrowly, this late version of Dionysus was especially challenging for Lawrence and Mann, since it proposed that sexuality was the primary life instinct and formed the basis of artistic and other kinds of creativity. In a broader sense, however, this myth animated the work of all his heirs in a great variety of ways. For, with the exception of the methods and issues associated with Nietzsche's polaristic thinking, which was itself bound up with his early version of Dionysus, the Dionysus of *Twilight* points the way to all the major themes in his literary legacy. I say "points the way" because the links and connections are fragmentary and glancing; they would be meaningful only to an experienced reader of Nietzsche who was already familiar with the topics discussed in this chapter. Furthermore, they are associative rather than strictly logical, as is the way with mythic thought, and would undoubtedly bend or even break before the onslaught of rigorous philosophic analysis. But when viewed from a certain distance, they result in a web of vividly expressed values and ideas that radiate back through much of Nietzsche's work. Dionysus comes to stand at the center of a highly poetic construction.

From this perspective, the otherwise mysterious tendency among modernists to prefer this myth over eternal recurrence becomes explicable. The bare formulas of the "Dionysus moral" would seem to offer little to the literary imagination; but these abstractions at the center had been well chosen to activate the haunting resonance of the whole. Once all the memorable ramifications had been added in, Dionysus could become an electrifying figure. Equally striking were the claims advanced by this myth, which served to embody Nietzsche's aesthetic naturalism. At the heart of this dream of power and life, which appeared all the more desirable because of his graphic accounts of everything that threatened it, was a vision of human possibility. Perhaps this vision of active creativity and a full adequacy to existence was something never to be realized; perhaps it was surrounded by much that was questionable or contradictory. But those writers who felt the appeal of this myth—and who struggled with any of the numerous values and ideas that Nietzsche attached to it, values and ideas that were at once suggestive and enticingly incomplete in their literary expression—were well on their way to becoming heirs to Dionysus in a much larger sense. The rest of this book will tell their story, by following up the trajectories briefly sketched in this chapter and showing how the Nietzschean inheritance was embedded in a number of major creative projects.

III

From Nietzsche to the Savage God:
An Early Appropriation
by the Young Gide and Mann

At the end of "The Tragic Generation," a section of his *Autobiography* that looks back on his life in the 1890s and which he published in 1922, William Butler Yeats recalls the first performance of *Ubu Roi* in Paris. Despite the excitement of this avant-garde event, the play ultimately saddened him because it suggested that "comedy, objectivity, has displayed its growing power once more."[1] A death of tragedy had occurred, a death all the more notable because it contrasts so sharply with the stories that Yeats has just chronicled of his doomed fellow-poets at the Rhymers' Club. For Yeats, Jarry's play was simply one more example of the growing force of abstraction in modern culture. Earlier in the *Autobiography* he had described this tendency in his famous litanies against the scientism of Huxley and Tyndall, but it was also at work in the "anxious study" he discerned in a portrait of Woodrow Wilson, and in the "logical, glittering road" chosen by Bernard Shaw, his chief rival as a playwright.[2] But as Yeats finishes his vignette, he abruptly shifts his ground. His highly Nietzschean meditation on the fall of tragedy before the forces of theory gives way to an end-of-epoch mood; but rather than foreseeing a cultural rebirth, he predicts the overthrow of the modern world by an equally excessive counter-movement. He exclaims: "After us the Savage God!"[3]

It is uncertain whether this anecdote accurately reflects Yeats's mood in the 1890s, for he could have given his impressions this special cast only after discovering Nietzsche in 1902. But the story does capture the main line of response followed by the young André Gide and Thomas Mann. Their interest in Nietzsche had begun in that decade, thus coinciding with the first great surge in his reputation; as in Yeats's anecdote, this interest was based largely on *The Birth of Tragedy*. In 1899, Gide could write that *Birth* epitomized Nietzsche's whole philosophy—"all of his future writings are there in germ" (PR, 83)—and many years later, in a retrospective on his life-long fascination with Nietzsche that appeared in 1947, Mann closely echoed this judgment. In its main outlines, Nietzsche's thought "was completely there from the beginning, was always the same, and . . . not only the germs of his later teaching" but the entire doctrine was already present in early writings that included *Birth* (W:IX, 684–685). Eventually Gide's and Mann's interest would prove to be imaginatively fertile, for it would contribute to some of the best creative work they produced in their long and remarkable careers. Thus the heroes of *The Immoralist* and *Death in Venice* face situations that closely resemble the one in Yeats's anecdote. They turn away from worlds distorted by abstraction and theory only to discover that the Dionysus Nietzsche had invoked as his guide to a better, "tragic" culture is in reality a savage god.

As these remarks have begun to suggest, my approach to these stories will combine an analysis of their relation to Nietzsche with the international perspective of a comparatist. In previous scholarship on Gide and Mann, these two aims have been pursued only in isolation. On the one hand, Kenneth Burke and Albert Guerard have drawn attention to the striking resemblances between *The Immoralist* and *Death in Venice*, but Burke sees them as illustrating a modernist preference for "the problematical, the experimental" while Guerard explores how they testify to an emerging psychological sensibility in fiction that anticipates the Freudian system.[4] Both points are valid and important, but these stories are also part of a Nietzschean current within the larger modernist configuration. On the other hand, though practically every critical discussion of *Death in Venice* gives some attention to Nietzsche's role, and though there have also been several studies of his influence on *The Immoralist*, these findings have not been placed in relation to each other.[5] Within a broad set of interests largely defined by *The Birth of Tragedy*, Gide and Mann have written stories whose strong similarities provide the backdrop for interesting variations in detail. If we join these two tendencies in previous criticism and develop them further, we shall come to see the special place of *Death in Venice* and *The Immoralist*. They are outstanding examples of an early, founding stage in the appropriation of Nietzsche's literary legacy that also shows the special importance that *The Birth of Tragedy* could have for writers.

The term "appropriation" usefully pinpoints the main interpretive principle I shall be following both in this chapter and in my discussion of more ambitious works later on. When writers drew on Nietzsche's literary legacy for major artistic projects, they made it into something characteristically their own. So thorough was their assimilation or incorporation of the legacy into the work that the process can fairly be called an appropriation; the heirs take over. As a result, the critic must do more than simply map the numerous after-shocks of Nietzsche's ideas over a literary landscape. He must respect the integrity of imaginative literature, must shift at some point from Nietzsche to works which exist as systems with intrinsic characteristics of their own. Therefore, the need to add a third factor to the two discussed in Chapter I, the problem of idea and image and the shift from model to rival. For direct contact to be critically meaningful, it must affect some main feature in a literary work. In other words, the Nietzschean elements should not be scattered haphazardly, but must gather along some interpretive axis within the work like a basic formal pattern, an underlying thematic concern or assumption, a structural element, or an autonomous aspect of a larger whole. Only by setting out from one or several of these axes can the critic do justice to the intrinsic qualities of the artistic projects conceived by the writers, and also capture their profound and complex linkage with Nietzsche.

Let me put the issue of appropriation in perspective by discussing several Nietzschean parallels in *The Immoralist* and *Death in Venice*. It might be noticed that Nietzschean guides play a decisive role in the lives of both Gide's and Mann's heroes. Michel, in *The Immoralist*, has listened to the pronouncements of Ménalque, whose appearance recalls pictures of the insane philosopher and suggests something of his values. He possesses an "enormous drooping mustache," and the "cold fire of his gaze" expresses "more courage and decisiveness than kindness" (I, 431). As for Aschenbach in *Death in Venice*, when he notices the mysterious stranger on the steps of the funeral hall in Munich, this man is the first of several messengers of death (among them Tadzio) whose ever closer association with music suggests a growing influx of the Dionysian. Equally Dionysian is their generally exotic appearance, which ties into a system of motifs that at their most specific and memorable point to Asian origins: Aschenbach's vision of an Indian swamp after he notices the first stranger, the "orientalism" of Venice, the English clerk's account of the spreading cholera epidemic. In both stories, this Nietzschean guidance leads to recognition scenes in which a savage god replaces a Dionysian rebirth. Among the Greek ruins at Paestum, Michel reaches the demoralizing insight that in comparison to the "dark god" he now serves this whole culture means nothing (I, 467), while Aschenbach's experiences with the musical and the exotic culminate with his shattering dream of barbaric rites offered up to "the alien god" (V, 516).

My discussion has touched on several problems of idea and image. Gide's choice of specific details in describing Ménalque evokes a certain way of interpreting Nietzsche's thought, and Mann invents a series of concrete equivalents for both the musical and Asian elements in the Dionysian. There is also a striking example of the shift between model and rival, for the decision by both writers to emphasize a savage god represents a radical reworking of Nietzsche. But even in analyzing these isolated parallels, it has been impossible to proceed without paying some attention to the work from which they came. Thus Mann's systematic use of motifs raised an important problem of structure, and the link of the guides with the recognition scenes depended on their being joined by a meaningful sequence of events. Parallels become critically interesting only when they can be related to leading features in the works, so that their "textual function"—as Guillen puts it—can be assessed.

But to establish appropriation, the critic would have to push the analysis of motifs or action further. Only if he kept finding new evidence of the writer's involvement with Nietzsche would he be sure that he was dealing with an energizing influence that had penetrated to the mainsprings of the work. In short, he would have to reverse the method followed in the examples above. Rather than setting out from Nietzsche to analyze the work, he would begin by identifying some main feature in the work that was closely bound up with Nietzsche, and then move through it back to Nietzsche. His approach would thus have an element of what Sartre, in outlining an interpretive strategy concerned with different problems, has called the progressive-regressive method.[6] In Chapter II, we analyzed lines of development that reach forward from Nietzsche to the writers; but now, as we turn to the writers, we shall look backward through them to Nietzsche. We shall thus give appropriation its due, and—far from abandoning our concern with questions of idea and image or model and rival—shall have gained a method for selecting those examples with the greatest critical interest.

□

In a moment we shall see that the examples discussed above do not do justice to the young Gide's and Mann's relation to Nietzsche; motifs and action are both aspects of a larger pattern in both stories. But to understand the full significance of this comparison, it will be necessary to consider some biographical data about Gide and Mann, data that concern their direct dealings with Nietzsche and with each other. Given the similarities between their stories, it is perhaps surprising that the two writers were not familiar with each other's work during the pre-war decades when they wrote them.[7] But at some point both of them formed an intense imaginative identification with Nietzsche. This identification, when joined with their special preference for *The Birth of Tragedy*, helps account for the parallels between *The Immoralist* and *Death in Venice* despite the lack of direct contact. However, at the time of writing—for Gide probably from 1899 to 1901, for Mann from 1911 to 1912—they stood at different distances from their first discovery of Nietzsche and were not equally conscious of the extent of his influence on them. These differences were to affect the way they handle Nietzschean material in the stories.

When Gide wrote *The Immoralist*, he was still very close to the moment of discovery, so close that at first glance it is hard to see how Nietzsche could have had a profound impact on the story. In fact, when Gide himself discussed this period in his career in later years, he would insist that he had already planned the whole book and begun to write it when he first read Nietzsche. The philosopher's role had been largely negative: he had spoken so well about some issues that Gide found it possible to cut certain theoretical passages, thereby intensifying the concrete, "imagistic" qualities he felt were primary in art.[8] But some scholars have questioned the full accuracy of this account. Though it has been impossible to establish a precise chronology for either his readings or his work on the story, it seems likely that Gide learned a good deal about Nietzsche from intermediaries and secondary accounts before he actually picked up one of his works.[9] At any rate, he did publish a critical essay on Nietzsche in December 1899, well before he gave *The Immoralist* its final shape. In this essay, there are indeed hints that Gide's first direct encounter had been preceded by information from other sources: "I entered into Nietzsche in spite of myself, I was waiting for him before I knew him . . ." (PR, 85). But this remark is even more interesting for the conflicting attitudes embedded in it, attitudes which give a valuable insight into Gide's state of mind at the time. Along with a surprised acknowledgment of Nietzsche's priority ("I was waiting for him"), it suggests the possibility of resistance and revolt so as to maintain his independence ("in spite of myself"). Evidently *The Immoralist* emerges from a period in which strong responses have not yet sorted themselves out, and can fluctuate rapidly between the acceptance of a model and the need to surpass a rival.

In contrast, at the time of *Death in Venice*, Mann's involvement with Nietzsche had lasted for more than fifteen years and had become highly self-conscious. As indicated in Chapter I, he felt that in some of his earlier works—and most notably in his play *Fiorenza* (1905)—he had fallen so completely under Nietzsche's influence that he had to defend his creative independence. But he didn't let this experience affect his underlying conviction that Nietzsche's philosophy could inspire valuable artistic work. Several years after *Death in Venice*, in *Reflections of an Apolitical Man*, he is still willing to announce that Nietzsche's thought "could have become a windfall and a find for a great imaginative writer in precisely the same way as Schopenhauer's did for the creator of Tristan . . ." (W:XII, 84). At the time of his story, Mann had passed through a period of fascinated admiration and was moving toward a more deliberate and carefully discriminated response which would allow him to realize his own ambitions to produce a major work. Nonetheless, Nietzsche could continue to serve as a model in a looser, more general way.

When Gide and Mann did learn about each other, Mann at least showed a pronounced interest in Gide. But he largely ignored *The Immoralist* itself in favor of its biographical context, by which I mean events in Gide's life which had either entered the story after a fictive reworking or simply occurred during the actual process of composition. As a result, Mann's comments on Gide failed to touch in any substantial way on the similarities between *The Immoralist* and *Death in Venice.* His observations are, instead, a part of the prehistory for another major Nietzschean work, Mann's late novel *Doctor Faustus.*

Mann's first contact with what I have called the biographical context of *The Immoralist* occurred in 1922 thanks to a postwar discussion about German-French cultural relations. After reading Gide's 1899 essay on Nietzsche, Mann wrote him a cordial letter in which he mentioned his interpretations of the philosopher's insanity: "I am charmed to the point of rapture by such statements as, say, 'The most important thing is that these things should be said; because now, it is no longer necessary to be mad to think them.' Also your conclusion—'I prefer to say that Nietzsche made himself mad' shook me with delight."[10] This enthusiasm would become artistically fruitful in *Doctor Faustus*, where the hypothesis that Nietzsche willed his insanity becomes a basic donnée of the novel. From the viewpoint of the biographer-narrator at least, the composer-hero knowingly infects himself with syphilis; though the disease helps him to overcome his inhibitions, it also leads in the end to a Nietzsche-like breakdown. Moreover, in an interview with the devil, the hero is given the Gidean promise that his feverish creativity will become an accepted cultural possession: in the future, "the young will swear by your name, who thanks to your madness will no longer find it necessary to be mad" (F, 324). Mann has absorbed something of Gide's response to Nietzsche at the time of *The Immoralist*, if not the response in *The Immoralist* itself.

Several years later, in 1929, Mann reviewed Gide's autobiography *If It Die . . .*, paying special attention to the shorter, second part which deals with Gide's first two trips to northern Africa. Mann was struck by its qualities of "literary historical imitation" (W:X, 716), a suggestive phrase that could easily be applied to the appropriation of Nietzsche and *The Birth of Tragedy* that we shall be exploring in this chapter. But Mann focuses on *If It Die . . .*, which from this perspective becomes a double-layered narrative; in the foreground are Gide's personal experiences, while the background contributes patterns laid down by both Goethe and Nietzsche. Once again *Doctor Faustus* looms on the horizon. As a fictive biography, it too sets personal experience in a pattern given by Nietzsche's life, though Mann is much more emphatic in working out the possibilities for imitation that he had discerned in Gide.

But was Mann really thinking only of *If It Die . . .* ? Michel's journeys to northern Africa in *The Immoralist* were a fictional reworking of the experiences described in this second part; and when Mann defines Gide's imitation of Nietzsche as a discovery of "the dangerousness of Christian morality for life, the 'most powerful instincts' " (W:X, 716), he might be speaking of Michel. He might also be speaking of Nietzsche's own autobiography, which builds up to a denunciation of Christian morality for secretly intending "*to revenge itself on life*" (E:IV, 7). It suggests that Mann had noticed, or at least had a subliminal awareness of, the parallels between Gide's story and *Ecce Homo*. Not only is the term "immoralist" sharply emphasized in Nietzsche's autobiography, but at several points he interprets his life in ways that strikingly recall Michel. He describes how he drifted into a precocious scholarly career without really choosing it; he is grateful for having fallen ill because the experience heightened his feelings for life; he sees the emergence of his true self as taking place slowly and unconsciously.[11] Such parallels certainly could be called "literary historical imitation."

And yet Mann's term does not do justice to the full intricacy of Gide's relation to Nietzsche. At the time of *The Immoralist*, he could not have read *Ecce Homo* because the book was not to be published until 1908. The similarities with Nietzsche's life story must have been the result of an interest so great that Gide discovered the essential points elsewhere, either in the numerous autobiographical asides in Nietzsche's prefaces to his other books or in the growing critical literature about him in the 1890s. Thus he already demonstrates a great deal of knowledge in his 1899 essay where he speaks of "a sort of charming fatality" that "led me to places he had passed through, in Switzerland, in Italy—caused me to choose to spend a winter precisely in Sils-Maria . . ." (PR, 85). But this comment is even more noteworthy for revealing the extent of Gide's fascination with the life, his sense that he was fated to repeat Nietzsche. So strong an identification would explain how his current work-in-progress, *The Immoralist*, could contain so many "anticipations" of *Ecce Homo*. In fact, the identification was still very active more than thirty years later when, after rereading *Ecce Homo*, Gide could comment: "Every time that I take up Nietzsche again, it seems to me that there's nothing more to say and that it's enough to quote him."[12]

In effect, then, *The Immoralist* could also have been a model for Mann's conception of *Doctor Faustus* as a fictional biography with Nietzsche's life in the background. He was therefore misleading when, in 1951, he criticized Gide's story for its "rather faded originality" and for the "sheer philosophical deadweight" injected by its Nietzschean title (W:X, 806). Probably the comment only shows how much a writer's interest in a complex of ideas can cool once he has put them into a book. For there is no doubt that over the years Mann had been greatly stimulated by Gide's fascination with Nietzsche during the years he wrote *The Immoralist*.

□

But in *The Immoralist* itself the main line of Gide's response to Nietzsche follows *The Birth of Tragedy*, and not the pattern of his life. Accordingly, although Mann's assimilation of new material for a project yet to come prevented him from experiencing a shock of recognition, the most fruitful comparisons are with *Death in Venice* instead of *Doctor Faustus*. At no other point in the careers of the two young writers is the Nietzschean current as prominent or as influential. Gide goes on from *The Immoralist* to make a counter-statement in *Strait is the Gate* in 1909; the Nietzschean impetus slackens as other problems enter his fiction. Mann's many uses of Nietzsche in his stories before *Death in Venice*, at their most successful in *Tonio Kröger* in 1903, often draw on other aspects of his thought and usually lack the high polish and precision of this culminating achievement in his prewar career. In addition, it is these two works by Gide and Mann that had a role in later developments among Nietzsche's heirs. *The Immoralist* was a useful model for Malraux when he was starting out as a writer, while D. H. Lawrence was engaged in a major shift in his aims as a novelist when he encountered *Death in Venice*.

The appropriation of Nietzsche in both of these stories has been so thorough that it accounts for their very movement. At this level, Gide and Mann have patterned events according to a three-part structure, whose parts can have a differing relative importance within the whole; since allusions and images comment on the progress of the action, they also contribute to this structure. The opening stage introduces us to heroes who have suppressed their passionate, spontaneous selves and live in a state of precarious abstraction. Then, as they rediscover hidden parts of their character, they begin to experience a new joyous fullness of life. But eventually they surrender to the savage god: their sense of a more highly integrated humanity gives way to behavior that is ever more obviously compulsive and nihilistic. To rephrase this plot line in terms that bring out its relation to Nietzsche's polarities in *The Birth of Tragedy*, it begins with a period of Apollinian excess, either Doric or theoretical; then moves to a brief achievement of bipolar unity; and finally swings on to the polar nullity of Dionysus in isolation. So important are the polarities for them that Gide and Mann pay careful attention not simply to these psychological issues but also to the social and political implications that Nietzsche had associated with Apollo and Dionysus.

It will be noticed that the sequence of events in this three-part structure reverses the pattern that Nietzsche found in Greek culture, which moved from an influx of the Dionysian through the tragic age to the establishment of theory. Mann and Gide are not retelling the "plot" of *The Birth of Tragedy*, but are writing fictional sequels to it which weigh its meaning for the present. They have accepted the challenge of envisioning what Nietzsche had called, in the course of *Birth* itself, *"the reverse process, the gradual awakening of the Dionysian spirit* in our modern world!" (B, 19). In the course of evaluating this rebirth of tragedy, *The Immoralist* and *Death in Venice* touch on both its best possibilities and its worst dangers. Discussing this method in a preface, Gide comments that his purpose had been "to state a problem properly" (I, 367) while being careful not to take sides. The story becomes a vehicle for presenting a wide spectrum of attitudes toward the reinstatement of the Dionysian, with the hero's ultimate fate being only one of a number of situations, all requiring their own assessment, through which the reader is taken.

I have suggested that in Mann and Gide the initial stage of Apollinian excess takes somewhat different forms. Gide's Michel starts out as a precocious scholar who has "looked at almost nothing but ruins and books" (I, 374); blind to his own instincts and emotions, he is a theoretical man at home with mental abstractions but completely alienated from life. Indeed, his ignorance extends to basic questions of character and personal commitment, for although his father has overseen his education in every detail, Michel has always been prevented by "a kind of insurmountable reticence" (I, 373) from discussing his beliefs with him. This combination of extreme intellectuality and obtuseness about the self parallels, as we have seen, Nietzsche's account of his young manhood. But it may be assumed that Michel's study of Phrygian religious customs (I, 374) treated Dionysian cults with far less sympathy and psychological insight than *The Birth of Tragedy*. His arranged marriage with Marceline epitomizes the sharp split between his abstracted, "theoretical" mode of being and the immediacy of lived experience. It does not occur to Michel to question his father's wisdom in choosing a bride or to doubt that he can build a relationship with her on respect alone; he replaces love with the elaborate masquerade of "cool gallantry" (I, 375). As he tells his story to his friends three years later, he comments bitterly: "I pledged my life without knowing what life could be" (I, 373). The split between mind and impulse had been complete.

By taking as his hero a creative writer, Mann considers a less extreme form of Apollinian one-sidedness. It remains an art drive, though its relationship to the Dionysian is one of stubborn resistance; it recalls the situation of Doric art in *The Birth of Tragedy*. This orientation is described in the second chapter where Mann gives a highly compressed account of Aschenbach's career; he anticipates *Doctor Faustus* by providing his fictive artist with a whole opus that is highly revelatory of his innermost state of being. As a young writer, Aschenbach showed a strong tendency to break with art entirely. Even as he built his reputation with work that provided "lively delineation making no demands on the intellect" (V, 454), he was flirting with abstractions and questioning the justification of art. Though the two tendencies intermingle in his books, one imagines that the first stood out in his "prose epic" about Frederick the Great and in his Maia novel "rich in figures" while the second found expression in his treatise *Intellect and Art* (V, 450). We have an artist whose Apollinian delight in vivid depiction teeters on the verge of a theoretical denial of art.

Then comes the decisive change in Aschenbach's career, the short story "The Wretch" which runs through his mind during his stay in Venice. With this work he opts for Doric art. He rejects the attractions of theory, "the sharp and bitter stimulus of knowledge . . . insofar as it is capable of crippling, discouraging, or degrading to the slightest degree, our will, acts, feelings, or even passions" (V, 454-455). But even as he admits the validity of his art drive, he resists the instinctual realm that this decision apparently justifies; he becomes a devotee of form, of "cold, strict service," of "a discriminating purity, simplicity, and evenness of attack which henceforth gave his productions such an obvious, even such a deliberate stamp of mastery and classicism" (V, 455). This compromise guides Aschenbach's behavior in the early part of *Death in Venice*. Thus, on the one hand, his Dionysian vision after seeing the stranger at the funeral hall is at once "moderated and adjusted by the force of his reason and self-discipline" (V, 448). But, on the other, his deepening infatuation with Tadzio is marked by typically Apollinian reveries: he repeatedly admires him as if he were a statue, sees him as an embodiment of his own devotion to form: "What rigor, what precision of thought were expressed in this erect, youthfully perfect body! . . . was not he, the artist, at home with this?" (V, 490). Aschenbach struggles to uphold an Apollinian artistry that can ignore the Dionysian.

Aschenbach's social and political allegiances are in keeping with the Doric qualities of his art: he is accustomed to a rigidly hierarchical world with a strong, centralized state. The offspring of generations of Prussian bureaucrats, he has been elevated to the aristocracy for his epic celebration of Frederick the Great; his style has acquired an elaborate formality that recalls Louis XIV, and an "official didactic" tone that has endeared him to the editors of German textbooks (V, 456). In his image of the artist, Aschenbach rejects "chronic vagabondage" for an attitude of conscious dignity that makes his trip to Venice a matter of first-class travel and luxury hotels (V, 456). Here again his response to Tadzio sums up the bent of his character. He admires his whole family for its nobility—its "self-respecting dignity, discipline, and sense of duty"—but the boy stands out for the "aristocratic advantages" he enjoys over his sisters and for his ability to get his friend Jaschu willingly to accept the status of a vassal (V, 472, 470, 477).

Even as Mann and Gide sketch in the broadly Apollinian traits of their heroes, they show how precarious this state of being is, how much it undermines the very capacity for life. In emphasizing this theme, they have widened their frame of reference, for although the topics of decadence and life-denial may be found in *The Birth of Tragedy* they are much more prominent in the late Nietzsche. Thus Michel's trip to Africa tests his low, "theoretical" level of vitality by bringing him into contact with sensations that are more direct and intense but also more dangerous for his stability. To use Gide's images for the conflict, the disappointing Tunisian ruins he has come to study give way before the terrific desert wind and the jolting terrain of his journey (I, 377). Michel's inability to deal with this Titanic, Dionysian landscape manifests itself in his illness, the late Nietzsche's favorite symbol for decadence. But elsewhere Michel's retrospective interpretations are more important than the narrative in itself. He tells us that his precocious studies and his delicate health had reinforced each other, both of them being expressions of an underlying inability to live fully that revealed itself at the first opportunity: "The excessively sedentary life I was leading weakened and protected me at the same time" (I, 374). He also insists that during his illness his distanced attitude toward life prevented him from sensing the danger and delayed his recovery: "I was exhausted. I simply let myself go. . . . 'what does it matter?' I thought, rather admiring my stoicism" (I, 379).

As an original conditioning factor for his life-denial, Michel fixes on his mother's piety; her "stern Huguenot teachings" had encouraged the "taste for austerity" that made him a scholar (I, 373). The late Nietzsche's essay on ascetic ideals had also stressed the dependence of the modern theoretical outlook on Christianity. In a similar spirit, during Marceline's illness later on, Michel detects an interconnection between religious sentiment, modern science, and life-denial. Once a doctor takes charge of her case, she loses some of her desire to live: "Marceline complied quite meekly with the most wearisome instructions; a kind of religious resignation broke the will which had sustained her till now . . ." (I, 434). Michel's prodding has greatly enlarged the implications of the story's images, for not only his own "theoretical" bent as a scholar but religion and science in general have been viewed as manifestations of a failure to achieve existential immediacy.

In *Death in Venice* this loss of immediacy becomes an artist's problem, the crisis that Aschenbach faces in his style of creativity. More and more aware of an "increasing exhaustion of his strength" (V, 444), he has reached an impasse in his writing that has left him stymied for several days running. He has come to fear that his deliberate, "Doric" control of emotion has reacted upon the very sources of his inspiration: "Were these enslaved feelings now taking their vengeance on him by leaving him in the lurch, by refusing to forward and accelerate his art?" (V, 449). Nor is the problematic nature of his creativity a short-term matter; it has colored his whole career. His very name is eloquent: a stream of ashes (externalized later in the stagnant and infected waters of Venice) has replaced the traditional fountain of inspiration. Mann presents the situation in Nietzschean terms. Aschenbach's works have not been "the product of sustained power that came forth, as it were, in a single breath" as in the writing of *Thus Spoke Zarathustra*; they were built up, like the decadent art analyzed in *The Case of Wagner*, out of "hundreds of isolated inspirations" (V, 452). As with Michel, this separation from the immediate and elemental in life expresses itself physiologically. Even before the final crescendo of the cholera epidemic, illness is an important theme; a sickly child, Aschenbach has never had a strong constitution (V, 451). And Tadzio again mirrors his state: the writer's sudden perception that the boy is not healthy strengthens his passion for him (V, 479).

But Aschenbach differs significantly from Nietzsche's portrait of the decadent artist. In a move characteristic of Mann's mature response to his master, he plays with Nietzschean positions, combining them in new ways and often arranging them to produce an effect of ironic qualification. Thus Aschenbach's painful accumulation of small flashes of inspiration does not result in an "anarchy of atoms"; his works do not consist of details placed more or less arbitrarily together but form wholes with a classic unity of effect. He has attained Nietzsche's ideal for healthy art in an un-Nietzschean way: tenacity of will substitutes for an inspired eruption of the will to power. Restated, the basic formula for his creativity is weakness, but a weakness that becomes strength in spite of itself—a heroism of weakness. This paradox may recall Nietzschean attitudes like tragic affirmation and pessimism of strength. But Yeats, with his attitude of tragic gaiety, is the heir to their vitalistic urgency rather than Mann, who seems to have coined the phrase as a result of his fascination for the ascetic priest. This figure showed great living strength not in spite of great obstacles but even as he denied life.

This line of descent from Nietzsche is apparent in *Death in Venice* itself. Among the examples of Aschenbach's heroes of weakness is one that closely resembles the portrait of Savonarola in *Fiorenza* which Mann later criticized for being modeled too closely on the ascetic priest: "a pallid powerlessness which draws from the glowing depths of the spirit the force to bow a whole proud people before the foot of the cross, before *its own* feet" (V, 453). From this passage it is evident how Mann emphasizes that aspect of Nietzsche where the normally opposing values of force and spirit, of pride and powerlessness intertwine and undercut each other to greatest effect. The result is a more deliberately ironic attitude toward an Apollinian alienation from life than we saw in Gide. Even as it shows us Aschenbach's exhaustion, *Death in Venice* reminds us that ascetic life-denial can be unexpectedly alive; *The Immoralist* merely relies on our sensing a distance between Michel's perspective and other possible interpretations of the events he narrates to moderate his condemnations of ascetic positions. This distance, necessarily more uncertain, allows Gide to handle his less settled response to Nietzsche.

□

As we move into the next phase of the action, a change of emphasis takes place. If Apollinian excess had a larger role in

Mann due to his packed summary of Aschenbach's career, Gide's lyrical account of Michel's convalescence gives relatively more weight to the discovery of new possibilities. His initial resignation to his illness drops away before a fierce desire for recovery and a passionate affirmation of the most immediate forces of life. No longer a despiser of the body, he reverses his field so completely that "it will seem to you . . . I am forgetting the mind's share" (I, 386). Instead of abstracting himself from the world, he cultivates concrete perceptions and sensations, finding in them the joy that comes from the awakening of a long suppressed part of his being.

Gide's descriptions, deceptively terse and apparently confined to a precise account of Michel's experiences, work on the reader's imagination by evoking exceptional states of being within nature. The result is a brilliant, "southern" Dionysian world: one thinks of the spaciousness and open air of the terrace at Biskra, of the flowing water that seems ever-present in the oasis, of Michel's plunge into the ice-cold pool high on the Amalfi coast followed by his communion with the vegetation that recalls Birkin in *Women in Love*. This last scene (I, 402) which shows that he has learned to open himself fully to nature without being shattered by it as in Tunisia, sets him apart from Nietzsche's theoretical man who shunned "the icy current of existence." The scene where he feels an intense pleasure while reading the *Odyssey* had marked an earlier stage in this transformation (I, 391), since the Homeric was already a less excessive form of the Apollinian than the theoretical. Placed in counterpoint to these allusions are a number of motifs that link his new self to the Dionysian: his feeling of intoxication on entering the public garden at Biskra, the sound of the flute when he first visits the oasis, the "springtime frenzy" joining him with nature after the rains, the primitivism that begins to shape his research into the Goths, and—perhaps less convincingly—the awakening of his sexual desire for Marceline.[13] As he looks back on this period of his life, Michel realizes that his convalescence has given him a new character, one that is more energetic, more direct, more natural, more than simply mental: "This was an increase, a recrudescence of life, the afflux of a richer, hotter blood which would touch my thoughts one by one" (I, 399). All of the falsifications which had once confined his existence seem to be vanishing.

Yet there is already reason to be dubious about Michel's liberation. Often his feelings of renewal come at times when he sees the bodies of adolescent boys, while the splendidly energetic Goth who catches his attention in his research is a person who burned himself out in three years. Factors more dangerous and more complex than he realizes enter into his joyousness. If hints at the beginning of *The Immoralist*—the three-year separation from his friends that measures the period of his own demoralization, the Arab boy they find in his garden—have not alerted the reader to the importance of these details, their significance is certainly evident on a second reading.

But Gide can use methods that are more direct than narrative irony to qualify his hero's celebration of life; several episodes reveal crucial inadequacies in Michel's perceptions and in his character. Thus he fails to understand his excitement at overseeing Moktir's theft of Marceline's scissors, and he seems unable to cope with the Nietzschean challenge of facing up to the "tragic sense of my life" when he has his intimation of death the night before leaving Biskra (I, 396). Despite his resolve never to forget this moment in the moonlight, it has little effect on him; indeed, part of his fascination with adolescent boys may come from the desire to offset this sense of mortality with their youth. Perhaps the most revealing episode occurs on his trip back to France, when Michel decides to shave his beard. He is distressed at having no greater results to show for his liberation, and speaks of his decision as a "puerile" act, failing to see the literal force of the word; his new, more boyish appearance is better suited to his pederastic inclinations (I, 402). Thus facial hair will be the key to his disenchantment with Charles later on (I, 443).

At a level that goes beyond sexuality to include his whole attitude toward existence are the surprising emotions that his act arouses, fear rather than joy. For all his triumph at gaining a new being, Michel continues to feel an inner timidity that blocks an honest and direct development of the self. We begin to sense his divergence from Nietzsche's ideal of a self-propelling sovereign individual.

Our response to irony can be overly facile, limited to seeing how it undercuts attitudes without asking about its exact force. During the first of the three parts of *The Immoralist* the qualifications do not reach as far as the issues they qualify. Michel's rediscovery of the joy of existence in an immanent world, which endorses the vision of Gide's previous book, *Fruits of the Earth*, affirms values that are not necessarily linked with the special psychological factors of his case. As a result, Gide encourages in the reader a special kind of divided reaction in which he may continue to acquiesce in some of his hero's aims even as he becomes aware of difficulties. The presence of irony does not rule out various positive possibilities. Indeed, as the second part of the story begins, Michel's situation briefly stabilizes. Surrounded by "a beauty at once human and natural" on his Norman estate, he no longer feels the ambiguous turmoil of his trip but envisions a state of bipolar unity that would join the best qualities of his old self and of the new forces within him. Just as "intelligent effort" and "powerful savagery" interact on his farm to produce "the most perfect alliance," so Michel seeks to balance intellect and impulse in "a science of the perfect utilization of oneself by an intelligent constraint" (I, 410-411). As his life ranges through a continuum from the energies of the self to disciplined consciousness, his old Apollinian strength of mind and his new Dionysian richness of instinct will develop to their fullest potential.

Aschenbach's discovery of a fuller and more joyous life comes later and is of shorter duration. For a long time he shows more strength of will than Michel and withstands repeated onslaughts of the Dionysian in forms that recall

Nietzsche's categories of the barbaric and the Titanic. Mann displays considerable inventiveness in rendering the first possibility as a series of unmannerly strangers and the second as natural conditions that dwarf and even threaten the human. After the uncanny traveler with the aggressive stare and the visionary swamp in the opening chapter, Aschenbach must deal in the third with a growing feeling of "a dreamlike estrangement, a peculiar distortion of the world" (V, 460). Still, he manages to show at least some inward resistance to the made-up old man whose drunken familiarity is so annoying on the boat to Venice and to the gondolier who refuses to obey his orders. But, in the case of the Titanic, though he flees the rugged cliffs of the Adriatic and is disgusted by the foul-smelling canals in Venice, he does give in to intimations of "empty inarticulate space" in gazing at the sea (V, 461).

But in spite of Aschenbach's efforts to view Tadzio in strictly Doric terms, it is only through the Polish boy that these mounting forces win full entry into his sensibility. As in Gide an allusion to the *Odyssey* marks a slackening of the hero's Apollinian excess (V, 473). Then, when the writer first sees the boy on the beach, Tadzio's statuesque appearance merges with the two forms of the Dionysian against which he has been struggling. One complex paragraph presents this coalescence, moving us from Aschenbach's submission to the ocean's immensity—"a forbidden hankering . . . after the unorganized, the immeasurable, the eternal"— to Tadzio, who brings his attention back "from the unbounded" to focus on "a human figure," then on to the child's scorn and hatred for the Russian family, a new variation on the theme of a "barbaric" failure in the amenities between strangers. Tendencies in the writer's character which had previously worked against each other come together for the first time, and he immediately feels "a deeper sympathy" for the boy (V, 475-476).

This crucial episode has a twofold impact on Aschenbach, for it releases an unfamiliar fullness and immediacy of emotion in the man while it awakens the mythical imagination of the writer. After the frustration of his plans to leave Venice has overwhelmed him with inexplicable feelings of "adventurous joy," he discovers the reason when he sees Tadzio again and becomes aware of "the exhilaration of his blood" (V, 484, 486). Transformed, the man whose cold and severe life had been likened to a clenched fist turns his palms upward in "a spontaneous gesture of welcome, of calm acceptance" (V, 486). At this point in the story his passion does not seem a debasement but a reawakening. Mann has shown us how Tadzio compensates for some of the human failures in Aschenbach's life: a man whose own childhood had passed without comrades and who never had a son is warmed by paternal feelings and by the sight of the boy's popularity among his playmates.[14]

Meanwhile, the sensation he had gotten from earlier strangers of an uncanny and malevolent distortion of reality gives way before a triumphant mythical heightening of the world. He has applied classical allusions to Tadzio from the first, but now his imagination transforms the boy's surroundings as well: "To see how this vital figure . . . came up out of the depths of sky and sea, rose and separated from the elements—this spectacle aroused a sense of myth, it was like some poet's recovery of time at the beginning . . ."(V, 478). This tendency culminates in the fourth chapter, which mimics his state of consciousness with its extended mythological set pieces that often fall into the epic rhythm of German hexameters.

Aschenbach's mythical world provides another good example of how Mann looks to Nietzsche as both a model and a rival. Apollo is central to both *The Birth of Tragedy* and *Death in Venice*; but the story elaborates on his role, describing his activity as a sun god and his relations with other gods when they serve the purpose of the story, though they have little to do with the Apollinian art drive.[15] Aschenbach's vision of Socrates clearly derives from Plato. Although, given the themes of theory and decadence in the work as a whole,

Nietzsche's portraits of the Greek philosopher could have been relevant, Mann deliberately turns to another source which dramatizes different issues of equal importance, most notably sublimated homosexuality. He makes no direct allusion to Socrates' famous snub nose, which would have been an excellent motif linking him to the messengers of death and thus provided some justification for seeing him as a Nietzschean personification of declining life force.

Mann's positive response to Nietzsche is evident elsewhere in this chapter, when Aschenbach overcomes his writing block and breaks through to a new form of creativity. With Tadzio before him on the beach as a kind of muse, he suddenly falls into a mood in which idea and feeling are perfectly joined to form "a pulsating idea . . . a precise emotion" (V, 492). Bipolar unity replaces Doric one-sidedness, and he writes a piece of prose which is widely admired.* In Aschenbach the interaction between Apollo and Dionysus is defined in terms of intellect and passion, but Tadzio's presence suggests a further interplay, one between form and formlessness. Regularly appearing against the backdrop of the ocean, he represents a humanized definiteness of outline rising out of the disordered, the vast, the chaotic. In Nietzsche's words he embodies "the Apollinian impulse toward beauty" as it grows out of the Dionysian "titanic forces of nature" (B, 3).

□

---

* Aschenbach's pretext for writing is a "large burning issue . . . in the intellectual world" so that his last work is not fiction but an essay with strong literary appeal. Echoing Nietzsche's self-proclaimed achievement in *Zarathustra*, his moment of inspiration joins theory and art and thus resolves another conflict that has run through his career. The corresponding situation in *The Immoralist* is Ménalque's discussion of the Greek ideal for writing: "instead of ignoring each other, philosophy could nourish poetry, poetry express philosophy, and together achieve an admirable persuasiveness" (I, 436). This union reminds us of Lawrence's program for the novel as the form where philosophy and fiction could meet. But we have seen that Gide's own intentions for *The Immoralist* were different, since the story was to be a concrete image growing out of abstractions expressed elsewhere; it was not a synthesis in its own right.

This brief creative episode caps Aschenbach's discovery of a new fullness in life. Inasmuch as Tadzio shared some of the characteristics of the messengers of death, there had always been a certain irony in this reawakening; but from now on a negative perspective dominates. Bipolarity is no sooner achieved than it breaks down, with his fascination for the boy providing the impetus. Qualities of Dionysian excess have appeared even as Aschenbach writes. Ambiguously inspired by "creative intercourse" between his mind and Tadzio's body—the German phrase "zeugender Verkehr" is even more pointedly sexual—his work leaves him enervated as if after a debauch; and Mann repeatedly describes his hero's mood in terms of *Rausch*, Nietzsche's own word for Dionysian intoxication.[16] Other allusions heighten the impression of a tilting balance. Aschenbach has begun to appreciate the musical rather than the statuesque in Tadzio, and in such a way that he denies his own Apollinian verbal art: "Aschenbach did not understand a word he said. . . . So the foreignness of the boy's speech turned it to music" (V, 489). This suppression of the word underlies the crucial incident in which Aschenbach overtakes Tadzio on the way to the beach and finds that he is unable to talk to him. His sudden inarticulateness transforms the nature of their relationship, from an interest that still could have become a "casual, friendly acquaintance . . . on a sound, free, and easy basis" into an illicit passion with all "the hysteria of an unsatisfied, unnaturally repressed desire" (V, 493, 494, 496). When the chapter ends, the moonlit scene in which he at last recognizes and accepts his homosexual love indicates that he has come full circle from the Apollinian set piece describing the sun with which it had opened.

The breakup of bipolar resolution occurs less abruptly in Michel's case. The first signs of trouble appear in his public life, a side of his character that becomes important after he returns to France, since his foreign travels and his illness have kept him apart from any real life in society. In Normandy, where he takes up the position of a landowner, he enjoys the authority and responsibility and makes ambitious plans to become more active in management. His experiences with the colt catch the spirit of this period of his life especially well, having a charged intensity of image that Gide underlines by having Michel exclaim at the vividness of his memories. By refusing to accept his tenants' assurances that the horse is too wild to be worth anything, he shows his determination to live up to his position; and his success in having it tamed shows how well he is realizing his program of balancing powerful savagery and intelligent effort. Then, as he rides the colt while overseeing his estate, it becomes a symbol of his authority, giving him "that proud joy of taking precedence and having power over the workers" (I, 417).* Like Aschenbach he has assumed the Apollinian social role of hierarchical order. Yet, once again, there is another possible motive for his actions—an infatuation with a young man. It is his bailiff's son Charles who convinced him of the colt's value, who tamed it, who accompanies him on his rides, who has awakened his whole interest in the estate. Even though Michel's memories of his first summer in Normandy end on a note of managed instincts, with his description of the ducks being penned up before their migratory patterns can take hold, things are evidently less serene beneath the surface. In his other public role, as he prepares a set of lectures on the Goths, a kind of compensatory outbreak has occurred: "I insisted . . . on exalting and even justifying savagery" (I, 418). An exaggerated primitivism, which emphasizes an unalloyedly barbaric version of the Dionysian, has begun to challenge his concern for order and discipline.

This latent conflict grows rapidly during the winter that Michel spends in Paris. Even as he continues to assert his social position by setting up a lavish establishment, he begins to find the role restricting. In his lectures he attacks fixed

---

* My translation brings out one meaning of a complex phrase—"cette joie fière, de précéder et dominer les travailleurs"—in which the verbs may be taken in a concrete as well as in an abstract sense.

form and conventionality, relating them to a process of cultural decline which "stiffens and hardens, makes impossible the free and perfect contact of mind with nature, hides under the persisting appearance of life the falling off of life" (I, 424). With this doctrine, which criticizes abstraction so sweepingly that it approaches a total disavowal of the Apollinian, Michel has started to break with his bipolar ethic. Meanwhile, Ménalque is uncovering conflicts in his way of life. When he tells Michel that his mysterious tolerance of Moktir's theft is to be interpreted as restlessness with being a property owner, he has revealed the fragility of his devotion to an Apollinian hierarchy of social roles. Far from resisting Ménalque, Michel goes further in the same direction and becomes fascinated with the fresh information that the boy had willfully destroyed the scissors after he stole them (I, 428, 430).

By the next summer when Michel returns to his estate, there has been a complete reversal in his social sympathies. At first, it takes a relatively mild form as he seeks to establish a Dionysian sense of community with his farm workers. He has an experience which includes the characteristic motifs of intoxication with nature and delight in music; he stops playing the landowner and starts to feel a "strange sympathy" for his workers and their way of life (I, 440-441). But this idyll of dissolving social barriers soon passes, for Michel's single-minded animus against Apollinian excess offers him no protection from contrasting Dionysian versions of polar nullity. He becomes ever more obsessed with mindlessness and the most direct expressions of all instincts, and listens eagerly to one of his workers, Bute, as he tells lurid stories about his neighbors, the Heurtevents. As yet, however, this vicarious participation in a primitivistic "witches' brew" has no clear-cut effect on his conduct. When he gets involved with the young poacher Alcide, and so satisfies both his unacknowledged taste for boys and his growing discomfort with property relations, the only result is ridiculous and humiliating conflict with his role as a landowner. At first Alcide tricks Michel into paying him first for setting snares and then for finding them; later, when Charles discovers what has been going on, Michel must submit to a scolding for playing poacher and gamekeeper at the same time. In exasperation he abruptly decides to sell his estate and to return to a life of travel; he has given up his commitment to Apollinian social consciousness, thus justifying the question with which *The Immoralist* began: "How can a man like Michel serve the state?" (I, 369). In the third part of the story his disgust with luxury and his close identification with outcasts and the poor show a persistence of Dionysian communal tendencies, but the main emphasis has shifted to private experience.

To establish this spectrum in Gide's handling of Apollinian and Dionysian social visions has required a lot of reading between the lines. Gide's art is admittedly one of subtle implication, multiple levels of meaning, and extreme compression; but in this case one suspects that difficulty in coming to terms with Nietzsche has contributed to Gide's lightness of touch. Social issues did not enter his art easily; his phase of direct political engagement in the 1930s was one of imaginative paralysis. This failure seems all the more telling given the success of his young disciple Malraux, who—as we shall see in a later chapter—was writing novels at that very time that greatly enhanced the social implications of the polarities. By showing Gide as he treats uncongenial themes in an oblique manner, this part of *The Immoralist* suggests how unsettling the moment of first contact with Nietzsche had been for him. The corresponding part of *Death in Venice* illustrates the greater self-consciousness and assurance of Mann's longer-term response. Selecting that aspect of the Nietzschean polarities which fits with his own emphasis on social upheaval and disaster (the story begins with a timely reference to a European diplomatic crisis of the period just before the First World War), he develops a thematic sequence which results in one of the story's most memorable scenes.

When Aschenbach declared his love for Tadzio, he had

been caught by surprise, prevented from assuming the pose of dignity that went with his social station. This loosening of the Apollinian hierarchy reaches a crescendo in the fifth chapter. A brief but pointed incident occurs just before the writer's death: in the absence of rules, the children's play on the beach degenerates to the point that "merciless brutality" replaces Jaschu's "servile feelings" toward Tadzio; an allusion to the psychology of inadequacy attributes this attack to a desire "to get vengeance for a long period of slavery" (V, 523). Throughout the chapter there has been an atmosphere of social demoralization, caused by the city government's refusal to acknowledge the cholera epidemic, a refusal bringing a "weakening of the bourgeois structure" in which Aschenbach glimpses "the advantages of chaos" (V, 500, 515). Clearly, the story presents Dionysian social feeling in a state of excess, but in stressing nihilism and class hatred it passes over the more moderate possibility of an awakened communal sense.[17]

The most vivid and, in an understated way, the most appalling image for Mann's vision is the last of the messengers of death. More Dionysian than the others because he is the only musician, the Neapolitan street singer dissolves social boundaries with a laughing song that unites his audience at the Grand Hotel with the performers below: "the ungovernable laugh broke out of him, burst into such real cackles that it was infectious . . . on the terrace also an unfounded hilarity, living off itself alone, started up. But this seemed to double the singer's exuberance. He bent his knees, he slapped his thighs, he nearly split himself; he no longer laughed, he shrieked. He pointed up with his finger, as though nothing were more comic than the laughing guests" (V, 510). Far from suggesting the social reconciliation that Northrop Frye has seen in the comic vision,[18] this laughter is aggressively mocking, savage, malevolent. Though to some degree the image is limited to issues of the day—conservative anxieties about the decline of the aristocracy or the stability of Prussian authoritarianism that reappear in *Reflections of an Apolit-*

ical Man—its enduring power lies in its prophetically addressing the longer-term problem of a total dissolution of civilized restraints occurring by and through the civilized order itself. Everyone joins in this pandemonic laughter. Mann remembered this street singer—"half pimp, half comedian" (V, 507)—when he created the avatars of the devil in *Doctor Faustus*.

□

Following the crisis in their social roles, Michel and Aschenbach enter the final phase of their fall from bipolar unity. The Dionysian overwhelms the last recesses of their inner being, and they surrender to the dark or alien god of instinctual excess. Their fates raise complex and disturbing questions about the whole project of liberating the impulses. *The Immoralist* in particular must make most readers feel something of the "strange uneasiness" (I, 470) that Michel inspires in his friends. To ponder his treatment of Marceline would ultimately lead one to problems in Gide's psychobiography and to the history of his relationship with his wife. But because we are concerned with literary responses to Nietzsche, we shall limit our attention to the story itself.

The drama of Michel's inner life turns on the growing pressure that Ménalque and Moktir exert on his relationship with Marceline. This echo chamber of initial M's suggests that the real conflict occurs between different potentialities or states of being within a single personality. But we should not overlook the primitive, even melodramatic horror of a story that describes the devastating results of Michel's actual choices among these people. When Ménalque or Moktir succeeds in usurping Marceline's place, she undergoes the bloodletting of her aborted pregnancy and her tubercular hemorrhaging (I, 438, 469). These scenes provide only too graphic a basis for Michel's guilty fear that he may have exceeded his rights. In seeking to transform himself from an abstracted thinker to a man of strong passions, he becomes responsible for the death of another person. Such is the final nullity of his Dionysian liberation that he ironically ends up where he began, as a denier of life; his restless urge for travel destroys Marceline. Should we wonder how she could have let herself be victimized, feeling that the story provides insufficient information about her motives, this limitation may be taken as a symptom of Michel's inadequacy. Only briefly has he been capable of seeing her as having "a life of her own—and a real one" (I, 376), and his failure affects the tale he tells.

Enriching this stark chain of events are the more subtle insights into Michel that emerge from his conflicting allegiances to the other characters. The ideological tensions between his former ascetic self and his new affirmation of life pass over into Marceline and Ménalque. The latter is not simply a mouthpiece for ideas, since Gide is careful to stress the lived context of "terrible anxiety" in which he develops his thoughts (I, 433). Though much has been made of biographical similarities between him and Oscar Wilde, we have seen that his features resemble Nietzsche's. Equally Nietzschean is his philosophy of existential immediacy and creative self-fulfillment. But we oversimplify Michel's transformation if we say that he devotes himself to Ménalque's ideas after refusing Marceline's prayers. After all, he vacillates again and again: he turned to the Bible on his night of tragic awareness, he could echo his wife in a moment of disagreement with his new mentor, while at the end of *The Immoralist* he regrets the "great steadiness of thought" he once possessed (I, 397, 432, 471). Though Michel is emphatically not to be identified with his author, such moments of hesitancy suggest something of the outlook Gide has said he held during this period, in which he hoped to reconcile the "struggle between Dionysus and Apollo" with Christianity.[19] If the course of Michel's development embodies the first possibility, then his lingering attachment to Marceline shows the importance of the second.

Quite apart from his difficulties in maintaining his wife's values, Michel proves unable to live up to the alternative vision proclaimed by Ménalque. His cardinal tenet is that self-knowledge must accompany instinctual liberation: "the important thing is to know what one wants." But in their long conversation before Ménalque's departure from France, Michel gets angry with his friend for having gone "too far ahead of my own thoughts" and presumably showing him more of himself than he wanted to see (I, 435, 436). The narrative suppresses all this information, as Michel again reveals the inner timidity and "insurmountable reticence" that surfaces whenever sharpness of vision about himself and his goals is called for. His effusions over the transparent Alpine air at the beginning of his fateful journey with Marceline will jar mockingly with his later failures in self-perception. Michel also ignores several crucial points that Ménalque makes about the Dionysian. In a paradox that reflects his continued allegiance to the Apollinian, Ménalque had defined the "more powerful intoxication" as one "in which I keep my lucidity" (I, 426). He also insists on the centrality of life-enhancement as a criterion: "I seek in drunkenness an exaltation and not a diminution of life." Dionysus takes a different form in the dark god Michel discovers during his compulsive and death-dealing treatment of Marceline.

The most pointed analysis of this aspect of the Dionysian emerges from the portrayal of his conflicting loyalties toward Marceline and Moktir. Gide's layer-by-layer revelation of the situation is an artistic triumph. We have seen how he begins with the bare facts of Michel's surprised enjoyment of the theft of the scissors, then moves to an underlying social tension between bourgeois stability and a disordered freedom. Now he presents the breakthrough of an instinctual core of sexual turmoil and aggressiveness. These tendencies have, of course, been visible throughout the story, particularly in Michel's preference for the society of boys. But Moktir is the catalyst who separates them from other motives and greatly accelerates the process that enables them to appear in a pure state. In retrospect, the reader is brought to see Michel's fascination with the theft as a crystallization of his uncertain sexual identity (Moktir rouses stronger passions

than Marceline), and of aggressive impulses against his wife
(the scissors were hers, and in stealing them Moktir has
turned against a woman who had befriended him). The
power of this incident becomes apparent after Marceline's
miscarriage when, even as Michel sympathizes with her, he
suddenly sees her as a "chose abîmée," with the phrase
placed at the end of a section for maximum resonance (I,
439). He had used the same adjective to describe the ruined
scissors, and in calling her a thing he has heightened the
symbolic identification. Later these aggressive sentiments become a factor in the disastrous second trip to Africa over
which Moktir becomes something of a presiding spirit;
Michel is overjoyed to see him when he returns to Biskra,
and Moktir is their guide during the exhausting trip to Toug-
gourt that kills Marceline. He also intervenes to bring about
the decisive change in Michel's sexual identity. By leading
him to his own mistress and staying in the room during their
encounter, Moktir separates Michel's sexuality from his marriage and starts to attach it more closely to boys. This episode foreshadows Michel's veiled acknowledgment of his
homosexuality at the end of *The Immoralist,* which occurs
after he has entered another relationship involving both a
woman and a boy and finally realizes that he prefers the boy.

This sorry story of compulsive behavior gives the lie to
Michel's exalted feelings of personal liberation. The conflict
of Moktir and Marceline shows him as he lives through a
highly particularized version of "that horrible mixture of
sensuality and cruelty" which Nietzsche had identified with
Dionysian excess. But when Michel's story ends, as he complains to his friends that "something in my will has been
broken" (I, 471), he has reached the state of lethargy or nausea that follows Dionysian excess. Gide breaks off with his
ultimate fate in doubt. If Michel follows the pattern set by
the Gothic prince in his scholarly research, he would confirm
the wisdom of Silenus by dying quickly; Malraux, for one,
read *The Immoralist* in this spirit.[20] But it is just conceivable
that his final moment of self-recognition might herald a turn

to some better way of coping with his impulses, one that would fulfill his cry that "my real life hasn't begun yet" (I, 471). In any case, Ménalque's apparent attainment of a freer life of the instincts suggests that Michel's pathological behavior need not be taken as the norm. Thus, even as Gide in his graphic account of his hero's turmoil gives much more weight than Nietzsche to the possible dangers of a Dionysian rebirth, he still leaves some room for his glorification of an integrated human nature. Right up to the end his story maintains the double perspective appropriate for presenting this issue as a problem.

Aschenbach's final days have a Nietzschean movement that stands out more plainly than the subtle psychological drama behind Gide's quick-paced recital of events. His nightmare of the alien god sums up the Dionysian experience. It opens with the distinctive motifs of flute music and of a word that has dissolved into the inarticulate, Tadzio's name as an "u" sound. It builds up to an orgy that is both sensual and cruel: "they drove each other on with lewd gestures and wanton hands . . . they thrust their pointed staves into each other's flesh and licked the blood as it ran down." From this excess the writer wakens into the lethargy of will-negation, "shattered, unhinged, powerless" (V, 515-517).★ Then he reenacts the pattern of the dream in his life. The savage drives are sublimated so that sensuality expresses itself as a passion causing Aschenbach to yearn after Tadzio shamelessly but from afar, while cruelty becomes a willing acquiescence in the raging spread of the epidemic. In the next stage, as Aschenbach's feverish excitement collapses into torpor, Mann finds an equivalent for instinctual nullification: he has his hero fall victim to the gentle form of cholera that leads to coma (V, 513). Drained of all desire, the writer sees

---

★ Though Mann is following Nietzsche very closely, he characteristically manages to keep a certain distance from him, here by amplifying the description of the dream with details drawn from Erwin Rohde's account of Dionysian ceremonies in *Psyche*.[21] In this case, however, the distance is not at all great, since Rohde was a close friend of Nietzsche's and indeed defended *The Birth of Tragedy* from attacks by hostile classicists.

the statuesque boy as "a pale and lovely Summoner" gestur-
ing into the natural immensity, "promising and vast," of the
ocean (V, 524–525). In this context, the familiar motifs suggest the fading of the Apollinian into that version of the
Dionysian whose only promise is death.

With no space ,for further growth and development in the
hero, Mann's story has a finality missing from Gide. Indeed,
Aschenbach's second vision of Socrates, after he has eaten
the strawberries that will cause his death, is a denunciation
of the whole aesthetic outlook for assuming that beauty can
have spiritual value. The artistic way is "truly a wrong and
sinful way"; there is a fatal logic through which beauty
awakens the senses, excites the passions, leads to intoxication
and the possibility of "frightful emotional excess" (V, 521–
522). Aschenbach reverses Nietzsche in all of these positions
except the last one; if the philosopher upheld the senses and
the passions, and defended the value of his notion of intoxication, he did admit the existence of dangerous forms of excess. And as the writer rejects Nietzsche's celebration of art
drives that grow out of man's full instinctual nature, he realizes the value of a Platonic-Christian tradition. Alongside
the condemnation of the poets urged by the Socrates of his
feverish vision is the religious phrase quoted above that overturns Nietzschean ironies about sin and guilt; it perhaps reflects Mann's interest in Tolstoy's *What is Art?* with its wide-
ranging attack on modern art.[22]

But to what extent can these condemnations be equated
with the total impact of *Death in Venice*? Aschenbach's words
hark back to his youthful "theoretical" phase in which he
questioned the very basis of art; they also contrast ironically
with the cosmetics he is presently wearing to hide his age, a
degraded aestheticism that can hardly bear the weight of his
generalizations. We are reminded that his outlook could be
the product of a special situation, that of "this particular artist" who has become the spokesman for an age of "the over-
burdened, the used-up" (V, 450, 453). The result is that
Mann has not completely ruled out a Nietzschean perspec-

tive on Aschenbach; his Platonic and Christian ideas about art may only be symptoms of the decadent denial of life that he has come to represent. Again Mann has created a fictional situation which intricately balances values that collide head-on in the philosopher. In such a response he is taking Nietzsche as a rival at the same time that he continues to see him as a model.

Lawrence would admire this portrait of a decadent artist in a decadent society, though he missed the careful qualifications in Mann's portrayal of Aschenbach. A life open to the instincts need not result in excess; though the writer swings from one extreme to the other, he does experience the reawakened but still disciplined emotions that made his last piece of writing possible. Here, if anywhere in his tragically limited life, he glimpses a vision, admittedly faint, of a fuller, better integrated humanity and communicates it to others. To this complex of issues focusing on the nature of creativity and the possibilities of humanism, but also touching on social crisis, Mann will return in *Doctor Faustus*. By then three decades of historical upheaval, of continued meditation on Nietzsche, and of constant practice in the art of fiction will combine to produce a much richer, if perhaps less carefully controlled, work of art. But in the meantime both Lawrence and Malraux will have completed their own major efforts in appropriating Nietzsche, efforts that were encouraged in some measure by the young Mann and Gide. It is therefore appropriate to consider their work in the next two chapters before proceeding with the later Mann.

IV

Holding Forth against Nietzsche: D. H. Lawrence's Novels from *Women in Love* to *The Plumed Serpent*

Readers of Lawrence soon discover his ingratitude toward those who taught him. Convinced of the possibility of a creation *ex nihilo*, he spurns the past as an obstacle to the future and thus differs sharply from Mann with his attitude of revisionary veneration. As a young writer he was capable of saying that "we have to hate our immediate predecessors, to get free from their authority" (CL, 182). Lawrence puts the entire emphasis on discovering rivals rather than acknowledging models; he overlooks the persistent action on him of writers who had helped to mold his imagination. His disavowal of Nietzsche no more deserves to be taken at face value than his rejections of Hardy or Tolstoy or Whitman.

We have seen that Lawrence first became "engrossed" by Nietzsche, and especially by the will to power, in his early twenties; somewhat later he portrays a heroine who mentions Nietzsche in a Wagnerian context, while in a review he salutes the philosopher for having demolished "the Christian religion as it stood."[1] No doubt his relationship with Frieda von Richthofen, which began in 1911, increased his awareness of German culture in general and of Nietzsche in particular. But only with the outbreak of World War I some five or six years after the initial contact does his interest come to a head. Overwhelmed by the war's "colossal idiocy" (CL, 290), he was driven inward to undertake a searching of conscience that would explain his mood of repudiation. He begins to formulate a "metaphysic" that floods in upon the literary criticism of his "Study of Thomas Hardy," eventually broken off and first published as a fragment after his death. In 1915, his brief association with Bertrand Russell, based on their shared opposition to the war, deepens his philosophic aspirations and results in the essays in "The Crown." During this period he is also revising some travel sketches which had previously come out in magazines; when they appear in book form as *Twilight in Italy*, he calls them "a plainer statement of a 'message'" (CL, 422-423).

This venture into abstract thought, for all its appearance of homespun originality, occurs under Nietzsche's aegis. Dominating "Study" is a mood of cultural crisis which sees Christian forms of consciousness on the verge of collapse. They have reached the stage that Lawrence identifies with Sue Bridehead in *Jude the Obscure*, who "had come to life only to spread nihilism like a pestilence" (P, 509). The reason for this situation is the breakdown of relationship between two fundamental "Wills," which are normally polarized in states of tension and struggle but which are capable of a momentary reconciliation when they achieve a bipolar balance that Lawrence sees as transcendent. The constitutive principle for this system of dualistic interaction is sexual; as Lawrence puts it: "we start from one side or the other, from the female side or the male, but what we want is always the perfect union of the two" (P, 515). Lawrence's metaphysic reenacts the drama of Apollo and Dionysus, but he gives primary emphasis to what was previously just a sexual analogy. Themes from Nietzsche's later work intrude when Christianity replaces theory as the determining factor in the modern crisis.

Given such close agreement in their general outlooks, Lawrence's attack on Nietzsche in "Study" seems surprising. The doctrine of the *Wille zur Macht*, he insists (using Nietzsche's German phrase), is a "spurious feeling" based on a misinterpretation of the sexual attitudes of Old Testament Jews, ancient Greeks, and Italians both in the Renaissance and later. Nietzsche glorifies their "sense of power, of dominating life" but fails to consider their unconscious attitudes, which reveal a "sense of richness and oneness with all life" (P, 491–492). Lawrence may have a valid point to the extent that he stresses sexuality more than Nietzsche; there is little "richness" in the philosopher's often silly comments about women or in his failure to form a meaningful sexual relationship. But to phrase his disagreement on this single issue as a blanket condemnation is certainly unfair. Lawrence says nothing that indicates how much he agrees with Nietzsche's general approach; indeed, he goes so far as to turn some of the philosopher's favorite arguments against him. Thus he charges the discoverer of the Dionysian side of Greek life with paying too much attention to the conscious attitudes of his own favorite cultures, and Lawrence's critique of the *Wille zur Macht* makes better sense as a description of Nietzsche's outlook. The philosopher's admiration of Goethe, for standing "amid the cosmos with joyous and trusting fatalism" and believing that "all is redeemed and affirmed in the whole," expresses an affirmative naturalism very similar to a sense of "richness and oneness with all life." In attacking theoretical man's disregard for instinct, in insisting that the conscious will was a "phantom," Nietzsche had shown his own dislike for the domination of life.[2] Clearly Lawrence has an uncommon need to present the philosopher as a rival if he must hide his role as a model with such deceptive mystifications.

The underlying engagement with Nietzsche begins to surface as Lawrence continues work on his metaphysic. During his dealings with Russell, he seeks to establish his philosophic credentials by giving his speculations the title of *Le Gai Savoir*, a French translation for Nietzsche's *The Gay Science*. Then, in "The Crown," he does accept the term "power," giving the name to one of his polarized wills.[3] Because it counters the disintegrating Christian principle, it has special importance in the modern crisis; it represents "the pagan eternity, the eternity of Pan . . . the eternity some of us are veering round to. . . ."[4] With *Twilight in Italy*, as he

again expounds his polarities, Lawrence openly acknowledges his indebtedness to Nietzsche's conception of power:
"We are tempted, like Nietzsche, to return back to the old
pagan Infinite."[5] And Pan is not the only mythical figure that
is constitutive of this world. Northern Europe, Lawrence
later observes, is "crying out for the Dionysic ecstasy"; and
he sees the pagan substratum of Italy in terms of Dionysus,
conceived as "the triumphal affirmation of life over death,
immortality through procreation."[6] Here Lawrence is para-
phrasing *Twilight of the Idols,* and thus his choice of title for
this book (he had trouble coming up with one) may also
reflect his fascination with Nietzsche.

Even as Lawrence's thinking develops, it remains closely
bound up with concerns that are characteristic for a writer of
fiction; his ideas find their most pointed expression in imagery. Thus in "Study" figures of wheel and poppy play a
central expository role, while the concurrent analysis of
Hardy's works extends the metaphysic to such broader novelistic senses of image as choice of setting, conception and
development of character, or shaping of plot. In "The
Crown" Lawrence's figurative language has become more
vigorous. At this time he was responding to images with a
visionary intensity that frightened him; Richard Aldington
has reported the following comment: "Everything has a
touch of delirium, the blackbird on the wall is a delirium,
even the apple-blossom. And when I see a snake winding
rapidly in the marshy places, I think I am mad."[7] The systematic manipulation of the imagery in "The Crown" is
equally remarkable. In the ceaseless struggle of the lion and
the unicorn beneath the crown, Lawrence has found a central
symbol for the dynamic of polarization and bipolar unity.
Itself susceptible of differing emphases depending on the
state of the struggle, the symbol also gives birth to secondary
images derived from certain of its aspects: thus vultures,
swans, water lilies, and the like become figures for the polar
nullity of the "flux of corruption."

With *Twilight in Italy* Lawrence turns to the problem of

constructing narrative patterns of his own which will express his philosophy. Though discursive interpretations often accompany his accounts of experience, his method has also become directly presentative. Lawrence can be explicit, for example, in relating his polarities to a contrast between an Italy of "southern" Dionysian power and a northern Europe which, along with America, is working out the last consequences of Christianity. But the descriptive and narrative parts of *Twilight* enact this idea concretely and, to a large extent, independently of doctrinal comment. Thus, many of the sketches have a shared structural principle, the borderline situation where the two worlds collide with varied resolutions. There are portraits of Italians who have been exposed to modern industrial society, returning from America or remaining in Switzerland; of Italian actors struggling to interpret northern European plays; of Bavarian and Tyrolean crucifixes on the way to Italy; of an Italian who has trouble using an American gadget; of Swiss and English hikers who approach the Italian frontier. These episodes depicting partial interaction or nullity give way to bipolar unity in a scene where two Englishwomen dance with Italian peasants: "there was a moment when the dance passed into a possession, the men caught up the women and swung them from the earth, leapt with them for a second, and then the next phase of the dance had begun, slower again, more subtly interwoven, taking perfect, oh, exquisite delight in every interrelated movement, a rhythm within a rhythm, a subtle approaching and drawing nearer to a climax. . . ."[8] A rhythmic prose collaborates with vividly concrete description to enact a balanced relationship of polarities that are sexual as well as geographical and cultural.

Nor has Lawrence abandoned fiction during this period of taking stock. In early 1915 he completes *The Rainbow* where the presentation of sexual conflict[9] and of the change from an agricultural to an industrial society, by virtue either of anticipating or of paralleling his work on the metaphysic, seems at times to image forth his ideas. Work on final versions of *Women in Love* overlaps still more with the theoretical writing. Nietzsche has now become a force that Lawrence must reckon with explicitly, with references to him apparently dating from the initial period where he felt him as a rival. The rejected first chapter to the novel depicts Birkin, at the age when Lawrence first encountered the philosopher's works, as a "youth of twenty-one, holding forth against Nietzsche."[10] In the final version Birkin outlines familiar positions: in admitting that "there's no God" he accepts the Nietzschean critique of Christianity while he continues his attack on the *Wille zur Macht* as "a base and petty thing." But when he objects to the "Dionysic ecstatic way," his attitude seems more sharply negative than the one expressed in *Twilight*.

But Lawrence's involvement with Nietzsche in *Women in Love* reaches far beyond such brief comments. The evolving attitudes apparent in his metaphysic should alert us to the presence in his fiction of massive unacknowledged influence beneath his resistance. Still more significant, for a novelist who is returning to a congenial form, is the dynamic of idea and image. In *Women in Love*, because it fulfills the possibilities sketched out in both "The Crown" and *Twilight*, this process has two aspects. We shall have to explore the novel's symbolic action, the engagement with Nietzsche evident in its systematic use of imagery. But we must also consider imagery in the broader sense of character and action; it will be convenient to divide this side of Lawrence's response to the philosopher into the two topics of crisis and life-affirmation. Finally, we need to follow the Nietzschean element in his fiction onward to its dubious culmination in *The Plumed Serpent*. In usually viewing *Women in Love* as the end of a first phase in Lawrence's career, critics have overlooked its role in initiating a second one.[11]

CRYSTAL AND STAR: NIETZSCHE AND THE SYMBOLIC ACTION OF *Women in Love*

Without a doubt *Women in Love* has Lawrence's most powerful and subtly organized imagery. When he first conceived of the novel in 1913, he set himself the goal of going beyond an art of vivid realistic description to one "all analytical—quite unlike *Sons and Lovers*, not a bit visualized"* (CL, 193). This statement, of course, exaggerates his actual achievement. In giving an intellectual intensity to *Women in Love*, Lawrence does not sacrifice vision to analysis but joins them. But he has identified an important reorientation in his creative energies. By turning away from the invention of images, Lawrence has freed himself for an exploration of their significance and relationship. Because *Women in Love* keeps the Midlands setting of much of his earlier fiction, he can take his world for granted. As he returns to the troubling presences of these works—to moon and pond and coal, to local flower and farmyard beast—he is now able to render them with the greater depth and complexity that his new goals for fiction and his "metaphysical" speculations require.

Never again will Lawrence strike so fine a balance between description and thought. *Twilight in Italy*, in which he sets himself the double task of assimilating fresh impressions from his travels and developing his philosophy, already suggests the difficulties of his later "thought adventures." He tries to push ahead on too many fronts at once. Nor would circumstances again permit the sustained effort that went into the writing of *Women in Love*. Unable to travel because of the war, unable to publish novels after the suppression of *The Rainbow*, Lawrence was forced to concentrate on this single project.

To do full justice to the imagery of this novel would re-

* Lawrence is probably referring to his work on *The Insurrection of Miss Houghton*, later published as *The Lost Girl*. But his comment is valuable for showing the direction his interests were taking at a period of great creativity in March and April 1913. Shortly afterward, he begins *The Sisters*, originally conceived as a "pot-boiler" because *Insurrection* was becoming too difficult a work. But *The Sisters* turns into even more of a new departure, "like a novel in a foreign language I don't know very well," develops into *The Wedding Ring*, then splits into *The Rainbow* and *Women in Love*. Mark Kinkead-Weekes has shown that the first version of *The Sisters* was probably a draft for *Women in Love*; Lawrence returned to this version after he finished *The Rainbow*, which had grown out of a second version of *The Sisters*.[12]

quire a phenomenological approach like the one J.-P. Richard uses in his book on Mallarmé.[13] Such an approach could not limit itself to the strands formed by particular families of images and to their use in shifting contexts. Also important are the relationships suggested by "symbolic clusters" in which several strands are united, the dynamic movement of some images from state to state in the course of the book, and the extraordinarily precise interaction of images in the novel's great symbolic scenes. Lawrence's response to Nietzsche as registered in the imagery of *Women in Love* will provide a revealing cross section of this broad subject. Four topics are especially important: the images Lawrence uses to render the polarized extremes of the Dionysian and the theoretical, the complex patterns of associated images used to evoke processes of declining life, the somewhat briefer development of countervailing images that suggest renovation, and the role played by explicit allusions to important Nietzschean ideas in key symbolic scenes.

□

The West African statues in Halliday's apartment provide the basis for a polaristic interpretation of cultural history. To Birkin and Gerald they suggest a world completely alien to their northern European sensibilities, one defined as "the extreme of physical sensation, beyond the limits of mental consciousness" (L, 83). The implied situation is one of polar nullities, where interaction between dualities of mind and body, of abstract and concrete has broken down. Much later, Birkin explicitly draws this conclusion as he ponders one of the statues: "the relation between the senses and the outspoken mind had broken, leaving the experience all of one sort" (L, 288). Unbroken relationship would be a bipolar unity, what Birkin calls "pure integral being." But energies limited to a single pole turn upon themselves and enter the lengthy process of nullification; thus "knowledge arrested and ending in the senses" ultimately results in "knowledge in dissolution and corruption" (L, 289). The two statues which Lawrence describes in detail epitomize this cultural process. In "Totem" we have the arrested knowledge of the woman in childbirth, given over wholly to "utter physical stress" (L, 88), while in "Moony" we have moved onward to the knowledge in dissolution of the woman with the "face crushed tiny like a beetle's" (L, 288). The sculpture traces a lapse from an affirmation that is still creative to an absorption with destruction.

Birkin's cultural reflections in "Moony" parallel his denunciation of the "Dionysic ecstatic way" (L, 286) in conversation with Ursula on the previous day; on both occasions his attitude grows out of a disillusionment with passion. As images for a Dionysian culture, the statues show Lawrence's penchant for conflating motifs from different periods of Nietzsche's philosophy. Evoking a non-European world and defining it as a polar nullity, they are primarily related to the Titanic and barbarian forms of Dionysus presented in *The Birth of Tragedy*. But the first statue also draws on the procreative Dionysus that Lawrence mentions in *Twilight in Italy*, while Birkin's allusions to Egypt and the Sahara in connection with the second statue recall the African setting in "Deserts Grow" from *Zarathustra* and the *Dionysus Dithyrambs*.

But in a novel focusing on the condition of northern Europe, Dionysian primitivism and exoticism cannot be the central concern. It is the opposing nullity of theoretical man that occupies Lawrence's attention. In the preface to *Women in Love* he attacks disembodied intellectuality, contrasting the "superimposition of a theory" with the continuity of mind and instinct that occurs during a "passionate struggle into conscious being" (L, p. x). Lawrence insists, in Nietzsche's spirit, that Apollinian lucidity is a drive, joins him in admiring "logic in passion." Thus the theoretical culture of northern Europe represents as much of a nullity as the world of the statues; as its energies turn on themselves, they will produce the "snow-abstract annihilation" that Birkin senses in Gerald when he contrasts him to the "burning death-abstraction of the Sahara" (L, 289). In a later section we shall turn to Gerald and the other characters of *Women in Love*; at present we need to consider the image of snow. Though it is just conceivable that Lawrence decided to focus on this precise image as a result of the metaphor in the *Genealogy of Morals* that pictured European nihilism as an explorer in a snowy landscape, there is nothing in Nietzsche to compare to the richness with which he develops it. It is central to the kaleidoscopic variety of complex and powerful imagistic patterns that are so striking a feature of this novel. Snow—or rather the more general notion of crystallization—comes to represent the constitutive principle behind northern European culture.

□

Snow is used dynamically in *Women in Love*, suggesting on a grander scale the process of development embodied in the sequence of statues. Because it represents a terminal stage it becomes dominant only in the Alpine scenes at the close of the novel, culminating in Birkin's communion with Gerald's "frozen carcass" (L, 543). The image has previously taken the form of incipient crystallization. In one aspect it appears as water that has lost its fluidity of motion. The reservoir in front of the Criches' estate is the setting for several important scenes, and entrapment of water is associated with members of the family in other ways. Thus Winifred plays outside on a rainy day and boasts "I've made a proper dam" (L, 327); thus Gerald's mind after his first night with Gudrun, so agonizing for her, is likened to a still pool (L, 399). This strand of imagery continues as we move from Shortlands and the Criches to Breadalby and Hermione Roddice. We find no fewer than *three* ponds which are "large and smooth and beautiful" and correspond to Hermione's "static magnificence" (L, 113). Even Birkin's new lodgings at the Mill Pond place him by enclosed water; but whether he throws stones or flowers into the pond or opens the sluice to the Criches' reservoir his role is to resist the encroachment of stasis by bringing water into motion. Another aspect of incipient crystallization is the emphasis on cold water. In "Diver" the energy with which Gerald swims on his lake derives from "the violent impulse of very cold water" (L, 51). When he dives below the surface in "Water Party" in search of his sister Diana's body, he discovers "a current, as cold as hell" (L, 208). Indeed, her very name, shouted out over the reservoir, becomes an incantation to the force symbolized by the contained and chilled water, the growing deathliness of an abstract culture: "Di—Oh Di—Oh Di—Di" (L, 204).

In that it develops through various preparatory stages, the snow imagery is dynamic; it also relies on associative links to spawn a wide assortment of secondary images in the manner of "The Crown." Thus, when Gudrun sees Gerald for the first time, she finds his "northern" appearance attractive, particularly his hair with its "glisten like sunshine refracted through crystals of ice" (L, 15). The phrase obviously anticipates his eventual fate in the snow, but it also functions as a "symbolic cluster" which relates freezing water to other strands of imagery. Here the connection with crystallization has become explicit, while the glisten of refracted sunlight given off by the crystals contrasts with the self-generated light that comes from stars.

Though refraction is relatively unimportant in *Women in Love*, there are other forms of illumination that do not come straight from a source. Reflected light is especially noteworthy; witness Lawrence's numerous descriptions of the moon. The most famous instance, when Birkin stones the moon in "Moony," has lighting that is doubly indirect since his target is the moon's reflection on the water of the Mill Pond. This family of images acquires a crucial psychological interpretation in the scene where Birkin compares Hermione, with the priority she gives to consciousness, to the Lady of Shalott experiencing life in the reflections of a mirror. Willful compulsion of the self joins theoretical understanding in bringing about a break with instinct: "You've got that mirror, your own fixed will, your immortal understanding, your own tight conscious world, and there is nothing beyond it" (L, 45-46). Reflected light also accompanies the disaster in

"Water Party"; the crying of the girl's name is counter-pointed by the effects of the boat lamps: "lovely darts, and sinuous running tongues of ugly red and green and yellow light on the lustrous dark water" (L, 205). These wavering lights on the dark water, in turn, directly foreshadow the descriptions of Birkin's attack on the moon.

Patches of reflected light take another form in the vividly colored clothing which readers of Lawrence will recognize as a special feature of *Women in Love*. In the drab world of "Coal-Dust" the Brangwen sisters stand out as "white and orange and yellow glittering in motion" (L, 129). But Ursula has been identified at the beginning of the novel with self-generated light—"that strange brightness of an essential flame" (L, 10)—so the description serves to place only Gudrun, who becomes notorious for her bright stockings (L, 497). In the case of Hermione, her house party at Breadalby reveals another facet of her affinity for reflected light. When she sees her guests in evening dress with "its rich colors under the candle-light," she has a "sudden convulsive feeling of pleasure" (L, 101). Even more uncanny is the "brilliant and striking" Bokhara robe that Gerald dons in "Gladiatorial"; Birkin's interest in *Blutbrüderschaft* with his friend fades almost immediately, and he returns to thoughts of Ursula (L, 311). The underlying significance of these descriptions becomes clearer on one occasion when the reflected colors of clothing modulate into a sinister direct light. To Gudrun's eye in "Sketch Book" Gerald's white clothes transform his movements into a "stretching and surging like the marsh-fire," a "rocking of phosphorescence" (L, 136). This is the cold light of dissolution, a new image of deathliness that also appears on Hermione's face, "soft and pale and thin, almost phosphorescent" (L, 158), and on Birkin's after his illness when it gleams "with a whiteness almost phosphorescent" (L, 223).

The motif of crystal is even more fertile than modes of illumination in joining together a wide variety of images for abstracted and declining life. Developed into the idea of precisely cut stone or a jewel, it can mark a break in relationship; we come to see polar nullity as a failure of interaction between couples as well as between dualisms. Thus Ursula's hatred for Birkin in "Sunday Evening" is a "sharp crystal" which turns him into something "fine as a diamond, and as hard and jewel-like" (L, 225). His proposal to her in "Excurse" is false so long as it is symbolized by jeweled rings; she responds "half unwillingly," he is "angry at the bottom of his soul" (L, 348). Only after she has rejected them can they move on toward a more adequate relationship. Similarly, Birkin's intimacy with Hermione reaches a crisis when she attacks him with her "ball of jewel stone." In this scene the image's underlying connection with crystallization is particularly clear. Before she seizes the weapon, Hermione's suppressed anger has combined a sense of enclosure—"fearful agony, like being walled up"—with a feeling of immersion in "swirling water" (L, 118). The psychological process depicted here parallels the icy transformation going on in Gerald's cold depths.

But the image of precisely cut stone has a larger function than characterizing personal relationships; it too sums up an entire culture which has lost its capacity for life and growth. Once again, Lawrence is conflating different aspects of Nietzsche, for here the implications of crystal have shifted from the philosopher's early interest in theoretical consciousness to his late concern with Christianity. This sense of cultural crisis appears in the first chapter in the groom's pursuit of the bride: their spontaneous behavior contrasts with the church, viewed as an "angle of silent stone" (L, 21). Then, after Birkin and Ursula break through to their "new universe" in "Excurse," they pass by Southwell Minster, which "looks like quartz crystals sticking up," fit to be relegated to the distant past of "dim, bygone centuries" (L, 356-357). For Gerald as well crystallization and Christianity are closely intertwined. Just before he freezes to death in the Alps, amid the snowy phosphorescence of "the rocking, pale, shadowy slopes," he sees "a half-buried Crucifix, a little Christ" (L,

540). By releasing his subconscious fear of being murdered, the sight hastens his death: "Lord Jesus, was it then bound to be—Lord Jesus! He could feel the blow descending, he knew he was murdered." This imagined blow recalls Hermione's crystalline attack on Birkin; but Gerald's surrender contrasts with his friend's resistance. Despite his strong reaction against his father's religious ethic, he remains inwardly attuned to a cultural form drifting into decay and deathliness.

Indeed, images of crystallization in *Women in Love* suggest something of Nietzsche's broad, "generative" view of cultural forms, in which an overarching, epochal presupposition gives rise to varied, even contradictory historical consequences. For Lawrence there was an essential continuity—to be seen in such attitudes as willful compulsion of the self, oversocialization of the individual, and radical suspicion of nature—that led from Christianity to urban, industrial civilization. In *Twilight in Italy*, as a result, he could view the secular, industrial world of northern Europe and America as Christian, the piety of underdeveloped Italy as pagan. And in *Women in Love*, as he moves from religion to images of urban enclosure, of mechanized vitality, or of coal mining, he repeatedly introduces the notion of hard, geometrical surfaces which impede free flow. Perhaps Lawrence's personal experience had predisposed him to give these particular meanings to crystallization. His only prolonged stay in a modern metropolis was in the London area when he taught at a school within sight of that famous emblem of industrialism, the Crystal Palace (P, 252).

In *Women in Love* the urban world is summed up by the cab that Birkin and Gerald take when they arrive in London. Described as a "little, swiftly running enclosure" (L, 68), it makes a telling contrast with the wedding scene of the first chapter. There the emphasis had been on the removal of barriers and the release of water. The bride, briefly trapped in her carriage, had asked the thematically resonant question "How do I get out?" before descending into the rural landscape "like a sudden surf-rush" (L, 20). In this context, Birkin's language in the cab has the force of a pun—he calls himself "one of the damned." Another key image for the urban world is the Brangwen family home, made to typify the English industrial north (L, 11) or even "the ordinary life" of modern society in general (L, 428). In "Flitting," in a scene that parallels the novel's opening, the sisters return to the house one last time. The domestic comfort that once surrounded them has vanished, and they feel "the sense of walls," of "enclosure without substance" that lay beneath the appearances (L, 426, 427). The course of the action has served to cut them loose from the social and historical conditions into which they had been born.

A second strand in this radiating network of images is epitomized by Gudrun's view of herself as "a new Daphne, turning not into a tree but a machine" (L, 131). The mechanization of vital, organic forces can be linked directly to the crystallization of freezing. Thus Gerald's passion for Gudrun, likened to "the ringing of a bronze bell," makes him feel "strong as winter"; it is both metallic and "a flame of ice" (L, 457-458). But the most memorable examples of mechanization present the containment of living fluidity in ways less closely tied to the underlying image. A psychological factor is introduced in the famous symbolic scene of "Coal-Dust" when Gerald compels his horse to stand at the railroad crossing. The exertion of the "almost mechanical relentlessness" of his will transforms the animal's natural spontaneity: "the mare pawed and struck away mechanically now . . . the heavy panting of the half-stunned mare sounded automatically" (L, 126). The imagery used to convey this metamorphosis is metallic rather than explicitly crystalline. Gerald's will is swordlike, the sight of his "bright spurs" fascinates Gudrun, while the passing train—with its "clanking steel connecting rod," its trucks thumping over the rails "striking like horrible cymbals," its "grinding and squeaking" connecting chains—is a nightmare of hard, clashing surfaces (L, 124-126).

In "Rabbit," a later symbolic scene that also centers on an animal under Gerald's control, the imagery fuses machinery with enclosure. The rabbit "exploded in a wild rush" while shut up in its hutch (L, 272); it lunged "like a spring coiled and released" while held in Gudrun's hands (L, 273); it ran "as if shot from a gun" when released in a court "shut in by old red walls" (L, 276, 275). The emphasis has moved from the mechanistic degradation of the horse's vitality to the perverse energies of mechanized life. This confusion of life and machine reappears in Loerke's frieze of workers at a fair, carousing with the gadgetry of rides and booths: "the machine works him, instead of he the machine" (L, 483). It would seem, in addition, that Lawrence wishes to correlate the unpredictable explosiveness of the rabbit with the plunge of industrialized Europe into the world war. The war's bitterness, Lawrence tells us in his foreword, should be taken for granted in the novel (L, p. ix); and the rabbit's name of Bismarck encourages this historical interpretation.

On several occasions Lawrence links mining to the imagery of cold water. In "Diver" Ursula compares Gerald to a Nibelung (L, 51), an allusion that joins his roles as coal magnate and swimmer; in *Das Rheingold* Alberich is identified with the two realms of river and underground. Later, this connection is reaffirmed when we learn that the reservoir supplies the mines with water (L, 209). Equally telling is Gerald's decision to reorganize the family firm, conveyed in language which can refer to both freezing water and the petrifaction of vegetation: "His vision had suddenly crystallized" (L, 254).

Crystallization as incipient petrifaction had appeared at the very beginning of the novel when the two sisters walked through Beldover. A transformation of organic life into coal is hinted at in images like the "sooty cabbage stumps" and the "glamour of blackness . . . over the fields and wooded hills" (L, 12, 13). Then, when Gudrun voices discontent with her existence, she speaks in a revealing way. She subsumes life to an inorganic process by implying that blossom-

ing and materialization are equivalents: "*Nothing materializes!
Everything withers in the bud*" (L, 9). But the motif of petrifaction is expressed most strikingly through its reversal. In
one of the novel's leading symbolic scenes Birkin, who has
avoided the rock of Hermione's lapis lazuli, escapes to a hillside whose luxuriant vegetation suggests the primeval coal
age (L, 120-122). The scene counters other images associated
with crystallization as well: hard, clashing surfaces give way
to "fine, cool, subtle touch" and movements that are "dis-
criminate and soft"; clothing that encloses and reflects light
is discarded; ponds are replaced by the running water of a
stream.

But the constitutive role of crystallization is not always as
clear as it is in these examples; Lawrence has not been completely systematic in setting up symbolic patterns for the ex-
tinction of vital energies. Thus he uses some images that are
fully organic, untouched by mechanization or some other
process of solidification. Water plants carry over from "The
Crown" as a particularly sinister presence, either when Pussum appears "unfolded like some red lotus"* (L, 77) or
when Gudrun becomes fascinated with them in "Sketch
Book" (L, 134). Another organic image would be Gudrun's
tendency to give a sharp gull-like cry at seeing animals dominated, either when Gerald coerces the horse or the rabbit or
when she herself frightens the cattle.[14]

Even more remote from crystal is the emphasis on mud,
fertile shapelessness contrasting with sterile rigidity. In this
case, however, Lawrence's use of his material can show a
lack of imaginative engagement. At times the image does
combine concreteness and centrality to the action as in the
exposure of "horrible raw banks of clay" after the draining
of the reservoir (L, 215) or the mud at the roadside where

---

* In revising this passage for the first British edition, Lawrence changed
the simile to "ice flower" in an apparent effort to tighten the symbolic
structure of *Women in Love*. Most of his changes are of little interest since
they were dictated by fear of a libel suit; some are confusing, such as Lawrence's inconsistent handling of the primitive statues. He shifts them to the
West Pacific but forgets to change several references to West Africa.

Ursula throws the rings (L, 353) or the clay that sticks to Gerald's boots the night he visits his father's grave (L, 387). But sometimes the image is not fully realized, and mud becomes a bare emblem of horror in Birkin's lectures on flowers of mud and rivers of dissolution.[15] Elsewhere the image is not integrated into the narrative; thus Gudrun tells her anecdote of beggars wallowing in the mud alongside a pleasure boat (L, 183). Perhaps Lawrence's interest in systematically exploiting the notion of crystallization has interfered with the thorough development of this symbolic strand.

But there are indications that Lawrence wanted to bring even these patterns into a closer relationship with the dominant family of images. Thus in "Breadalby" Birkin explains to Hermione what a picture of some geese means to him: "the hot, stinging centrality of a goose in the flux of cold water and mud—the curious bitter stinging heat of a goose's blood, entering their own blood like an inoculation of corruptive fire—fire of the cold-burning mud—the lotus mystery" (L, 100). This passage functions as a symbolic cluster linking a water bird, mud, and the water plants of "the lotus mystery" to cold water and the "corruptive fire" of phosphorescence.* We get the sense of degraded life persisting on the verge of snow annihilation, involved with cold water but not captured by its dynamic. The imagery suggests a distinction that roughly corresponds to the implied contrast between decadence and nihilism in Nietzsche, but only when we turn to the characters will we find that this distinction has become pronounced.

---

* In the unpublished prologue to *Women in Love* there is a symbolic cluster that has a similar function in linking the two separate families of images. It speaks of "men with eyes like blue-flashing ice and hair like crystals of winter sunshine, the northmen, inhuman as sharp-crying gulls, distinct like splinters of ice, like crystals." This fusion of characteristic motifs associated with Gerald and Gudrun would support Scott Sanders' interesting conjecture that Gudrun as we now know her "split off" from Birkin's feelings for Gerald rather late in the composition of the novel. According to Mark Kinkead-Weekes, Gudrun did appear in *The Sisters* but then dropped out of a later version of the novel.[16]

□

Contrasting patterns of imagery in *Women in Love* present possibilities for renovation and the achievement of bipolar unity. Moving from the extremes of England and Africa to the midpoint of Italy, the novel's geography points hesitantly toward resolution. Italy's "dark fruitful earth" challenges the "silent, frozen world of the mountain tops" to which the northern European process has led with seemingly irresistible logic (L, 495). Though Birkin can doubt whether the voyage southward was really a way out (L, 545), it was in this direction that Gerald's "remaining instinct of life" had taken him (L, 540).

In "Excurse" Birkin himself had briefly experienced a unity of the faculties which included a cultural synthesis of north and south. In discovering a "strange and magical current of force in his back and loins, and down his legs," he began to resemble "the great carven statues of Egypt," while "his arms and his breast and his head were rounded and living like those of the Greek" (L, 363-364). This last comparison recalls the Apollinian statuary of *The Birth of Tragedy*, while the allusion to Egypt suggests an accommodation with the "African" Dionysus of this novel. But the passage places more emphasis on Birkin's personal achievement of integral being; instinct joins with theory, "immemorial potency" with "free intelligence." The physiological references associated with the Greek and Egyptian statues, which unite upper with lower and front with back, look ahead to Lawrence's essays on the unconscious which appeared shortly after the publication of *Women in Love*. Bipolar interaction has overcome disembodied theory and replaced it with an intellectuality taking its natural place in a harmoniously functioning organism.

But the presentation of Birkin's momentary integration is marred by turgid, even ludicrous language like "subtly, mindlessly smiling" or "suave loins of darkness" (L, 364). The most compelling images for renovation are associated with neither cultural patterns nor the individual personality.

Rather, they emerge during Birkin's struggle to form a relationship with Ursula. As elsewhere in Lawrence, flowers are central. In *Women in Love* the image serves to accentuate the contrast between organic vitality and connection, on the one hand, and isolation, degraded life, and deathly petrifaction, on the other. Dominating Ursula's meeting with Birkin in "Class Room" are catkins, flowers in bloom which contrast with the withered or materialized flowers of her sister's complaint. Similarly, right after Gudrun's vision of the sinister water plants comes the scene in "An Island" where Ursula is deeply moved by the daisies which Birkin has thrown upon the water, "tiny radiant things like an exaltation" (L, 148). Floating on the surface, not anchored in the mud beneath, grown on dry land which has resisted the encroachment of the millpond, the flowers oppose the destructiveness of dammed-up water. In "Excurse," of course, Ursula reaffirms her relationship with Birkin by returning to him with a wildflower after she has thrown the crystalline rings into the mud (L, 354).

These scenes of daisy and wildflower are among the most deeply moving in Lawrence's fiction, brief instants of resolution in the couple's continuing struggle for connection. But a more intellectually demanding image for renovation, and one that evokes bipolar unity with greater precision, appears in "Mino" when Birkin develops his idea of stars in equilibrium. In general terms, of course, this image stands in opposition to the indirect light of crystals, moons, bright clothing, and mirrors. More specifically, its concrete details join self-assertion and interaction in an even proportion. Thus the solipsism of self-generated light mingles with the reception of illumination suggested by "discernible fire" (L, 171); thus the distance between the stars, "a maintaining of the self," coexists with interconnection, "a conjunction with the other" (L, 173). Birkin even draws on the physics of orbiting bodies when he balances centrifugal forces leading to "the possibilities of chaos" (L, 172) with centripetal forces that threaten "meeting and mingling" (L, 168).

To read the scene in this way, however, is to ignore its movement; in Joseph Frank's terms, we have spatialized writing that also has a temporal dimension.[17] It is significant that Birkin arrives at his most satisfactory formula for bipolar unity—"mystic balance and integrity" (L, 173)—only after his argument with Ursula has given him a direct experience of this state. Foremost in Birkin's mind is interaction: after having opened with words about "a pure balance of two single beings" (L, 168) which show an awareness of the full image, he moves to the more limited notion of "a star in its orbit" (L, 170). This phrase prods Ursula in the opposite direction; she takes a self-assertive stance, attacking the dependency that his image might suggest: "You want a satellite" (L, 171). Added to their complementary stands on individuality and interaction is a further polarity suggested by their previous experience. Ursula's insistence on integrity compensates for her previous emphasis on loving relationship, while Birkin has turned against his mood in "Breadalby" where he had praised the absolute separateness of stars and had sought among the vegetation on the hillside a total isolation from humanity (L, 117, 121). Thus, the verbal skirmish serves to give substance to Birkin's conclusion, showing us the couple's richly complex involvement in bipolarity before it becomes a formula.

With its tight organization, rapid movement, and casual but intensely suggestive language, this passage shows Lawrence writing at his best. Yet he not only draws on Nietzschean ideas of bipolar unity but even echoes star imagery from key passages of *Thus Spoke Zarathustra*. The motifs of self-generated light and orbital dynamics appeared, we have seen, in "On the Way of the Creator"; and Birkin even calls his doctrine of relationship "the law of creation" (L, 173). Meanwhile, if the longing for connection of Nietzsche's isolated star in "Night Song" were to be fulfilled, one would get a metaphor like Birkin's two stars in equilibrium. This last point brings out a larger truth, that Nietzsche has not overwhelmed Lawrence's imagination. The novelist has freely elaborated and refined the philosopher's images, given them a new unity within a lively dialogue, provided an intellectual precision based on his response to works other than *Zarathustra*. We sense how reading Nietzsche could be a vivifying experience for Lawrence.

□

"Mino" also contains the first of the explicit allusions to Nietzschean doctrines that are closely associated with important symbolic scenes. The behavior of the two cats provokes a discussion of the *Wille zur Macht*. Ursula connects the Mino's treatment of the stray with Gerald's compulsion of the horse; she sees the will to power as domination of others, "a lust for bullying" (L, 170). It results in a relationship which has no regard for the integrity of the other. Birkin restates the issue by appealing to a conception of power that emphasizes how connection awakens previously latent areas of the self, resulting in a new fullness of being. What he calls "a transcendent and abiding *rapport*" replaces existence as "a fluffy sporadic bit of chaos" (L, 170). To sum up his attitude, he uses a French translation of Nietzsche's phrase: "It is a volonté de pouvoir, if you like, a will to ability, taking pouvoir as a verb" (L, 170). Such careful attention to shades of connotation indicates the depth of Lawrence's interest in the will to power.

Indeed, Birkin's rejection of the *Wille zur Macht* is misleading, since his emphasis has been thoroughly Nietzschean; the philosopher would have agreed with him that in personal relations *Macht* should be construed as *pouvoir*. Zarathustra's great hope was that his power over others could be transformed into an aroused power of the self, that his followers would become individuals. He chides them in a passage repeated in *Ecce Homo*: "You had not yet sought yourselves when you found me." Only when his dominion over them had ended could a new form of relationship be established: "with another love I shall then love you."[18] Here, as with the star imagery, Lawrence's real revision of Nietzsche lies in his much more detailed portrayal of this other love which affirms connection along with individuality.

At this point readers might object that much of Birkin's discussion of power sounds like an ideology of male dominance. But to read it in this way is to misinterpret the complex status that theory has throughout this chapter; to recur to Lawrence's distinction in the foreword, it can be superimposed or it can emerge from passionate struggle. Ursula's image of the satellite is superimposed theory; even as she speaks Birkin admires in her a starlike luminousness that contradicts her words about the moon's reflected light: "She was so quick, and so lambent, like discernible fire" (L, 171). If we remember that for Lawrence "quick" often has the archaic meaning of "alive," we see even more clearly that an elemental vitality is breaking through the veil of language and argument. Similarly, Birkin's defense of the male cat for hitting the stray clashes with the tenor of his own life: after all, it was Hermione who had struck him. Indeed, as he argues for relationship, he resembles the stray more than the Mino since he too is leaving a state of total isolation. Birkin's irritatingly confident diagnosis is undercut by the mystery of immediate experience: " 'She is a wild cat,' said Birkin. 'She has come in from the woods.' The eyes of the stray cat flared round for a moment, like great green fires staring at Birkin" (L, 169). Life has asserted a connection unstated in the theory; the cats have a symbolic richness larger than the interpretations their human spectators put on them. The sexual politics of the chapter may be symptomatic of a festering bitterness Birkin feels toward Hermione, but as doctrine it is unimportant. The significant thinking, affirming both balance and integrity, grows out of his passionate struggle with Ursula. By being enacted, it is authenticated.

We must now return to Birkin's condemnation of Dionysic ecstasy in "Moony," because it provides the link between two other symbolic scenes and Nietzschean doctrine. His speech likens the Dionysian to "going round in a squirrel cage" (L, 286), an image of frenetic animal energy bounded by enclosure that reminds the reader of the rabbit's behavior in the previous chapter. The mysterious bond that Gerald had felt with the frenzied beast would thus justify Ursula's earlier view of him as a Dionysus (L, 114). Meanwhile Birkin's attack on the moon seems directly related to his condemnation of the Dionysian. Just before he starts throwing stones into the water, he curses Cybele, the Magna Mater he had criticized earlier in the novel.[19] In the ancient world her orgiastic cult had centered in Phrygia (we recall Michel's scholarly investigations) and was closely associated with the worship of Dionysus.

The tendency of these allusions is to make these scenes into symbolic critiques of a Nietzschean idea. But Lawrence has handled the Dionysian in as misleading a way as the will to power; once again, he caricatures Nietzsche as he attacks him.

His bias may be observed in *Twilight in Italy* where he emphasizes how deliberate northern Europe is in "practicing on itself the Dionysic ecstasy."[20] This phrase summons up the self-conscious cultivation of passion and instinct, the attempt to will an unconscious spontaneity that Birkin analyzes in Hermione. In the nondiscursive mode of imagery, the trapped violence of the rabbit and the reflected incandescence of the moon suggest a similar situation. We have seen how carefully these images have been fitted into the elaborate and emotionally riveting pattern of snow annihilation. This overarching pattern, so closely associated with theoretical abstraction and willful compulsion, has little to do with Dionysian instinct and passion.

Indeed, if we were to look for a Nietzschean analogue for these images, it would be his description of the post-Dionysian tragedy of Euripides, set within the emerging culture of theoretical man: "the Euripidean drama is a thing both cool and fiery, equally capable of freezing and burning. . . . It requires new stimulants, which can no longer lie within the sphere of the only two art impulses, the Apollinian and the Dionysian. These stimulants are cool, paradoxical thoughts, replacing Apollinian contemplation—and fiery *affects*, replacing Dionysian ecstasies . . ." (B, 12). Nietzsche would not have seen the violence and incandescence of rabbit and moon, associated with a world of frigid crystallization, as Dionysian ecstasies; they are fiery affects that are the result of a willed attempt to create spontaneous impulse. Lawrence's attitude is thus much closer to the philosopher's than he allows himself to admit. Even as he follows him in attacking the one-sidedness of theoretical culture, he makes room for himself by misunderstanding Nietzsche's positive aspirations, interpreting them as products of the outlook they were meant to overturn.

For Lawrence, then, Dionysic ecstasy is an ultimately contradictory state of willful letting go. But if Gerald's identification with the rabbit places him squarely in this situation, Birkin's act of stoning the moon is not simply a sign of his desire to get beyond it. The richness and precision of this scene's symbolic context make it necessary to follow it in greater detail. We then realize that, despite the negativity of the doubly reflected light on the pool's surface, Birkin's behavior is essentially sterile, for it reverses the situation in "An Island" where there had been a promise of renewal. As Birkin approaches the pond in "Moony," he touches "unconsciously the dead husks of flowers," then ineffectually tosses the husks on the water (L, 280-281). Evidently it is no longer possible to throw flowers; in shifting to stones, Birkin is identifying himself with an image that has repeatedly been associated with the crystalline realm. To echo Gudrun's words, things for him have withered in the bud and materialized.

Moreover, the awakening relationship between Birkin and Ursula has given way to separation. In this scene she is hiding from him, while his horror at the Magna Mater has led him to view even her intrinsic luminousness as a sinister force: "He saw the yellow flare in her eyes, he knew the unthinkable overweening assumption of primacy in her" (L, 228). He is no longer capable of distinguishing a satellite from a star; there is thus something excessive and misplaced

in his attacking the moon's reflection as a symbol for Dionysic ecstasy. And Ursula is aware of this excess: as the scene
begins, with her discomfort at the "moon brilliant hardness"
(L, 280) of the night, she seems to share his mood; but after
watching him she understands that it is "horrible, really"
and begs him to stop (L, 283). Though the immediate object
of his attack is indirect light, he is hostile toward light in
general; his desire for escape from an obsessed and inadequate world has turned into a destructive frenzy that undermines the very sources of life.

It is Ursula's decision to reveal her presence that opens up
genuinely new possibilities by ending his isolation and re-
newing the dynamics of relationship. To be sure, Birkin's
attack has seemed to produce an image of bipolarity when it
turns the pond into "a battlefield of broken lights and shadows." But the emphasis on "broken" suggests a failure of
interaction, and later stones only result in "a few broken
flakes . . . without aim or meaning" (L, 282); we recall that
"Water Party" has already created a powerful link between
flickering reflections on water and destructive forces. Equally
suggestive of deathliness is the repeated insistence on the
"rocking" of the waves, which points to the uncanny visual
effects produced by snowfields and phosphorescence. In any
case, Birkin's efforts have no abiding effect; the moon's om-
inous image inevitably returns to the pond, with Lawrence
noting on one occasion that the patches of light move "en-
viously" (L, 280). This realm of deflected illumination includes the forces of *ressentiment* as well as willful control and
theoretical consciousness.

So Ursula is the catalyst of real change. In a movement to
be reenacted with the jeweled rings and wildflowers of "Excurse," Birkin turns back from stones to flowers, asking her
"why are there no daffodils now?" (L, 283). He now can see
the distinction between her and the reflection he was attacking: "he remembered the beauty of her eyes, which were
sometimes filled with light" (L, 284). When he mentions this
intrinsic luminosity to Ursula, she responds with another of
the casual questions in *Women in Love* which have an intense

thematic resonance: "What kind of a light?" (L, 284). They have reestablished the possibility of a star equilibrium that recognizes both the integrity of otherness and the necessity of connection. The back-and-forth of rhetorical battle between the couple will continue, but they will never again go back to so pure a state of isolation.

□

With *Women in Love* the wonderful hermetic vigor of the imagery in "The Crown" has passed into the novel. Lawrence's capacity to render direct sensual particulars—his material imagination—had always been remarkable; but now, as he systematizes those impressions that moved him most, he goes beyond realism to attain a visionary intensity. Nietzsche's role in this transformation of his art is clearest in "Mino," where Lawrence takes the philosopher as a model not only for his ideas but even for Birkin's image of balanced stars. The rivalry that surfaces in the critique of the will to power seems excessively defensive, since the scene as a whole has an inventiveness far beyond the capacity of an epigone. Elsewhere in the novel Nietzsche's impact, acknowledged or resisted, has affected the imagery less directly. It has influenced the tenor of specific symbols like the African statues or the rabbit or the moon. More importantly, it has contributed to the emphasis on broad continuities in Western culture and to the themes of declining life, theoretical consciousness, and alienation from the self and nature that underlie the network of images centered on the basic notion of crystal. But only Lawrence, let it be repeated in conclusion, could have created this impressive kaleidoscope of associations that binds together concrete presentation, powerful feeling, and a struggle for values.

CRISIS AND LIFE-AFFIRMATION: NIETZSCHE ENTERS THE LAURENTIAN LOVE STORY

Up to this point the discussion of *Women in Love* has been a bit one-sided. In the years that Lawrence worked on this novel, so much of his artistic development centered on imagery that it provided the natural axis of interpretation along which to follow Nietzsche's impact. But, to appreciate the full significance of Lawrence's images, it was often necessary to refer to the context of person and event within which they functioned. Character and plot are, of course, the traditional concern of prose fiction, a concern that still has a prominent place in *Women in Love* in spite of all of Lawrence's experimentation. As we turn now to consider this second axis of interpretation, we shall find that Nietzsche's impact still remains considerable.

By following two couples as they form and dissolve relationships, *Women in Love* conforms to one of Lawrence's earliest pronouncements on the art of the novel. Steeped in nineteenth-century fiction, he had asserted at the age of twenty: "The usual plan is to take two couples and develop their relationship."[21] This method accounts for the double plot of *Women in Love*; but despite the emphasis on the Brangwen sisters in the title, the two stories are best identified with the characters who are involved in the most dramatic changes of relationship. From her early interest in Palmer, Gudrun moves to her affair with Palmer's employer Gerald Crich, then shifts at the end of the book to an involvement with the sculptor Loerke. Birkin is tied to Hermione as the novel opens but soon enters into a relationship with Ursula which, punctuated with short bursts of concern for his friend Gerald, eventually leads to marriage. The two stories complement each other, with the destructiveness of the Gudrun plot balancing the hesitant life-affirmation of the Birkin plot. In some form, of course, Lawrence's interest in these interrelated themes must have preceded his study of Nietzsche; perhaps, as I suggested in Chapter II, their urgency derives in part from his own experience with cycles of sickness and health. But in *Women in Love* the themes have gained a substantial Nietzschean component. Gudrun's story dramatizes the issue of crisis in its two phases of decadence and nihilism, and Birkin's story examines the borderline situation that looks toward renovation.

In fact, it is possible to observe Lawrence's shock of rec-

ognition and his revisionary impulse when he encounters one
of these Nietzschean themes in the hands of another artist. In
1913, in the period he first conceived of *The Sisters*, he writes
a review of *Death in Venice*. F. R. Leavis has rightly stressed
the importance of this article.[22] But alongside the criticisms
of Flaubert which may mark a parting of ways in modern
literature are some revealing remarks about Thomas Mann.
After the previous section we shall not be surprised to find
Lawrence praising his careful use of motifs and his ability to
create a "gruesome sense of symbolism" (P, 310). But he
also admires the choice of subject, though in equating Aschenbach with Mann Lawrence is too literal about the autobiographical impulse in Mann's writing.* This portrait of
the decadent artist, he remarks, is "genuine," "perfect in a
world of corruption," "too well done" to be morbid (P,
312); he sees it as "a kind of Holbein *Totentanz*" that reveals
a "real suicidal intention" (P, 310, 312). Lawrence's response
shows his appreciation for the masterly treatment of themes
of decadence and nihilism; in Gudrun's story he will shape
this material in his own way. At the end of the review, however, a new attitude appears. Lawrence dismisses Mann as
"somewhat banal" and asserts the importance of a different
theme, "the fulsomeness of life" (P, 313) which he symbol-
izes with the familiar image of a flower. Here we have the
basis for the Birkin story. Lawrence's critique, of course, is
fully Nietzschean in spirit: to a story that reflects Mann's
fascination with "the greatest and most experienced psychologist of decadence," he restores the philosopher's mood
of renovation and life-affirmation. Then, with the outbreak
of World War I, Lawrence's easy confidence in the banality
of crisis-thinking was shattered. When he completes *Women
in Love*, he has allowed for the power of *Death in Venice* by
striking a balance between the Gudrun and the Birkin plots.

□

* In addition, Aschenbach's "Doric" tenacity of will may well have encouraged Lawrence in his misconstructions of the role of deliberate effort in
Nietzsche's philosophy of power.

In his portrayal of Gudrun herself, Lawrence has synthesized a remarkably wide range of issues concerned with declining vital force. As the novel opens, she is in transition, having returned to her native coal country from London, where she moved freely among artists, Bohemians, and cultured aristocrats like Hermione. This art world is a laboratory of cultural crisis that brings to a focus tendencies that are latent in the larger society; it is later characterized as a "small, slow, central whirlpool of disintegration and dissolution" (L, 435).

Characters like Halliday and the Pussum are obviously pathological specimens, but Gudrun's life as an artist represents a more complex form of declining vitality. Views of her creative process in action indicate that it is tainted, split off from the directness and fullness of life it seeks to emulate. Hence the questionable intensity with which she responds to the sinister water plants. The art lesson in "Rabbit" is also symptomatic. She has been drawn to Winifred by her cry of "Di, Di, Di" (L, 266); while beneath her preference for animals as models are the impulses, violently domineering yet ending in self-mutilation, that break loose from her in this scene and prevent any real communion with their natural vitality. Nor does her dancing enact the harmonious integration envisioned by Nietzsche or Yeats. When she takes the role of Ruth in the masquerade at Breadalby, she reveals the deep-seated conflict of her "subterranean recklessness and mockery" (L, 103); an enforced, rather than spontaneous, release of instinctual energies is closely bound up with an ultimate indifference and distrust. Similarly, she begins her Dalcroze movements in "Water Party" with the "desolating, agonised feeling that she was outside of life" (L, 188), but her attempt "to throw off some bond" (L, 189) does not bring her any closer. Instead, she is finally driven to attack the cattle, an act that again sets her apart from the possibilities of direct, living immediacy as embodied in animals. As an artist, therefore, Gudrun is torn between willfully affirming and being forced to deny her creative impulses. In Birkin's view, this fatal irony will keep her from developing her

talent: "Her contrariness prevents her from taking it seriously—she must never be too serious, she feels she might
give herself away" (L, 106).* Her character is a Laurentian
version of the fall from instinctual fullness and unity that in
Nietzsche led to various forms of decadence, whether the
death of tragedy or the rise of Christian life-denial.

As the novel ends, Gudrun is again in transition, but in an
opposite direction from the beginning. Her infatuation with
Loerke takes her back to an art world whose scope has now
broadened from the simply English to the northern European. The discussions of these two artists add up to an incisive vignette of art and society in crisis. Loerke's sculpture
celebrates the mechanization of life in the new industrial
world, thus capitulating to the dehumanizing tendencies of
his age. Yet, by advocating pure form and the sharp separation of art from reality, he has developed doctrines that prevent him from seeing the implications of his own work.
These theories naturally stir Gudrun's enthusiasm, since they
justify her alienation from her creative impulses: "*I* and my
art, they have *nothing* to do with each other" (L, 493). Lawrence is presenting a vicious circle in which an ever growing
disturbance in the artist's psyche corresponds with an ever
lessening ability to sense the disorders rendered in one's art.
Thus, even as Gudrun and Loerke invent disturbing stories
about a perfect explosive that destroys the world or about
the degeneration of mankind to a state of "ice cruelty," they
cannot take their visions seriously. Though they have captured the age's pathological features, they possess only
"mocking imaginations of destruction" (L, 517). It may be

---

* Birkin goes on to speak of Halliday and the Pussum in similar terms:
"It's the old story—action and reaction, and nothing between" (L, 107).
Despite the tantalizing similarity in the key terms, this psychological syn-
drome of lacking faith in one's spontaneous self or being unable to find it
has little in common with Nietzsche's distinction between nobility and *ressentiment* as active and reactive modes of being. Lawrence's characters recoil
from their own impulses, but Nietzsche's man of *ressentiment* is ruled by the
impulses of others. Later in this section we shall see that Gudrun does become reactive in Nietzsche's sense in her relation with her sister.

that their loss of instinctual wholeness and their refusal to see
themselves clearly reflect the Nietzschean categories of artificiality and innocence. In any case, when Ursula criticizes
Loerke's statue of Lady Godiva for being "a picture of your
own stock, stupid brutality" (L, 493), she has explicitly introduced the philosopher's third characteristic for decadent
art.

But comparison with Nietzsche's portrait of Wagner or
with Aschenbach brings out Gudrun's individuality; not simply an artist at the center of cultural developments, she is
rightly seen as a person who has "touched the whole pulse
of social England" (L, 476). She resembles Lawrence himself
in the exceptional breadth of her social experience. Her return to the coal country at the beginning of *Women in Love*
is particularly important because it involves her directly in
the economic realities of industrialism.

At first, Gudrun's aesthetic sensibility finds the "amorphous ugliness" of Beldover repulsive (L, 11). But for someone like her this phrase contains a telling ambiguity: it implies that the social world resembles one of her art works
from which the shaping spirit has departed. Eventually Gudrun finds that she is attracted to Beldover, as she experiences
Laurentian nostalgia, the overwhelming desire to return to
a more primitive condition of existence. She begins to identify the world of the colliers with her life in art, seeing in it
a "foul kind of beauty" (L, 130). Mingling with the crowds
on market day, she has fantasies of being caressed by labor-
ers, in whom she senses not some greater vitality but merely
the voluptuousness of machinery. As she searches for a man
who can give her some all-inclusive sense of participating in
this world, she fixes first on Palmer. This electrical engineer
charged with modernizing the mines prefers to view the colliers as a "new sort of machinery"; in the last analysis, Gudrun's relation with him simply epitomizes the degradation of
the whole society. They are on a higher level, and yet merely
concentrate the tendencies in the whole community. Thus
Gudrun and Palmer are defined as "two elegants in one

sense: in the other sense, two units absolutely adhering to the people, teeming with the distorted colliers" (L, 133).

But Palmer is just a forerunner of Gerald, apex of the social and economic pyramid and the source for all the changes which are transforming the community. Chapter 9, which marks a key stage in their developing relationship, presents him in this role. This is the chapter in which Gerald forces the mare to stand at the railroad crossing; yet the central symbol emphasized by the chapter title is not "Horse" but "Coal-Dust." The image of Gerald on horseback must be joined to "the roads silted with black dust" (L, 130) along which he rides; his obvious qualities of masterful supremacy coexist with the essential formlessness of his industrial world, a formlessness that is far more radical than amorphous art. And Gudrun's passion for Gerald clearly derives from his being the fullest embodiment of Beldover's foul beauty: "Under this bridge the colliers pressed their lovers to their breast. And now, under the bridge, the master of them all pressed her to himself!" (L, 378). In loving Gerald, she satisfies her nostalgia for the spirit of a shapeless place.

Gudrun crosses an important divide in *Women in Love* when she throws Gerald over for Loerke. By reaffirming her vocation as an artist, she conquers her lapse back into an industrial world ruled by an even greater disintegration and loss of vitality. For all her shortcomings, Birkin has admired her for being "somewhere" a true artist and as such probably Gerald's superior (L, 236, 237), while Gerald himself rather pathetically admits "that only an artist is free, because he lives in a creative world of his own" (L, 316). Yet even as Gudrun acts on her perception that marrying Gerald would mean entering a world where, in a Nietzschean metaphor for modernity, "the whole coinage of valuation was spurious" (L, 476), we come to see the negative aspects of her decision.* Rejecting Gerald also reinforces the fatal irony of her character, her persistent failure to achieve a passionate immediacy of life: "Everything turned to irony with her

* Gide draws on the same metaphor in *The Counterfeiters*.

. . . ," "she recognized too well . . . the mockery of her own impulses" (L, 476). Tragically, the manner in which she struggles toward a fuller existence puts strict limits on what she will be able to achieve. In moving from a coal magnate to an artist for factories, she has not gone very far.

Commentary and symbolism help to clarify the implications of Gudrun's decision: on the spectrum of declining life she has moved from nihilism to a decadence that is more congenial for her. Earlier Birkin had grouped her with Gerald as an example of "destructive creation" (L, 195-196). Then, in the letter that Halliday reads in the Pompadour Café and that wakens such intense emotions in Gudrun that we realize that it applies not only to the Bohemians but to her and Gerald as well, he holds forth on "the flux of corruption" (L, 437-440). But when Birkin vacations with them in the Alps, he discovers that the tempo of the destructive process can vary. In distinguishing between Gerald, who wants "to take the quick jump downwards, in a sort of ecstasy," and Loerke, who "ebbs with the stream, the sewer stream" (L, 488), he echoes the themes that Nietzsche had personified in Wagner with his sudden plunge into the abyss and in the long illness of Socrates.* Symbolically, this distinction had appeared most memorably in the gull motif that characterizes Gudrun's involvement with Gerald. He is the diver, who impetuously throws himself ever deeper into the chilling element; she is a bird who plunges in momentarily but quickly darts back to a distanced, uninvolved vantage point. Versions of this distinction return during their final struggle in the Alps. Gerald numbs himself with the "perfect, soaring trajectory" of winter sports (L, 480), while Gudrun manages to break his hold over her in the mysteri-

---

* This distinction is imaginative. Conceptually, of course, Nietzsche often saw Wagner as decadent, and so it was possible for Loerke's and Gudrun's fantasies to recall the Wagnerian categories of artificiality, innocence, and brutality while lacking the nihilistic sense of a recklessly accelerating fall from life.

ous scene where she asks him to look for a box with the picture of another diving bird, a cormorant, on it (L, 473).

Gerald's nihilism deserves careful scrutiny on its own. The destructive tendencies in his psyche had declared themselves in his boyhood when he "accidentally" killed his brother; they surfaced again in his frantic, self-lacerating response to his sister's drowning. But they become absolute after his father's illness and death, when he has an elemental experience of nothingness, feeling himself "suspended on the edge of a void, writhing" (L, 385). Though Gerald's closeness to his father dated only from adulthood, he is suffering "the lapse towards death, following in the wake of his beloved" of Paul Morel in *Sons and Lovers*.[23] In *Women in Love*, however, the family drama of losing a supportive parent has wider implications. Part of Gerald's despair comes from his sense that with his father a whole cultural form is coming to an end: "The whole unifying idea of mankind seemed to be dying with his father, the centralising force that had held the whole together seemed to collapse with his father, the parts were ready to go asunder in terrible disintegration" (L, 251-252). This nihilistic loss of all structure has the dimensions of Nietzsche's "God is dead."

Lawrence describes old Mr. Crich's cultural legacy to Gerald in "The Industrial Magnate." Defined in the broadest terms, his unifying idea is Christian; more specifically, his religion centers on a "Godhead of humanity" (L, 245) which motivates his acts of charity toward his workers and the poor in general. In so doing he might have exaggerated one aspect of Christianity, and Lawrence's critique of his partiality in interpreting a mythical form anticipates his own effort to shift interest in Christ's passion from the crucifixion to the resurrection:[24] "Perhaps he loved his neighbour even better than himself—which is going one further than the commandment" (L, 245). In any case, Mr. Crich's religious ethic conflicts with his role as a mine owner; the anomaly of his position becomes clear during a labor dispute when his employees fight a reduction in their wages. They are motivated by a desire for equality which is seen as another deduction from Christianity, "a religious creed pushed to its material conclusion" (L, 256). As an employer Mr. Crich joins other coal magnates in a lockout, but as a Christian he must admit that the workers are right. The whole situation is interpreted by Lawrence as a breakdown of cultural form: Christian myth can no longer deal inclusively with reality, and the myth itself is dissolving into partial fragments, "the last impulses of the last religious passion" (L, 257). Mr. Crich is "trapped between two half-truths and broken" (L, 258) and contracts the lingering disease he suffers from throughout *Women in Love*. His role in symbolizing the end of a cultural epoch is underlined by Birkin's later comparison of England itself to "an aged parent who suffers horribly from a complication of diseases, for which there is no hope" (L, 451).

But Mr. Crich lives on with the illusion of stable mythical form; it is left to the next generation to feel the breakdown in all its intensity, to know the nihilism of "the living death, the ensuing process of hopeless chaos" (L, 244-245). When Gerald enters the firm, he resolves his father's dilemma by choosing economic values over religious ones; for the "whole Christian attitude of love and self-sacrifice" of his father and the "whole democratic-equality problem" of the workers, he substitutes devotion to the "great social productive machine" (L, 258-259).

Lawrence turns to Nietzsche for help in describing this change, again conflating different periods in his work. In aiming at the rational organization of industry, Gerald establishes a "great and superhuman system" (L, 263), a notion that Gudrun echoes in the Alpine snows as she reacts to that symbolic analogue for the industrial system: "It is simply marvellous. One does really feel *übermenschlich*" (L, 450). And, since Gerald's reforms correspond to profound desires in the whole society, he takes on the attributes of its ruling principle; he becomes "the God of the Machine, Deus ex Machina" (L, 260). Reference to this phrase from *The Birth of Tragedy* is particularly revealing. Just as for Nietzsche the stage device marked the death of tragic myth and prepared for the subjection of nature to technology, so Gerald's ethic of organization puts an end to the organic purpose and unity still apparent in his father's mythical world. For him, too, nature is simply inert matter to be controlled by machinery, though Lawrence emphasizes will rather than theory as the usurping faculty behind this cultural transition. This close adaptation of Nietzsche to a new context brings out what is misleading in other allusions that link Gerald to his ideas. Representative of a period in which myth and the unity of the personality are disintegrating, he is no more a Nietzschean *Übermensch* than he is a Dionysus. Again Lawrence has used one of the philosopher's insights in order to criticize others.

After the economic development of the last half century, this equation of industrialism with nihilism may seem even more paradoxical and willfully wrongheaded than when *Women in Love* was written. Yet Lawrence's childhood in the coal country and his anguished response to World War I gave an urgent immediacy to issues like the abuse of nature or the mechanized intensification of violence. Symbols that convey his engagement with these issues, symbols like the blighted landscape of Beldover and the frenzied rabbit, still have an extraordinary power. The portrait of Gerald raises an equally cogent problem in modern industrial society: the emptiness of making productivity an end in itself. Gerald's singleness of purpose in reorganizing the family firm prevents him from attaining any full vision of life. Indeed, beneath the goal of efficiency that leads him to eliminate all the arrangements made by his father's Christian spirit lies a "furious and destructive demon" (L, 261). Gudrun's question about Gerald is justified: "Where does his *go* go to?" (L, 53).

Gerald himself senses the need for a larger mythical wholeness when he admits that life "as far as I can make out . . . doesn't centre at all"; he wakes up from his feverish activity to discover a world whose only cohesiveness lies in its being "artificially held *together* by the social mechanism" (L, 64).

At times the possibility of a new system of values attracts him, and he becomes intrigued with Birkin and his quest for meaning in a world where "there's no God" (L, 64). More characteristic, however, is his reliance on the social mechanism even though he doesn't really believe in it; thus he objects to the unconventional behavior of the bride and groom when they dash into the church (L, 35-36). Even more revealing of his dependence on traditional forms he partly rejects is the continuing hold over him of his father's religious ethic. His assault on it presupposes its existence: "For Gerald was in reaction against Charity; and yet he was dominated by it, it assumed supremacy in the inner life" (L, 249). Culturally as well as personally, therefore, his father's death deprives him of essential support; when the obstacle vanishes against which he has defined himself, he confronts a void. Later on, of course, this creation of a cultural identity through negation turns into a negation of the self. Gerald lives out the process of suicidal nihilism that Birkin outlines in his letter to Halliday: "There is a phase in every race . . . when the desire for destruction overcomes every other desire. In the individual, this desire is ultimately a desire for destruction in the self . . ." (L, 438). It is appropriate that Gerald's will to live should give out after his vision of the crucifix in the snow, symbol of a dissolving world of myth that he must attack yet without which he cannot live.

Taken separately, Gudrun's and Gerald's characters have raised a rich array of cultural and social issues. But even their love story itself is drawn into Lawrence's sense of crisis, for he uses it to dramatize the psychological basis for his distinction between two phases of declining life. Like Gerald's parents, Gudrun and Gerald have a "relation of utter interdestruction" (L, 248) whose inner logic is pointed up by the chapter title "Death and Love." The course of their affair confirms Birkin's theory of murderers and murderees who are ruled by the "profound if hidden lust" of destructive impulses (L, 36). As a decadent, Gudrun directs them outward, seeking a person she can victimize, someone onto whom she can project—in a largely unconscious process—her own fall from fullness of life. Because Gerald as a nihilist has reached the stage where he turns his destructive impulses against himself, he accepts the transference. Some of the most vivid moments in *Women in Love* are concerned with presenting these unconscious tendencies as they well up in their characters.

Before Gerald stumbles up the stairs to Gudrun's bedroom, tracking in clay from his father's fresh grave, the nature of her hold over him has already been established. In a series of sightings—at the wedding, as he swims or maneuvers a boat, as he handles horse and rabbit—she gradually comes to realize that he is a victim. At first her basic emotion is relatively undefined, though we already recognize it as the quick plunge of a gull: viewing Gerald outside the church, Gudrun momentarily feels "a paroxysm of violent sensation" (L, 16) in place of her normal attitude of ironic distance. But the horse bleeding from Gerald's spurs confronts her with literal violence, while the true direction of the violence becomes apparent when he shows her the gashes in his arm made by the frenzied rabbit. The crucial transition in this ripening of Gudrun's instinctual bent comes when she terrifies the cattle with her dance. Her behavior imitates Gerald's compulsion of the horse, since she has appropriated for herself the possibilities of aggression that she had discovered in watching him. When he appears and lectures her about the cattle, the dreamlike strangeness of her words and gestures suggests an attempt to force some elemental transfer of potencies: " 'How are they yours! You haven't swallowed them. Give me one of them now,' she said, holding out her hand" (L, 193). Gerald's initial response in this battle of wills is to resist her with a "faint domineering smile" (L, 193), but when Gudrun strikes him on the face the character of their relationship is set. The blow gives vent to her "unconquerable lust for deep brutality against him" (L, 194), while in him it releases a new form of aggressiveness. Rather than flowing outward, his anger floods back upon himself: "It was as if some reservoir of black anger had burst within him, and swamped him" (L, 194). Feeling a delirious loss of all accustomed guidelines, he is soon confiding to Gudrun that he does not feel anger but love for her (L, 195). Her blow has opened up his true identity.

Looking back at the development of Gerald's character, we see that there has been a precedent for this dramatic reversal of psychic energies. When Halliday quarrels with him over the Pussum, Gerald is about to respond in a manner befitting a former soldier and jungle explorer when strange new emotions come to the surface: "Gerald was on the point of knocking-in Halliday's face; when he was filled with sudden disgust and indifference, and he went away . . ." (L, 90). The pendulum swing that transforms aggression to suicidal self-denial is completed in the Alps when Gudrun strikes Gerald again. As he starts to strangle her, Lawrence marks the emergence of his destructive instincts with an impersonal construction: "Then it laughed, turning, with strong hands outstretched . . ." (L, 538). But at the moment of crisis his violence burns itself out to become the characteristic "revulsion of contempt and disgust" (L, 538), and Gerald wanders off into the mountains to freeze to death. With his aggressive manner he has the appearance of a murderer, but at heart he is a murderee, and rouses Gudrun's gull-like instinct for carrion.

As a dance of death, the Gudrun story rivals Mann in dramatizing a complex of Nietzschean themes; for all its inventiveness of character and situation, it bears the stamp of Lawrence's wide-ranging and eclectic response to the philosopher. Gudrun is the representative artist of a period in decline, self-divided and cut off from instinctual spontaneity like Euripides and Wagner. But though she shares the latter's inner brutality, she does not have his frenetic aura of nihilistic disintegration. In prefiguring a lingering process of dissolution, Loerke and Gudrun are closer to Nietzsche's portrait of the dying Socrates. Lawrence's Wagner is Gerald; his personal experience made him see catastrophic possibilities in the industrial system that dwarfed the problems of contemporary art and culture. To characterize Gerald he gives special weight to a rare passage in Nietzsche that deals directly with industrialism. But alongside the *deus ex machina* there are a host of more characteristic concerns which enter into his picture of the Crich family: the notion of an epochal cultural form based on Christianity; the sense for the continuities between this mythical origin and varied, often conflicting phenomena in the modern world; the awareness of cultural breakdown and death-directed tendencies in the present. In this last area, Lawrence gives a sharper emphasis than Nietzsche to a final stage of murderous rages and self-destructive frenzies.

Complicating Lawrence's acceptance and further development of these themes of decadence and nihilism is a smoke screen of resistance. In presenting Gerald as someone who has fulfilled Nietzsche's prophecy of the superman, and in showing Gudrun as endorsing that prophecy, Lawrence tries to implicate the philosopher in their world of destructive creation. In that case, Birkin's and Ursula's attempt to escape this world would represent an alternative beyond Nietzsche. But actually, though an early version of *Women in Love* did characterize Birkin as "holding forth" against Nietzsche, Lawrence's hero does not escape his influence.

□

Birkin's story begins within the destructive world of the Gudrun plot and remains there for a long time. Entering the novel in the company of Gerald's father, he appears "thin as Mr. Crich, pale and ill-looking" (L, 22); recurrent bouts of disease mark his course through the book. He is evidently on intimate terms with the London Bohemians, while his liaison with Hermione involves him yet more closely with a world in crisis.

As a "*Kulturträger*, a medium for the culture of ideas" (L, 17), Hermione resembles Gudrun in bringing together the problematic tendencies in modern life. Basic to her character is a lack of natural self-sufficiency that causes her to become possessive; she needs to manipulate others so as to contribute to her notion of herself. In particular, her craving for Birkin as "someone to close up this deficiency" and her efforts "to bring him to her" despite his resistance (L, 18) illustrate the avoidance of one's own identity and the exploitation of one's partner which Nietzsche had castigated in some of his analyses of love. Then, when Birkin asserts his independence at Breadalby, her murderous attack on him epitomizes the process whereby this implicit denial of the fullness of life can become destructive and then suicidal. Because she is unable to accept his otherness as an opportunity for interaction and growth, she seeks to eliminate it; and in the end her violence against him comes to include a feeling of pleasure at injuring herself: "But her fingers were in the way and deadened the blow. Nevertheless . . . it was one convulsion of pure bliss for her, lit up by the crushed pain of her fingers" (L, 119). If Hermione's aggressiveness from a sense of personal inadequacy anticipates Gudrun, this self-destructive tendency looks toward Gerald; and, indeed, in one of Lawrence's more curious symbolic transfers, he shows up a few scenes later with a mysterious bandaged hand (L, 182).

As far as Birkin is concerned, however, even this attack is not enough to break the hold that a declining culture has over him. Right up to the time that Ursula's gift of a flower seals their relationship, he remains drawn by Hermione's world. When Ursula sees them both together in "Woman to Woman," she understands that they belong to "the same withered deadening culture" (L, 342). Birkin analyzes his continuing interest in Hermione in terms of this abiding strain in his character: "There really *was* a certain stimulant in self-destruction for him—especially when it was translated spiritually" (L, 353).

It is important to realize that the problem of infected spirituality carries over from the conditions of Birkin's existence to his apparently positive role as a prophet of renovation. Always ready to deliver sermons to fellow decadents, he draws on ideas that show he has indeed studied Nietzsche.

We have already touched on his interest in suicidal nihilism and relationship between individuals; he also echoes the philosopher when he calls for a revaluation in which people would "smash up the old idols" (L, 59) and redefines nobility by seeing the true gentleman as one who can "act spontaneously on one's impulses" (L, 36). But Birkin's thinking is often merely theoretical, lacking in lived immediacy. As we saw in interpreting the symbols of "Mino" or "Moony," he can superimpose his preconceptions on a situation that is more complicated than he realizes. Another failure at making his ideas correspond to his experience comes out in his letters to the Bohemians. Ignorant of what has been happening between Birkin and Ursula, they do see how much his warnings to Halliday were a projection of his own problems: "He must be corrupt himself to have it so much on his mind" (L, 439).

But the most damaging limitation on his authority as a prophet is the ease with which Hermione parrots his teachings. Anticipating Kangaroo's travesty of Somers's writings, she shows Birkin's tendencies toward "spiritual translation" in full-blown splendor. In "Class-Room," for example, Hermione can mouth phrases about spontaneity and passion that are very close to speeches of his own; his theorizing has made her outlook possible. The savageness of his attack on her for having knowledge only "in the head" (L, 47) should be understood, therefore, as stemming in part from uneasiness with the status of his own thinking. Birkin's case looks ahead to a major tenet in Lawrence's theory of fiction, that though a novel should contain philosophy it could have no "didactic absolute."[25]

But Birkin's character does not belong entirely to Hermione's world. Beneath his words there exists a genuine passionate self that Ursula is able to perceive: "a curious hidden richness . . . like another voice, conveying another knowledge of him" (L, 48). In "Breadalby" his joyous dancing shows him to be a chameleon, capable of breaking loose from the scheme of values given to him by his environment

(L, 104). He might be seen as a borderline character like Zarathustra, since he is the product of a culture in crisis and is thoroughly implicated in its characteristic problems yet has the power to get perspective on it and glimpse possibilities for renewal. At times, in fact, Birkin's experiences as well as his thoughts directly echo Nietzsche. Introduced to us as "a man on a tight-rope" among the Criches (L, 22), he recalls the maladroit performer in the marketplace at the beginning of Zarathustra's quest. By "Excurse" Birkin has moved on to achieve the third metamorphosis of the spirit, that innocence and creative self-affirmation of the child which Nietzsche's hero had only preached: "He breathed lightly and regularly like an infant, that breathes innocently, beyond the touch of responsibility."[26]

It is this power for growth and change, "a strong spirit" which awakens at the moment of crisis (L, 119), that saves him from Hermione's murderousness. But Birkin's response is more than simply instinctive: he wards off the blow by covering "his head under the thick volume of Thucydides" which he was reading. This specific book is relevant since Lawrence found *The History of the Peloponnesian War* to be a warning example of the cultural suicide threatening Europe (CL, 466). There is thus a place in this symbolic scene for mind and theory to oppose the deathliness of an epoch in crisis. As a prophet, Birkin may often be attracted by the disembodied thoughts of declining life but he also possesses valid interpretations of deep-seated impulses toward vitality and growth.

Driving him beyond Hermione's emphasis on will and theory, these new tendencies in Birkin's character come to fruition in his developing relationship with Ursula. Because so much of their story flows into symbol and image, we are already familiar with the most important events: the botany lesson, the flotilla of daisies, the argument over the two cats, the attack on the moon, the pledge with rings and wildflower. The values of immediate life, of spontaneity and passion rather than the deliberate control of creative energies, are embodied in the figures of plant and animal and self-generated light. But the progress of this plot is not a simple one; in the menacing presences of calm water, reflected light, or crystal, the old world repeatedly threatens Birkin's and Ursula's dynamic adjustment to each other. We are made to see that crossing the borderline is no easy transition.

Less directly affected than Birkin by the sickness of the time, Ursula nonetheless faces difficulties almost as great. Much in her ideology of love—her "war-cry" as he styles it (L, 287)—is as false to the actuality of relationship as any of his theories. When Ursula enters the novel, the essential flame that sets her apart is "caught, meshed, contravened" (L, 10); and we remember that in "Mino" she is shown to be partially alienated from her creative selfhood even though her radiance gives Birkin his clearest vision of renewal. Along with this split in her being, she suffers from the dead weight of false human attachments. Unlike Birkin with Hermione, she has gotten over her love affair with Skrebensky and the sense of baffled development that it brought;[27] but she has not yet detached her intrinsic self from the confining pressures of her family.

Her father is the most obvious obstacle. With an essentially incoherent personality that is likened to "a roomful of old echoes," Brangwen is jealous of the fullness of being that gives his daughter "a light of her own" (L, 294, 295). As in *The Rainbow*, their relationship is conditioned by the "bullying and denial" of his constant irritation and sudden rages (L, 419). He is ruled to such an extent by this psychology of inadequacy that he can only resent her happiness with Birkin. When Birkin comes to propose to Ursula, Brangwen takes the words out of his mouth and turns the occasion into a fiasco (L, 296); later, when Ursula tells him that she will get married, he lashes out at her in another of the novel's moments of murderous passion (L, 419). Her ability to break with him completely, so different from Gerald with his hidden dependence on his father, reveals the vigor that Birkin admires in her inner self: "She had the perfect candour of creation. . . . How could he tell her of the immanence of her beauty!" (L, 422, 423). This insistence on the immanence of the moment of creation is interesting, given the emphasis on transcendence when Birkin called star equilibrium the "law of creation." The earlier passage is more typical of Lawrence's conception of bipolar unity, while here he comes very close to Nietzsche's eternal instant of life-affirmation. Ursula has brought Birkin down to earth, at least momentarily, though it must be admitted that Lawrence is seldom very rigorous when he speaks of transcendence.

The more subtle pressure that Ursula faces from her sister does not lead to a dramatic crisis. But Gudrun's awareness that she lacks Ursula's self-sufficiency distorts their whole relationship, from the tensions of their opening conversation to the resistance and veiled insults of their last intimate meeting in the Alps. At times Gudrun tries unsuccessfully to imitate her; thus, her motive for dancing in "Water-Party" is the desire to capture Ursula's state of being as she sings "strong and unquestioned at the centre of her own universe" (L, 188). More characteristic are feelings of envy and suppressed hostility springing from the psychology of inadequacy: "she always envied, almost with resentment, the strange positive fulness . . ." (L, 432). The dance between Naomi and Ruth which they enact at Breadalby sums up the relationship between the two sisters: "The interplay between the women was real and rather frightening. . . . Gudrun clung with heavy, desperate passion to Ursula, yet smiled with subtle malevolence against her" (L, 102). Ursula's growing attachment to Birkin frees her from this unhealthy situation in which her assured selfhood arouses others to alternating moods of spiteful resentment and anguished clutching.

We should be careful, however, not to view the marriage of Birkin and Ursula as some ultimate form of renewal. Their discovery of "a new, paradisal unit regained from the duality" (L, 423) does represent an advance over the troubled worlds in which they have previously lived. But bipolar relationship is by nature variable, swinging from these moments of reconciliation into periods of polar conflict. Though the married couple no longer goes through the periods of venomous repulsion that appeared during their courtship, they continue to struggle back and forth right down to the unresolved argument with which the book ends. Further qualifying this necessary relativism are problems that make Birkin and Ursula's quest for renovation even more precarious. In their failure to be "*quite* together" sexually (L, 496) are hints of a maladjustment that seems especially grave because Birkin has placed so great an emphasis on immediate sense experience. However, the main event darkening the outcome of the Birkin plot is Gerald's death.

Since the publication in 1963 of the canceled prologue to *Women in Love*, with its frank discussion of Birkin's homoerotic longings, the nature of the relationship between the two men has provided fertile ground for psychosexual criticism.[28] Yet it is possible that Lawrence's conception of his characters changed radically between the writing of the prologue and the final version of the novel; in any case, *Women in Love* as we now have it is not very explicit about what it calls "a strange, perilous intimacy" (L, 37). But this vexed question would lead us too far afield, and we would do better to turn to the social issues raised in the course of the two men's friendship, issues which have a direct bearing on the theme of renovation.

In proposing blood brotherhood to Gerald, Birkin takes a first step toward extending bipolarity beyond marriage to all human relationships; as he assumes the congenial role of a "Salvator Mundi" (L, 145), his ultimate goal is nothing less than the regeneration of the modern world. But his renovating impulse cannot overcome Crich's deep-seated nihilism. Though Birkin argues for the bipolar standard of "intrinsic difference between human beings," Gerald looks back to social conventions he no longer finds convincing; he wobbles, to use Lawrence's expressive verb, "upon a tacit assumption of social standing" (L, 238) and defines himself according to his function as an industrial magnate. In other words, while Birkin advocates his "volonté de pouvoir," Gerald contents himself with the "Wille zur Macht," a distinction that crops up explicitly in a later scene where for all his driving will the industrialist is said to reveal a crucial "absence of volition" (L, 404). The wrestling scene in "Gladiatorial" registers their differing modes of power in the greatest detail. Birkin achieves the spontaneity of being he has preached, showing a "physical intelligence," a "fine, sublimated energy," a "potency" that enable him to vanquish Crich (L, 308), whose seemingly greater strength is "frictional" and "rather mechanical" (L, 307). Paradoxically, Gerald's body is "more solid, more diffuse" (L, 308): lacking fullness of selfhood, he can have a closer resemblance to inert matter while at the same time failing to reach the highest pitch of living wholeness and unity.

Birkin and Gerald are fatally at odds. Though in their wrestling they do experience a "tighter closer oneness of struggle" (L, 308), the result is neither dynamic bipolarity nor a redirection of the industrialist's mode of power. Gerald shows how little he understands what has happened when he mythologizes the episode, telling Birkin that "you came here to wrestle with your good angel" (L, 313). He has reversed their real roles as he makes one of those misinterpretations of a symbolic moment that are characteristic of Lawrence's art. The error shows his distance from renovation; its consequences soon become apparent during his nihilistic plunge into self-destruction. Ursula's valedictory to the relationship between the two men suggests broader, historical implications: " 'I didn't want it to be like this,' he [Birkin] cried to himself. Ursula could not but think of the Kaiser's: 'Ich habe es nicht gewollt' " (L, 546). These words about the beginning of World War I are another of the glancing allusions that connect Gerald with the tragedy of Lawrence's Europe. Birkin's quest for renovation ends on a hesitant note, not only because of personal failures but also because it is overshadowed by the disasters of his epoch.

The Birkin plot is one outgrowth of the aspirations for renewal that Lawrence voiced in his review of Mann; in its final form, though it was closely identified with his resistance to Nietzsche in the rejected prologue, it draws upon several versions of renewal in the philosopher's work. Birkin searches after and occasionally attains a wholeness of integral being which Ursula achieves more readily and with less deliberation. This transformation of theory from alienated consciousness to a natural expression of passionate impulse hearkens back to the new values that the young philosopher saw emerging from the rebirth of tragedy. But allusions at crucial points in the action also connect Birkin with Zarathustra. He resembles Nietzsche's hero by living in a borderline situation where renovation comes through overcoming the crisis of the age in oneself. In addition, he is centrally concerned with Zarathustra's doctrines of creativity and power, giving special emphasis to the way they redefine human relationships. Ursula, in turn, suggests the values of noble morality: unlike Hermione, the nominal aristocrat, she maintains an affirmative self-sufficiency despite pressures from people gripped by the psychology of inadequacy.

Of course, these various strands intermingle as they appear in the concrete details of event and character. As a response to Nietzschean ideas, the Birkin story does not possess the clarity of outline of the Gudrun story. Perhaps this situation reflects an inherent fuzziness in utopian desire, Lawrence's random selections from Nietzsche's profusion of wares. In any case, *Women in Love* severely qualifies the theme of "fulsomeness of life." The Birkin plot has its moments of real joy, of fulfillment, of vivid interchange; but the dominant impression it conveys is of frustrated possibilities. An episode in "A Chair" suggests the ultimate contrast between Lawrence's and Nietzsche's visions of renewal. Imitating Zarathustra, Birkin and Ursula flee the marketplace, but *Women in Love* does not provide them with the refuge available to Nietzsche's hero. When they look back at the city, it has the appearance—in a rich phrase that evokes so much in the novel's symbolic universe—of "a vision of hell that is cold and angular" (L, 414). But when they reach a mountain landscape, the snow simply offers them more of the same.

Lawrence's comment on *Women in Love* when he finished it in the midst of the world war is well known: "The book frightens me: it is so end-of-the-world" (CL, 482). At least in part, these words imply dissatisfaction with the limits he had placed on the theme of renewal, for he adds that "it is, it must be, the beginning of a new world too." This imperative will guide his next major effort as a novelist. In *The Plumed Serpent* and the novels leading up to it Lawrence will continue his involvement with Nietzsche even as he attempts to right the balance between crisis and renovation in his artistic vision.

THE QUEST FOR POWER: THE NIETZSCHEAN CONTEXT OF LAWRENCE'S LONG FICTION TO *The Plumed Serpent*

When Lawrence worked on *The Plumed Serpent* from 1923 to February 1925, he did so with the sense that it was a major undertaking; he rewrote and revised the manuscript with the care he had devoted to *The Rainbow* and *Women in Love*. Looking back over the years since those novels, he undoubtedly felt that he was on the verge of a creative breakthrough. As a writer of prose fiction he had produced the short stories that make the second volume of his collected stories stand out above the others. As a poet he had composed the free verse lyrics of *Birds, Beasts, and Flowers*, some of which are his best and most original poems. As an essayist and prophet, he had devised the forceful, colloquial style in which he writes about American literature, or the unconscious, or the diverse topics in *Reflections on the Death of a Porcupine*. And as a writer of travel sketches he had created the delightful renditions of spontaneous experience that appear in *Sea and Sardinia* and in his memoirs of Maurice Magnus.

With *The Plumed Serpent*, which combines narrative and

free verse, Mexican travel impressions and speculation, Lawrence seems to be trying to bring all of these new departures to bear upon a single work. Even after he sent the book off to the publisher, having suffered an almost fatal bout of tuberculosis that may have cut short his writing,[29] he persisted in thinking that it was his best. It was "nearer my heart than any other work" (CL, 844); it was without question "the most important of all my novels" (CL, 859). But Lawrence soon began to have doubts, which most of his critics have shared. In retrospect, his failure to create a long work with the richness and control of *Women in Love* gives a quality of fragmented brilliance to his career in the late teens and early twenties. He never succeeds in consolidating the advances he had made on many fronts.

Throughout this promising outburst of creativity, Nietzsche's impact on Lawrence's imagination continues to be important; it can be sensed in all the varied directions taken by his work. But it becomes crucial in the long fiction. A direct line of development that interrelates Nietzschean images and ideas becomes steadily more important as we move from some episodes in *Women in Love*, through *The Lost Girl*, *Aaron's Rod*, and *Kangaroo*, to the central symbol of *The Plumed Serpent*. But this concentrated emulation of the philosopher is accompanied by an overall decline in Lawrence's narrative art. His previous depth and sureness of touch give way to flatly schematic conceptions and passages that are only loosely relevant to the whole. There are exceptions to this adverse judgment—especially the attempt to break new ground by dealing with the politics of renovation and some very successful scenes that dramatize aspects of Lawrence's response to Nietzsche. The concern in these areas, as in the central ideological and symbolic complex, is to explore the implications of taking power as a central imperative. We shall see that this intellectual quest leads Lawrence to several distinct assertions of value and to a number of dilemmas.

The evolution of symbol and doctrine that occurs in these

novels begins with episodes in the "Mino" and "Excurse" chapters. A first suggestive step is taken in *The Lost Girl*, started at the time of *The Sisters* but completed after *Women in Love*. The heroine of this novel wonders over a tattooed Japanese wrestler in a variety act: "Who could have imagined the terrible eagle of his shoulders, the serpent of his loins, his supple, magic skin?"[30] The man is an embodiment of Lawrence's plumed serpent symbol; right after him there arrives a troupe performing Indian dances which points even more directly to his North American experiences and his later novel. But the scene also looks back to "Excurse." The tenor of the image recalls Birkin's brief attainment of a balance between the upper and lower centers of his body, while this influx of cultural exoticism into the Midlands parallels the Egyptian element in Birkin's posture. In addition, Lawrence has followed the strategy he used with the constellated stars in "Mino." Conflating ideas and images from different parts of Nietzsche, he elaborates on the notion of bipolar interaction, then reinterprets Zarathustra's proud eagle and wise serpent in those terms.

In *Aaron's Rod* doctrine dominates over symbol. If Aaron's flute is an image for the Dionysian, it is much less inventive than the African statues. To be sure, after an anarchist's bomb has destroyed it near the end of the novel, Aaron has a wonderfully mysterious dream: "The impalpable Aaron in the bows saw the whitish clay of the bottom swirl up in clouds at each thrust of the oars, whitish clayey clouds which would envelope the strange fishes in a sudden mist. . . . They were drawing near a city. A lake city like Mexico. . . . when Aaron woke up . . . he could remember having just seen an idol. An Astarte he knew it as . . ." (AR, 277, 278). This boat trip over pallid and opaque water prefigures Kate Leslie's journey in *The Plumed Serpent* while echoing the mid-Eastern exoticism associated with Birkin.

But these fragmentary images give way to Rawdon Lilly's harangue about the "great dark power-urge which kept Egypt so intensely living for so many centuries" (AR, 288).

Once again Lawrence has created a character who defines his outlook by reacting against Nietzsche. Even as Lilly comes closer to the philosopher's terminology—for he has broken with Birkin's grudging acceptance of love—he continues to lash out against the "will-to-power" for being overly conscious and self-compelling: ". . . not in Nietzsche's sense. Not intellectual power. Not mental power. Not conscious will-power." Instead, he advocates a "living, fructifying power" which "urges from within, darkly." But the vision of polar interaction in human relations has begun to fade, since Lilly argues for a special form of submission, of men to a greater man, of women to men: "No slavery. A deep, unfathomable free submission" (AR, 289). As a result, Lawrence's response to Nietzsche, though now displayed prominently at the end of the novel, lacks the intensity of "Mino." Elsewhere in *Aaron's Rod* he still shows his ability to explore issues by presenting conflicting viewpoints that lead to firmer insight—in the argument between Lilly and Jim Bricknell that ends with the "punch in the wind" admired by Norman Mailer, in the debate about modern marriage on Argyle's balcony that T. S. Eliot has praised, in the clash of political ideas cut short by the explosion of the bomb.[31] But some of this creative tension has vanished from the rendition of his involvement with Nietzsche; brief questions and gruff negations from Aaron serve only as token interruptions to the flow of Lilly's words.

In *Kangaroo*, though the haste with which it was written is obvious to any reader, the handling of Nietzschean symbol and doctrine is much richer than in *Aaron's Rod*. Combining the polaristic interpretation of a national emblem in the manner of "The Crown" with the close attention to nonhuman life of *Birds, Beasts, and Flowers*, Lawrence makes the kangaroo the central image in the novel. His hero Richard Somers has come to Australia in search of cultural values ignored by modern Europe. During his first experiences he discovers a split between the spirit of the place and the character of its people: despite the strange place names, the new constellations in the sky, the reversal of the seasons, and the exotic plants and animals, he senses that the society is "one step further gone" in the direction of Europe (K, 45). This split is epitomized by the political leader Ben Cooley whose appearance is kangaroolike: "He leaned forward in his walk, and seemed as if his hands didn't quite belong to him. . . . He seemed not much taller than Somers, towards whom he seemed to lean the sensitive tip of his long nose . . . and approaching him with the front of his stomach" (K, 105). Later on, this final detail is developed further: "You felt . . . that your feet were nestling on his ample, beautiful 'tummy' " (K, 117). But Cooley's resemblance to the national animal is a frontal one only. At the end of the novel, when Somers has already decided to leave Australia, he finally glimpses the full possibilities of the kangaroo: "And one golden brown old-man kangaroo, with his earth-cleaving tail and his little hanging hands, hopped up to the fence and lifted his sensitive nose quivering. . . . The female wouldn't come near to eat. . . . Her little one hung its tiny fawn's head and one long ear and one fore-leg out of her pouch, in the middle of her soft big, grey belly. . . . The gentle kangaroos, with their weight in heavy blood on the ground, in their great tail!" (K, 347). Somers's wife Harriet has been more perceptive. Watching Cooley as he sprawls on a chair with "his big hips sticking out," she has exclaimed much earlier: "you needn't turn the wrong end of you at me quite so undisguisedly" (K, 122). In terms of Lawrence's physiological theories of the unconscious, Cooley possesses the sympathetic centers in the belly but not the voluntary centers in the back.[32] As a kangaroo he is a fraud, being capable of loving intimacy in the mode of Christian Europe but lacking a vigorous sense of his own identity, both as an individual and as the inhabitant of a new continent. Lawrence has made of the image a brilliant expression of the possibility for bipolarity and of its failure. For power of concrete detail, it stands up to a comparison with the distinction between balanced star and satellite in *Women in Love*. Only the relative absence of associated images radiating outward from this central symbol suggests a certain slackening in Lawrence's inventive power.

Lawrence presents the issues clustering around the kangaroo image with his old dialectical urgency. Somers and Cooley show themselves to be worthy antagonists in some half-dozen arguments throughout the novel; the give-and-take is vivid and there is a genuine dramatic development. The Australian sees himself as a disciple of the English writer and initially echoes his most cherished opinions. But Somers remains aloof, and it gradually becomes clear that the two men are loyal to completely different first principles. Thus Cooley can wonder aloud, "you have your *own* idea of power, haven't you?" and can burst out with passionate professions of love (K, 112, 120). Matters finally come to a head in "A Battle of Tongues." Cooley has already aligned himself with Dostoevsky as a prophet of love and of "living life" (K, 110, 111), while Somers proclaims a dark god "who enters us from below, not from above" (K, 134). In its essentials his doctrine is closely allied to Lilly's dark power urge, except that he is more stubborn in stressing the isolated self over any social vision.

He is, moreover, more relaxed in his attitude toward Nietzsche. In discussing power, he never quarrels with the philosopher and even identifies with him in his disillusionment with politics: "like Nietzsche, I no longer believe in great events" (K, 162). Even the continuing polemic over "Dionysic ecstasy" is muted. After his debate with Cooley, Somers receives advances from Victoria Calcott and considers giving in to this "bright, swift, weapon-like Bacchic occasion" (K, 143). But he realizes that his motives have been contaminated by consciousness, having been "bred in the head and born in the eye"; his dark god leads not to Bacchus but to "Egyptian darkness." Unlike Birkin, Somers no longer finds it necessary to react against Nietzsche's characteristic term, the Dionysian.

As the debate over power and love reaches its peak, Lawrence draws on yet another current in Nietzsche's thought, the master-slave dichotomy from *The Genealogy of Morals*. Cooley attacks Somers by identifying himself with religious imagery of absolute good and evil: "I'm the hound of heaven after you, my boy, and I'm fatal to the hell hound that's leading you" (K, 135). Somers, meanwhile, argues for the impulsive spontaneity of a gannet—"one seizure and away again"—and interprets his opponent's central premise as an ideal that masks weakness: "It's a world of slaves: all love-professing" (K, 138). Perhaps Kangaroo's very name is intended to evoke Nietzschean slavishness—Cooley as a coolie. But despite these sharp distinctions, Lawrence is aware of the underlying complexities in the *Genealogy*. He suggests some interaction between the modes of being of his two antagonists when Somers is reminded that his middle name of Lovat means that "Love is in your name, notwithstanding" (K, 151). And his hero can find it difficult to separate his own outlook from Cooley's insistence "on the Power of Love rather than on the Submission and Sacrifice of Love" (K, 270). But the crucial resolution of their conflicting viewpoints occurs after Kangaroo's death. No longer forced to defend one side in a debate, Somers still criticizes abstracted absolutes but does admit the importance of self-consciousness: "I'll give up the ideals. But not the aware, self-responsible, deep consciousness that we've gained" (K, 356). In this credo he echoes Nietzsche's praise of the sovereign individual for his "extraordinary privilege of responsibility," a power over the self that after generations had penetrated "to the profoundest depths." In the *Genealogy* this affirmation had included aspects of both master and slave; it provides a fitting conclusion to the arguments between Cooley and Somers by suggesting a certain reconciliation.

In *The Plumed Serpent* the intellectual battles are not usually so vivid, but Lawrence has become more elaborate and suggestive in his manipulation of the central symbol. Reversing the tendency of *Kangaroo*, the polaristic interpretation of a national emblem has now become the vehicle of a polemic against Nietzsche. Eagle and snake were animals sacred to the Aztecs and still appear on the Mexican flag, but they also continue Lawrence's challenge to the handling of crucial images in *Zarathustra*. Indeed, the collocation of Mexico and Nietzsche is not arbitrary, though Lawrence may not have been aware of the fact. The original conception of *Zarathustra* coincided with comparisons of the refuge in Sils Maria to "the high plateaus of Mexico," while after writing the first part the philosopher had become so disgusted with Europe that he longed to move there.[33] As a polemic with Nietzschean imagery, *The Plumed Serpent* returns to the probable source for Zarathustra's animals.

Perhaps because it is intended as a major work, the novel is sharply revisionary in its stance toward other writers, most notably Conrad, Tolstoy, and E. M. Forster. Lawrence had been a great admirer of the early Conrad (CL, 527), but he creates in his hero Ramón a revalued Kurtz. As a Westerner presiding over native rites in a non-European landscape, he has become a positive figure who is able to see "the heart of all darkness in front of him, where his unknowable God-mystery lived and moved" (S, 379-381). Ramón breaks with another model when he appears in peasant's clothing, taking on the role of "Señor Peon, like Count Tolstoy became a Señor Moujik" (S, 184). The Russian novelist's identification with the people had been, in Lawrence's view, one last expression of "the absolute of love."[34] But Ramón goes beyond these limits when he rejects even the Christian faith of the Mexican peasantry as something imposed upon them from the outside. Then in the final chapter, Lawrence resolves his divided response to Forster, whom he called "just about the best" of contemporary English novelists (CL, 800) while objecting that his treatment of India "doesn't go down to the root to meet it" (CL, 811). The triumphant title "Here!" celebrates Kate's acceptance of Cipriano; it reverses the elegiac last words of *A Passage to India* when Fielding and Aziz drift apart: "the sky said, 'No, not there.' "[35]

But these polemics are subordinate to the crucial relationship with Nietzsche. It is no exaggeration to say that Zara-thustra's animals permeate the novel, taking on various forms to comment on its tendencies. A normative example would be the emblem for Ramón's Quetzalcoatl movement: "a snake with his tail in his mouth, the black triangles on his back being the outside of the circle: and in the middle a blue eagle standing erect, with slim wings touching the belly of the snake with their tips, and slim feet upon the snake, within the hoop" (S, 191).[36] Eagle and snake have joined to suggest bipolar unity. Each creature limits and contains the other: the eagle grasps the snake with its claws while the snake coils around the eagle. In the delicacy of contact be-tween the two creatures, Lawrence shows how fragile and momentary the resolution is between his warring antino-mies. The eagle evokes the temper of modern Western cul-ture. As it spurns the earth, it suggests the idealism and ab-straction through which man evades the limiting conditions of existence. Its sharp eyesight recalls both Apollinian vision and an important image for mental knowledge in *The Plumed Serpent* and throughout Lawrence. Meanwhile, the accept-ance of the snake, the animal cursed in Genesis, indicates a reappraisal of the Christian basis to modern culture. As a creature in close contact with the earth, it suggests Zarathus-tra's insistence on wisdom of the earth over otherworldly hopes; and its resemblance to a phallus implies a full, non-ascetic involvement in the life of the body. There are over-tones of Laurentian "phallic mysteries," in which sexuality connects man with the forces of the cosmos and takes on a religious intensity. In this sense, the snake recalls the pro-creative Dionysus which had contributed to one of the Af-rican statues in *Women in Love*.

Elsewhere Lawrence comments on the action by dividing this symbol into its component parts. The early stages of Kate's relationship with the Indian Cipriano show the Eu-ropean heroine becoming aware of Mexico's profoundly al-ien qualities. The snake has just begun to impinge on her consciousness when she thinks back on their meeting in the

downpour after the bullfight: "Something so heavy, so op-
pressive, like the folds of some huge serpent . . ." (S, 22).
This sinister and limiting image that suggests polar nullity
soon modulates to a more complex sense of attraction as well
as repulsion: "She could well understand the potency of the
snake upon the Aztec and Maya imagination. . . . And her
fascination was tinged with fear. She felt somewhat as the
bird feels when the snake is watching it" (S, 71). Though a
mesmerized bird is a poor substitute for the soaring eagle,
we see the outlines of the central image. This sense of dis-
proportion can intensify in one of Kate's frequent moments
of hesitation: "And she had been beating her wings in an
effort to get away. She felt like a bird round whose body a
snake has coiled itself" (S, 77). But the general tendency is
toward bipolarity; once Kate has finally married Cipriano,
she can be "softly alert" when she happens upon a snake.
She feels a sense of connection between herself and the creature: "Perhaps it had its own peace. She felt a certain reconciliation between herself and it" (S, 466). The converse to
Kate's deepening awareness of polar interaction would be
certain moments of violent negation on the part of Mexican
characters. Ramón's comparison of his country to "a dirty
egg that you take from under the hen-eagle" reduces the bird
to a mere embryo (S, 210). And it wakens destructive fantasies in Cipriano: "wouldn't it be good to be a serpent, and
be big enough to wrap one's folds round the globe of the
world, and crush it like that egg?" (S, 211). Or, when Kate
catches sight of a child torturing a bird, she reflects that there
was a "curious void" in him preventing him from understanding that it "was a real living creature with a life of its
own" (S, 241).

In comparison to these and other variations on the plumed
serpent symbol, Lawrence's use of the kangaroo seems rather
simplistic for all its vividness. But if we recall the multiple
facets and interlocking associations that make the imagery of
Women in Love so striking, even this symbol appears insistently schematic. Lawrence has proved that he can surpass

Nietzsche in both the intrinsic suggestiveness and the structural role he gives to eagle and snake. But in challenging the philosopher so explicitly, he loses the rich variety and the emotional intensity of crystal and star. And the presentation of ideas of bipolarity suggests a similar impoverishment in Lawrence's art. Closely tied to the plumed serpent and the associated symbol of the morning star, these ideas no longer emerge through a dramatic cut-and-thrust of argument that explores the implications of an image. Enactment often gives way to assertion. Thus the following reflections imputed to Kate: "We are all fragments. And at the best halves. The only whole thing is the Morning Star. Which can only rise between two: or between many" (S, 426).

This blurring of polar tensions in Lawrence's manner of expressing his ideas carries over to the ideas themselves. Kate comes to realize that there are two forms of power, one of which leads her to "spread the wings of her own ego" but is merely "a sort of power, purring upon her own isolated individuality" (S, 481, 480). The other is the "power so much greater than her own will" which she senses in the presence of Cipriano when he seems "turned into a sort of serpent" (S, 421, 480). This way of stating the dichotomy twists the plumed serpent symbol by exalting snake over bird and points toward her one-sided resolution of the issue: "I ought to be *glad* if a man will limit me . . . I will make my submission . . ." (S, 482). I have omitted qualifying clauses to which we shall return in a moment. But it is easy to understand Simone de Beauvoir's objections to this relationship;[37] in *The Plumed Serpent* Lawrence often seems to endorse the simplified version of power, stressing control over life-enhancement, that he had sketched out in *Aaron's Rod*.

□

If we move on from the developing interaction of image and idea at the center of these novels and consider Lawrence's art of narrative in general, we see even greater difficulties. Birkin's exasperated outburst in *Women in Love* might stand as an emblem for what has occurred: "Why bother! Why strive for a coherent, satisfied life? Why not drift on in a series of accidents—like a picaresque novel?" (L, 345). As he transforms his postwar wanderings into fiction, Lawrence often captures the spontaneity of a moment in the manner of his travel sketches. But his method can also produce renditions of experience that are disappointingly superficial, and there can be a drastic decline in formal coherence. The plot of *Aaron's Rod* consists simply of "breaking loose from one connection after another" (AR, 174) as its hero disowns his wife and the Midlands, then England itself, and finally the very possibility of any binding relationship. *Kangaroo* becomes for Lawrence himself a "gramophone of a novel" (K, 286): he quotes passages directly from Australian newspapers, and whole sections—such as the silly allegory of Somers's marriage as a "hymneal bark" or the long digression about his experiences in England during the war[38]—are only loosely related to the main action. On reflection, the reader can find connections beneath this "drifting structure," but they are the product of Lawrence's persistent concerns rather than of any "bother" with the form of this particular book.

The Plumed Serpent returns to the method of *Women in Love*. The two-couple structure had surfaced at times in *Aaron's Rod* and *Kangaroo*: there is the implicit parallel between Lilly's and Aaron's marriages, or the friendship between the Somerses and the Calcotts. But now Lawrence goes back in earnest to the old pattern. We have paired relationships—Kate and Cipriano, Don Ramón and Carlota; and we have characters involved in dramatic changes in relationship—Kate with her memories of previous marriages, Ramón with his new wife Teresa at the end of the novel. Once again, however, the art has become more schematic.

The loss of psychological depth is especially striking; Lawrence's characters suggest sociocultural situations of great interest, yet the reader often feels that these situations have not been sufficiently internalized. Thus Kate Leslie continues the Celtic theme that had entered *Kangaroo* in the Cornishman

Trewhella and in Somers's memories of Cornwall. Her marriage to an Irish activist has given her an "Irish spirit" that makes her more responsive than most foreigners to the Mexican scene. As a result she feels drawn to Ramón and Cipriano in early meetings, can sense the appeal in the name Quetzalcoatl, is able to identify with the Indians after she moves into the country.[39] Yet, vital though this Celtic trait is for understanding Kate's motives, it remains simply a vague mystique; Lawrence cannot render it as a basic pressure in the personality like Gerald's death wish or Ursula's passionate selfhood. Cipriano's background creates similar difficulties. Patronized by a bishop who hoped he would enter the priesthood, then educated in England, he has become a Mexican general and a firm supporter of Ramón's efforts to bring back the old gods. But only rarely can Lawrence present him as a person who has actually had all these experiences. For every moment of psychological complexity—such as when he sees Kate as a "goddess, white-handed, mysterious" (S, 75) like the saints of his Catholic childhood—there are many which rely on mystification. Cipriano turns into a presence with glittering eyes and the capacity to awaken obscure sensations of heaviness and dark power. The flatness of invention becomes most obvious with Carlota, Ramón's Europeanized and devoutly Catholic wife. She remains a mere token except for a few fiery attacks on the Quetzalcoatl movement; when her continued presence would seriously interfere with her husband's plans, she conveniently breaks down and dies. Not only is Lawrence content with baldly asserting the bankruptcy of her principles, but he also leaves unexplored her motives for ever having formed a relationship with Ramón.

Yet major problems such as these should not blind us to important local successes in all three novels. There are situations and patterns which suggest that if Lawrence had given the same attention to these works as to *Women in Love*, he might have achieved something equally fine. In particular, his response to Nietzsche and to the issue of power can often activate his full powers of narration. F. R. Leavis has praised the first chapter of *Aaron's Rod* for its "marvellous reality," "enough to establish that the author was a rare kind of genius."[40] Yet this description (AR, 5-7) of a home in the mining country and of the breaking of a Christmas ornament, the "blue ball" of the chapter title, serves to express the sense of cultural crisis and its psychological underpinnings that Lawrence got from Nietzsche. The ornament itself evokes the very widest ramifications of the Christian tradition; as a long-time family possession which had "never been broken all those years," it represents a whole mode of life. As husband and wife and daughter discuss the decorations, their words run through a gamut of implied attitudes toward this tradition. The child begins with the neutral word "beauty," her naive mind not yet conditioned by cultural values. But the mother responds with a loaded expression. "Lovely" suggests a complete identification with what Lawrence saw as the defining characteristic of Christianity, an unqualified insistence on love. The daughter picks up on this word as she turns to her father, showing the process of acculturation: "don't you love it!" Then he shifts her exclamation to a question, for he has become "ironical over the word love." This split between cultural form and psychology reappears later, when the ball breaks with a "curious soft explosion" that prefigures the anarchist's bomb at the end of the novel. The child's mixed reaction—"half of pure misery, half of satisfaction"—reflects the dilemma of judging a partial truth; she has sensed both its inadequacy and its worth. Lawrence has succeeded in creating a narrative situation that renders with careful detail his sense of a crisis in values.

Kangaroo stands out for the dynamism of some of its imagery, which can recall the developing patterns associated with water in *Women in Love*. Lawrence uses natural descriptions to express fluctuations in Somers's mood and outlook; they allow him to combine a traveler's observations of a new country with the polarities of love and power that are central to the novel's intellectual movement. A first brief contrast juxtaposes the alien presence of the West Australian bush, suggesting completely different human possibilities, with Somers's memories of Europe. But the ocean soon takes on this role of calling modern culture into question, of substituting intimations of power for an insistence on love.

In Sydney the Somerses get their first sense of "the wide fierce sea, that makes all the built-over land dwindle into non-existence" (K, 19). Then, when they move to an ocean-front cottage, it becomes a presence to be feared as well as to be longed for; buffeted by the surf, Somers learns the difference between "looking at it from the outside" and being "even on the edge of it" (K, 82). But because it is an opposing force, "the dark sea" becomes the main emblem for his alternate values, the "everlasting gods" of the power urge (K, 89). First it feeds his resistance to Calcott's offer of solidarity, then it counters Cooley's sermons on love: "As for loving mankind . . . it was all rot. . . . He liked the sea, the pale sea of green glass that fell in such cold foam. Ice-fiery, fish-burning. He went out on to the low flat rocks at low tide, skirting the deep pock-marks that were full of brilliantly clear water and delicately coloured shells and tiny, crimson anemones. Strangely sea-scooped sharp sea-bitter rock-floor, all wet and sea-savage. . . . [H]e watched the gannets gleaming white, then falling with a splash like white sky-arrows into the waves . . ." (K, 123-124). Aspects of this powerful description continue to guide Somers's reaction to Cooley—hence his use of the gannet metaphor, cited above, and his offering of seashells to the dying man, who can see them only as "bits of uninteresting printed paper" (K, 329). But once Kangaroo dies, the ocean collapses as a polarized alternative. As the result of a terrific storm, it gives way to the violent chaos of polar nullity, and even Somers is repulsed: "Its great yellow fore-fringe was a snarl of wave after wave, unceasing. And the shore was a ruin. The beach seemed to have sunk or been swept away, the shore was a catastrophe of rocks and boulders. . . . Richard would wander cold and alone on this inhospitable shore, looking for shells, out of the storm. . . . He crooned to himself, crooning a kind of war-croon, malevolent against the malevolence of this ocean" (K, 360-361). Ending on a muted note of frustration, the novel returns to this sense of inhospitality: "The sea seemed dark and cold and inhospitable. It was only four days to New Zealand, over a cold, dark, inhospitable sea" (K, 367). No longer in relation to an opposing tension, the ocean has become as inadequate for Somers as Cooley's one-sided doctrine of love had been.

The junglelike scenery near the Somerses' cottage undergoes a similar collapse. When Richard discovered it after quarreling with Harriet over the meaning of love, it suggested some of the nonhuman vastness that entered into his conception of power. He looked down "into the center of the great, dull-green whorls of the tree-ferns, and on to the shaggy mops of the cabbage palms. . . . The previous world!—the world of the coal-age" (K, 179). This landscape also loses its hold over him after the storm. To escape the beach, he goes with Harriet into the bush, itself changed from a brooding presence to something "lovelier"—a "heaven," "a corner of paradise" (K, 362, 363). As they pass by the ferns and palms, the mystery and fascination of the vegetation have disappeared. This pattern of imagery is relatively unimportant in *Kangaroo*, but it is central to Lawrence's imaginative world considered as a whole. The coal-age jungle reverses the processes of crystallization and petrifaction in *Women in Love* which transform vegetation and flowing water into coal and ice.

In *The Plumed Serpent*, the first ten chapters or so bear out Lawrence's claim that it was one of his best works. The action is well paced and varied; the descriptions are precise and vivid. The dominating impression is of deathliness, epitomized in an image of Ramón's : "I think of all the Mexican revolutions, and I see a skeleton walking ahead of a great number of people waving a black banner with *Viva la Muerte!* written in large white letters" (S, 40). In this passage Lawrence might be remembering the *Genealogy of Morals*

with its "evviva la morte" of religious nihilism (G:III, 21).
In any case, Ramón's reference to Mexican revolutions is secondary to a general evaluation of Western culture: "Instantly
Kate and he, Europeans, in essence, understood one another.
He was waving his arms to the last *Viva!*" (S, 41). European
models have been so important in recent Mexican history
that Lawrence can present the local situation as a special case
of the larger failure of life he had discovered in his culture
during the war. His outlook is apparent in the stark description of the bullfight in the first chapter. The place may be
Mexico, but the spectacle is European, so derivative that
even the bulls have been shipped over from Spain. The
crowd, with its Western clothing and its anonymity, could
have come from any modern city; and as it moves with "a
crash like a burst reservoir" (S, 8), it displays an undercurrent of violence and mass hysteria. This vaguely murderous
potential becomes explicit in the bullfight itself. Kate's
friends might view it as "Life" (S, 4, 13), but she understands it for what it is. The sight of a bull goring a horse
suddenly assaults her with the force of a visionary experience, surprising her as never before in her life: "Human cow-
ardice and beastliness, a smell of blood, a nauseous whiff of
bursten bowels!" (S, 13). European culture has degenerated
to this sordid, sickening ritual of death.

Later, when Kate moves out of Mexico City, she passes
through nihilism and ruin to intimations of renewal; Lawrence mobilizes travel impressions to suggest the loosening
hold of the modern world. There are long, unexplained halts
during the train trip into the back country, the passengers
are terrified of attack from bandits, the provincial towns are
raw and unfinished (S, 90-95). The lake shore, from having
been the "Riviera of Mexico," has "lapsed back into barbarism and broken brickwork." Kate's bleakest moment comes
from hearing the bitter complaints of a local hotelkeeper and
the story of José, murdered by bandits among the cactus that
"thrust up their sinister clumps, like bunches of cruel fingers" (S, 107-113). But her boat trips on the lake, with its

"fish milk water gleaming and throwing off a dense light" (S, 115), calm her with the sense of other possibilities. And the plaza in Sayula presents her with a borderline situation like the ones in *Twilight in Italy*. Jazz age flappers are contrasted with the drums and Indian dancers of Ramón's Quetzalcoatl movement; almost in spite of herself Kate joins in the dancing, where she finds "her sex and her womanhood caught up and identified in the slowly revolving ocean of nascent life" (S, 143). She has discovered the life-affirming force of the procreative Dionysus.

With this shift from a nihilistic world to visions of renewal, the real difficulties with *The Plumed Serpent* begin. Ramón's sermons and hymns vaguely recall the style of *Zarathustra*, with its exhortations and dithyrambs. But his thought is so loose and repetitious that it makes even Nietzsche's most lyrical effusions seem rigorous and probing. Meanwhile the refurbished Indian rituals and the Aztec mythology show a more unconditional acceptance of a suppressed Dionysian culture. Yet this aspect of the novel often becomes tiresome or bathetic. When Ramón and Cipriano chat with Kate about her possible apotheosis as "the First Woman of—say Itzpapalotl, just for the sound of the name" (S, 347), the reader wonders whether Lawrence himself was really serious about the Quetzalcoatl movement.

Partially offsetting these failures is the characterization of Kate herself, in whom the pressures and counterpressures of the polaristic outlook are vividly apparent. More than Lawrence's other heroines of his North American years, she tries to strike a balance between accepting the primeval power of a cosmic sympathy with nature and of Indian or Celtic myth and maintaining some contact with a modern world whose Christianized and egotistical love has become rotten but cannot be denied completely. She contrasts on the one hand with the Princess, who blots out her experience with Romero, and with Mrs. Witt, who fails to capture Lewis. But she does not go to the extreme of the woman who rode away, who passively accepts the role of a sacrificial offering to the gods of the Chilchui, or of Lou Witt, who retires to the isolation of her ranch in the Rockies.[41] Thus Kate is not only a Celt wise with primeval wisdom but also a contemporary emancipated woman; even as she becomes the goddess Malintzi, she cries out: "For heaven's sake let me get out of this, and back to simple human people" (S, 407). After Ramón's movement supplants the Catholic Church in Mexico, the interplay between her leanings toward power and love persists, for she is still capable of dreaming nostalgically of Christmas holidays in England (S, 471). And the qualifying phrases I omitted above suggest other counterpressures; the limiting man she envisions has a "warm touch" as well as a "strong will," and she will submit "so far as I need, and no further" (S, 482). The ending of *The Plumed Serpent* is as unresolved as *Women in Love*. Kate gives in to Cipriano with words that remind us of the strength of the forces pulling her in the opposite direction: "You won't let me go!" (S, 487). At least a remnant of Lawrence's polaristic approach has survived in her character, so that a more dynamic outlook continues alongside the insistence on achieved renewal.

□

So far I have not discussed the political issues raised in the novels after *Women in Love*, though the social unrest of the early twenties has a prominent place in them. Lawrence's awareness of the key long-term factors is apparent in Lou Witt's vision of evil in *Saint Mawr*; she identifies bolshevism and fascism as "a rapid return to sordid chaos,"[42] thus anticipating the disasters of the thirties and forties. It was his travels and his international connections that gave him a breadth of outlook shared by few other writers. A brother-in-law of Frieda's had been a member of the short-lived *Räterepublik* in Bavaria, Lawrence himself lived in Italy during the postwar disturbances that brought socialists and then Fascists to the fore, he observed the Mexican Revolution in its early stages, and he visited Germany shortly after. Hitler's beer hall *Putsch*.[43] These experiences have left vivid traces in his novels. The opening paragraph of *Aaron's Rod* sets the stage by presenting the postwar world as "the violence of the night-mare released now into the general air." Later, in Italy, Aaron is the witness of a violent street demonstration and loses his flute to the anarchist's bomb. *Kangaroo* begins with its hero being mistaken for a "Bolshy"; during much of the novel Somers vacillates between the nationalistic and author-itarian Diggers led by Kangaroo and the socialists of Willie Struthers. Whatever the justice of this picture to Australian politics, it does epitomize Lawrence's wide experience with political upheaval. An equally broad perspective is apparent in *The Plumed Serpent*. The young ideologue who shows Kate through the art museum is a Mexican socialist, but the novel also uses the Italian word "Fascista" and introduces a German who mentions national socialism.[44]

But these political situations are of more than documen-tary interest. They inspire Lawrence to some of the most compressed and suggestive writing in these novels; these passages are essential for understanding the nature of his de-veloping concern with renovation. And as Lawrence's imag-ination becomes more directly involved with broad social problems, his conception of power undergoes further im-portant refinements. In *Aaron's Rod* the crucial incident is the explosion of the anarchist's bomb. A brilliant aposiopesis, it cuts off an argument about the meaning of power just as Levison was about to admit the logic of Lilly's ideas: " 'You have no doubt, like most of us, got a complex nature which—' CRASH!" (AR, 273). From supporting Argyle in his praise of slavery, Lilly had shifted suddenly to an attack on "bullying" and a defense of the "sacred and holy individ-ual" in every man. More clearly than in his concluding ha-rangue, he is seeking a definition of power that will join self-sufficiency in a complex union with the acknowledgment of authority. But he lives in a society that values love exclu-sively so that "what I think is ineffectual" (AR, 272). In in-terrupting him, the bomb dramatizes his isolation; it also suggests the consequences when a world based on a one-sided conception of man breaks down, "the awful gulfing whirlpool of horror in the social life" (AR, 273). The political event has become the symptom of a larger cultural crisis.

Somers's vacillations between the socialists and the proto-Fascistic Diggers make *Kangaroo* the most political of Lawrence's novels. As a result it provides the best insight into how he related his concern with power to the issues of the day. The crucial scene occurs when Somers watches the Diggers break up a socialist meeting; in a moment of confusion that strikingly parallels the bombing in *Aaron's Rod* his wavering feelings suddenly crystallize: "There was a crash, and the hall was like a bomb that has exploded. Somers tried to spring forward. In the blind moment he wanted to kill—to kill the soldiers" (K, 321). The hesitation in the final sentence suggests the process of discovering one's real impulses, or to use the language of *Kangaroo* the promptings of the dark god who enters from below. It is this version of power that motivates Somers in his rage against the Diggers and makes him, in effect, an ally of the socialists despite his previous denunciations of them. This emergence of a "popular-front" Somers seems less surprising once we recall his distrust for Kangaroo's plausible speeches on social renewal, his insistence that he had an underlying love for working people (K, 204), or the horror of bullying that links this scene with his own experiences in wartime England. The event has proved that power as authority over others is less important to him than power as the realization of selfhood. Soon, however, Somers has returned to his normal aloofness, declaring that "I can't be on either side" (K, 323). Trewhella has been the agent of this neutrality, having restrained him in his anger and led him away from the meeting; as a Cornishman, he has remained in touch with a Celtic world of myth that seems a more genuine source of power. He points ahead to *The Plumed Serpent*, where myth has become the essential counterweight to modern politics.

Not that Lawrence's Mexican novel ignores political matters. There are some striking vignettes in the first chapters as Kate moves among various groups in the capital and observes the impact of the recent revolution. One might consider the Americans she meets at Mrs. Norris's tea party. A Judge Burlap is tense with exasperation at the current situation and needlessly insults a native guest by refusing Mexican food (S, 42); a military attaché named Law ridicules Aztec and Mayan art as "dirty stones" (S, 36). Yet the play of shifting perspectives is such that the scene suggests more than a Yankee blindness to other cultures. A young Mr. Henry can be good humored and understanding, while Mrs. Norris questions the fairness of identifying Americans with a soulless cult of the dollar. The discussion leaves caricature behind and builds up a more complex and nuanced political vision. But Kate's response to the tea party is truer to the novel's general intent: "the table was like a steel disc to which they were all, as victims, magnetised and bound" (S, 45). During the rest of *The Plumed Serpent* political themes retreat to the background. Ramón concentrates on mythic regeneration, emphasizing that he "must stand in another world, and act in another world—Politics must go their own way, and society must do as it will" (S, 210). To be sure, he does reach a grudging accommodation with Montes, the newly elected socialist president, thus ratifying Somers's momentary identification with Struthers. But this aspect of the novel's action is sketchy: one-sentence asides often suffice for the reporting of great historical changes, and it is difficult to believe that the main characters actually have the important public roles that Lawrence assigns to them.

For most readers, however, it is precisely with Ramón's "other world" of myth that the novel's social implications become most questionable. The Indian rituals build up to the Huitzilopochtli ceremony, in which Cipriano proclaims that "The Lords of Life are Masters of Death" (S, 416) and executes most of the people who plotted to assassinate Ramón. The scene is vulnerable on artistic grounds alone; the monotonous chants and gaudy costumes and the reliance on mystique instead of psychology epitomize the failures of the last two-thirds of *The Plumed Serpent*. But the executions might also suggest that Lawrence's conception of power has coarsened to the point that he asks us, in Graham Hough's words, "to celebrate the virtues of the hangman and the con-centration-camp guard."[45] There would then be a tempting parallel with Nietzsche, whose philosophy is often assumed to take a similar path to a brutal and more or less explicitly Fascist ideology. Has Lawrence, after all his quarrels with his master, finally succumbed to this wretched error? This line of thinking may be attractive, but it is difficult to reconcile with the facts. Just as those who want to see Nietzsche as a forerunner of the Nazis fail to explain why he should fanta-size about ridding the world of anti-Semites, so the Huitzi-lopochtli ceremony inconveniently deals with the execution of Fascists. Despite the vagueness of the political plot, it is clear that the assassination was engineered by the "reaction-ary Knights of Cortes," themselves closely allied with Fas-cists and a mysterious " 'black' faction."[46] Though there is little enough imaginative force in the execution scene, it does not demand the glorification of a Mussolini or a Hitler.

One guiding motive behind the Huitzilopochtli ceremony is Lawrence's sardonic and audaciously satirical attitude to-ward the pretensions of modern civilization. These human sacrifices, unlike the one in "The Woman Who Rode Away," can easily be justified by an appeal to legal procedures. As a general in a period of rebellion, Cipriano would have the right under martial law to execute the conspirators; after all, in attacking Ramón, they were attempting to assassinate an unofficial member of the government, and they actually did murder several of his servants. Indeed, Cipriano shows an unusual honesty and directness when he carries out several of the executions himself. Unlike Dean Vyner in *Saint Mawr*, who points out to Lou that "you can shift the responsibility" when it is a question of having the stallion shot,[47] he refuses to hide behind some bureaucratic chain of command. On a more profound level, the whole situation represents a mock-ing contrast with the world war, itself touched off by repris-als for a political assassination. The refurbished Indian rituals seem less shocking alongside the historical event which Lawrence viewed as a catastrophic reawakening of a primitive cult. In a letter from Cornwall he had spoken of the war in the following terms: "*we* shall roll with ecstasy in blood, get our fulfillment out of the hot bath of blood, like communicants bathing in the sacrifice-blood . . ." (CL, 452). The same savage irony had surfaced earlier when Ramón burned the religious ornaments in the local church. By titling the chapter "Auto da Fé," Lawrence drew attention to a far more violent episode in Western history.

But Lawrence had other motives than showing up the hypocrisies of his own culture. He believed that a death ritual could have affirmative elements, that it could express "the passion of its own mystery" instead of being a "ragged, squalid, vulgar" spectacle like the bullfight (S, 51). Thus, though the Huitzilopochtli ceremony repels Kate at first, she eventually accepts it because it served to renew "the old, terrible bond of the blood-unison of man, which made blood-sacrifice so potent a factor in life. . . . Sometimes it made her revolt. But it was the power she could not get beyond" (S, 457-458). By reawakening a vivid sense of bodily existence and establishing a basic biological feeling of community, the rituals have shown themselves to be life-enhancing. Their use of Mexican mythology differs profoundly from that of the Aztecs, whose mass sacrificial killings were the symptom of a people "in a cul de sac so they saw nothing but death" (S, 64-65). Lawrence tries to make a similar distinction as he describes how Ramón made the decision to have the executions. Before the attempted assassination, he had earnestly sought to avoid the vicious circle of violence; he realized that "death was not so easily wiped out of the air and out of the souls of men, as spilt blood was washed off the pavements" (S, 287). But during the attack, as his eyes take on "a certain primitive gleaming look of virginity" (S, 325), Ramón himself enters a state of death lust in which he exults in killing and makes the vow that will result in the executions: "We have got to kill them all"

(S, 330). The ritual does not purge or even greatly deflect this obsession with death, but does initiate a movement away: along with the five conspirators who die, there is one who is pardoned. There is also the renewed dedication to life symbolized by the green leaf of Malintzi.

Given the artistic shortcomings of the Huitzilopochtli ceremonies, it is difficult to grasp Lawrence's full purpose in the scene. But enough has been said to show that his conception is highly complex. He has imagined a scene that expresses his trauma at World War I as well as his revulsion from rationalized and bureaucratized modern societies, that includes both his concern with managing man's potential for violence and his disillusioned recognition of how deeply rooted these murderous tendencies are. We would be falsifying the intricacies of Lawrence's art if we labeled his attitude as fascistic even in some "higher sense" that would permit us to disregard his explicit political statements.[48]

The real problems with the mythical material in *The Plumed Serpent* lie elsewhere. For one thing, the Huitzilopochtli rituals are inadequate as an expression of a deeper concern of Lawrence's, that the consciousness of death could be a source of power. His serious illnesses from adolescence on and the worsening condition of his health during his work on the novel had forced this outlook on him. Its pressure can be felt behind the phrases quoted above like "the passion of its mystery" or even Cipriano's "Masters of Death." But there is an evasiveness in Lawrence's handling of this theme; ancient rites of human sacrifice are a peculiar vehicle for suggesting the existential demands of living in the presence of death. By raising the issue of taking human life, they obscure the drama of coping with mortality and make one wonder whether Lawrence might have been trying to blot out his personal situation. In any event, the hope of finding the power to confront one's own death emerges with greater clarity in "The Ship of Death" a few years later, where the poet envisions "the deep and lovely quiet / of a strong heart at peace."

The use of myth in *The Plumed Serpent* also testifies to a failure of social vision. Lawrence's travels after the war had given him a new breadth of outlook, which can sometimes result in prophetic insight; but they also increased the estrangement from any settled society which was already a conspicuous trait in his character. As a result, he can be superficial and even incredible in his assessments of group behavior. There is, therefore, a certain dishonesty in his satiric stance in the Huitzilopochtli ceremonies; the difference in social scale between the sacrificial ritual and a war involving an entire continent is too great. Were the myth to be generalized, particularly to the bullfight world of mass hysteria and an unconscious yielding to destructive instincts, one could easily imagine a disaster of equal proportions. But Lawrence subordinates social actuality to polemical intent. In effect, he has willingly accepted the difficulties he had recognized in Cooper's novels dealing with Indian material: "let me put aside my impatience at the unreality of this vision, and accept it as a wish-fulfillment, a kind of yearning myth."[49] But is this approach acceptable in a novel where the yearning myth that transcends social reality is joined with an urge for renovation that is more than merely personal? Caught between hasty observations and the projection of individual desires, Lawrence's portrayal of a new basis for power in a group fails to satisfy all the expectations it raises. To move from *The Plumed Serpent* to *Man's Fate* is to realize the much firmer grasp of social experience in Malraux.

Nietzschean issues persist in Lawrence's work after his Mexican novel: they color his response to the Etruscans and help mold the new commitment to life of the man who died. But there is a break after his serious illness and his return to Europe, and the concern with power is no longer the driving force of his career. At times this concern had led to profound ambivalence, whether toward Nietzsche himself as an acknowledged forerunner or toward the conflicting imperatives of selfhood and individuality versus relatedness and authority. But it also motivated some important assertions of value—an affirmation of the body, of the unconscious, of sexuality; a celebration of immediate contact with otherness in nature and in the cosmos; an exploration of myths and cultures that might provide an alternative to the Christian vision; a disillusioned look at the tendencies of the postwar world. In each of these areas Lawrence is elaborating on, or giving new emphasis to, themes that also appear in his predecessor. What makes this series of "thought adventures" compelling, of course, is Lawrence's continued success in finding symbols and imagined situations to convey his outlook. *The Plumed Serpent* and the novels leading up to it are far from being unqualified artistic triumphs. But there is real merit in them, despite the diffuseness caused by haste or some failure in creative ability, despite the decline when compared with the first product of Nietzsche's impact on Lawrence's imagination, *Women in Love*.

V

Preceded by Nietzsche's Madness: André Malraux as a Novelist in *Man's Fate* and *The Walnut Trees of the Altenburg*

For the young Malraux, precociously making his way in a postwar Paris of avant-garde movements, Nietzsche was a central intellectual experience. Characteristically, he has been very guarded in analyzing the effect of this interest on his writing, for he has none of Mann's confessional openness about the workings of his imagination. But he does admit how important Nietzsche was for him, and has given him first place in an account of his early years: "It is more difficult than one might believe to know the influences one has undergone. I admired Nietzsche and Dostoevsky, Anatole France and Maurice Barrès, Gide, Claudel, Suarès; and like all the young men of my generation the poets."[1] No doubt his heightened awareness for the obscure processes by which influence works came from his own studies of metamorphic changes of style in art history; but he shows none of Lawrence's impatience at acknowledging a predecessor. Another interview on the subject of his youth draws much the same picture: he dwells on the high prestige of the poets, then quickly shifts to "influences of a quite different kind, stemming essentially from Nietzsche, who, for us, was something of a giant. . . ."[2] His first wife Clara, who met him at this time, goes further, recalling that he was "obsessed with Nietzsche . . . even before we knew each other."[3] She was in a good position to strengthen Malraux's understanding of his hero: though French herself, she came from a German Jewish family and had a deep interest in German culture.

Even more than with Lawrence, another writer intervenes to reinforce Malraux's admiration for Nietzsche and to help condition his response. I am referring to his enthusiasm for André Gide, then at the height of his influence after years of semiobscurity before the war. His earliest published writings include two appreciations of Gide—one of them a fragment, like so much undertaken by Malraux—which provide a valuable insight into his developing attitudes. Emphasizing Gide's influence on contemporary youth and defining his greatness as both literary and didactic (but didactic in the open sense of setting minds in motion without rigidly channeling their development), Malraux is primarily interested in his significance as a cultural phenomenon. He sees him as a representative man in a post-Christian world, one whose "form of mind" still derives from Christianity though he has "put a space" between himself and God.[4]

But he also has some intriguing observations on his value as a "point of departure" in a more specifically literary sense.[5] He admires Gide's way of coping with predecessors, and notably Nietzsche, who had anticipated his intellectual outlook: "Some thoughts had been expressed, which were in him. Incapable of giving them up without ceasing to be himself, he transformed them so well that he gave them life."[6] Malraux's specific comments make it clear that this notion of transformation applies primarily to Gide's creation of characters in his fiction; and, though he discusses Alissa from *Strait is the Gate* in the most detail, it is apparent that he finds *The Immoralist* more fascinating. He argues that "it is Michel's sufferings which have given your teachings the force that one sees in them today," then complains that "you hide from us the death of Michel."[7] Concerning another character, he can remark that "it pleases me greatly, Ménalque 'with the face of a pirate,' to imagine you . . ."[8] This deep, collaborative involvement with Gide's story suggests that it had alerted Malraux to the possibilities of using fiction as a vehicle for his passionate interest in Nietzsche. He too could give new life to thoughts which had already been expressed;

he too could invent fascinating images for Nietzschean ideas. Perhaps it is revealing that the older writer hovers in the background of the two novels we shall be considering in this chapter: more than one critic has seen traces of Gide in the character of old Gisors in *Man's Fate*, while Malraux sought out Gide for a first reading of the manuscript of *The Walnut Trees of the Altenburg*.[9]

Several years after these appreciations, and with his Indochina adventure behind him, Malraux returns to the issue of post-Christian culture in "Concerning a European Youth." The representative role once given to Gide has now passed to Nietzsche, who "finds so many echoes in desperate hearts" (J, 139). One reason for the switch is the broadened scope of this essay. Having lived in the Orient, Malraux now chooses to take the general situation of the West as his subject, and the "good European" provided a much more useful starting point than Gide's popularity in postwar France. Nor is he concerned with Nietzsche simply as the prophet of the death of God, for he goes on to discuss the problems faced by post-Christian intellectuals. Malraux traces the outlook of these free spirits back to a faith in liberty and a reliance on rational intelligence (*esprit*), becoming somewhat Nietzschean in his methods when he reveals the religious underpinnings to such movements as the religion of humanity or the cult of the self. As he remarked earlier in the essay, cultural forms are persistent: "Our first weakness comes from our being forced to perceive the world through a Christian 'gridwork' though we are no longer Christians" (J, 137).

Nietzsche becomes the object of Malraux's analysis when he discusses the necessary conflict between the ideals of mind and liberty. The first was directed toward rational, lucid judgment while the second made the individual the measure of everything. But this double imperative broke down as soon as the individual was found to be essentially irrational and subject to compulsive behavior: "The Self, a palace of silence into which each person penetrates alone, conceals all the precious stones of our provisional madnesses mingled with those of our lucidity. . . . . Our involuntary life—almost always very far from being unconscious—would dominate the other without the exertion of a constant effort" (J, 142). Malraux's disagreement with Freud may be sensed in this insistence that "involuntary life"—the whole formless and chaotic side of the personality—should not be identified with an unconscious. In any case, the collapse of the rational self uncovers the stark absurdity of existence, an absurdity no longer softened by Christian appeals to human sinfulness or to a possible connection with God. The world as well becomes a chaos, an "infinity of possibilities, . . . an immense play of relationships" (J, 152). Thus in art Malraux sees an acceptance of merely provisional realities (J, 151), in science a recognition that it has become hopeless to try to discover the sense of the universe (J, 145). And the great forerunner for this confrontation with the absurd was Nietzsche: "Laden with the successive passions of men, it [individualism] has destroyed everything but itself; raised up by the most lofty minds of our epoch, preceded by Nietzsche's madness, and decorated with the booty taken from the gods, it is here before us and in it we see only a blind victor" (J, 145-146). The insane philosopher in the vanguard of the dubious triumph of individualism—here is a fitting symbol for the failure of the modern mind when faced with the chaotic self.

This vivid passage crystallizes several tendencies in Malraux's developing response to Nietzsche. Taking up the challenge he had found in Gide, he has begun his own process of transforming ideas into fiction: this unification of speculative concerns with an implied drama of combat foreshadows the characteristic world of his novels. Gide's impetus also lies behind the reference to Nietzsche's madness, which the older writer had once seen as a measure of the originality and daring of his thought.[10] Malraux is more doubtful, yet even as he creates a striking image of crisis he argues according to Nietzschean categories. This defeat of lucid consciousness by a chaotic mystery in the depths of the individual recalls the nullified extremes of Apollo and Dionysus, with

The Immoralist reinforcing the suggestions in *The Birth of Tragedy*. Malraux's fascination with Nietzsche's madness builds on his interest in the sufferings and death of Michel. On the other hand, he breaks with the philosopher when he refuses at this point to accept a science of hypothetical constructs or an art relying on a metamorphic succession of provisional styles (J, 151-153), though both could easily be justified by an appeal to the will to power. Yet he rejoins Nietzsche when he refers to the "nihilistic, destructive, essentially negative thought" of his time and criticizes "the taste for this disaggregation" that he finds in art (J, 148, 151).[11] The philosopher has become both symptom and diagnostician of a nihilistic formlessness in the modern world. With its sensitivity to early Nietzsche and late, to broad cultural speculation and probing psychological insight, "Concerning a European Youth" reveals the breadth and the general outlines of Malraux's interest in his thought.

The attitudes expressed in this essay and in others during the twenties are seminal for Malraux's entire career.[12] But for our purposes we may largely ignore the writings on art and the memoirs that make up a major part of his literary achievement. The problem of finding fictional equivalents that might dramatize and further develop a highly Nietzschean outlook will be crucial to him only so long as he is an active novelist. Over the fifteen-year period following "European Youth" Malraux shows such power in inventing characters and situations and images that, in Geoffrey Hartman's words, "it almost convinces us that the form of the novel is the natural medium for his view of life."[13]

Two novels are especially important. Judged simply on such artistic grounds as variety, attention to detail, and integration, *Man's Fate* decisively surpasses its predecessors that deal with Eastern material, *The Conquerors* and *The Royal Way*. Moreover, these earlier books were reductively Nietzschean in their concern with empire and conquest; the later novel conveys a deeper and more nuanced response that is truer to the character of Malraux's interest in Nietzsche.

Man's Fate is also the best place to observe Malraux's effort to integrate his growing interest in Marx with more basic categories of thought derived from Nietzsche. By contrast the more straightforwardly "engaged" *Days of Wrath* is a minor work; while *Man's Hope*, though much more varied intellectually and with an epic sweep rightly admired by Gaëtan Picon,[14] does not fully resolve the issues it raises. But Malraux's last novel, *The Walnut Trees of the Altenburg*, is an exciting new departure. In it he both abandons the technique of his most ambitious earlier work—the scenic method that captures the atmosphere of breathless news dispatches—and turns back to Nietzsche, who inspires him to explore fresh themes and situations. This book is not as well known as it should be, primarily because Malraux dismissed it as a mere fragment, part of a larger work destroyed by the Gestapo, and did not allow it to be reprinted after the first French edition of 1948. But he showed a continued esteem for *Walnut Trees* after taking up his semifictive "autobiography" in 1965, for he reworked several of its most important episodes for use in this latest project.[15]

The Temptation of the West: Nietzsche and the Sociocultural Basis of Malraux's Eastern World

Malraux's passage from Nietzschean speculation to *Man's Fate* had already begun in a book published a year before "European Youth." In *The Temptation of the West*, a work that he classified with his nonfictional productions and which consists of letters between a Frenchman visiting China and a Chinese in France, he confronts East and West in the manner of his first three novels. Though the correspondence is largely a vehicle for ideas, it already shows a certain interest in characterization and drama: Malraux's spokesmen not only explain but exemplify their cultures, and there are lively patterns of give-and-take as we read through the letters. This fictionalization of essayistic material is in accord with a conception of art that stresses the dependence of image on idea:

"a well-organized intelligence easily dominates human representations" so that the arts can be seen as "ornaments, adding savor to thought" (TW, 137). In literature, Malraux remains most sensitive to how this process of transformation
will affect characters; thus he can remark that "Werther is
the proposition of death" (TW, 169).

The preface to *Temptation* defines the book's purpose with
an elliptical reference to the split that would make Nietzsche's
madness such a compelling image for Malraux: "to characterize the movements of two sensibilities and to suggest to
readers some arresting thoughts on the life of their senses
and of their mind, a life which could seem strange" (TW,
12). Malraux develops this duality of mind and senses within
the sensibility in a way that anticipates the conflict in "European Youth" between Apollinian reason and Dionysian
forces of chaos in self and world. Thus his Chinese character
Ling, who prefers to "*sense* that beyond every act . . . a yet
hidden life extends its numberless ramifications" (TW, 44),
can revolt against Western rationalism: "My sensibility op-
poses itself to limitations set by the mind" (TW, 45). This
psychological premise underlies the cultural distinctions drawn
in the *Temptation*. The Apollinian West typically projects intellectual constructs, including actions, out onto the world,
thereby humanizing it; but the Dionysian East tries to submerge the mind with intuitions of a universe profoundly different from man. As Ling puts it in a peremptory maxim:
"The first wants to bring the universe to man; the other offers man up to the universe" (TW, 155). The Frenchman
A.D. has defined the specifically Western sensibility in similar terms: "This defense against the incessant solicitation of
the universe is the very mark of the European genius,
whether it expresses itself behind a Hellenic or a Christian
mask" (TW, 103). Malraux, it will be noticed, does not follow Nietzsche in emphasizing the radically non-Christian
elements of Greek culture; indeed, the initials of his hero's
name stamp him as a product of the Christian epoch. Still,
he continues to interpret statues of human beings as an Apol-

linian victory over a Titanic world of Dionysian terror. Eastern sculpture, by contrast, prefers "the monster—dragon, sphinx, winged bull" which correspond to "that part of the soul" which reappears "every time men ask more of life than thought can give them" (TW, 66).

This way of using Nietzsche's polarities extends the contrast between Eastern and Western cultures in *The Birth of Tragedy*. A young Frenchman investigating Buddhist temples in Indochina might easily have been fascinated by these hints about the differences between the Latin and the Indian traditions. But there is more at stake in *The Temptation of the West* than cultural typology. The title sums up the mood of crisis shared by both characters: the West is a source of temptation for the East and is also undergoing temptation itself. This theme has its political aspect, since Ling is bitterly aware of the European colonial presence in Asia while A.D. is uncertain about the vision and ability of postwar European leaders. But the basic crisis centers on the loss of cultural identity. For A.D., contemporary experimental art testifies to a breakdown in the inner law of the West: "Forsaken palace attacked by the winter wind, our mind disaggregates little by little, and its cracks with a beautiful decorative effect continue to spread" (TW, 140). And Ling, contemplating the assault of the modern world on Eastern civilization, cries out in despair: "How to express the state of a soul which is *disaggregating?*" (TW, 200). The forms of sensibility characterizing both worlds are in danger of disappearing, and the possibility of nihilism opens up. Again, concerns voiced more forcefully by the later Nietzsche have fused with themes from his early work.

Malraux pauses to give examples of this general situation, some consisting simply of a cluster of observations while others are partially transformed into characters. A.D.'s letter from Shanghai tells of his interview with an aging Confucian intellectual named Wang-Loh. Fully devoted to Chinese culture, the man analyzes the accelerating process of its destruction. A final image captures his mixed attitude; his trembling hands seem "to render homage to the misfortune he had just evoked with one of the brief salutes demanded by the rites of long ago" (TW, 189). Contrasting with this resigned despair is Ling's account of the frenzied nihilism among Chinese youth. They are "as desperate as Wang-Loh or myself, stripped of their own culture, disgusted with yours"; but in this void they discover a "strange, passionless desire for destruction and anarchy" (TW, 201). As with the bullfight in *The Plumed Serpent*, the West becomes the source of "all that you could want to die." Alternatively, A.D. finds possibilities for chaos in the enormous variety of cultural artifacts flooding into Europe from all over the world. Anticipating Malraux's later writings on art with their emphasis on the cross-cultural juxtapositions possible in the modern museum, he remarks that "it is no longer Europe or the past which is invading France as this century begins, it is the world with all its present and past which is invading Europe" (TW, 143). But rather than celebrating this broadening of horizons, he is troubled by it. It might unsettle even those artists who are most sure of themselves, and it encourages a superficial restlessness in searching after new impressions. Europeans are becoming like "sick kings to whom each morning brings the most beautiful gifts of the realm, each evening brings back an ever-present and desperate avidity" (TW, 142). Malraux is echoing the account in *The Birth of Tragedy* of a shapeless and fragmentary culture without myth.[16] Finally, A.D. can discern nihilistic possibilities in Western activism; at no level does the pursuit of power lead to truly satisfactory forms of organization. In the international system "the elements of Western strength oppose and combat each other in the service of an energy without a head" (TW, 208); in the state and the church "there is no longer any domination lofty enough to carry consciousness along with it" (TW, 209); for the individual "the development of self which has as its goal the acquisition of power is not supported by an affirmation . . ." (TW, 211). Even as he continues his activity, Western man finds he can neither believe in it nor justify it.

Alongside these doom-laden sketches of the future appear intimations of different possibilities. Malraux had polemical motives in choosing the title for his book, with his most immediate target being the French conservative Henri Massis, whose *Defense of the West* was soon to be published. Arguing that Western culture was threatened by "Asiaticism," this book favored suppressing the postwar agitation in the East against European colonialism. Malraux counters by insisting that the cultural situation is just the reverse; the disorders prove that Asians are succumbing to the temptation of Western ideals and methods. As Ling reflects on the general strike in Canton that became the subject of *The Conquerors*, he points out that "it is no longer her defeats, but her victories, which mark the destruction of China's past" (TW, 195). This incident serves a double purpose in *The Temptation of the West*, for it provides a counterweight to A.D.'s doubts about the adequacy of political activity in the West, and it briefly lightens the dominant mood of despair at the vanishing Asian past. Ling sees in it "a change in Chinese culture which heralds a complete transformation" (TW, 195). Is the West's real mission to contribute to a more inclusive and more satisfactory culture in the future? Malraux has glimpsed two guiding ideas in his later thought, the process of metamorphosis and the possibility of a universal humanism.

Malraux's title also expresses his resistance to a book which created a great stir in the twenties, Spengler's *The Decline of the West*.[17] The French word rendered as temptation is "tentation," which can suggest a testing or probing that determines the true importance of a quality and reaffirms it. Like Mann about this time, Malraux resists Spengler's deterministic fatalism; alongside the possibility of decline he sees an opportunity for energizing struggle. Thus A.D. counters his awareness of nihilistic tendencies in Western culture with efforts to discover the persistence in adversity of its most characteristic trait. He claims to find a commitment to the intellect among his contemporaries, both in their attempt to discover principles of artistic form among the hodge-podge of artifacts gathered in modern museums (TW, 139-143) and in their determination to reach some understanding of the disordered reveries and sensations created by the "passive imagination" (TW, 98-103). In his last letter A.D. himself, in much less ambiguous circumstances, gives his allegiance to this Western tradition: "Voracious lucidity, I still burn before you, a solitary and upright flame in this heavy night, while the yellow wind cries, as in all those foreign nights when the wind from the open ocean repeated around me the proud outcry of the sterile sea . . ." (TW, 218). This eloquent image transcends the sociocultural argument of *The Temptation of the West* and, returning to its psychological underpinnings, points to an ideal. Setting light against darkness, fire against water, a small center of calm against the threat of wind and waves, it binds polar opposites in a precarious resolution like the one in which Nietzsche's tragic Greeks affirmed Apollo in the presence of Dionysus. Hence for Malraux *The Birth of Tragedy* not only provides a scheme for juxtaposing Europe and Asia; it also becomes an assertion of rational intelligence against psychic disorder and inhuman immensity. The force of this assertion grows in proportion to the opposing term; as a result, crisis can furnish the occasion for a new access of strength.

□

As Malraux's commitment to fiction deepens in the years following *The Temptation of the West*, he will create characters who embody the confrontation of East and West far more vividly than A.D. or Ling. Thus the adventurer Grabot in *The Royal Way*, blinded and enslaved by savages in an inaccessible Asian jungle, or the terrorist Hong in *The Conquerors*, whose character is decisively altered by contact with Europeans. But only with *Man's Fate* does Malraux fully exploit the wealth of types and situations sketched out in *Temptation*. The Shanghai of this novel, like Andrei Bely's

Petersburg, is a place where East meets West. Built by European commerce on the shores of Asia, it provides the appropriate setting for an impressive array of characters who illustrate Malraux's sense of the possibilities facing both traditions. In one group, which includes several of the most vivid figures in his fiction, the dominating factor is the breakdown of cultural values. The barfly and sometime art dealer Clappique, the obsessed terrorist Ch'en, and the expatriate professor old Gisors all wander through a no man's land between Asia and Europe. The activists, meanwhile, are united by their dedication to the Western political will. Both the revolutionaries Kyo and Katov and their main antagonist, the French businessman Ferral, share the ambition of providing new forms of organization for a traditional Chinese society that is falling apart. But their conflict resolves little, and in its wake the sense of a crisis in social meaning has deepened.

The Baron de Clappique is a character who has had a strong hold on Malraux's imagination. In preparing the final version of *Man's Fate,* he had to cut a long scene involving him so as to preserve the novel's unity; and he comes back to him in *Anti-Memoirs,* though with a sad decline in imaginative power. The key word used to describe his case is "mythomania" (e.g., M, 208-209), a term which can refer simply to obsessive lying. But there are overtones of meaning to Clappique's situation that recall Malraux's interest in cultural fragmentation and the dissolution of governing myths as presented in *The Birth of Tragedy.* Thus Clappique has developed a certain expertise in Oriental art, to the point of once being "the foremost dealer in antiquities in Peking" (M, 209). Yet these broadened cultural horizons have not enriched his identity; instead, at the end of his visit to the Japanese painter, Kama, he confesses under cover of his clowning that "the Baron de Clappique does not exist" (M, 323, 324). It is appropriate that he should usually give "the impression of being in disguise" and that in the cosmopolitan but desperate world of Shanghai nightclubs he should "not do badly at evoking the spirit of the place" (M, 197, 196). Indeed, his typicality could be extended further, given his popularity not only with Ferral but also with the fashion designer Valérie and with König, the police chief under Chiang Kai-shek. In its broadest implications, Clappique's mythomania suggests the possibility of a general breakdown of cultural meaning in the West.

The Baron's first appearance in the novel presents his situation with special clarity. In need of his services as an arms dealer, Kyo looks him up in a nightclub and overhears him telling an anecdote to some dancing girls. It deals with his grandfather, an Hungarian landowner who had himself buried astride his horse in imitation of Attila the Hun. His greatest exploit had been to gather his peasants together in a ragged army to pursue his mistress, a circus performer he had abducted and who then ran off with a barber out of boredom (M, 198-200). The grotesque contrast between heroic model and actual performance recalls the inauthentic posturing of an actor that Nietzsche had seen in Wagner. The sense of a decaying cultural form is strengthened by the fact that for once Clappique is discussing his own background. Usually his stories have exotic subjects with a gruesome twist to them: East Indian pirates who revolt against a Dutchman planning to loot Mecca, an Afghan chieftain who tears out a rapist's eyes in front of the naked woman he violated, South American savages and ghastly Arab ships filled with victims of the plague.[18] But this anecdote, though it may be equally fictitious, is at least European; as a self-dramatization, it conveys the failure of a constitutive model from the past and the squalid, rootless existence that takes its place. And our very uncertainty as to how much Clappique might have embroidered the facts provides the key to his course through the novel. Disordered fantasies—moving from his exotic stories through his playacting at being rich to his persuading a prostitute that he is about to commit suicide and on to his successful masquerade as a sailor at the end—overwhelm reality again and again. Breaking loose from A.D.'s

Apollinian ideal of masterful lucidity, Clappique has plunged into the realm of the passive imagination.

Several later scenes give further insight into this cultural situation. When Clappique visits the gambling house in a last-ditch effort to raise money for his escape from Shanghai, his mood is unusually resolute. This commitment to some form of planned activity recalls A.D.'s rather desperate hopes that the fragmented West might return to its basic principles; the Baron's perception of his surroundings is in accord with his mood: "as though it were answering him, the fragrance of the wet boxwood and spindle trees rose from the garden. That bitter fragrance was Europe" (M, 357). But when he leaves, having lost most of his money and missed a meeting with Kyo due to his feverish involvement with the game, the cultural landscape has shifted. Looking out on the moon-lit city, he feels its human meaning dissolving into an unearthly void, "an extraterrestrial life as if the moon's atmosphere had come and settled in the great sudden silence with its light" (M, 361). This dissolution of his cultural identity reappears when he finally does escape by disguising himself as a sailor. Delighted at his success in "living a story, not merely telling one," he remembers the joyous estrangement he had felt on first coming to Asia: "it was the same feeling of being taken out of one's country, the same happiness that had seized him the first time he had entered a Chinese crowd" (M, 399). Unfortunately, he has committed himself to returning to France, and he suddenly realizes that he will lose the floating state of indefinite cultural possibilities in which he has lived for so long: "Europe . . . the party is over" (M, 400). Already feeling trapped, he decides to get drunk.

The futility of these attempted evasions of his identity had been made evident in the scene where he makes faces at himself in the mirror. Isolated for once in his room and increasingly anxious about the prospects for escape, he diverts himself by seeking to reproduce "all the grotesques that a human face can express" (M, 372-373). He enters an orgy of trans-

formations—gargoyle, carnival samurai, monkey, idiot, toad
face—that often betray the humanized ideal of the West. But
when he laughs in a manner that reminds him of his mother,
the illusion is abruptly shattered. Once again he recognizes
himself in the mirror. His response, characteristically, is to
recoil and make another attempt at self-evasion through automatic writing. The alternation here between imaginative
frenzy and a desolating awareness of the real self recalls Malraux's earlier image for the cultural breakdown of Europe.
Like the sick king, Clappique vacillates between the "beautiful gifts" of a worldwide experience and a sense of "desperate avidity" conditioned by an inner void. Due to the
broadened cultural horizons of his century he has a large rep-
ertoire of possibilities for escaping himself, but in the end his
attempts at flight are abortive. The scene in front of the mirror epitomizes the diversity and instability of the fictions by
which he lives in a world without mythical form.

With Ch'en, who is probably the character in *Man's Fate*
that Malraux portrays with the greatest care, the cultural
contradictions have become more intense. At first glance he
might be thought to represent a decisive break with Chinese
tradition; thus an early scene shows old Gisors, his former
sociology professor, contrasting him with an aged mandarin
who defends the subjection of women and ancestor worship:
"Order! Crowds of skeletons in embroidered robes, lost in
the depth of time in motionless assemblies: facing them
Ch'en, the two hundred thousand workers of the spinning
mills, the crushing horde of the coolies" (M, 220). But just
as the mandarin expresses his die-hard attitudes in English,
so Ch'en cannot be taken as a simple emblem of the shift to
an urban and industrial society based on a Western model.
His face suggests the difficulties of this interpretation. As he
comes into the room, Gisors remembers the picture of an
Egyptian bronze hawk that Kyo had saved because of its
resemblance to Ch'en (M, 220). This Westernized Chinese
can also evoke a Dionysian monster of the Orient, and the
sociologist must revise his view of him: "In short, a hawk

converted by Saint Francis of Assisi." The epigram has to allow for the irreducible bird of prey while asserting the humanizing Western impulse of the saint who assimilated even the animals to the world of language.

Ch'en's tangled relationship with his Chinese heritage permeates the opening of the novel. When old Gisors talks with him about his sexual initiation, he bitterly distances himself from its typically Chinese form: " 'I am Chinese,' Ch'en answered with rancor" (M, 222). Ironically, of course, the very fact that he has turned to Gisors testifies to the persistence of the traditional respect felt by a pupil for his master (M, 221). Similarly, after the assassination of the gun dealer he is startled by the shadow of a stray cat passing before the window. Although he is certain that he has purged himself of the old superstitions, his response expresses more than nervous surprise: "Although Ch'en did not believe in spirits, he was paralyzed, unable to turn around" (M, 184). Then, after he leaves the gun dealer's room, the contradictions become even more involuted and disturbing. Wearing Western clothing, he passes through a cosmopolitan bar; but he avoids an Asian who addresses him in English by pretending to have the native identity he thinks he has surpassed: " 'I don't know any foreign languages,' said Ch'en in Peking dialect" (M, 186).

These moments of tension between cultures recall Malraux's analysis of Chinese youth caught between their own tradition and the West and unable to find stable values for themselves. But *Man's Fate* does not simply present Ch'en's current state; it also explores his development. The opening scene in which he murders the gun dealer exposes feelings from the past, "a dread at once horrible and solemn, which he had not experienced since childhood" (M, 184), that are crucial for an understanding of his character. Later on we learn the deep impact upon Ch'en of the disintegration of his society: he grew up an orphan, his parents having been killed by bandits or warlords in the pillage of Kalgan (M, 225).[19] His feelings beside the gun dealer's corpse probably reproduce his mood at that time, when he might well have felt "alone with death, alone in a place without men, limply crushed by horror and by the taste of blood" (M, 184). Gisors's memories of his education show that he reacted to this experience of dispossession by striving to find a new cultural identity through a succession of contacts with the West. A first, preliminary stage is represented by Ch'en's uncle, who sent him to a Lutheran college to learn French and English, perhaps because of their usefulness in business. Since he intends to raise his nephew according to Confucian principles, he wants no large-scale Western influence; thus he warns him against the school's religious teachings (M, 225).

But Ch'en does convert to Christianity. The significance of this act is complex. On the one hand, it teaches him that Apollinian sense of a personal identity as opposed to a Dionysian submission to the cosmos that Malraux thinks distinguishes Western from Eastern culture: "His faith had detached him from China, accustomed him to isolate himself from the world instead of submitting to it" (M, 226). But it also reveals a profound ambivalence in his emotions. Though Ch'en does respond to Christianity as a religion of love, he also senses the intense anguish and terror that his mentor feels at the possibility that divine grace might be withheld (M, 225). For someone with Ch'en's character, this mood must have provided a fateful link between his childish sense of dread and the emotional world he will enter as a terrorist.

First, however, Ch'en's development enters an intermediate stage. He switches to the University of Peking where the Marxist teachings of old Gisors cause him to give up his religious beliefs and become a revolutionary. Both the source of the ideology and the choice of an activist role demonstrate his continuing commitment to the West, while the death of his uncle in another episode of internal disorder severs his last tie with the past. It suggests something of the secondary status of the Marxism in *Man's Fate*[20] that Ch'en's new ideology should result in a highly Nietzschean challenge: "What good is a soul, if there is neither God nor Christ?" (M, 226). From his childhood experience with an Eastern society in crisis, Ch'en has moved in a very few years to a crisis point in the Western tradition. Indeed, his new dilemma recalls the reflections in "Concerning a European Youth" on the post-Christian predicament; not only does East cut against West in Ch'en's character, but he has been unable to discover a firm set of values in either culture.

In the course of *Man's Fate* this unstable compound "disaggregates," to use the Nietzschean term Malraux admired. There are profound psychological motives behind Ch'en's fascination with terrorism and his cult of suicide that are best taken up in the next section. But his story also dramatizes the failure of his cultural experiences, suggesting an irresistible smelting down of his identity as he passes through the stages of his development in reverse order. His ideological commitment wavers as early as his assassination of the gun dealer, when he senses that "below his sacrifice to the revolution was stirring a world of depths" (M, 181). By the time of the siege of the armored train he is dismissing Kyo's and Katov's political analyses as meaningless talk (M, 273). And when he visits the headquarters of the International in Hankow, he has become impenetrable to argument (M, 284). Then, after his return to Shanghai, he breaks with an earlier cultural layer when he happens to meet Smithson, his teacher at the missionary school. His divided attitudes toward the West surface once more in his response to this man, for whom he feels an affection "not without rancor," an anger that does not exclude "a furtive pity" (M, 301, 302). But at last he tears himself away by brutally interrupting a discussion of religion with the announcement that he plans to kill Chiang Kai-shek.

Ch'en must now cope with the earliest stage of his upbringing. The scene of his first attempt on Chiang Kai-shek's life is especially well done. He chooses to wait in a shop selling Chinese antiquities that recalls his cultural heritage, but his success in fooling the shopkeeper as to his intentions dissolves traditional structures. He glimpses a terrible freedom where everything seems arbitrary: "Things, even ac-

tions, did not exist; they all were dreams which take possession of us because we give them force, but which we can
just as easily deny" (M, 307). But he has not, in fact, tran-
scended all cultural forms. In a masterful twist to the action,
the antiquary assumes that Ch'en must be looking for pieces
of jade for a Japanese geisha girl and in his eagerness to make
a sale gets in the way of the assassination. His mistake is
absurd; yet it was based on Ch'en's actions and remarks,
which included a veiled reference to his childhood misfor-
tunes: "I used to live in the interior. The war forced me to
leave" (M, 304). Thus, despite his efforts, the terrorist has
still been assimilated to a Chinese system of values. But
when he angrily shoves the merchant aside, he has thrown
off the last and most profound of the cultural influences that
have formed him.

The backdrop for Ch'en's second assassination attempt
will enlarge on the implications of this scene. As he waits,
the immemorial world of the peasant enters the city built by
European commerce: "The desolate night of the China rice
fields and marshes had reached the almost deserted avenue"
(M, 352). Ch'en himself thinks of an ancient Chinese legend,
and Chiang Kai-shek's automobile also evokes the distant
past when it arrives as if from "the times of Buddhism"
along a street whose signs "sunk in confused perspectives,
disappeared into that tragic and blurred world as if into the
centuries" (M, 353†). These various long perspectives combine to enforce a sense, not of continuity, but of crisis. When
Ch'en runs toward the car "with the joy of an ecstatic" (M,
354), his act no longer has meaning within the tradition to
which it refers. As in Bely's *Petersburg*, the explosion of a
terrorist's bomb implies the absolute destruction and collapse
of a cultural form.[21]

In old Gisors the conflict between Eastern and Western
values has a gentler outcome. But in its unusual complexity
the conflict testifies to the large role Malraux can give to
choice over early environment in cultural matters. Despite
his European origins, old Gisors has devoted himself so fully

to Oriental art that he, more than any other character, has Wang-Loh's intense consciousness of the Asian past. The doctrines held by his brother-in-law Kama, a talented painter in the traditional Japanese manner, suggest the extent to which Gisors had once sought out an Eastern submission to the world in preference to a Western assertion of the individual self: "The more your painters paint apples, and even lines which do not represent objects, the more they speak of themselves. For me it is the world which counts" (M, 319). As a result old Gisors can have an insider's view of the breakdown of cultural form in the East. In his home filled with masterpieces of Asian art he senses, with desperation, the irrevocable death of the values for which he once had lived: "His exquisitely pure sense of Chinese art, of those bluish paintings which his lamp barely lit up, of the whole civilization of suggestion which China spread about him, from which, thirty years earlier, he had profited with such refined taste—his sense of happiness—was now nothing more than a thin cover beneath which anguish and the obsession of death were awakening, like restless dogs stirring at the end of their sleep" (M, 229). Perhaps this mood of disillusionment has helped to reawaken his sympathy for Western modes of consciousness in recent years. But the major factor was his son's choice of a political vocation. Turning his attention from art history to sociology, old Gisors began to argue for an activist creed based on the premise that "Marxism is not a doctrine, it is a will" (M, 228). The emphasis on will implies a reversal of cultural identity; thus he welcomes his former student Ch'en as a decisive break with Chinese tradition or becomes impatient with the apparent irrelevance of Kama's artistic goals in a world where "Today serenity was almost an insult" (M, 319). When he visits Clappique to have him intercede with the police on Kyo's behalf, this new orientation is even clearer. In assuming that "if the world was without reality, men—and especially those who are most opposed to the world—have themselves an intense reality" (M, 375), he glorifies the West's humanizing projection

of the self upon the world. For old Gisors Marxism represents another stage in a cultural migration between two
worlds.

Old Gisors's addiction to opium introduces a new twist to
his case. One of its effects is to free him from the tormenting
pressure of the chaotic, involuntary self: "This force, the furious subterranean imagination which was in him . . . ready
to take on all forms" (M, 229). Thus he avoids A.D.'s dedication, in a similar situation, to Western lucidity; in the last
issue, his commitment to will and to humanized illusion
turns out to be hollow.

Opium also serves to reawaken his sensitivity to the Asian
past. The beautifully cadenced prose that describes his vision
after the interview with Ch'en evokes a peaceful scene from
the old China (M, 230). In a normal state of consciousness
he would have concluded that it was gone beyond recall, but
now he loses himself in a landscape where a lake, a Buddhist
priest near an ancient temple, and some peasants among the
waterlilies combine to produce a mood of solemn melancholy. Ultimately the dream becomes Eastern in a more general sense, as he finds serenity in contemplating the whole:
"His eyes shut, carried by great motionless wings, Gisors
contemplated his solitude: a desolation that joined the divine,
while at the same time the wave of serenity that gently covered the depths of death widened to infinity." The specific
scene has expanded, through a series of metaphors (the
wings and the wave derive from the wake of the peasants'
boat), to a sense of release in the infinite and the divine. This
experience corresponds to Kama's somewhat enigmatic remarks on the Oriental mode of consciousness; he uses the
word "sign" to refer to a Chinese ideogram: "The world is
like the characters of our writing. . . . Everything is a sign.
To go from the sign to the thing it signifies is to deepen the
world, is to go toward God" (M, 319-320). Just as the ideogram yields meanings that go beyond its origins as a repre-
sentational equivalent to some object, so objects in the world
point beyond themselves to broader truths. But these truths

are taken as inherent in the world, not as projections of the perceiving self as would be the case in Malraux's vision of Western consciousness. It is, of course, tellingly ironic that old Gisors can achieve this Dionysian cosmic sense only in a state of intoxication and not in everyday life.

In the epilogue to *Man's Fate* the weakness of old Gisors's attachment to Western values and the tragic hopelessness of his engagement with the East become fully evident. Kyo's death has removed the main force pushing him westward, and he has gone to live with his brother-in-law in Japan. It is appropriate, therefore, that he now interprets his interest in Marxism as the expression of an Asian sense of destiny rather than of European activism. Its appeal lay not in its promise of transformation but in the rationale it provided for his cultural despair: "Marxism has ceased to live in me. In Kyo's eyes it was a will, wasn't it? But in mine it is a fatality, and I found myself in harmony with it because my anguish before death was in harmony with fatality" (M, 428). The underlying Nietzschean coordinates to his cultural dilemma become clearest when he remarks that a new spirit has recently entered his life: "Since Kyo died I have discovered music. Music alone can speak of death. I listen to Kama, now, whenever he plays" (M, 429). In turning from ideology to music, old Gisors has crossed the same borderline as Nietzsche's Socrates. But in *Man's Fate* this Dionysian rebirth is specifically Asian; in an earlier scene Kama had defended his music as a means of preserving Eastern attitudes and withstanding Europe (M, 321). In addition, old Gisors continues to rely on opium to evade the imperatives of Western intellect and join himself with the cosmos. For the first time he finds that "the idea that the time which brought him nearer to death was flowing away in him did not separate him from the world but joined him to it in a serene accord," and he resolves that "one must not think life with the mind but with opium" (M, 430). But as Kyo's widow May looks at his drugged face, it does not express discovery but seems to return "from the deep regions of death, foreign like one of the corpses in the common ditches" (M, 431). The transition that in Nietzsche's Socrates had promised cultural renewal suggests in Malraux a resigned apathy within a disintegrating tradition.

□

In all three of the characters we have examined so far, the rational, planning will that typifies the West is either weak or radically infected. Hence, though they each play some role in the political drama of *Man's Fate*, the center of interest is clearly their equivocal cultural situation. Only when we turn to Ferral and the revolutionaries does social action become a leading issue. The historical resonance to this side of the novel is remarkable: as so rarely happens in Lawrence, we see people making decisions and carrying them out in a specific and solidly realized social situation. And in dramatizing the events in Shanghai in the spring of 1927, Malraux—always eager to find elements of unconscious prophecy in his works—evokes larger issues than he could have realized when he wrote. Notwithstanding the reservations reported by Jean Lacouture, that the Chinese leaders "wanted their revolution to be rural, intensely Chinese, optimistic, and impelled by the 'masses' themselves," while Malraux's China is "urban, cosmopolitan, metaphysical, and emotional" and his "native revolutionaries are all terrorists seeking foreign aid,"[22] *Man's Fate* does look ahead to such developments as the civil war between Chinese nationalists and communists, the Soviet-Chinese split, and indeed the whole reawakening of China in the twentieth century.

Given this historical perspective, it might be tempting to view the social conflict in the novel as one episode in the clash between capitalism and communism. But such an interpretation would drastically oversimplify Malraux's viewpoint. For one thing, he does not let the political differences among his activist characters outweigh what for him is an essential similarity—the sharp break with the cultural past that they hope to initiate in China. For another, he does not conceive of his businessman or his revolutionaries as typical figures; in fact, he stresses their deviation from their expected social roles. Finally and most importantly, the adventures of his exceptional activists lead to reflections on power and community which center, not on the struggle of twentieth-century economic systems, but on Malraux's interest in and resistance to Nietzsche.

Ferral's actions take place within an economic and political situation that Malraux describes in some detail. He has undoubtedly brought a vast transformation to the East: among his ventures in Indochina are new agricultural projects, mines, factories, and railroads (M, 241-242). The human dimensions of this change are equally far-reaching, as suggested by the pride he feels at having "torn from their straw huts the thousands of peasants now housed in the sheds of corrugated iron sheets around his factories" (M, 341). But Malraux seeks to be even more precise in defining Ferral's role. Insofar as his hero compares himself with "a feudal lord, a delegate of empire" (M, 341), he has an imperial sense that recalls A.D.'s fantasies in *Temptation* about ancient empires or Grabot's scheme in *The Royal Way* of becoming the ruler of a native kingdom.

To what extent, however, does empire mean twentieth-century colonialism? Certainly Ferral takes European dominance over Asia for granted: he is interested in the East simply as a springboard for his political ambitions in France; he intervenes in Shanghai to safeguard his investments in the Yangtze Valley; he bases his plans on what he feels will be the expectations of possible sources of credit. Yet there is a grandiose and anarchic streak in his personality that makes him a special case. When he says to old Gisors that "I am my roads" (M, 349), he identifies himself with his actions, even in their most remote consequences, even though the actual deed depends on the work of many others. This is an outlook, as old Gisors observes, that ignores the organization ethic of modern economic life (M, 350). He goes further when he accuses Ferral of "looking at himself through the eyes of a romantic petty bourgeois" and insists that "The

roads had to be built" (M, 350, 349). Perhaps the businessman's vision of himself as a solitary and all-powerful empire
builder is only an illusion when compared with the overarching historical process of Westernization to which he contributes. Still, the portrait of Ferral usually focuses our attention on his special qualities rather than his typicality.

Old Gisors isolates these special qualities when he contrasts the will to organization of modern capitalism with this
businessman's devotion to the will to power. The starting
point for his reflections is Ferral's way of defining the Western urge to assert the mind and impose structures on the
world. Intelligence, he insists, is the "possession of the
means of coercing things or men" (M, 347). In terms of the
Nietzschean polarities in back of Malraux's cultural analysis,
Ferral is moving toward that version of the Apollinian which
favors "cruel and relentless" political arrangements. But in
linking this tendency to the will to power, old Gisors has
expanded on the early Nietzsche by drawing on a broader
but related topic in his later work. And there is a further
nuance in Malraux's position, for his sociologist actually distinguishes between two forms of power in a closely written
passage that needs to be clarified by reference to the French
text (M, 349†). There is power as the capacity to govern,
that sense of responsibility and social fitness which would
prevent a general who could have an entire city machine-
gunned from actually doing so. By the time he writes *The
Walnut Trees of the Altenburg* during World War II, Malraux
would be less confident of the soldierly ideal to which he
appeals in this example. But his general point is sufficiently
clear. Power can be exercised as a trust, in the interests of
society as a whole. So as to focus on the awakening and
furthering of human abilities of this version, Gisors turns to
the same French word that Birkin had used—"pouvoir." But
Ferral's emphasis on constraint suggests a different version
of power, one that derives from the desire "to be more than
a man, in a world of men." It is this outlook that Gisors
identifies as the will to power, which he calls the intellectual

justification of a will to godhead. Here power becomes "puissance," a word that can have overtones of domination and compulsion.

These distinctions reveal a deeply ambivalent attitude toward Nietzsche's philosophy of the will to power. There are certainly passages in his work that would align him with "puissance," particularly his most literal statements on aggression or some of his discussions of a human desire to rival the gods. But when he praises the "gift-giving virtue" or defines power as a generous overflow of strength in the interests of others, he becomes a spokesman for "pouvoir." To the extent that Ferral represents one strand of Nietzschean doctrine that has been detached from the whole, he should be compared with Gerald Crich in *Women in Love*. Both men illustrate the dangers of a limited or partial interpretation of the will to power, though Malraux seems less compelled than Lawrence to misinterpret the philosopher's position.

Nor is the attitude toward Nietzsche registered in the portrait of Ferral simply ambivalent; it is also revisionary. Several other scenes in *Man's Fate* expand on the notion of "pouvoir" as the capacity to govern, providing sharply focused vignettes of political man that would be unimaginable in the philosopher. During Ferral's first appearance in the novel, for example, we learn how his narrow conception of power had contributed to the failure of his career in France. He had been unable to show his associates even an elementary respect that would have enhanced his authority. Rather than "giving the illusion of appealing to each one individually, of wishing to convince them, of involving them in a complicity in which a common experience of life and men united them," he had had an "insolent indifference," "a unique talent for ignoring their existence" (M, 238).

Ambivalence and revision are both apparent in the epilogue, when Ferral returns to France in an effort to raise money. Sitting helplessly by while bankers decide to dismember his enterprises, he tries to understand his situation by toying with a Nietzschean idea: "Perhaps great individualism could be fully developed only on a dungheap of hypocrisy: Borgia was not a pope by accident. . . . It was not at the end of the eighteenth century among the French revolutionaries drunk with virtue that the great individualists were most visible, but in the Renaissance, in a social structure which was Christianity, obviously" (M, 420).[23] It is significant that Ferral considers a Borgia who actually did become pope; he is more literal-minded than Nietzsche who singles out Cesare Borgia instead, and uses him as a vehicle for maliciously ironic comments within a symbolic historical scheme. Like Michel in his failure to understand nuances in slogans advocating life and intoxication, the businessman arbitrarily limits the philosopher's play of meanings so as to justify his thirst for absolute, constraining power.

And yet his interest in the Borgia pope also suggests that he has gained some perspective on himself. In admitting, in however cynical a fashion, that the strong individual is dependent on the assumptions of a community, he acknowledges the problems raised by his own deviation from type. Failure to project the image of a trustworthy, conventional businessman has put him at the mercy of the bankers, who mouth stock phrases and wear identical decorations in their lapels. Malraux makes us see the basic lack of social realism in Ferral's conception of power. But his sarcastic tone here, along with his final outburst of anger and contempt, shows his unwillingness to accept this insight. Corresponding in some measure to Malraux's vision in *Temptation* of a decline in the West's capacity to organize itself, he represents a special case. He pushes the ethic of a forceful will that imposes itself on the world to such an extreme of individualistic assertion that it becomes self-defeating.

Meanwhile, the efforts of the two revolutionaries Kyo and Katov have been directed toward a transformation of the East as wide ranging as the one undertaken by Ferral. The very make-up of Kyo's character, as captured by an image during his first appearance in the novel, suggests the magnitude of the change he represents. Just after the assassination of the gun dealer, Ch'en rejoins his comrades in the record shop, shutting the door in such a way that the lamp begins to swing. The curious effect of the light on Kyo's face testifies to his mixed French and Japanese parentage, but in more general terms it suggests the clash between European and Asian cultural traditions that will be such an important theme throughout *Man's Fate*: "in passing over his head the lamp accentuated the drooping corners of his mouth which had a Japanese stamp; as it swung away it displaced the shadows and his half-breed face appeared almost European" (M, 187†). This image echoes Nietzsche's striking assertion in his autobiography that he had access to separate worlds, that he had "a 'second' face in addition to the first." But if other characters in *Man's Fate* experience sharp cultural divisions and are incapable of resolving them, Kyo will apparently be successful: "The oscillations of the lamp became shorter and shorter: Kyo's two faces reappeared by turns, less and less different from each other." This wholeness of personality arising out of cultural diversity suggests both a metamorphosis of the East and a new universality for the West.

In its most concrete form the Western influence that the revolutionaries bring to Asia is Marxist activism. The first episodes of the novel focus on their decisiveness and rationality, whether in their careful preparations for the insurrection that captures Shanghai for the nationalists or in the hastily improvised plan for seizing the guns once it is learned that the delivery order stolen by Ch'en is worthless. But before the unfolding of these events several images have stressed the connection between activism and an underlying habit of imposing mental constructs upon a formless world. As Kyo walks with Katov through a district he has organized, his lucid insight transforms his surroundings: "he had ceased to see the streets: he no longer walked in the mud but on a map. . . . Though veiled by the beating rain, the street preserved nevertheless in his mind its full perspective" (M, 192, 193). Thus Kyo is a character with Asian roots who has learned the basic tendencies of the Apollinian West; Katov, on the other hand, is a European whose traits point up the great differences between the activist mentality of the revolutionaries and that of Ferral. He replaces coercion and solitude with a generous and social *pouvoir*. Meeting a combat group that sees in tanks "the power [*puissance*] of demons," he shares with them specific plans for defense; rationality becomes the instrument of heightened morale, "a token of a victory" that liberates rather than constrains (M, 205). Katov is also the first among the revolutionaries to understand that Ch'en "shouldn't have gone off all alone" after the assassination (M, 189†), a remark that points up his sensitivity to others as well as the dangers of an isolated selfhood.

This initial commitment to Marxism becomes problematic as the novel progresses; among Communists, Kyo and Katov come to seem as exceptional as Ferral among the capitalists. From having been units in a tightly organized party with a doctrine of social revolution, they turn into lonely individuals who are uncertain about the positive content of a desirable social philosophy. This reversal begins during Kyo's visit to Hankow where he confers with Vologin, the man in charge of Shanghai at the headquarters of the Communist International. Forced to argue his own ideas, he realizes how dependent he is on the organization for his sense of social mission: "he had never ceased to feel how poorly informed he was, how difficult it was for him to get a solid basis for his activity, if he no longer consented purely and simply to obey the instructions of the International" (M, 287). Yet despite the precariousness of his situation as an activist he refuses to accept the party line and returns to Shanghai intending to follow his own strategy. As a result there is a crucial reservation in the statement of faith he makes to the police chief König after his arrest; he defends communism, but only in negative terms (M, 394). Though the party may not really have a program that can realize the urge for human dignity, it at least combats social systems which refuse even to acknowledge the validity of this urge: "I think that communism will make dignity possible for those with whom I'm fighting. What is against it, in any case, forces them to have none."

But the novel places even this distinction in question. Kyo's ideals are incompatible with the secret police force instituted by the Communist party. In an ideological discussion much earlier, Katov had shown some uneasiness with the special powers of the Cheka despite his admiration for Lenin (M, 272). Now, at the end of his interview with Kyo, König contrasts him with a Chekist he had questioned previously; the members of the opposing organizations for repression had soon discovered their shared contempt for human dignity. In an effort to make this contempt prevail, König decides to break Kyo's spirit and gives orders that he be tortured (M, 395). As a result of these associations, the locomotive boiler in the famous scene of the deaths of the two revolutionaries becomes a symbol not only of the world they sought to change but also of ambiguities within the party in whose name they fought.

This scene is a complex one, and I shall have to postpone discussion of some of its crucial features until the next section. At present, the most striking quality about Kyo's and Katov's deaths is that they bear witness to their cultural backgrounds rather than to their revolutionary ideals. The scene illustrates the general phenomenon noticed by old Gisors, who surveyed the varied peoples of Shanghai and decided that "a man becomes separated from his nation in a national way" (M, 222). As in "European Youth," Malraux raises the issue of an underlying "gridwork" of values that persists in spite of efforts to break away. In this episode the pattern first appears when Lu-Yu-Hsüan, one of the owners of the record shop, presents himself for execution: "Lu was reciting in a loud voice, without resonance, the death of the hero in a famous play; but the old Chinese solidarity was indeed destroyed: no one was listening" (M, 405). Though it is clear that traditional cultural forms have lost their authority, there is no new form—and certainly no revolutionary ideology—that has an equivalent power to give meaning to the whole of human existence. For Nietzsche, as he analyzed Socrates' importance to theoretical culture, one key test for the viability of a cultural form was whether it could overcome the fear of death. In this moment of supreme crisis it is significant that Lu finds his best support in a model from the Chinese past; the gridwork has reasserted itself.

Similarly, Kyo's decision to commit suicide with a cyanide tablet reflects his Japanese heritage. We learn from Ch'en that he had insisted on the need for a sense of hara-kiri (M, 315), and he returns to this topic as he lies among the prisoners: "He had seen much of death, and, helped by his Japanese education, he had always thought that it is fine to die by one's own hand, a death that resembles one's life. And to die is passivity, but to kill oneself is action. As soon as they came to fetch the first of their group, he would kill himself with full consciousness" (M, 405). As rendered in this passage, Kyo's choice of a Japanese death does not exclude his characteristic dedication to lucid intelligence and an activist outlook. The full importance of this continued assertion of Apollinian values will become apparent in the next section; but it should be noticed at this point that they no longer connect with a specific political ideology, as they did earlier in the novel.

A similar situation arises with Katov's actions when he decides to give his cyanide capsule to the frightened young Chinese and face torture in their place. As with Kyo one aspect of his behavior reminds us of Malraux's vision of the Apollinian, for he shows generosity in offering what is called "the greatest gift he had ever made" (M, 409). But there is also an underlying cultural pattern about which Malraux could be less explicit because he was writing for a Western audience which would recognize and respond to it, at least in a subliminal way. It is evident that Katov is drawing on Christian premises when he sacrifices himself for others in a gruesome death. The whole scene has a certain mythic intensity: the Chinese recall the two thieves at the crucifixion, the record dealer Hemmelrich had compared the Russian to Jesus

(M, 331), and Katov's peculiar exclamation of "O resurrection" on recovering the dropped capsule (M, 409) suggests how much his own thinking is dominated by this model. The final moments of both revolutionaries affirm the force, not of their social ideals, but of a basic psychological commitment that now must work through their cultural traditions.

The aftermath of their deaths raises similar questions. The power of cultural gridworks remains apparent in the choice of setting for the two-pronged epilogue to the novel. In shifting from Shanghai to Paris and Kobe, it moves from a point of interaction between East and West back to long-established centers of both traditions. More importantly, the ultimate social mission of the two heroes is uncertain. It is true that Kyo hopes that their death might contribute to a revolutionary myth which would spread "wherever men labor in pain, in absurdity, in humiliation" (M, 406). But this vision of the future is a momentary response to despair at his own fate, and thus serves personal needs. After the event, there is little sign that such a myth is taking hold. Even the people who knew Kyo best seem to have forgotten the meaning of his political activity, for his father has renounced Marxism entirely and his wife is dominated by a bitterness that renders her commitment questionable.

The fate of a man Katov did manage to help is also ambiguous. In the final pages we hear that Hemmelrich has a job in a Russian factory and finds his work to be meaningful for the first time in his life. But the news comes from Pei, who has forgotten his admiration for Ch'en and whose "fanatic intellectuality" has now taken up the cause of Soviet industrialization (M, 427†). His account of Hemmelrich justifies his enthusiasm so neatly that one wonders whether it is the whole truth. In any case, and quite apart from what history tells us about the thirties in the Soviet Union, the novel itself has raised too many doubts about the International and the Russian Revolution for Pei's attitude to have much validity. There is no return at the end of *Man's Fate* to the definite and unhesitating activist commitment apparent at the beginning. Apollinian social ideals have collapsed.

Instead, Malraux's Marxists turn to a preideological sentiment of community among men. In a complex sequence of thoughts during the execution scene, Kyo's attention shifts from the outer world to the courtyard of the condemned, where he feels a "brotherly quavering" uniting him with the others (M, 406). Alongside his hopes for a revolutionary myth, he discovers a more basic social sense in which "the virile heart of man" outweighs the constructs of the intellect (*esprit*). This communal sentiment depends on an awareness of shared human dignity, an ideal that exists in its own right despite Kyo's guarded effort to identify it with communism during his interview with König. It shows Malraux's priorities that when Clappique spoke with the police chief about Kyo's ideas, König found the activist's belief in a "will to dignity" more upsetting than his subversive political opinions (M, 378). Katov's experiences during the execution scene show the consequences of this belief. As a result of having spoken with Kyo before his suicide, he makes his decision to give his cyanide tablet to the Chinese with his friend's defense of human dignity in mind (M, 408). Concern for this ideal produces the communal feelings so powerfully expressed in his wordless handclasp with the men, the sign of "a wretched fraternity without a face" (M, 409).

But the value of dignity is even more prominent in Ferral's philosophical discussion with old Gisors at the French Club. The words of Kyo's father here have a special weight because he uses the phrase "man's fate" the only times it appears in the novel; in between these speeches he pauses to reflect: "He thought of one of Kyo's ideas: all that men are willing to die for, beyond self-interest, tends more or less obscurely to justify that fate by giving it a foundation in dignity: Christianity for the slave, the nation for the citizen, communism for the worker" (M, 348). In recalling Kyo's notion, old Gisors has made the crucial distinction that these ideologies serve only as "more or less obscure" vehicles of human dignity; they

cannot be taken as full expressions of the communal sentiment his son was seeking. Still, this passage at the heart of
Man's Fate marks a drastic revaluation of Nietzsche. The philosopher had placed elemental social feeling at the center of
his thought only when he described the Dionysian in *The
Birth of Tragedy*. And he had very little sympathy with
Christianity, nationalism, or socialism, which for him were
prime examples of how men could discover in groups a
fraudulent sense of purpose that they lacked as individuals.

Yet it would be a mistake to argue that *Man's Fate* responds to cultural and political crisis by overturning Nietzsche.
Without a doubt these reflections on community go much
further than the philosopher in stressing social or collective
concerns. Malraux has passed beyond the powerful individual who generously awakens power in others; he envisions
a shared set of values that will knit together leaders and followers. But he has arrived at this moment by way of his
special version of the Apollinian, which is rational, activist,
and "gift-giving" and which incorporates aspects of the will
to power. Thus Malraux attacks one tendency in Nietzsche
by exploring the possibilities of another tendency and emphasizing them. The relative unimportance of this critique as
compared with his entire outlook becomes even clearer if we
look beyond *Man's Fate*. A decade later, in an unpublished
speech to which Horst Hina has drawn attention,[24] the novelist used the phrase "Nietzschean socialism" in describing
his friend Leo Lagrange, who had been a member of the
Blum government in the thirties. Among the values he seeks
to capture with this slogan is precisely the uncompromising
insistence on human dignity that is so crucial to Kyo and
Katov. Evidently the two revolutionaries should be seen as
followers of Nietzsche first and critics later, people who
strive to bring the best aspects of his thought to fruition.

And there is another factor to bear in mind in evaluating
this passage: Malraux may be expounding a social vision, but
in the novel itself his heroes remain individuals. Estranged
from the party in whose name they struggled, and misun-

derstood by their closest associates, Kyo and Katov end up as isolated as Ferral among the Parisian bankers. From their perspective as well as his, "all that had happened in Shanghai was to be dissolved, here, in a complete meaninglessness" (M, 425). As *Man's Fate* comes to an end, having depicted a world conditioned by a temptation of the West of various kinds—whether it refers to the reactions of Ch'en and old Gisors to the destruction of Eastern civilization, or to the inner weakness of the West as shown in Ferral and Clappique, or to the process of metamorphosis and reaffirmation in Kyo and Katov—we realize that everything remains to be done. In a book that begins by evoking a "night of last judgment" (M, 193†), the mood of crisis has simply intensified.

THE VOICE OF THE THROAT: NIETZSCHE AND THE LIFE-PSYCHOLOGY OF *Man's Fate*

There is more to Nietzsche's impact on *Man's Fate* than is amenable to a sociocultural approach. In a famous remark published some fifteen years later, Malraux has stated: "I once told the story of a man who does not recognize his voice which had been recorded, because he is hearing it for the first time through his ears and no longer through his throat; and because our throat alone transmits to us our inner voice, I called this book *Man's Fate*."[25] This comment is important because it retrospectively locates an alternative center for the book. In contrast to old Gisors's reflections on the justification of man's fate, which stressed communal aspirations, the scene in the record shop where Kyo is startled by the sound of his own voice emphasizes psychology. Beneath man as he appears in society is an inner self that has priority; the ears of others do not catch the voice of the throat. Later on, as Kyo reflects on the dichotomy that has suddenly opened up before him, he returns to the psychological premise that preceded the cultural interpretation of Nietzsche in *The Temptation of the West*. He draws on the versions of the Apollinian and the Dionysian that pervade *Man's Fate*, not as a means of distinguishing East from West, but as general categories of the mind. On the level of his ears man is a planner of rational actions—"to others I am what I have done"—while the voice of the throat conveys the underlying forces of the psyche—"A kind of absolute affirmation, an affirmation of an idiot: an intensity greater than that of all the rest" (M, 218). Kyo has discovered the involuntary self, that chaotic area of the mind which in Malraux's psychology is far from being unconscious and for which he found Nietzsche's madness to be such a vivid image.

This seminal moment in the record shop also makes Kyo reconsider the meaning of his marriage. It is the only relationship he has that takes this level of existence into account, and hence May is different from everyone else he knows: "Men are not my kind, they are those who look at me and judge me; my kind are those who love me and don't look at me. . . . With her alone I have this love in common" (M, 219). These thoughts closely parallel some questions that interested Malraux in D. H. Lawrence, whom he had saluted as "the foremost novelist of his country" when he commented on some of his work in the *Nouvelle revue française* a year before the serialization of *Man's Fate*.[26] His whole discussion of the English writer's attitudes toward sexuality and relationship is broadly relevant. But one specific remark, in which he quoted from the systematic contrast between eyesight and sexuality in *The Plumed Serpent* is especially important. Malraux was probably remembering this contrast when he opposed "look" and "love" in the passage above; in effect, he has subordinated Lawrence's notion to his own opposition between voices heard through the ears and through the throat. The way he presents the contrast is equally significant. In the review the Frenchman ultimately distanced himself from what he saw as Lawrence's reliance on "guarantees which must be sought in the depths of the flesh and the blood,"[27] but in the novel Kyo discovers the validity of just such a guarantee. He finds in his marriage "something primitive which was at one with the darkness and caused a warmth to rise in him, resolving itself into a motionless embrace, as of cheek against cheek—the only thing in him that was as strong as death" (M, 219). Perhaps Malraux was encouraged in this Laurentian acknowledgment of sexuality and the Dionysian by a sense that the English writer was another follower of Nietzsche from whom he could learn. But whether or not his shock of recognition included this specific perception, there is little doubt that he found Lawrence to be a kindred spirit.

The psychological explorations that Malraux undertakes in *Man's Fate* expand greatly on the insights of *Temptation of the West*. His general method, which aims to render and evaluate the involuntary selves of his various characters, might be called life-psychology. In coining this phrase, I have assumed, as René Girard has done with Dostoevsky,[28] that the best writers often invent their own psychologies; in that case, one of the critic's tasks is to consider how the writer's outlook has shaped his novel. For Malraux in *Man's Fate*, the basic problem is to present and judge the quality of that elusive "intensity" that lies below the threshold of the lucid mind, to characterize the "absolute affirmation" that is the voice of the throat. Normally he depicts these drives and energies as they surface to form some fascinating or obsessive image. The degree to which this image aligns itself with "life" provides the means for evaluating the quality of the involuntary self. It is Malraux's reliance on this implied standard that justifies the name of life-psychology.

We have already seen this psychology in action in Kyo's thoughts about his marriage which build up to an imagined scene: "a motionless embrace, as of cheek against cheek." Perhaps the orientation of this scene toward "life" can be grasped intuitively, but its psychological significance is further emphasized by the sharp contrast with Kyo's momentary fantasies of beating May when he first discovered her infidelity and by the explicit remark that these new emotions are "the only thing in him that was as strong as death." Insofar as life-psychology is concerned with distinguishing between levels of vitality, it is highly Nietzschean in its general outlook. And, as we look along this axis of interpretation at the characters of *Man's Fate*, we shall see that Malraux dramatizes specific issues that are equally Nietzschean. With several characters he portrays the dynamics of nihilism and of less extreme forms of life-denial. With others he investigates the psychology of inadequacy both in Nietzsche's classic example of vengeful feelings produced by *ressentiment* and in the loosely related case of pity. The struggle of his heroes against these states of inadequacy gives Malraux the opportunity to portray self-overcoming, while in Kyo and Katov's final scene he is especially concerned with exploring their capacity for tragic affirmation. Most of these concerns derive from Nietzsche's later philosophy and especially from *Thus Spoke Zarathustra*, which Malraux greatly admired. But in spite of this wide-ranging impact, the imaginative power of *Man's Fate* is such that it gives new precision and force to the themes of life-psychology.

□

Certainly the famous abrupt opening of the novel is one of the most successful of these scenes; at the heart of Malraux's gripping account of the assassination of the gun dealer is a problem of life-psychology. We have already noticed the wavering of Ch'en's ideological commitment and the reawakening of childhood dread during the event. The decisive moment comes when he suddenly confronts the fascinating image that lies, for him, somewhere in the act of murder. As he hesitated before striking the blow, he felt a vague repugnance for the sleeping man, seeing him as a corpse; but afterward his mood reverses itself, and he experiences a powerful sense of identification: "A current of anguish passed between the corpse and himself, through the dagger, his stiffened arm, his aching shoulder, to the very depth of his chest, to his convulsive heart" (M, 183). The linkage of corpse and heart is suggestive in itself, but elsewhere in the scene there appear indications of a conversion of life into death that are more specific, though more limited. Before stabbing the gun dealer, Ch'en had cut himself in the arm, supposedly to test the resistance of flesh to the blade (M, 182); now he confusedly equates his own bleeding with that of the man on the bed (M, 183). His sensations during the murder itself were such that the death-dealing act became obscurely identified with sexual feelings: "Sensitive to the very tip of the blade, he felt the body rebound toward him, flung up by the springs of the bed" (M, 183). And when the cat startles him, he can feel enraged at its very status as a living creature (M, 184). Clearly Ch'en has discovered an orientation toward death among his impulses that is far in excess of what is demanded by the simple act of killing;[29] he has momentarily confronted the nihilism at the core of his being. As yet, however, his awareness of these tendencies is limited. Stepping to the window and gazing out at Shanghai, he returns to the realm of life; the view of the city contrasts with the "death which was withdrawing from him," causing him to feel an "infinite gratitude" for a reversal that returns him to what he believes are the normal conditions of his existence (M, 184).

During the insurrection the next day the death-directed image at the core of Ch'en's self becomes more explicit. In fact, Malraux's portrayal of the revolutionaries' most successful undertaking focuses on the ripening of this obsession to the exclusion of other possible themes. For example, during the first stage of the attack on the police station Ch'en freezes at the sight of an injured prisoner: "But with a hole of flesh instead of a leg, but tied up! The feeling he experienced was much stronger than pity: he was himself that bound man" (M, 249). Apparently feeling a fraternal empathy so intense that it transcends pity, he cuts the man's bonds at great danger to himself. But his impulsive act really testifies to something else. Rather than freeing the man, whose injuries were so serious he couldn't really escape and who dies moments later in a fire, Ch'en is liberating an image of violent death in himself. It is on this level that his acts make sense—his strong identification with the prisoner, his exposure to danger, his absurd cutting of the ropes. Somewhat later, during a pause in the action, he shows some consciousness of these psychological factors while providing some further indirect confirmation of their existence: " 'Why did I go and cut the rope? It couldn't make any difference.' Even now, would he have been able to ignore that man who was struggling, tied up, with his leg blown off? Because of his wound, he thought of the gun dealer Tang Yen Ta" (M, 251). There is a fine ambiguity to "his" in the last sentence; in context it can refer to Ch'en's self-inflicted wound from the night before as well as to the injured prisoner. The two wounds are equivalent in that they are both expressions of his impulses toward death, and the memory of the gun dealer at this point completes the pattern.

As the fighting continues, the revolutionaries begin tossing grenades from the roof of the building, and Ch'en sees one blow up in a man's hand: "A moment later a violent explosion resounded on the sidewalk; despite the smoke, a splash of blood a yard wide appeared on the wall. The smoke lifted: the wall was spattered with blood and shreds of flesh" (M, 254). He decides to join his men on the roof, wishing to show an elitist officer how closely he could work with them. But again he is really responding to an image: soon he has placed himself in a situation where he too could be killed by an exploding grenade. His compulsive imitation of the scene he has just witnessed brings out the force of the French word for "spattered" which is "constellé." The punning relationship with "constellation" suggests a deterministic psychological influence similar to the one astrologers ascribed to the stars.

After the bungled attempt on Chiang Kai-shek near the antiquary's shop, these images of violent death come to fruition. Ch'en's special psychology can begin to work its will once he has broken through the various cultural restraints provided by his education. Thus he is amazed by the intensity of his emotions when he argues for suicidal terrorism over simple bomb-throwing (M, 314). Driving a fragment of glass into his thigh, he reenacts the confused identification with his victim that had occurred when he stabbed himself in the arm at the gun dealer's bedside (M, 316, 317). Then, during the suicide mission itself, he is haunted by what he had seen when the grenade exploded during the insurrection: "He would blow up with the machine, in a blinding flash that would illuminate this hideous avenue for a second and cover a wall with a sheaf of blood" (M, 352). The very scene of his death casts him in the role of the mutilated prisoner: "He felt for his trouser pocket. No more pocket, no more trousers, no more leg. . . . Hacked flesh" (M, 354). As he maneuvers himself into events that correspond to the tendencies of his inner self, he has brought his earlier flashes of recognition to fulfillment. Ch'en's psychology is based on a tightly structured bundle of images that realizes the possibilities that Malraux had seen in Werther—his character is indeed a "proposition of death."

During the reflective section where Kyo and Ch'en visit Hankow, Malraux had offered two Nietzschean perspectives on his predicament. When Ch'en describes his obsessive nightmares about octopuses, Kyo thinks of them as "familiar visions of horror" which reveal "the presence of the inhuman" (M, 290), a formula that applies just as well to his fascination with death through self-mutilation. These dreams and images testify to the presence of Dionysian excess in him, an excess that is hostile to humanity and identified with a universe of terror. Ch'en's resemblance to the bronze hawk has already made the same point. Later in the section Kyo watches moths burning up in a flame whose light had mesmerized them. When he considers Ch'en to be "a moth who secretes his own light—in which he will destroy himself" (M, 295-296), he is interpreting the obsessive images welling up from the involuntary self as one stage in the fruition of a suicidal urge. Symptoms of the basic impulse toward death in Ch'en's character, they recall Nietzsche's analysis of the death-directed tendencies in nihilism. The problems of polar nullity and nihilism were, we have seen, not incompatible even in the philosopher.[30] But in his portrait of Ch'en Malraux welds them together with much more care; he is so attentive to detail and to the development of character that this extreme case in life-psychology becomes a riveting drama. In fact, his suicidal terrorist is so striking that he threatens to become the psychological norm for the whole novel. Perhaps all people are to be seen as self-immolating moths, and living in the interests of life is an impossibility.

In the course of his visit to Hankow, Kyo actually does think of generalizing Ch'en's example to humanity at large (M, 296). His father is more emphatic at the end of the novel when he gazes at a crowd of Japanese workers and sees "each one nursing his deadly parasite in a secret recess of his being" (M, 430). But actually, in spite of these ideas, the psychology of *Man's Fate* ranges over a much broader spectrum. In fact, when the two men discuss Clappique's character, they have themselves brought up another possibility. Kyo, who has not yet confronted the full meaning of Ch'en's experiences, takes the position that "no man lives by denying life," while his father responds by observing that "one lives badly by doing so. . . . He feels the need to live badly" (M, 209†). When life-psychology follows this pattern, someone negates life but not to the extent of Ch'en's self-destructive frenzy; in the end such a person contrives to maintain a tenuous attachment to life.

Malraux vividly dramatizes this state in the episode where Clappique visits the gambling house. Within the cultural "frame" of East and West we have already discussed, the Baron discovers that his method of raising money contains a fascinating image that corresponds to his involuntary self. Because Clappique must get out of Shanghai to avoid reprisals for having helped the revolutionaries, he veers toward death whenever he loses money and moves back to life when he wins. As a result, his changing fortunes at the roulette wheel become an exact equivalent for the fluctuating state of his life-psychology: "he had the feeling of seizing his life, of holding it suspended to the whim of that absurd ball. Thanks to it he was able for the first time to gratify at once the two Clappiques that composed him, the one who wanted to live and the one who wanted to be destroyed" (M, 359). Later in the scene the balance seemingly shifts as he gives himself up to the ecstasy of losing. But Clappique manages to avoid any real commitment to suicidal urges. The only person harmed by his absorption in the game is Kyo, whom he fails to warn about the impending crackdown against the Communists; as for himself, he is attracted to gambling because it represents "a suicide without death" (M, 360). His successful masquerade as a sailor shows that he has life-furthering strategies to fall back upon when faced with real danger. Similar tendencies had appeared right after the gambling bout. The lunar landscape Clappique finds on leaving the casino suddenly takes on an uncomfortable immediacy when "the smell of corpses from the Chinese city was borne on the wind which was again rising"; typically he finds that he "could endure the idea of death more easily than its smell" (M, 362). In the last analysis his inner self remains oriented toward life, although it is a "bad" life. Thus, soon after swerving away from this brutal and overly direct image, he is playacting before a prostitute whom he convinces that he is about to kill himself. The gruesome tinge to many of his stories testifies to the same element of life-denial that will sap his existence so long as it can be kept sufficiently fictive.

It is appropriate that old Gisors should be sensitive to Clappique's need for living badly, since he clearly feels this need himself. In drawing a contrast between Ch'en's passion for death and his own addiction to opium, he saw it as a form of "intoxication as terrible as his own was not" (M, 224). Carefully limiting himself to five pellets a day, he is far from the obsessions of an all-devouring suicidal drive; still, his use of drugs does express a negation of life, as May realizes when she notices his deathly appearance in the epilogue. His basic psychological bent is apparent in his response to Kyo's death. His decision to throw the opium out the window suggests a transformation, but then he feels "the basic suffering trembling within him, not that which comes from creatures or from things, but that which gushes forth from man himself and from which life attempts to tear us away" (M, 414). When he surrenders to this mood of hostility toward life that is generated in the inner self, he has returned to his previous state of partial negation. It is appropriate, therefore, that in the epilogue he should have gone back to his opium. And the last ideas voiced by this agile intellectual are symptomatic of his psychological division, for alongside his notion of a parasite in the psyche that drives men deathward he comes out with the affirmative maxim that "one must love the living and not the dead" (M, 432).

□

In Ferral's case, partial negation converges with the issue of *ressentiment*. When he conceives of power in ways that eliminate generosity and community, he has shifted the direction of life-denial so that it diminishes the vitality of others rather than his own. In his erotic life, where the tendencies of his involuntary self are revealed more clearly than in his public career, life-denial occurs when he humiliates and dehumanizes an admirable woman so as to reduce her to a function of her sexual passions. During his first appearance in the novel he describes this process in mythological terms; it involves stripping away the "superb mask" of a Minerva so as to discover "the expression of your face when you're making love" (M, 240). Thus the importance of the light switch during his assignation with Valérie, a clever and successful dress designer. He has to see her sensual smile, which pleases him because it proves that she is "no longer a free and living being, but only the expression of gratitude for a physical conquest" (M, 268). Similar motives cause him to treat an elegant Chinese courtesan as a common prostitute (M, 351). If this woman is simply stupefied by his behavior, Valérie is more eloquent; in breaking up with him, she writes that "Your presence brings me close to my body with irritation, as springtime brings me close to it with joy" (M, 340). She has echoed one of Nietzsche's most positive images for the

Dionysian so as to show by contrast how great an impoverishment of life Ferral has caused.

However, in extreme situations Ferral's need to humiliate others turns upon himself, and a kinship becomes evident between his form of denial and those of Clappique and old Gisors. Just as he brings his power to bear with the greatest force, he suddenly identifies with his victim; he undergoes the negation he usually inflicts. He can picture himself as Valérie in the aftermath of the light-switch episode, "inhabiting her body, feeling in her place that enjoyment which he could experience only as a humiliation" (M, 268). Then, when she breaks with him, these mixed emotions become much more intense. After a series of violent fantasies—he remembers one of Clappique's stories, he imagines Valérie being beaten—he is suddenly possessed by an image of a very different character: "the legend of Hercules and Omphale brusquely seized his imagination—Hercules dressed as a woman in soft, flimsy garments like these, humiliated and content in his humiliation" (M, 343).[31] At the core of his psychology there exists a defeatist element that is intricately bound up with his drive for mastery and is so basic that it probably contributed to his failures in public life as well.

Ordinarily, of course, Ferral's life-negation is directed outward, leading at times to a dependence on others that approximates *ressentiment*. His thoughts as he approaches the Chinese courtesan are especially revealing: he realizes that it is only by manipulating the responses of the outside world that he can get a sense of his own identity. "He had possessed, he would possess through this Chinese woman who was awaiting him, the only thing he was eager for: himself. He needed the eyes of others to see himself, the senses of another to feel himself" (M, 352). At this point he notices a picture of two embracing skeletons, an image that comments graphically on his psychology. Earlier, Malraux had dramatized the vengeful core of *ressentiment* in the scene where Valérie rejects Ferral. She has made him look ridiculous in the lobby of Shanghai's best hotel; he retaliates by buying up a pet shop and leaving the animals in her room. But even though he takes care that his act not seem "the blatant image of his anger," it is evident that he has been motivated by reactive feelings: revenge is on his mind, he wants to defend himself from the stories she will tell at his expense, he chooses a way of getting back at her that simply builds on her malicious wit.[32] Thus, even as he tries to shield himself from the judgment of others, they have the initiative over his life. Nor does he really cease to appear ridiculous when he leaves Valérie's room, where parrots are fluttering about, a kangaroo is hopping on the bed, and the hotel keeper is fretting about bird droppings. Again, an image has measured the extent of his degradation.

Vengeful obsessions are more rigid in König, whose character may be seen as an extreme version of Ferral's. The two men are connected in several ways: the story puts the police chief in close contact with the businessman's functionaries (M, 258), while Ferral's coercive sense of power has become more intense in König's prison, which makes it seem that "power were enough to change almost every man into a beast" (M, 389). The psychological link between the two men is apparent during Clappique's visit on Kyo's behalf. König answers him indirectly, by talking about the horrifying torture he underwent during the Russian Civil War as a prisoner of the Communists. The experience is more than a political parable; it has become a ruling image that gives him an excuse for making others suffer as he did: "Beyond a doubt he told this story—or told it to himself—each time he had a chance to kill" (M, 379). He is so committed to revenge that he has turned into an automaton of *ressentiment*, his attention wholly fixed on this searing moment in the past when the outside world injured him. Therefore he disregards Clappique's hesitant but unusually penetrating advice: "there is forgetfulness" (M, 379). Incapable of giving himself to life and growing beyond his past, he remains trapped within his murderous obsession. He has to feel contempt for Kyo's

code of human dignity because it questions the very basis for
his psychological state.

Kyo's response to his wife's infidelity had provided a
counterexample of someone striving to overcome vengeful
feelings. The two of them had agreed to allow each other
sexual freedom within marriage. But when May confesses
that, in the anxious hours before the insurrection, she had
slept with another doctor, he feels obscure emotions he had
not reckoned with. True to character, he makes an effort to
understand them; in the process he must come to terms with
his *ressentiment*, which expresses itself as a sense of injury at
the imagined judgments of others. Thus he is sensitive to the
possible role of his mixed racial status: " 'If I were not a half
breed . . .' He was making an intense effort to push back the
hateful or base thoughts all too ready to justify and feed his
anger" (M, 214). He also imagines the attitude of the man,
contemptuous of May now that he has "possessed" her (M,
216). The outcome of these vulnerable feelings is the vengeful fantasy of beating her we have already glanced at; but
then Kyo experiences a different mood. He moves from "the
fierce craving for an intense contact with her . . . even one
that might lead to fright, screams, blows" to a contrasting
vision: "The revelation of what he wanted finally flashed
upon him, to lie with her, to find refuge there against this
vertigo in which he lost her completely" (M, 216-217). A
process of overcoming that began with a deliberate act of
self-appraisal concludes as a battle in the involuntary self between two forms of instinct, a battle in which sexual desire
and an elementary yearning for human contact finally prevail
over resentment and impulses toward revenge. At the core
of his being Kyo has come upon an "intensity" that is oriented toward life and community. In effect, he has found a
new basis for his dedication to human dignity, a mood of
fellowship that depends on a finer responsiveness to his own
psychology and not on the imperatives of a questionable ideological commitment.

Malraux dramatizes this breakthrough to an irrational and

primitive vitalism in a way that suggests qualifications and complications. For example, he presents his hero's self-searching as occurring at intervals during preparation for the insurrection; Kyo may decide that the voice of the throat is more basic than the world of action, but he does not ignore the demands of public life. Old Gisors clarifies the situation when he distinguishes between his son and Ch'en, whose inner needs totally dominated his activity: "The heroic sense had been given him as a discipline, not as a justification of life" (M, 227). Kyo retains a complex awareness of interacting frames of reference that keeps him from taking his vitalistic experience as more than a starting point. Nor does his experience simply affirm his essential nature; to stay in touch with this source, he must struggle repeatedly to overcome inadequacies. Hence he goes through a similar psychological crisis in the scene where he refuses to expose May to danger by letting her go with him to a meeting. Almost immediately Kyo recalls their earlier quarrel; feeling "familiar demons stirring within him," he gives way to resentful fantasies of violence before he detects the presence of more tender feelings (M, 328). But he knows they will force him to reverse his decision, and he resists them. Only after he has left does he realize that May was right in saying that there was an element of vengeance in his attitude (M, 330). This perception finally releases his deepest emotions and, having lived through the process of overcoming once more, he returns to get her.

Malraux's psychology of vengeance becomes especially intricate and illuminating in the portrait of Hemmelrich, co-owner of the record store with Lu-Yu-Hsüan. The situation is sketched in very lightly, and yet it plays an important role in defining the reader's response to the end of the novel; in addition, the contrast between *ressentiment* and psychic states more fully aligned with life is less clear-cut than it was with Kyo and König. Hemmelrich's leading trait at the outset is impotence, the very opposite of the ideal of adequacy that he glimpses when he says: "The important thing would be to want what one is capable of" (M, 311†). Trapped by his poverty and his responsibilities to a helpless wife and a sick child, he is condemned to passivity; his resentment expresses itself in "outbursts of impotent anger," while his morale sinks to the point that he feels death to be "the only dignity he could ever possess" (M, 312, 313). But when his wife and child are killed during the crackdown against the Communists, active revenge becomes a possibility: "Now, he too could kill. It came to him suddenly that life was not the only mode of contact between human beings, that it was not even the best; that he could know them, love them, possess them more completely in vengeance than in life" (M, 369). Ironically, his family means more to him as pretexts for the discharge of *ressentiment* than they did when alive.

Hemmelrich's obsession with reprisal and fixation on images of death may recall König, but Malraux also hints at a very different undercurrent of feelings: thus his genuine tenderness for his wife or the sense of fraternity that paradoxically mingles with the "atrocious craving" of his rage (M, 312, 313). Hence, when he finally does kill, ambushing the first man to enter the local Communist office after it falls to the nationalists, the scene is ambiguous. His desire for revenge bursts out in a frenzy of violence and hatred, but then he discovers with the force of revelation that he has a basic urge to live (M, 386). He puts on the dead man's uniform and escapes unharmed from a situation that seemed to promise certain death; his masquerade, like Clappique's, testifies to the vitalistic elements in his psychology. But rather than undergoing a process of overcoming in the manner of Kyo, he has passed through an intensification of *ressentiment*. As he moves from impotent passivity to active vengeance, he suddenly attains an enhanced state of being where the more life-affirming elements in his character can become effective.

Hemmelrich's character points the way toward a substantial revision of Nietzsche. His is the situation that the philosopher contemplated with horrified fascination, the "slave revolt" whereby essentially reactive states of being could become active. Malraux's version is more positive, but it already suggests some hesitancy in revaluing Nietzschean psychology that he should portray Hemmelrich in less detail than the more straightforward cases of Kyo or König. The oblique manner in which he goes on to treat this theme in the last pages of *Man's Fate* indicates that these doubts were in fact deep seated. Hemmelrich's transformation recedes into the distance. To be sure, the account of his life in Moscow is consistent with the previous development of his character; now that desire and capacity are in accord he can live up to his ideal of adequacy: "It's the first time in my life that I work and know why I work and don't wait patiently to die" (M, 426). Yet the source for this report is Pei, whose poor qualifications as an objective observer we have already noticed.

In the foreground, meanwhile, Malraux has placed a picture of May that offsets the tendency of this fable, whether true or not. After Kyo's death, she gives in to a mood of extreme negation that causes her to become "all tense with passivity in the vain welcome she offered wildly to nothingness" (M, 413). The consequences of this psychological state become apparent in the epilogue, where she suffers from the sense of vulnerability and the vengeful feelings of *ressentiment*; she confesses that "there is no grace left in me of any sort" and looks forward to serving the revolution as "a way of avenging Kyo" (M, 427). Not only does this bitterness clash with the warning against vengeance that meant so much to Kyo during their last conversation; but her last words, bringing *Man's Fate* itself to an end, leave the reader wondering whether she will ever rediscover a fuller and more flexible conception of life: " 'I hardly ever cry any more now,' she said, with a bitter pride" (M, 432). The full negativity of her mood becomes apparent when she rejects some advice from old Gisors that recalls Hemmelrich's transcendence of *ressentiment*: "On the road of vengeance, little May, one finds life . . ." (M, 432). But of course an old man in an opium trance, even when he is voicing his inclinations toward life, is a dubious oracle. At the close of Malraux's novel the intensification of *ressentiment* has become problematic.

Hemmelrich also contributes to the portrayal of another central issue in Nietzschean psychology, the inadequacy of pity as the basic emotion in valuable human relationships. Here Malraux takes a different approach than in his treatment of *ressentiment* and vengeance, for he concentrates on the process of overcoming and does not render the psychological state itself in any detail. As a result the theme of pity serves mainly to highlight the value of a vitalistic selfhood beyond inadequacy. As we have seen, even Ch'en has glimpsed these ideals, for when he misinterprets his fascination with the mutilated prisoner he sees it as an emotion that surpasses pity in the fullness of its concern for others. The issue is raised more straightforwardly during a brief interchange on the eve of the insurrection. Aware of Hemmelrich's self-hatred at his inability to take an active role, both Kyo and Katov realize that if they showed they were sorry for him they would only discourage him further. When they leave the record shop, they make a point of emphasizing fellowship instead: "both shook Hemmelrich's hand warmly. Pity would only have humiliated him more" (M, 192). Later episodes in the stories of both characters will develop the implications of this moment.

When Katov meets Hemmelrich again, his mood of bitter despair has deepened (M, 332-335). The Russian tries to help, but the record dealer becomes exasperated and accuses him of acting out of pity; the rest of their exchange takes place at the very edge of articulate speech. Katov's first response is to deny pity in favor of an unnamed emotion which he tries to describe with a story. It illustrates the point that when it is a "matter of life and death" people become "capable of going beyond" and discover the basic qualities of the heart. Then Katov realizes that the story is a parable of his own experience. He remembers how, as a young man, he made up for a sense of personal futility by inflicting pain on the woman he was living with. But at last her affection prevailed over the sadistic elements in his character, and he came to know "the obsession of the limitless tenderness concealed in the heart." This process of overcoming in his past corresponds to the transformation of Kyo's violent fantasies into a feeling of communion with May; Katov too has made contact with the vitalistic and irrational self. By this point, of course, it is no longer the value of pity but the problem of resentment that is at issue. But clearly, whatever the inadequacy to be surpassed, the final goal is the same—the attainment of a more inclusive and demanding form of fellow-feeling. So basic is this sentiment that in the end Katov succeeds in conveying it to Hemmelrich without words, through "gestures, looks, mere bodily presence."

In accord with the life-psychology of *Man's Fate*, Katov's acts, words, and memories in this scene should all be related to another image, evidently more basic since it repeatedly "takes possession of his mind" (M, 231-232). As with König it involves a moment of extreme suffering during the Russian Civil War, but the spirit of this experience is ultimately very different. Katov remembers standing among a group of prisoners awaiting mass execution: they have finished digging their own graves and have been ordered to take off their clothes in the sub-zero temperature. But then, instead of fixing his attention on death and revenge, the incident speaks to him of life and shared humanity. Because of the cold the prisoners began to sneeze, and "those sneezes were so intensely human, in that dawn of execution, that the machinegunners, instead of firing, waited—waited for life to become less indiscreet." It is this moment of hesitation, rather than its aftermath when the execution actually takes place, that Katov finds so haunting; and well he might, since the image crystallizes his overcoming of coercive modes of power, his awareness of fellow-feeling, his essential vitalism.

And alongside this contrast with König is one with Ch'en, who is just as obsessed with gruesome scenes of combat.

The siege of the armored train revealingly juxtaposes the two men. As they watch from a clockmaker's shop, Ch'en is transfixed by the impassive motion of the clocks (M, 270). This mysterious image perhaps suggests that for him the living interval has been swallowed up by the deathly end; in any case, when Kyo asks him to delay his assassination of Chiang Kai-shek, he paces beneath the clocks and finally takes the attitude that more or less time is meaningless, "a childish whim" (M, 273-274). Katov, meanwhile, has become fascinated with the rails that hold the train to its fate. But he finds a way of counteracting this image of death with one that shows his immersion in life: "he made a forward movement with his arm to prove to himself that he at least wasn't paralyzed" (M, 275). It is appropriate that on the day of the suicide bombing the Russian will try to find the terrorist and dispel his deadly obsessions by warning him of the futility of his act.

Like Katov, Kyo also struggles to get beyond pity to the more life-affirming forms of connection that he senses in moments of psychological crisis. At the very moment that he detects vengeance among his motives for leaving May, he is also questioning the "pitiful protection" he had shown in not wanting to expose her to danger (M, 330). When he returns to get her, he discovers a communion in risking death together that is "perhaps the total expression of love," and realizes that his pity was a pretext for evading the full meaning of their relationship. In prison, when the sadistic guard gratuitously beats the madman (M, 390-392), he experiences a more complex process of overcoming. Kyo's cell mate has reacted oddly by shutting his ears to the screams while keeping his eyes open because, he says, "it seems to me that by looking at him I'm helping him, that I'm not deserting him. . . ." Immediately suspicious, Kyo detects elements of cruelty in this compassion; to be a passive spectator of the sufferings of others awakens ambiguous feelings: "What is base, and also what is most susceptible to fascination in every man was being appealed to with the most savage vehemence." This fascination he locates in the part of the psyche revealed by Ch'en's dreams of octopuses or his own nightmares of gigantic insects and crustaceans, images that deny the value of human life itself. But Kyo is successful in resisting this inclination; and when he bribes the guard to stop, he expresses his fellow-feeling in constructive action.

Malraux's development of the scene is characteristic in that he emphasizes both the effort of overcoming and the fragility of this victory over inadequacy. Kyo shows force of will when he defies the guard's whip by returning his hands to the bars of his cell, but he must also recognize his kinship with the man when the guard shakes his hand. He leaves the prison with mixed feelings, with the sense that he has abandoned "a loathsome part of himself" and with a sobering memory: "in his whole life he would not forget that clasp." But he has reaffirmed his goals; as we have seen, when he appears before König in the next scene, he prefers to identify his resistance to humiliation with an urge for human dignity and not with pity. The latter evidently implies too great a complicity with suffering.

□

In all of these scenes Malraux's portrayal of the inadequacies of vengeance and pity has proceeded in close alliance with his presentation of a self that is capable of repeatedly asserting its vitality. Kyo and Katov reach high points of insight and intensity at these moments of overcoming; on the spectrum of life-psychology their experiences stand at the opposite extreme from Ch'en's ripening obsession with death. But what happens to their vitalistic drive when they must confront not inadequacy but death? This is an issue that underlies the scene where the two revolutionaries await torture and execution. In the last section we saw how it evokes the lingering power of traditional cultural models and dramatizes the priority of an elemental social bond over political ideology, but in addition Kyo's and Katov's last experiences display a psychology that remains recognizably Nietzschean. However, there has been a marked shift in emphasis, for

Malraux moves from Zarathustrian overcoming with its lyricism of an "unexhausted procreative will of life" to a more somber and extreme state of mind, that "condition of *fearlessness* in the face of the fearful and questionable" which the philosopher had discovered in the tragic affirmation of the Greeks.[33] In this psychology, confrontation with Dionysian excess is followed by a reassertion of the powers of the conscious self; it may be viewed as a continuation of A.D.'s ideal of voracious lucidity, if the ideal is interpreted liberally to mean a disciplined intensity of the will.

The execution scene opens by posing the challenge of Dionysian terror. Even before Katov learns that the locomotive whistle means that prisoners are being burned alive, he notices the psychological impact of the sound: "he sensed about him such a startling terror that it made him motionless. . . . not fear, but terror, that of beasts, of men who are alone before the inhuman" (M, 401). There are several possible responses that fall short of tragic affirmation because they do not summon up countervailing forces. Both revolutionaries are fearful of being unable to meet the challenge, and hence their anxious scrutiny of the prisoner who has a nervous attack when called before the firing squad (M, 405, 407); and another possibility would be Ch'en's submission to Dionysian terror through involuntary identification. But Kyo, as we have seen, was capable of summoning up Apollinian traits when he decided to commit suicide. He continues this classic Nietzschean response to the very end, when his lucid thoughts and activist behavior show that he has neither failed nor submitted: "No, dying could be an exalted act, the supreme expression of a life which this death so much resembled. . . . He crushed the poison between his teeth as he had commanded . . ." (M, 407). Kyo realizes that in taking the cyanide, and thereby substituting a fate of his own making for König's locomotive, he has avoided the demoralization of the prisoner with an act of self-assertion. Moreover, he kills himself in deliberate response to a specific situation that has been evaluated beforehand, not from the pressures of a death-driven psyche like Ch'en's. The very self-consciousness and control of this moment argue that he has mastered Dionysian terror.

Katov's decision to give his cyanide to the terror-stricken Chinese has similar results. As he transforms death at König's fiat into his own deliberate choice, he discovers the psychological strength that will surmount the challenge facing him: "But a man could be stronger than this solitude and even, perhaps, than that atrocious whistle" (M, 408). His tenacious lucidity is equally apparent, as in his last-minute plan for forcing the guards to shoot him or, when that fails, his ruse for combatting the anguish of facing torture—he imagines that he is dying by accident in a fire. But what stands out in Malraux's treatment are emotions which, like Katov's fellow-feeling for Hemmelrich, accompany his thoughts but can barely be articulated. At first, even before Katov shares his cyanide, he remembers an unidentified quotation, so Nietzschean in its enthusiasm for confronting the unknown, whatever its dangers—"It was not the discoveries, but the sufferings of the explorers which I envied, which attracted me. . . ." These thoughts lead to a mysterious feeling of "repose he had encountered, found again, in the worst moments of his life" (M, 407). Then, at the culminating moment when he announces that he has given away his cyanide, he moves beyond this calm to a more powerful emotion: " 'There was only enough for two,' Katov answered with a deep joy" (M, 410). He has attained the paradoxical emotion of tragic joy, that awakening of the full force of the will which can come as someone faces a desperate situation in all its clarity.

Despite the personal and cultural differences separating Kyo and Katov, their tragic affirmations are equivalent: both men have confronted Dionysian terror directly. There is little reason to believe that Kyo would not have been equally generous had he not already committed suicide before the arrival of the Chinese. After all, he had intervened on the madman's behalf in prison, and it was his account of his meeting with König that helped strengthen the Russian's resolve prior to his act. The tendency among critics to glorify

Katov is difficult to explain except as a subliminal response to the Christian gridwork behind his behavior.[34] Such a comparison of the two revolutionaries fails to do justice to the cultural pluralism of *Man's Fate*; both men have turned to their own traditions for lofty models of the good death. The real issue raised by this scene is Malraux's ambivalence toward tragic affirmation itself. With the exception of Hemmelrich, all of his previous explorations of Nietzschean psychology had followed the pattern of idea and image: he expanded upon and dramatized the philosopher's insights. Now, however, his silence about the final moments of his heroes suggests a revisionary impulse. He has already implanted doubts about these moments, both in the passage cited above where Katov senses that "perhaps" a man might be stronger than the locomotive whistle and in Kyo's reflections just before his death about "the savage indifference with which life unmasks us to ourselves" (M, 406). These doubts continue afterward: there is no evidence about how Katov met his end since his body cannot be found, while Kyo's body is convulsed and shows no trace of the serenity he had hoped for as a sign of "the dignity of even the most wretched" (M, 411, 405). Has either of them been able to maintain his tragic affirmation to the very last?

This question has profound implications for a reading of *Man's Fate* as a whole. If Malraux's heroes have faltered, the very possibility of a life-directed life-psychology is placed in doubt. Ch'en's death, which we do see and which has such graphic force, speaks against it; and the muted ending of the novel, where May gives way to the bitterness of *ressentiment* while old Gisors ineffectively counsels a more affirmative outlook, denies it more obliquely. It is easy to see why Cecil Jenkins, as he sums up the tenor of much criticism of *Man's Fate*, should define its basic standpoint as a "being-towards-death" which tends "in some sense to turn life inside out."[35]

Yet such a judgment is mistaken because it neglects differences of degree. A confrontation with death is the supreme test of the intensity of a life-psychology, but Malraux's silence on how his heroes meet this challenge does not negate

Kyo's and Katov's previous overcomings of inadequacy, or even the fortitude that they show throughout the execution scene. Moreover, he does not tell us that they did falter. At most he shows an uncertainty about Nietzschean tragic affirmation that he will explore in greater detail in *The Walnut Trees of the Altenburg*. As he imagines a scene which extends what was originally a psychology of art to existence in general, Malraux suddenly wonders whether the intensification of the will that can occur in contemplating a representation of disaster will necessarily carry over to the pressures and confusions of immediate experience.

And Malraux has been careful to limit the scope of his doubts in another way as well. Thus it is that even as they affect his conception of the story, he reaffirms the full spectrum of life-psychology for all but these extreme moments. As Katov limps awkwardly toward the unknown, the prisoners react "with love, with dread, with resignation as if, despite the resemblance among his movements, each one was unmasked as he followed this swaying departure" (M, 411†). His appearance has been transformed into a gamut of images with differing meanings. Katov inspires in some a continued dedication to the possibilities of life, evokes in others a mixed state that sees death but recoils from it, moves still others to abandon themselves totally to death. At this supreme moment, the prisoners have discovered an outer equivalent for that basic level of the self whose guarantees Malraux distrusted when he encountered D. H. Lawrence. But now his novel has taken them into account: as the prisoners watch Katov, they have recapitulated the main psychological alternatives so vividly dramatized throughout *Man's Fate*.

The Apocalypse of Humanity: Malraux's Return to Nietzsche in *The Walnut Trees of the Altenburg*

After *Man's Fate*, with its vivid contrasts and varied possibilities, Malraux's technical innovations in *The Walnut Trees of the Altenburg* can seem insufficiently dramatic. His narrative method in this novel is involuted and understated, and relies heavily on abrupt cuts back and forth in time and on the gathering significance of recurrent motifs and implied parallels. The result is a story that emphasizes a long, complex process of development in a single character; it might be seen as an expansion of what Malraux had undertaken in his portrait of Ch'en. In the end, the novel's psychological subtlety and its skillful revelation of undercurrents of meaning compensate, at least in part, for the relative diffuseness of its action.[36]

The prologue and epilogue of *Walnut Trees* deal with the experiences of Victor Berger during the French defeat in 1940. They are set off from the rest of the book by being printed in italic type; and, though Malraux wrote them first, he originally intended to place them in a later volume of a larger project called *Wrestling with the Angel*. The body of *Walnut Trees* was to have been the first volume of this novel.[37] It focuses on Victor's father, Vincent Berger, who was an Alsatian and thus a German citizen in the period before and during the First World War. Its three parts correspond loosely to the three major phases of his young manhood—his adventures in the Ottoman Empire and Central Asia as an adviser to the young Turks, his discoveries about himself on returning home in the summer of 1914 after an absence of six years from Europe, and his experiences while serving on the Russian front and especially when witnessing a gas attack. The last incident is the hinge on which the whole of *Walnut Trees* turns. Culminating with an "apocalypse of humanity" (A, 243) when some German soldiers break ranks to help the Russian soldiers poisoned during the gas attack, it is both an anticipation of the son's discovery of "the mystery of man" during the next war (A, 292) and the last in the series of "encounters with mankind" (A, 29) which give a certain unity to the disparate events of the father's story. But the starting point in this series of revelations, if we follow an historical chronology rather than the involuted sequence of the novel, is Nietzsche's madness. As in "Concerning a European Youth," but now with a much richer command of the resources of fiction, Malraux takes this episode to be deeply meaningful for understanding the situation of modern culture.

The story of Nietzsche's madness enters the novel through Vincent's uncle Walter, a retired historian who has purchased the Altenburg priory as a meeting place for intellectuals. This uncle, whose childhood dream had been to run the French Academy, sums up the tendencies of contemporary Europe on a number of levels. His secularized priory suggests the emergence of a post-Christian epoch, and in the room that is now the library he has replaced the crucifix with a new symbol, "a carefully polished figurehead, an Atlas [Atlante] in the grandiose and clumsy style of nautical carvings" (A, 111-112). Not only does this piece of sculpture embody man's responsibility to supplant the gods and hold up the heavens with his own efforts, but it could also serve as an emblem for Europe's transformation into an Atlantic civilization, for the exploring spirit of the maritime voyages of discovery which Katov had called upon, even for the more prosaic age of seaborne trade which created a city like Shanghai. The Altenburg also catches the spirit of the age in a more specific sense; out of the colloquia sponsored by Walter have grown papers by such leading intellectuals as Weber and Freud, Sorel and Durkheim (A, 44). Yet despite the wide sweep of these references and implications, it is clearly Nietzsche who has the dominant role. Walter had known him personally, has some letters from him which he considers to be the treasure of his library, and had helped Overbeck bring the philosopher back to Basel after his breakdown in Turin. Never, he confesses in telling of this last experience, had he felt the mystery of the human situation so strongly as when Nietzsche sang his poem "Venice" while their train was passing through the Saint-Gotthard tunnel (A, 96-97). No longer the sign of an impending intellectual crisis, his madness has instead become an obscurely affirmative image.

But the precise nature of this affirmation becomes a matter

for debate. As Walter tells the story to his nephew shortly after Vincent's return from Asia, he interprets Nietzsche's song as a revelation of the nature of artistic creativity. It is "sublime" (A, 96), something that "was just as strong" as life (A, 97), an example of how "we draw images from ourselves that are powerful enough to deny our nothingness" (A, 99). In appealing to power, he would seem to be using Nietzsche's own philosophy to explain what had happened; but actually Walter has a very different conception of the aesthetic. In place of a continuity between art and a naturalistic sense of life, he sets up a dichotomy in which the function of art is to replace or deny life, which he tacitly equates with nothingness. The same desire to give art a transcendent status leads him to call it "a response which, so to speak, imbues those who are worthy of it with immortality."[38] Thus, even as he admires Nietzsche's song, he has been separating culture from life in a profoundly un-Nietzschean way. It is not surprising to learn that the famous letters he had received from the philosopher consisted almost entirely of complaints (A, 103).

For Vincent, Nietzsche's song comes to represent a different kind of affirmation. Deeply interested by his uncle's story, for he admires the philosopher more than any other writer, he resists raising the song to an eternal "cultural" realm. Rather, he senses a vague kinship between this event from the past and his own experience, and he begins a terse and abruptly shifting series of reflections by thinking back to his father's suicide and funeral shortly after his return to Europe: "In my father's mind [the narrator here is Vincent's son Victor] Nietzsche's singing above the din of the wheels mingled with the old man of Reichbach waiting for death in his curtained bedroom, the funeral feast, the caricature that corpses make of those who approach them—the metallic thud of the handles of the coffin being carried along on men's backs . . ." (A, 99). Toward the end of this somewhat random flow of memories Victor's attitude suddenly becomes more precise, with the dash before the final phrase marking his recognition that there is a crucial link between the two stories that is to be found in the motif of metallic noise. In itself perhaps this image suggests forces hostile to life, but in context it has more specific implications. The train is carrying Nietzsche to the intellectual oblivion of his last years, and the coffin is the fruit of the old man's growing obsession with suicide. So the metallic noise evokes the internal pressures of self-dissolution and self-destruction against which both men struggled so doggedly, though in the end without avail. To Berger, therefore, Nietzsche's song testifies to something more basic than the triumph of art over life: it demonstrates the persistence with which life strives to assert itself against the inhuman.

The assertion by the father that is the equivalent of the song is itself highly Nietzschean. Vincent gives extraordinary weight to a statement he had made a few days before his suicide: "for my father, the whole starlit sky was contained in the sentiment which had caused a person already totally inhabited by the desire for death to say, at the end of a life without impact and frequently painful: 'If I had to choose another life, I would choose my own . . .' " (A, 99-100). This credo is, of course, a total affirmation of life in the style of eternal recurrence, but Malraux omits the scientific and esoteric aspects of Nietzsche's doctrine to concentrate on a simple and direct formula of full acceptance. This myth of power carries more weight with Vincent than his uncle's explicit appeal to power; and as he replaces a transcendent aesthetic realm with the existential vigor roused by great obstacles, he voices a characteristically Nietzschean outlook.

This fusion of Nietzsche with Berger's tribute to his father is merely the most explicit and dramatic response to the philosopher in this scene. It also presents a submerged confrontation between Nietzsche and Freud. The son's final reflections have touched on an earlier disagreement with his uncle, his definition of man's essence as a "wretched pile of secrets" (A, 99; cf. A, 90). The basic issue is still the status of crea-

tivity, for Walter was drawing on the Freudian unconscious—always highly suspect with Malraux*—in support of
the negative sense of life that is the necessary preliminary for
his transcendent aesthetic. But Vincent vehemently objects,
retorting that "A man is what he does!" (A, 90). This ringing statement might mean many things, but Berger clearly
has something more than political activism in mind since he
rejects his uncle's interpretation to that effect. Given his lectures in Turkey where Nietzsche was the main spokesman
for a "Philosophy of Action" (A, 47), it seems likely that he
wants to emulate his intellectual hero by placing creative activity at the center of human nature. For him men do not
follow the dictates of a secret; they realize themselves, and
he admires in his father "the resolution with which he had
chosen death" (A, 90). In the same spirit his son Victor has
written in the prologue of "an idea, no matter how elementary, that engages and directs a life" (A, 28). Though stressing conscious deliberation more than Nietzsche would, these
phrases do celebrate the inherent capacities of the self in the
manner of the will to power.

    If Walter's interpretations of Nietzsche's basic significance

---

    * We have already noticed his tacit disapproval of the unconscious in a
passage from "Concerning a European Youth." As for the specific allusion
intended in Walter's phrase, it will be recalled that Freud is mentioned as
one of the illustrious participants in the colloquia at the Altenburg; we learn
that he had given a striking talk just several days before, and that another
psychoanalyst had presumed to analyze Walter himself and had been thrown
out (A, 103). He has good reason, therefore, to be mindful of a concept that
a speaker on the next day will discuss as well: "It's unbelievable: in psychoanalysis, the unconscious that is suspected and still evil *a priori*, is the devil
once again" (A, 126). Previously, in the prologue to *Walnut Trees*, Victor
Berger has followed his father in repudiating a negative conception of the
unconscious on his way to affirming man (A, 27). Despite this polemic,
however, Malraux continues to be troubled by Freud. When he discusses
"The Rat Man" in his preface to *Anti-Memoirs*, he still has Walter's
"wretched pile of secrets" in mind: "the confessions of the most provocative
memorialist seem puerile by comparison with the monsters brought back
by pschoanalytic exploration, even to those who contest its conclusions.
From the hunt for secrets, neurosis brings back more, and with a sharper
accent."[39]

are false, the spirit of his remarks are equally so. As he tells his story, he causes Vincent to feel ill at ease (A, 95); and it becomes apparent that his friendship with Nietzsche had been poisoned by feelings of inadequacy: "beneath his voice . . . stirred all that there is of revenge in certain kinds of pity" (A, 96). This quick observation is important in its own right as a synthesis of two strands of psychological analysis that had been treated separately in *Man's Fate*; even Nietzsche didn't usually view pity as an aspect of *ressentiment* as Malraux does here. These deficiencies in Walter's attitude are all the more evident because Vincent has developed a truly affirmative response to Nietzsche. Admiring him "not for his preaching but for the incomparable generosity of intelligence he found in him" (A, 95), he has preserved the essence of what the philosopher meant by the gift-giving virtue. Specific doctrines and catchwords are secondary to the stimulus he offers to further development in his readers.

So far we have been discussing passages which, with a few minor exceptions, Malraux would again use some twenty-five years later in *Anti-Memoirs*. Along with events on the next day which we shall consider shortly—the speech of the ethnologist Möllberg and Berger's vision of the walnut trees—Walter's story of Nietzsche and his nephew's reactions make up the first section of this oblique autobiography. The result of this transposition is that Nietzsche and the problem of understanding him correctly take on the dimensions of a basic formative experience. As we have seen, the main emphasis falls on the uncle's failure to grasp his characteristic positions on creativity and inadequacy. But in *Walnut Trees* a second kind of misunderstanding is almost as important. Because the novel gives a much fuller account of Berger's experiences in Asia, it becomes clear that in dismissing Nietzsche's "preaching" he is attacking not his uncle's obtuseness but his own mistaken response to the philosopher as a younger man.

Let us look more closely at the lectures he gave to the Turkish students. Malraux is vague about Nietzsche's impact

on young Berger, hinting at multiple determination as a factor—"the echo of the still almost unknown voice of Zarathustra was not without a role in amplifying the taut eloquence of Professor Vincent Berger" (A, 47-48)—but one
point of contact is clear. His style was "all the more striking
in Turkish in that it replaced the traditional arabesques with
slogans" (A, 48). Nietzsche serves as a model for a society
that wishes to break free from its Oriental past, a conception
that recalls the younger Malraux's interest in him as the ty-
pologist of a cultural drama in which a dynamic West confronts the static East. It is therefore appropriate that Berger
gives his lectures in Constantinople, a city like Shanghai
where Europe and Asia meet. But this spokesman for the
activist West has not yet learned that a philosophy of slogans
is insufficient. His image of a man is superficial; he has to
break with his narrow political and historical attitudes and
go back to the psychological roots of action. Only then will
he discover the importance of an elemental commitment to
life.

The prelude to this deepened awareness is error. Berger
quickly moves from slogans to political intrigue, first as head
of German propaganda, then as an adviser to one of the leading young Turks, the Enver Pasha.* He later admits that his

---

* As he observes the decline of the Ottoman Empire, Berger identifies
two possible sources of social renewal—the pan-Islam movement covertly
supported by the Sultan and the nationalism of the young Turks (A, 55).
The prominence of these forces indicates that in *Walnut Trees* Malraux is
portraying what for him was an earlier stage in the historical process than
the world of *Man's Fate*. He is focusing on religion and nationalism, which
for Kyo were the most important social creeds before communism. Hence
Lucien Goldmann is mistaken when, in his sociological analysis of Malraux's
novels, he takes the young Turks to be an elaborate allegory for the Russian
Communists.[40] This part of *Walnut Trees* describes a world where socialism
has not yet become a burning issue; even Berger has no real interest in its
role in the German politics of the time (A, 55). Of course, it is possible that
in some oblique way Malraux's disenchantment with communism affected
his portrayal of his hero's eventual disillusionment with Turkish politics.
But the details of this specific world are directly relevant to his social and
historical vision.

motives were unclear, but one of his explanations—that he had a "need to get away from Europe" (A, 64)—is correct in only the most trivial sense. He is no Clappique; what really drives him is precisely his Western commitment to political activism. Thus he mentions "the lure of history, the fanatical desire to leave a scar on the face of the earth, the fascination of a scheme to whose definition he had contributed not a little" (A, 64). Except for having been transferred to Asia, these ambitions are the same as the Apollinian imperialism that A.D. had ascribed to the Western imagination: "Among us there is not a man who has not conquered Europe" (TW, 50). The young Berger comes out of the same cultural matrix as Ferral or the conqueror figures in Malraux's early fiction; indeed, his friend the Enver Pasha recalls the man who for A.D. was the apotheosis of the type: "Enver's youth and dash acted on the Turkish army in the same way as Bonaparte's had on the army of Italy" (A, 65-66). So far Berger's role has been to bring a European dream to Asia.

His unexamined cultural assumptions are abruptly punctured during his mission to Afghanistan, where he seeks to rally the Turkic tribes to Enver's cause. Weakened by dysentery and overawed by the inhuman presence of the desert—the situation is vaguely reminiscent of Michel's trip to Tunisia—he is reduced to equivocal negotiations with petty chieftains. He feels his Western capacity for planned, decisive action slipping away, and begins to have sentimental memories: "Oh for the green of Europe! Trains whistling in the night, the rattle and clatter of late cabs . . ." (A, 70). But Berger's mood crystallizes when he must endure the attack of a madman, who is protected by the customary Moslem respect for the insane. As if "inexplicably released from a spell" (A, 71), he suddenly realizes the profound otherness of Asian culture. Empire building is futile in a world where "The skeleton of Islam was the only framework supporting these people who were sleep-walking among their ruins, between the nakedness of the mountains and the solemn tremor of the white sky" (A, 72). This landscape and the violent madman suggest a Dionysian extreme that overthrows an Apollinian devotion to the state with the pressures of cosmic awareness and the disordered self.

More is at stake, however, than the collapse of Berger's mission in the face of Asian realities. For the first time he has an immediate sense of human possibilities outside his own culture, and his former naive and unquestioning acceptance of the West is no longer possible. As a result his return to Europe is startlingly different from his nostalgic dreams. Debarking in Marseille, he feels an intense estrangement, a "shock come from the most profound level of the being" which negates "the state of all-powerful distraction which permits us to live" (A, 78). In the wake of his discovery of Asia, all culture has come to seem provisional; among the evening crowds he has the vertiginous sense of losing his place in time: "Thrown up on some shore of nothingness or of eternity, he contemplated the confused flow of the race once familiar to him—as separated from it as from those who had passed, with their forgotten anguish and their lost legends, in the streets of the first dynasties of Bactria and Babylon, in the oases overlooked by the Towers of Silence" (A, 78). Berger goes on to stress the gravity of this psychological crisis by likening it to a political assassin's description of his changed perceptions after killing or to his own unpredictable reactions during his first communion. But although he does not know it yet, he is not undergoing a loss of faith or a burgeoning obsession with death in the manner of Ch'en. Rather, as he gazes at the faces of women who do not wear the Moslem veil, his culture shock gives way to an obscure intimation of a fundamental vitality: "What stamped these faces was not nakedness, but work, anxiety, laughter—life. Unveiled" (A, 71). For an instant the faces become a revelation of his inner state; in terms of Malraux's life-psychology, they turn into an image that registers the quality of his orientation toward life at this critical moment.

Berger has a similar experience when he goes into his father's darkened bedroom after his suicide; indeed, at the time he is strongly reminded of his feelings of cultural displacement in Central Asia and Marseille (A, 91, 92). But Malraux's involuted narrative technique places a special emphasis on this scene. He begins Vincent's part of the novel with a partial account of the suicide and funeral, then cuts back to his life in Turkey before he describes his reaction to his father's death. Because this crisis "brackets" the series of culture shocks, it stands out as the moment which fully realizes their potential. In other words, Malraux has developed a fictional strategy that stresses the dependence of cultural values on familial affections; in *Man's Fate* he had been more schematic, and simply stated that old Gisors felt his son's death as if it were "a suicide of God" (M, 413). As a result Berger's sense of alienation as he contemplates his father's deathbed is even more intense than before. He feels separated from life itself—"delivered—mysteriously alien to the earth" (A, 92)—and this mood infuses the images to which he responds at first, the closed curtains which give the impression that "no one—not even himself—had dared chase death away" (A, 90) and the "muffled, alien" quality of the sounds he hears "from the world of the living" (A, 91).

But then, as in Marseille, a new current of emotion makes itself felt, and he opens the curtains which have shut him in a world of death: "On the other side of the classical spirals of the huge iron doorway, the leaves had the bright green of early summer; a little further down the darker foliage began, culminating in the ranks of near-black fir trees. He realized that he was in the process of imagining all this vegetation as violet-colored" (A, 92).[41] Berger's first impression of the lush greenery and the forest in the background shows a basic openness to life, but his imaginings reveal a certain psychological inertia that carries over from his previous mood. Like Kyo when confronted with his wife's infidelity, his first reaction includes negative impulses. The dual potential of this moment is especially important because it anticipates the novel's major visionary landscapes of life and death—the grove of walnut trees outside the Altenburg and the gruesomely wasted vegetation left behind after the gas attack. Soon, however, as Berger continues to drink in the view through the window, and especially as he looks at people, the balance in his psyche shifts decisively toward life: "And from the mere presence of the people passing by out there, quick in the morning sunshine, as alike and different as leaves, seemed to bubble up a secret which did not come solely from the death still hidden behind him, a secret which was far less one of death than one of life . . ." (A, 93). It is this growing awareness of the active force in the mind which produces such basic commitments that underlies his insistence to Walter that simple political activism was not responsible for his image of man.

And, of course, these experiences have affected his attitude toward his philosophic mentor. If the failure of his Turkish mission has overthrown the Nietzsche who coined slogans, Berger's new sensitivity to fluctuating psychic intensities has helped open his eyes to the value of generous intelligence. A similar shift is implicit in Walter's story. The song in the tunnel counteracts the violent madman in Afghanistan, whose role in exposing the absurdity behind superficial cultural assumptions recalls the insane Nietzsche of "European Youth." Beneath the uncle's mistaken commentary on the events are the events themselves, which allow Berger to glimpse psychological depths where creative impulses persist even in a person claimed by madness.[42]

□

The immediate result of these new insights into Nietzsche is to reawaken Berger's curiosity about cultural issues. Unable to articulate the difference between his understanding of Nietzsche and his uncle's, he inquires about the nature of his relationship with the philosopher. But he prefaces his question with a comment showing that he believes the issues at stake to be very broad: "whatever concerns European culture interests me the most these days" (A, 103). This interest in the broad significance of his intuitions comes to a head during the next day's colloquium at the Altenburg. Stimulated by the remarks of Möllberg and others on the subject of man's permanence and metamorphosis, Berger rediscovers the contagious excitement in culture that he had known while giving his courses at Constantinople (A, 121). He speaks out, and then has the vision of the walnut trees that confirms the tendency of his thinking.

Malraux's portrayal of the Altenburg colloquium stands out for its success in catching the spontaneous flow and haphazard associations of excited conversation. Rather than simply expounding ideas, he causes them to emerge from a fully realized fictional situation. Thus Berger is stirred to formulate his intuitions after listening to an argument about artistic creativity that touches on the questions raised by Walter's story. The Count Rabaud has set things off by ascribing to artists "that great privilege, that divine quality, of finding in the depths of themselves, that which delivers us from space, time, and death" (A, 113). Described as a spokesman for Walter's views and cultivating a physical resemblance to Mallarmé, he favors a narrow and exclusive aestheticism which is vague about what the artist finds in these depths and assigns art to a special realm separated from the conditions of existence. In vehemently objecting to this stance, his two interlocutors Thirard and Stieglitz develop positions with which Berger repeatedly feels the closest affinity.[43] Thus the former insists that culture cannot be considered a "supreme value" (A, 115). Against Rabaud's view that the artist creates permanent types, he argues that his role is more modest, that he recognizes possibilities within the process of life. The novel is the primary domain for this form of knowledge which Thirard also contrasts with systematic theories of human motivation; he evidently shares Berger's distaste for Nietzschean slogans since one of his examples of these theories is the will to power (A, 117). Stieglitz's comments bring out the nature of the artist's descent into the self. A friend of his who had been sent to prison had found that the most fortifying books had all been written by people who were seeking to regain contact with life after having

known intense solitude. Out of their elemental sense of separation they won psychological insights that led them to a
new vision of the world; when Stieglitz says that "the great
artist draws his character from his discoveries" (A, 122), he
is drawing on the special case of characterization in fiction,
always so important for Malraux, to show the dependence
of artistic creativity on this basic psychological realm. He
explicitly mentions Nietzsche as an authority on these moments of discovery (A, 121), though he warns against using
them for the "sleight-of-hand" of preaching (A, 122).

The emergence of these ideas from the ebb and flow of
debate confirms Berger in his intuitions about his uncle's
story and about Nietzsche. It is not surprising that he should
feel that his thought has been crystallized, and in his remarks
he finds a single formula for what has come before: "Our art
is a humanization of the world" (A, 128). Implicit in
"world" is Stieglitz's awareness of estrangement. The artist
perceives "the independence of the world with respect to
himself" and thus comes to feel "the presence of destiny" as
an indissoluble part of the human situation (A, 127). But in
his work, by his very capacity to conceive of the world and
give it form, he recreates it according to a human scale; as
opposed to Rabaud's transcendence of space and time, this
humanization follows Thirard's emphasis on an immersion
in existence. Berger's formula also recalls the polarity of
Apollo and Dionysus, in that it emphasizes the overcoming
of inhuman immensities by human illusions. In fact, this admirer of Nietzsche makes tragic affirmation the key to his
conception of art. With particular reference to other notions
of Greek tragedy, he remarks that people have tended to feel
that "to represent a fatality is to submit to it. But it's not, it
is almost to possess it" (A, 128). Here the awakening of human powers in the presence of disaster is aesthetic, rather
than existential as it was in *Man's Fate*; but the qualification
of "almost" continues to register Malraux's residual ambivalence toward Nietzsche's insight.

What is the relevance of Berger's remarks to the colloquium's topic of man's permanence and metamorphosis? There is an implied dichotomy between East and West when he stresses the humanizing impulse in "our art" as opposed to the tendencies of Moslem art, which in his view is "concerned with God but with man never" (A, 125). But his broad definitions of human estrangement and the sense of destiny do leave open the possibility for fundamental continuities between cultures. No matter how diverse art might be in execution, it has its origin in a consciousness of fatality that wakens creativity. Thus Möllberg is right to open his disquisition on the wide disparity among cultures by attacking Berger's inclination to see destiny as a human universal (A, 129).

But as the ethnologist gives examples of strikingly alien conceptions of destiny, of birth, of the exchange of property, and of death, it becomes evident that he separates culture from life even more thoroughly than Rabaud. His basic premise is that "every mental structure holds for absolute and unassailable a particular sign which gives order to life, and without which man could neither think nor act" (A, 138). This conception of cultural form sees it as imposed on life rather than emerging from it; again and again Möllberg shows himself to be peculiarly resistant to any notions of growth. After tracing how the Egyptian belief in a surviving double evolved into a soul, he raises the end points of the process into fixed categories and dryly notes that "the difference of mental structure is, I believe, rather considerable" (A, 137-138). But he has neglected the intervening lived experience that gradually produced the change and furnished the common ground for such different views of an afterlife. Or, when he says that "I doubt that there's a dialogue between the caterpillar and the butterfly" (A, 148), he overlooks the fact that in the course of its life the caterpillar does become a butterfly. For him, metamorphosis is an "implacable" concept that serves to reduce life to a function of death (A, 141-142). Equally telling is the tendency of his metaphor when he uses the sculpture on the library wall to illustrate his ideas about culture: "Those two Gothic pieces and that figurehead are made from the same wood, you know. But beneath those forms there is no fundamental walnut, there are logs" (A, 146). Apart from the cultural artifact he is capable of discerning only dead wood.

Ultimately, Möllberg's intellectual failure to allow for life is the product of psychological inadequacies. Like Berger he has just returned to Europe after a deeply unsettling experience in the non-Western world. His researches in Africa have caused him to lose faith in his theory of civilization as conquest and destiny, which did see continuities in human development but with the limitation that German culture and not some universal was the final goal. As a result Möllberg reaches an impasse, destroys the book he had been working on for fifteen years, and becomes obsessed with visions of a desolate landscape of "trees gloomily soaring up in the prehistoric void" (A, 149). The aridity of this response contrasts strongly with Berger's rediscovery of life after the collapse of his mission for the Turkish nationalists. What we see of Möllberg at the colloquium is even more disturbing. He now shows a desperate and unhealthy obstinacy in maintaining his nationalistic ideas; despite the shattering effect of Africa on his whole outlook, he has brought a Cranach with him because "at this moment I feel the need for German painting" (A, 108), while reference to the cultural mission of Germany wakens in him "the suppressed violence of incurables to whom one has incautiously mentioned their disease" (A, 148). His inability to attend to life is also mirrored in the figures he sculpts; these monsters, as he calls them, "seemed to remember having once been men" (A, 105). Möllberg is the victim of an equivalent alienation from a wholeness of humanity, and doubtlessly suggests the rise of Fascism.

Berger seeks to rebut the ethnologist's presentation by briefly suggesting that one should look for a fundamental humanity beneath the diversity of cultural forms. But he counters Möllberg's denial of life more effectively after the colloquium. In another of the moments in which what he sees becomes symbolic of basic truths, he has his vision of the walnut trees. This vision has the effect of opposing transcendence and rigid dichotomies between culture and life; the wood appears "so old and so heavy that it seemed to be sinking into the earth rather than dragging itself out of it" (A, 151), thus echoing Zarathustra's "remain true to the earth" and the closely related motto of Garine's father in *The Conquerors*, that "one should never leave the earth."[44] As Berger continues to gaze at the trees, however, the aesthetic imperative of self-heightening development also becomes a factor. They appear to him as an "ageless thrust of living wood," as "two sturdy, gnarled jets which dragged up the forces of the earth to spread them in their boughs," and finally as a statue "which the forces of the earth carved out for themselves" (A, 152-153). Berger's vision offsets the gloomy trees of Möllberg's Africa and shows that the real source for the specific cultural form of Walter's walnut statues is living wood and not logs. His rediscovery of life has continued and become more precise: "the convulsed wood of these walnut trees . . . opened out into an everlasting life in their glossy leaves silhouetted against the sky and their ripening fruit, in all their solemn mass above the wide ring of young shoots and the dead nuts of the past winter" (A, 152). As part of a ceaseless process that also includes birth, growth, and maturity, death is no longer the dominant force in the scene; and yet, though muted, it still sounds the last note.

It is characteristic of Malraux that he should describe Berger's vision in terms of "life" instead of power, the Nietzschean word that Walter had misused and Thirard had criticized. Yet the will to power is not far below the surface in this scene, though it does not appear as an explicit formula. After all, for Nietzsche the tree was an image of power which he used to suggest the same naturalistic and aesthetic values as Malraux does here. But the novelist develops it in more concrete detail and places it in a dramatic situation that is much more fully realized; his intent is to let the image speak for itself. Thus the relationship between perception and abstract thought at the beginning of Berger's vision, when the trees "impose at the same time the idea of a will and of a metamorphosis without end" (A, 151). The concrete imposes an intellectual perspective; the image is not derived from preaching but is the source for an emerging idea. Of course, the will vaguely glimpsed by Berger is simply the will to power as the constant motive force behind the myriad transformations of cultural history. In fact, if we shift from general values to specific issues, the whole debate with Möllberg can be taken as an enactment of Nietzsche's first major exposition of the will to power. As in Zarathustra's speech on the "Thousand and One Goals," the seeming diversity of the thousand cultures of man have been resolved into the one goal of the human drive to create. Möllberg focuses on products and finds the chaotic multiplicity that troubled the young Malraux; but Berger has discovered an underlying unity by appealing to a basic psychological process.★

□

Vincent's vision closes on a premonitory note that blunts its affirmative impact: "It was forty years since Europe had been at war" (A, 153). In the third part of his story he is con-

---

   ★ I must disagree with Joseph Frank's criticism of this passage in his fine essay on *Walnut Trees*. He finds a disharmony in the imagery because the emphasis on trees, which are "only a part of nature," "clashes with Malraux's central thematic focus on *man's* freedom and creativity."[45] But it is a basic tenet of aesthetic naturalism that this clash is an illusion and that there is a continuity between the natural and human creativity. Moreover, insofar as the vision serves to distinguish the quality of Berger's inner being from Möllberg's, it is a manifestation of creative capacities. Frank also argues that Malraux confuses matters still further by setting the trees above a humanized landscape that includes Alsatian vineyards and Strasbourg Cathedral. But this emphasis is fully consistent with the theme of life's priority over cultural artifacts that has been so important throughout the novel. The one example of confusion that I have found is Berger's response to Möllberg's analogy: "Between the statues and the logs there were the trees with their design which was as mysterious as that of life" (A, 152). By placing the trees in the middle, this declaration obscures their symbolic function as an ultimate source and also distorts the literal process whereby trees must become logs before they can be carved.

fronted with specific choices during the war that both test his commitment to his insights and force him to develop them further. Thus, though Nietzsche has ceased to be a direct presence, he continues to be relevant in the sense that Berger is working out the implications of his earlier experiences. In particular, the war sharpens his awareness of fundamental man and of the universality of human creativity while revealing the precise nature of the life-enhancing emotions and their precarious situation within human psychology as a whole.

We have seen Berger moving toward universalism when he tacitly allows for a continuity between Western and Islamic culture and when he resists Möllberg's efforts to separate cultures into mutually isolated compartments. But the Altenburg is a place that sums up the European intellectual situation; and even his vision, though it came to him after the discussion and outside the priory, had centered on an intensely local scene. There is a contradiction in Berger's attitudes which becomes explicit when he explains why he volunteered for service on the Eastern front. Despite a resistance to nationalism, he still subscribes to a certain cultural exclusiveness: "Not that he placed his hopes in France, as a number of Alsatians had; his mother was German. But in the realm of art and thought at least, France and Germany were both necessary to him; Russia did not matter" (A, 158). His missions with Captain Wurtz and Professor Hoffman teach him to see the inadequacy of his reasoning and give him a renewed appreciation for the basic universals of humanity.[46] He becomes more certain about the persistence of one goal beneath the thousand goals; or, to use another Nietzschean formula, he moves from a simply European perspective to the more comprehensive outlook that perceives a Dionysian "new world."

Berger's indifference to things Russian first begins to crumble when he witnesses Wurtz's interrogation of a woman prisoner. Soon after she enters the room, he becomes aware of the distinctive cast of her features: "Her face was a perfect oval, the striking and strange Easter-egg oval of certain Russian women" (A, 161). Wurtz's methods reinforce this broadening of his sympathies. To check whether the woman is an important Russian spy, he has the spy's young son brought into the room; the child doesn't know that to recognize his mother would mean her death. It turns out that the prisoner is someone else, but Berger sees Wurtz's tactic as a violation of a shared humanity bridging the divisions of war. Thus he feels that it is impossible "to suffer so much shame" or to forget the boy's "small, smiling face chosen to become the perfect instrument of treachery" (A, 166, 167). Acting on his perceptions, he asks to be transferred out of the intelligence service.

But while awaiting a new assignment, he is ordered to accompany Professor Hoffman as he oversees one of the first attempts at chemical warfare. The night before the attack the evolution of Berger's cultural outlook has become still more pronounced. Even the setting mirrors the pull of his allegiances, for he is quartered with the professor at the Hotel Europa in the Polish town of Bolgako; in contrast to Hoffman, who sentimentalizes over home and family, Berger notices the Russian flavor of the room. Then, when the professor launches into a wild monologue on winning world supremacy through gas warfare, Berger sees his gestures as "beating time for the funeral march of humanity" (A, 176) and turns to the exotic world around him for a sense of man's creative potential: "beyond the rose-colored streets, the invincible Russian past was the only thing alive in the evening and the hanging silence of the war. The Professor's voice was summing up the advantages and disadvantages of phosgene, and my father was conscious of the depth of the Slavic world extending to the Pacific" (A, 175). This sweep of his imagination into the past and toward Asia represents Berger's final break with an exclusively European outlook. He has discovered the living qualities in an Eastern past that had seemed so futile during his mission to the Turkic tribes;

he feels the presence of humanity where the professor only finds an arena for his deadly fantasies.

The next morning, as he waits in the trenches for the gas to be released, Berger's new openness to man becomes an all-inclusive vision that reaches out to his own people. He suddenly experiences the aimless conversation of the German soldiers alongside him as a revelation of the basic qualities of mankind: "For the first time, listening to this living darkness, my father heard the people of Germany. Or perhaps simply people: men. A voice close to primitive darkness, like those silhouettes hardly to be distinguished from the shadows" (A, 190). The specific conditions of the war dissolve in the presence of this primordial level of being, which Berger compares to "a light hardly troubled by the passage of ephemeral human wills, ephemeral like this war and like the German army" (A, 199). Shortly thereafter, in the apocalypse of humanity where the soldiers disregard their orders and help Russians poisoned by the gas, these intuitions of an elemental shared quality prior to cultural differences are confirmed by action in which Berger himself takes part. Appropriately, the focus of Malraux's writing shifts from the evocation of emerging thoughts and perceptions to the simple rendition of events. Dawning possibilities become lived realities in a scene often compared with the peasants' rescue of the airmen in *Man's Hope* for its power of concrete presentation.

Even as the German soldiers show that there is a kinship among men, Berger is undergoing his most profound experience of elemental psychological states. On entering the area of the gas attack, he discovers a landscape of death which wakens in him "the disgust that life feels for carrion" (A, 218). The culminating horror in this "universe of rottenness" is the disfigured face of a poisoned man: "The lips and eyes of the Russian were violet against the background of his grey skin" (A, 220, 224). No longer the result of a psychic fluctuation registered by the imagination, as was the case when Berger stood by his father's deathbed, the unnatural change of color now testifies to an alienation from life that has become a masterful collective reality.

Berger's response, like that of the other soldiers, is a frantic effort to resist and overcome this situation of extreme negation. The protest of a noncommissioned officer captures the general mood: "No, man was not made to be mildewed" (A, 228). Because these emotions take the form of attempting to rescue the Russians, Berger identifies them at first as an "assault of pity" (A, 235; cf. 227, 241). But eventually he realizes pity does not do justice to the experience. As in *Man's Fate*, a more basic kind of fellow-feeling has come to the fore: "Pity? . . . it was an impulse [*élan*] a good deal deeper, in which anguish and fraternity were inextricably joined, an impulse that had come from very far back in time" (A, 243). This obscure "impulse" is an elemental reflux of life after a confrontation with death. Just a moment before Berger had been filled with wonder at the force of existence he had found in living things once he left the devastated zone: ". . . now life seemed to be reborn from one single element, from this straw whose tension as of a watch-spring animated both the lightest tufts of grass and the subtle impulse [*élan*] of the grasshopper . . ." (A, 242). Now the sight of a flourishing grove of walnut trees reminds him, perhaps all too conveniently, of the Altenburg and his vision of the persistence of life. But there has also been a less emphatic analogue for his psychological state: when one of the poisoned Russians revives after using an oxygen mask, the bluish color left by the gas fades from his face and it seems as though "death was leaving like sleep" (A, 239). As this part closes, Berger himself feels the symptoms of intoxication and is carried to the ambulance to undergo the same treatment. When he later used this episode as an installment of his autobiography, Malraux highlighted the basic shift from death to life by calling it *Lazarus*.

For all the magnificence of this climactic affirmation, Malraux is careful as always to indicate its precariousness. In a maneuver that corresponds to the ring of dead nuts around the walnut trees, he breaks off the story before Berger's treatment; this refusal to depict the climactic moment in which life is restored has led some readers to assume he died, though references to his later life elsewhere in the novel make it clear he survives.[47] There have been similar ambiguities during the apocalypse of humanity itself. Many soldiers flee without attempting to aid the stricken men, one of them kicks a feebly crawling Russian, another drops his burden once he feels the effects of the gas himself.[48] And when Berger, covered with hideously transfigured vegetation, leaves the area of the attack, he meets with incomprehension. He realizes that the unprecedented can quickly become routine, that as a result his mood of desperate resistance provoked by the horror of the gas "would not be effective several times. It's only dying that man does not get used to" (A, 241). Behind these words the reader senses not only Malraux's awareness that there were to be three more years of World War I but also the pressures of his experiences while writing *Walnut Trees* during World War II.

Of course, the most obvious impact of the Nazi years was on the final shape of the novel, which Malraux tells us in *Anti-Memoirs*[49] was partially destroyed by the Gestapo. But the very incompleteness of *Walnut Trees* has a thematic function, for in emphasizing the vulnerability of art, it dramatically illustrates the precariousness of life-enhancing emotions at yet another level. The destruction of writing has had an important role at several previous points. When Möllberg loses faith in the continuity of mankind, he strews the pages of his work-in-progress throughout the Sahara Desert, while in the prologue the French prisoners-of-war learned the extent of their degradation when they saw their undelivered letters blowing in the wind. Unlike Möllberg, however, the prisoners are able to carry on, motivated by the desperate knowledge that Victor Berger describes when he says that "here, writing is the only way to keep alive" (A, 30). The result of his efforts is the novel we read. But at the same time, having been alerted by Malraux to see it as a truncated fragment, the reader senses the vanity of even this affirmation of life through artistic creativity. This further element of precariousness makes the breaking off of *Walnut Trees* meaningful in a way that Malraux apparently overlooked when he called his last novel an unfinished work and refused to republish it.

The epilogue also provides a certain sense of resolution, in that the father's discoveries about mankind are shown to have descended to the son and been amplified. So highly did Malraux value this account by Victor of how his tank escaped from a trap during the brief French campaign of 1940 that, as with Walter's story of Nietzsche, he later reprinted it in *Anti-Memoirs*.[50] In this scene the analogue for elemental psychological commitments is the younger Berger's discovery of two forms of night, the deathly region of the pit from which he and his crew struggle desperately to free their tank and the vital realm of the open sky into which they finally emerge: "And yet the night which is no longer the tomb of the ditch, the living night appears to me like a prodigious gift, a huge germination . . ." (A, 284). The following morning, when the son wakes up in a farming village that has been abandoned because of the war, everything he sees testifies to the power of this living night. His delight in existence fixes on dogs, cats, chickens; while his awe at human creativity transfigures such simple artifacts as a clothespin, a broom, or a watering can. These experiences lead Victor to a first glimpse of the intimate connection between the world man makes and a basic psychological orientation toward life: "I still bear within me the invasion of the earthly night when we came out of the ditch, that germination in the shadow deepened by the constellations in the gaps of the drifting clouds; and, just as I saw the thundering, teeming night rise up out of the ditch, so now from that night rises the miraculous revelation of day" (A, 289-290). Even now, however, he tempers his celebration of the creative will with an awareness of its precariousness; the escape from the trap had been a near miss: "Perhaps anguish is always the stronger: perhaps the joy granted to the only animal which knows that it is not eternal is poisoned from the very start" (A, 289).

But then he has a culminating revelation when humanity itself appears on the scene in the form of a peasant woman who was too old to flee the village. Her smile corresponds to the walnut trees that framed the Alsatian countryside in that it makes everything at which he has wondered a mere appendage of the power of man: "Let the mystery of man but reappear in an enigmatic smile, and the resurrection of the earth becomes nothing more than a shimmering backdrop" (A, 291-292). Berger suddenly feels himself in the presence of an abiding quality of human nature, a pristine innocence with open possibilities for development that has been captured in myths of creation. "Thus, perhaps," run the final words of Malraux's last novel, "God looked at the first man. . . ." This all-encompassing affirmation of human universality, this revelation of the underlying vitality and creativity of the self—if such an affirmation can be maintained, for it is said that the smile merely "seemed" to express indulgence and irony as it regarded "death in the distance" (A, 291)—recapitulates the lessons learned by Berger's father and provides a fitting coda for the series of encounters with man that had begun with Nietzsche's madness.

VI

Enter the Devil: Nietzsche's Presence in *Doctor Faustus*

Along with *Felix Krull* and the Joseph novels, *Doctor Faustus* is one of the masterpieces of Mann's later career. Within the Continental tradition of the intellectual novel, it stands out for its range and power; and Mann himself valued it so greatly that he wrote a whole book about his work on it called *The Story of a Novel*. As we conclude this study of a Nietzschean current in literary modernism, it is especially fitting that we should consider *Doctor Faustus*. For Mann's hero is a German composer, and the reader is asked to consider him—in one of his several roles—as a typical modernist artist. In chapter 37, where the impresario Saul Fitelberg tries to lure the musician to Paris, this amateur sociologist of the avant-garde places him on equal footing with the surrealists, Pound and Joyce, Stravinsky and Picasso (F, 530-532). Moreover, Mann has been careful to invent a career for his composer that coincides with the zenith of modernism in the twenties, making it the decade of his greatest and most characteristic works, the *Apocalypsis* oratorio and the *Lamentation of Dr. Faustus*. Even more suggestive, however, is his penchant for seeing his hero Adrian Leverkühn in terms of Nietzsche.

It is, of course, well known that *Doctor Faustus* draws heavily on details from the philosopher's biography. But the reasons for this borrowing have not been sufficiently explored. One explanation emerges in *The Story of a Novel*, surely one of the most complete commentaries a writer has ever made on his own work. There Mann remarks, somewhat disingenuously, that he found this opportunity to place

facts in a fictive setting highly alluring, and then decided he
had gone so far that he could never mention Nietzsche in the
novel. Or, as he puts it, the name doesn't appear "precisely
because the euphoric composer was set in his [Nietzsche's]
place, so that it may not be used any more."[1] Such scruples
are curious, and it becomes apparent that the absorption of
Nietzsche into Leverkühn has allowed Mann to realize, in
yet another way, his old project of displacing the philosopher
with a creation of his own. As a result, and this is the second
advantage of his procedure, he achieves an historical double
vision which links Nietzsche to artistic modernism by shifting his biography forward in time. The Fitelberg episode
comments on this shift. In the midst of discussing the avant-
garde in literature, music, and painting, the impresario concedes that a mood of radical innovation can enter philosophy
as well. He names no thinker, but perhaps someone German
would serve, someone with whom Zeitblom—Leverkühn's
friend and the narrator-biographer of *Doctor Faustus*—might
be familiar: "And I have a vague feeling that it is in Germany
one should study metaphysics—perhaps the Herr Professor,
my honored vis-à-vis, will agree with me . . ." (F, 431).
Despite its playful evasiveness in saying so, Mann's novel is
on one level a dramatization of Nietzsche's affinities with the
modernist movement.

But Nietzsche's submerged role in *Doctor Faustus* involves
much more than this thesis. For the reader who comes to the
novel with some knowledge of the philosopher, Mann's
metaphor of haunting, which he uses to describe the impression created by his reliance on leitmotivs and the veiled interconnection of themes (W:XI, 170), seems well chosen.
The text may avoid any direct mention of Nietzsche, but it
teems with echoes, allusions, elaborations, critical reactions,
and revisions. Even more than *Walnut Trees*, this novel is the
product of an imagination that was saturated with Nietzsche
and his writings. For close to fifty years Mann had been fascinated with him, to the point of reading his most important
books many times and assembling a large library of second-

ary literature about him.[2] It is not surprising that the philosopher's presence in his novel should be so ubiquitous.

However, much of the indirect reference built into *Doctor Faustus* is relatively superficial. Unlike Malraux, who focused in his novel on a series of major Nietzschean questions, Mann often appropriates ideas and motifs with little relationship among each other and then goes on to treat them very freely and with little regard for contradictions. For example, Leverkühn signs a letter to Zeitblom with the name of a medieval composer whose aims he shares (F, 494-495). Zeitblom compares this act of "playful identification" to a letter of Wagner's in which that composer called himself a church councillor. Nietzsche tells of a similar incident in *Ecce Homo*, which Mann read twice while working on *Doctor Faustus*, and uses it as an emblem for the issues that caused him to break with Wagner. It is thus Zeitblom and not Leverkühn who for the moment is following the philosopher's biography, a reversal of roles that also occurs elsewhere. Furthermore, Mann has greatly elaborated on the kernel furnished in *Ecce Homo* by having Adrian's behavior merely resemble Wagner's and by giving Zeitblom some thoughts very different from the ones Nietzsche expresses in his autobiography.

Consistency of viewpoint is even less important in the portrayal of the Kridwiss Circle, a group of intellectuals whose discussions have a strong Nietzschean undercurrent and also anticipate the Nazis. When these men prophesy the "practice of not caring for the diseased in the grander style—the killing of the unfit and weak-minded" (F, 492), they seem to be enlarging on a notorious suggestion from the "Moral Code for Doctors" in *Twilight of the Idols* (T:IX, 36). The prediction sounds all the more menacing given its context in *Doctor Faustus*. Because Zeitblom is writing his friend's biography during the last years of Nazi Germany, the book has already featured interludes from the authorial present which make it clear where these ideas will eventually lead. Yet the Nietzschean echoes in this episode also point in a very different direction. Mann has shown how the intellectuals were guided in their thinking by the image of diseased teeth; the most modern dental technique is simple extraction. Nietzsche also relied on this image in *Twilight* when he argued against an ascetic denial of the passions by insisting that "we no longer admire dentists who pull *out* teeth to stop them hurting" (T:V, 1). It is apparent that the Kridwiss Circle has reversed the concrete force of this image and has shifted its meaning to different issues. The connection between Nietzsche and the intellectuals no longer seems at all direct.

Similar transmutations characterize much of the Nietzschean material in *Doctor Faustus*. But this practice is hardly limited to Nietzsche, for by this time Mann had perfected a method of composition which has been called the art of quotation or the montage technique.[3] He draws on a wide range of "sources," while insisting that he has transformed his borrowings through free artistic play; in appropriating outside material, he assimilates it so thoroughly to the themes and concerns of his own work that it loses the meaning it had in its original context.

Because Nietzsche wrote philosophy, Mann's attitude toward the "quotation" of ideas demands special attention. In *The Story of a Novel* he remarks that for an artist "an idea as such will never have much worth in itself or with reference to its author. The thing that matters to him is the way it functions within the intellectual framework of his creations" (W:XI, 175). This stance explains the freedom, even the opportunism, with which Mann develops Nietzschean insights and the arbitrary way in which he can combine them. At this level, one might wonder whether recognizing the Nietzschean background to a passage serves a meaningful purpose. The contradictory approaches taken by the Kridwiss Circle may be relevant to the novel's portrayal of German intellectual history. But elsewhere, as in the Wagner allusion, the Nietzschean passage fits so closely into the other purposes of the novel that knowing its origin is helpful only for understanding Mann's creative process. The philosopher's writings become little more than a reference book for vivid motifs and images which can be manipulated with no regard for their author's enduring concerns.

But is Mann always so serenely distanced and self-aware when he deals with Nietzsche in *Doctor Faustus*? The very practice of leaving the philosopher unnamed would suggest not, for Mann has effectively eliminated all occasions for explicitly scrutinizing his use of this source. And in any case such scrutiny would have been most difficult. Nietzschean material had been part of the fabric of Mann's thought for so long that it could have easily contributed to ideas and situations in the novel without his being conscious of it. There is an example of just this process in *The Story of a Novel*. Mann recalls that during the period of preparation before starting to write, he read several books dealing with Nietzsche's relationship to women (W:XI, 151, 156); in the novel itself the story of Adrian's courtship of Marie Godeau closely resembles some of this material. Yet Mann insists that the episode derived from Frank Harris's biography of Shakespeare (W:XI, 166-167). The contradiction can be resolved if we think of two layers of assimilation, one involving montage or quotation when the novel was being written, the other involving a deeper structure of persistent concerns and preferences. In other words, Mann's absorption of the Nietzsche story, which he must have known even before the gestation period of the novel, was a precondition for his choice of the markedly analogous story from Harris. Though at the time of writing he may not have meant to allude to the philosopher's biography, its underlying presence was so obvious that early critics noticed the parallel at once. In this case at least, an interest in Nietzsche has a privileged position among the diverse materials assembled to make the novel.

Mann himself makes allowances for a layering effect among his sources when he discusses his use of Theodor Adorno's *Philosophy of Modern Music*, the book that prompted the comments cited above on free artistic play in handling ideas. On reading Adorno he felt "an unhesitating readiness to appropriate what I felt to be my own" because his thoughts coincided so closely with concerns of his own dating from *Death in Venice* (W:XI, 174). But Mann's words "my own" need to be qualified. Having seen in Chapter III how much of that story grew out of a fascinated interest in Nietzsche, we realize that his openness to some of Adorno's ideas could have depended on this formative intellectual experience. Yet, even as he admits that long-term factors underlie his quotation of other writers, Mann refuses to consider the nature of these factors in any depth.

These two examples suggest an underlying Nietzschean presence in *Doctor Faustus* which Mann did not recognize or could not be candid about. It is my contention that this presence indeed exists, and on a grand scale. Once we deduct all the haphazard details introduced through montage, there still remains a core of issues and motifs that are specifically Nietzschean and which give *Doctor Faustus* much of its significance and power.[4] Style counts for surprisingly little here, though as someone who wrote in German, Mann was in a better position than any other author we have considered to profit from Nietzsche's example. Granted, the montage technique does have an affinity with the idea of metamorphosis outlined in the second essay of *On the Genealogy of Morals.* Mann shares Nietzsche's interest in a process of reinterpretation whereby fixed elements acquire new meanings on entering the field of a different will to power. But he shifts its focus from the transformation of cultural phenomena throughout history to the artist's manipulation of passages taken from his predecessors. It is also true that Nietzsche was his model for another striking feature of *Doctor Faustus*, the accounts the novel gives of the work of an imaginary composer. Mann regarded the philosopher's description of the overture to *Die Meistersinger* as a stylistic triumph, and long before beginning his novel he opened one major attempt at this kind of writing—a review in 1917 of Hans Pfitzner's opera *Palestrina*—by echoing the appreciation of *Carmen* in *The Case of Wagner.*[5] Otherwise, however, the important relationships involve what Mann called, in his overly broad declaration on the artist's freedom in playing with ideas, the "intellectual framework" of his novel. The rest of this chapter will show that Nietzsche is not simply the source for isolated details but that he has strongly influenced guiding conceptions and crucial scenes in *Doctor Faustus*.

Mann's comments in *The Story of a Novel* are of little direct help in studying this level of impact. The many critics of *Doctor Faustus* who draw on this book do not allow for the limited value of its information, which usually relates only to the actual period of composition. Indeed, Mann could hardly be expected to analyze Nietzsche's presence in this novel, shaped as it was through an entire career by the dynamics of idea and image and of model and rival. Only in a few scattered observations does he show some awareness. Thus he remarks that the novel absorbed his powers more completely than any other (W:XI, 147), that his first vague conceptions of it were associated with thoughts of Nietzsche (151), and that it soon became connected in his mind with the period forty years before when he struggled to release his own creativity from Nietzsche's shadow (155). Tantalizingly sketchy comments such as these point to an elemental substratum of concerns joining Mann's most intimate reactions to Nietzsche with some of his leading artistic aims. But, to gain an understanding of these concerns, our first priority must be *Doctor Faustus* and not Mann's commentary on it. As we consider this complex and challenging work of art, we shall find that its Nietzschean underlayer extends along three axes of interpretation: an ambivalent attitude toward Dionysian creativity, an interest in analyzing cultural and historical decline but also in looking beyond it, and finally a perplexed effort to sustain a humanistic faith which includes some religious attitudes.

THE TRANSFORMATIONS OF DIONYSUS: PERSPECTIVES ON THE INNER LIFE OF A MODERN ARTIST

At first glance *Doctor Faustus* divides into two irreconcilable parts: a biography of Adrian Leverkühn, the artist whose hermetically isolated existence barely touches the world; and a social and historical novel presenting key moments in the development of Germany and culminating in the early twentieth century. This break between inner and outer might well seem arbitrary, a threat to the unity of the novel. But such a dichotomy would be meaningless to someone like Mann who had absorbed two major concepts in Nietzsche's thought. In Chapter II we noticed the prominence the novelist gave to his idea of culture at the time of writing *Doctor Faustus*. Because culture is the constitutive form that defines both the solitary moments of artistic creativity and the history of a whole society, it provides a bridge between the two areas. The same is necessarily true of decadence, since it represents a single phase of culture; in *Reflections of an Apolitical Man*, Mann had praised Nietzsche for his skill in analyzing this phenomenon. The concept of decadence does much to illuminate Mann's two-pronged strategy in the novel. It has a psychological component which may be observed in an individual's diminished creative powers; hence the complex of issues centering on Leverkühn's precarious commitment to art. But decadence is also a crisis in the community at large as it undergoes an epochal process of decline and fall; hence the vignettes of German demoralization in the generations before Hitler.

Thus, though this section will deal with Leverkühn and the next with social issues, the two realms were aspects of the same thing both for Nietzsche and then for Mann. Our sharpened sense of their radical difference, at least in the United States, derives in part from the conflicting perspectives of aesthetic and sociological criticism. It suggests the force of Nietzsche's example that Lionel Trilling, whose career took him through the center of this controversy, invoked his name when he sought to resolve the split. Writing in the decade of *Doctor Faustus*, he saw Nietzsche as the critic who never thought "to separate his historical sense from his sense of art."[6]

The postulate of an intimate relationship between inner and outer worlds underlies one of Mann's basic formal decisions for his novel. He has said that in telling Leverkühn's story as a biography written by a friend he wished to get ironic distance on the story and to hold open the possibilities for comic effect (W:XI, 164). But this method had other advantages. The novel makes it clear that Zeitblom, the man of humanistic culture, has the role of mediator. Simply on the most literal level, he is the first audience for Leverkühn's compositions, thus suggesting their transmission to the world at large. But as he assists him with libretti and watches over him in sympathetic friendship, he also participates to some degree in his creativity.

In broader terms, Zeitblom's very position as narrator makes him the meeting place for the public and private aspects of culture. After all, everything that appears in the novel is there because it has been channeled through his mind. It is he, rather than Leverkühn, who witnesses such symptomatic events as the startling appearances of Dr. Chaim Breisacher, the meetings of the Kridwiss Circle, or the murder of Rudi Schwerdtfeger, and who then reports on the course of German history after the fall of the Weimar Republic. On the other hand, despite an appearance of obtuseness, he is also capable of responding to the innermost motives of his friend's artistic life. It is one of the triumphs of Mann's technique in *Doctor Faustus* that we usually remain convinced that Zeitblom's perceptions accurately reflect Leverkühn's isolated and buried self. Mann's reliance on recurrent, interlocking, and subtly varying motifs—which on one level is purely formalistic—serves an epistemological purpose. Because of the continuity among the motifs, the direct revelation of the artist's being which occurs in biographical "documents" and in expressive passages from his music generally confirms the less intensely concentrated observations of his meandering but sensitive biographer.

In general, therefore, the invention of Zeitblom allows Mann to view Leverkühn from the perspective of Nietzschean cultural analysis.[7] But the friendship of the two men also raises a more specific set of cultural issues centering on concepts from *The Birth of Tragedy*. In the opening chapters where Zeitblom gathers his forces to start writing his biography, he describes his public, humanistic values in Apollinian terms while he sees Dionysian traits in his friend's tortured and solitary genius. Out of this contrast comes the first and most discursive of the several versions of Dionysus that will appear in *Doctor Faustus*. And as he introduces some of the salient features of Nietzsche's myth, Mann transforms it by identifying it with "life" as defined by an opposition with "intellect." This opposition amounts to a sharp distinction between instinct and reason or between energy and order, thus breaking with the philosopher's growing tendency to view both Apollo and Dionysus as instincts with an inherent capacity to give order to themselves. Mann has even shifted his own position since *Death in Venice*, where he had shown some parallelism between the polarities by depicting Aschenbach's discovery that his "Doric" Apollinianism was as much a Nietzschean art drive as the Dionysian.

This new emphasis is apparent in the one place in *Doctor Faustus* where Nietzsche's concepts are mentioned with some explicitness. Dionysus is associated with "innocence of life" (F, 378†), innocence being a favorite word of Nietzsche's for the spontaneous expression of vitalistic energies. In connecting the Dionysian with "the relaxed and fraternal" atmosphere of a carnival, Mann shows an awareness of the primitive communal feelings he had suppressed in the partial and exaggerated version of *Death in Venice*.[8] Apollo he links to the interrelated values of form, measure, and consciousness (F, 368). So when Zeitblom at the beginning of the novel speaks of his "nature directed toward the rational" and of his "need for order" (F, 10, 18) he shows the extent to which he personifies Mann's current sense of the Apollinian. Meanwhile, his perception of "irrational" forces in his friend's artistic genius (F, 11) reveals Leverkühn's affinity with the Dionysian. And alongside this reinterpretation of Nietzsche's polarities there are hints of a more drastic transformation of Dionysus. In describing Adrian's artistic gifts as demonic,

Zeitblom evokes a religious universe of good and evil that is far removed from the creative spontaneity of innocence. Clearly the inner life of Mann's artist will bring reversals as well as shifts in Nietzschean positions. The devil has entered the sphere of Dionysus.

In addition to outlining and interpreting basic distinctions, Zeitblom's opening remarks allude to several subordinate topics associated with the polarities in *Birth*. His own concern with "human dignity" (F, 17) recalls the specifically human domain of Apollo;[9] Leverkühn's coldness, compared to an "abyss, into which one's feelings toward him dropped soundless and without a trace" (F, 13), reveals the indifference to the human implied in Dionysian cosmic consciousness. A later elaboration of this motif of coldness, in Leverkühn's Faustian contemplation in chapter 27 of the ocean deeps and interstellar space, brings out more explicitly the Dionysian characteristics of the primal and cosmic as opposed to the human and social. Similarly, Zeitblom's love for language and beauty is related to Apollo's sponsorship of poetry and the visual arts (F, 16). Leverkühn, on the other hand, is devoted to "that other, perhaps more intense, but strangely inarticulate language, that of tones" (F, 16), the elemental musical realm of Dionysus.

So many specific correspondences between *Birth* and Zeitblom's friendship with Leverkühn prompt a further question: does Mann, like Lawrence, develop the notion of polarity into an ideal for human relationships? The distinctions he makes between his heroes' characters at the beginning of the novel reverberate thereafter in their very names, the audacity of the Germanic "kühn" being countered by the moderation of the Latinate "Serenus." More fanciful perhaps is the contrast of initial letters in their preferred forms of addressing each other; Adrian cuts against Zeitblom as if they represented some alpha and omega of human experience. But there is no real polarized mutuality between them. If Zeitblom's loyal friendship strives throughout the novel to bridge the gap between their contrasting states of being, Leverkühn's coldness forestalls his efforts.

Since cultural issues were so important in shaping Mann's conception of the two men, perhaps the nature of their relationship is best defined by Zeitblom's insight into what culture is. During his travels in Greece he learns to see it as a "fruitful contact" between a "fullness of feeling for life" which embraces even the demonic and an attitude which, "pious and ordering," seeks to draw the "dark and uncanny into the service of the gods" (F, 17). The references to creative interaction between two realms and to the Dionysian quality of life and the Apollinian one of order may sound polaristic. But once again a religious vocabulary—"demonic," "pious"—has modified the Nietzschean categories. Furthermore, Mann places decisive emphasis on a dualistic process of transformation involving higher and lower realms: instinct ascends to reason, Dionysus is contained and channeled by Apollo. Here he becomes explicit about no longer construing Nietzsche's polarities as a composition of equivalent forces, but as a hierarchy where one sublimates the other. Except in brief passages, as in Zeitblom's reference to an "instinctive" resistance to the demonic (F, 10), Mann on this level usually avoids conceiving of Apollo and Dionysus as self-heightening drives.

The one-sidedness of the friendship in *Doctor Faustus* parallels this interpretation of *Birth* by elaborating it into character and action. Zeitblom fulfills his Apollinian nature by repeatedly attempting to absorb the meaning of his friend's existence; he certainly experiences fruitfulness of contact. But Leverkühn seems incapable of moving outside the boundaries of his self. He usually addresses Zeitblom by his last name, while the prime condition of his pact with the devil is a prohibition of love which apparently confirms his inability to form human connections. For Mann in this novel, there is no way in which an essentially Dionysian nature can get beyond itself. Given this outlook, it is not surprising that Leverkühn's later life should often resemble

Nietzsche's descriptions of polar nullity: he alternates between prolonged periods of lethargy and frenzied moments
of creativity, thus combining the two possibilities of immo-
bility and violence.

□

In their thorough engagement with Nietzschean issues, Zeitblom's opening remarks both illustrate Mann's continued
and developing response to the philosopher and illuminate
much that will come later in the novel. But once he starts
describing the formation of Adrian's artistic gifts up to his
young manhood, he provides a new perspective on his inner
life that involves yet another version of Dionysus. In this
part of Doctor Faustus, as throughout the novel, Mann shows
great mastery in arousing and manipulating the reader's curiosity about Leverkühn's character. His methods are an
elaboration of his practice in Lotte in Weimar several years
before, where he had also been concerned with progressively
illuminating the consciousness of a creative personality.
There he had combined a shift in point of view with a break
in style as he moved to Goethe's interior monologue in the
last chapter; he had previously presented him through a variety of outside views that tantalized the reader with partial,
diffuse perceptions.

In Doctor Faustus we are almost a third of the way into the
novel when Zeitblom interrupts his recollections of his
friend to produce two of his prized biographical "documents." After so much mediated portrayal we suddenly have
the letters on becoming a composer and arriving in Leipzig
in which Adrian speaks directly. The weirdly antique German in which he expresses himself heightens the impression
of moving to a character with a distinctively new point of
view. Mann will again draw on original stylistic devices and
will remove barriers to immediacy so as to emphasize key
episodes later on, especially in the interview with the devil,
the accounts of Adrian's works with their masked drama of
developing character, or the scene of his final breakdown.
Those who criticize the first half of Doctor Faustus for slow-

ness of pacing have not responded to this artful presentation. The delayed breakthrough to Adrian's viewpoint deserves comparison with the famous late entrance of the main character in Molière's *Tartuffe*.

With Mann taking such pains to focus our attention on Leverkühn, the basic quality of his creativity naturally becomes a leading issue. In the end, there will be dramatic confirmation of Zeitblom's early comments on the demonic. But until then the Dionysian remains prominent, though it is now conceived in somewhat different terms. Rather than being defined by a contrast with Apollo, as was the case in descriptions of Adrian's friendship with Zeitblom, it becomes the composer's goal as he struggles to overcome a disembodied intellectuality in his own character on his way to artistic maturity. This shift derives from a different reading of *The Birth of Tragedy*, and shows how much Mann's imagination was drawn to that shadowy Nietzschean type, the "theoretical man." It is appropriate that when he commented on *Birth* during his work on *Doctor Faustus* he mentioned Apollo only briefly as the principle of opposition to Dionysus, but then discussed "theory" in much more detail (W:IX, 686-687). This reading, it will be noticed, had the advantage of bringing the book closer to Mann's concern with dualisms of instinct and intellect. But it also recalls his interest in Gide's Nietzschean phase, since it follows the response to *Birth* dramatized in *The Immoralist* more than his own *Death in Venice*. And, finally, it provides Mann with a key to Nietzsche's own character, since "he is himself this theoretical man par excellence" (W:IX, 709).

Given the extent to which Leverkühn is modeled on the philosopher, this last statement is worth pursuing further. *Birth* contains several assertions about theoretical man which are already incipient character sketches and which have a direct bearing on Mann's conception of his composer. There is the portrait of Socrates, of course, who sees through the limitations of theoretical culture and resolves to practice music; latent here is Adrian's choice of a musical vocation when he finds nothing to absorb him at the university. Even more suggestive, however, is a reference to Faust "storming unsatisfied through all the faculties" (B, 18). The parallel with Adrian's years of schooling is more exact, while Nietzsche himself has chosen Faust to typify a crisis facing theoretical man. But the reference is especially interesting because it fuses Nietzschean material with the Faust myth. Standing in the background of *Doctor Faustus* and running through the entire novel, these two stories guide and comment on the narrative in the foreground. In many ways they do not mesh with each other: after all, Mann draws attention to the myth in his title while he is resolutely silent about Nietzsche's presence until *The Story of a Novel*. But here it is possible to see how these two aspects of the book formed a unity in Mann's conception of it; the phase of theory in Adrian's life is equally Faustian and Nietzschean. Indeed, one might argue that the Nietzschean element has priority since it is the philosopher's interpretation of Faust that justifies the coalescence of the two bodies of material. And a similar set of priorities reaches far back in Mann's career; decades before, he had already been quoting as a favorite passage—as "a symbol for a whole world, *my world*"—a phrase in which Nietzsche identified himself with a "Faustian fragrance" (W:XII, 541).

Mann's fascination with theoretical man has other, more specific consequences as well. We have seen how theory serves as a general model for the first stage of Adrian's life and how it illustrates the persistent assimilative powers of Mann's imagination, but it also affects the texture and character of his writing in two complementary ways. At times he conveys the sense of disembodied intellectuality through a vivid image or a telling phrase or incident; elsewhere he develops this theme through symptomatic discourse. By this term I mean passages that present ideas which may have value in themselves but which are equally important for suggesting general psychological attitudes; in this case, theories—even theories of attaining existential immediacy—overwhelm direct experience and testify to an underlying state of alienation from the instincts. As a result, whether Zeitblom recalls concrete details or abstract discussions in his role as sympathetic observer, the story he tells has the same tendency, that of revealing the outer contours of a personality cut off from its own life and struggling with its situation. A few examples from this part of the novel will suggest the range of Mann's methods.

Among the formative influences on Adrian's life is his mother's attitude toward music. Her speaking voice, Zeitblom recalls, had a quality of "natural harmony defined by instinctive taste" (F, 34); but because of her "chaste reserve" she never developed her talents as a singer (F, 41, 33). As a result Adrian's initiation into music came from Hanne the cowherd, linked to the "animal smell" of the barnyard (F, 41). But his mother's denial of her inborn capacities returns to blunt the force of this naturalistic image. Eventually the composer will announce that his aim is to overcome the "stable warmth" of music, cooling it off by the application of sternly rationalistic and arbitrary laws (F, 94).

Adrian's achievements as a student reveal a similar abstraction from instinct. His easy absorption of knowledge brings him praise for his "natural merits" (F, 114), a phrase from Goethe whose ambiguities attracted Mann's attention on several occasions. Here, as the director of Adrian's school bids him farewell, he stresses the second word so that the expression takes on a religious meaning. It refers to a transcendent realm of spiritual values: "You know too that He above, from whom all comes, entrusted your gifts to you . . . natural merits are God's merits in us, not our own" (F, 114). But later Leverkühn tells Zeitblom that the emphasis should fall on the first word. The phrase would then refer to an antithetical outlook which is purely immanent and which defines qualities by their natural basis; Goethe sought "to take from the word 'merit' its moral character, and, conversely, to exalt the natural and inborn to a position of extramoral, aristocratic worthiness" (F, 114). Ironically, the very intellectual agility that Adrian shows in this conversation points up his continued allegiance, in spite of his keen awareness of an existentially immediate world, to a split one that separates idea and nature. A telling phrase has generated symptomatic discourse.

An even more ironic use of such discourse occurs during Adrian's theological studies. His friends criticize him for his coolness and cleverness (F, 160), qualities which contradict a religiosity whose locus should be "the immediacy, the courage, and the depth of personal life; the will and the capacity, the naturalness and the demonic of existence" (F, 160). Their comments do catch the basically theoretical bent of his character; but later, when the realm of this theology is defined tersely as "the instincts" (F, 167), we become aware of the ideological convolutions of their own position. The ironic undercutting here is analogous to the scene in *Women in Love* where Birkin attacks Hermione for parroting ideas that he himself knows only as theories.

Especially significant, because they decisively influence Adrian's interests in music, are Kretzschmar's lectures in chapter 8. This torrent of abstractions, by encouraging the young man's tendency to "speculate in the void" (F, 82) without a basis in lived experience, extends the domain of theory to include even art. Kretzschmar also moves him to start exploring his own personal situation. The modern world, Adrian tells Zeitblom after one of the lectures, lacks the instinctive naturalness of "naïveté, unconsciousness, taken-for-grantedness"; by remaining in a narrow sphere of technology and comfort, it is shut off as well from the fullness of outer nature (F, 83). But this highly Nietzschean critique of a theoretical culture is the product of a theoretical mind; whatever its validity as an objective judgment, it at least testifies to the state of Adrian's psyche. The outer world he perceives is his inner world writ large. Thus, when he begins composing music himself, a "mania" for contriving technical problems masters him to such an extent that it threatens to overcome more important creative impulses (F, 100). The magic square that he hangs in his apartment is a memorable image for his tendency to treat art simply as an intellectual puzzle (F, 125).

Mann's varied renditions of a split between theory and instinct come to a head in Adrian's first letter, in which he writes to Kretzschmar about pursuing a career in music. Like Nietzsche's Socrates, he learns to appreciate art by having arrived at the outer limits of knowledge. Thus he argues that the very mental powers which propelled his rapid Faustian advance through the disciplines to "the highest science" of theology had also kept him from being satisfied with his achievements (F, 175). Thinking came so easily for him that he never made contact with the instincts; he had never known how "blood and mind really warmed up for the sake of a subject and by effort over it" (F, 174). He considers his chronic headaches to be the symptom of a purely theoretical existence at the end of its tether, when the mind turns against itself "from disgust, from cold boredom" (F, 175).

Yet it is clear from his letter that similar problems will arise should he become an artist. Music interests him primarily for its "mysteries of theory" (F, 177), and he uses a revealing alchemical metaphor to convey his sense of the creative process. By emphasizing the action of "spirit and fire" in refining matter which he sees as essentially passive and with no inherent tendencies toward form, he sets up a strong dichotomy between the material shaped in art and a shaping force that is transcendent to it.[10] This outlook simply repeats his characteristic psychological split between an active but ungrounded intellect and an inert instinctual self. Ultimately Adrian shows a certain awareness of this irony. He ends the letter with a discussion of what he fears will be the only mode of creativity possible for his "quickly satisfied intelligence" (F, 178). His gift for abstracting musical techniques and forms, when joined with his inability to experience the "robust naïveté" (F, 178) of more profound artistic energies, will produce a dominant mood of mocking disgust at earlier achievements, which will seem to him to be merely repetitive stereotypes.

The development of Adrian's career will show that there is some basis for his fears. His first major project is an opera inspired by Shakespeare's *Love's Labour's Lost.* Zeitblom's phraseology in describing the libretto epitomizes the involuted mockery to which Adrian doubtlessly responded—"a spirit of the most artificial persiflage and of the persiflage of artificiality" (F, 218)—and Adrian himself composes in a style which "in every way ridiculed and parodistically exaggerated itself" (F, 290). Later, he is drawn to subjects from the *Gesta Romanorum* that undercut the "swollen pomposity" with which the German opera treated the Middle Ages and thus satisfied his "penchant for parody" (F, 425, 420). This trait in Mann's version of a music-practicing Socrates puts in question Nietzsche's whole project of converting theoretical man to an artistic world view that releases the creative-affirmative forces of the instincts. Leverkühn's art is often one that exists "at the edge of impossibility" (F, 290), in a region where the abstractions of theoretical consciousness have almost completely effaced the energies of a Dionysian art.

Only after Adrian's first letter does attention turn to the irrational elements Zeitblom found in his character. In retrospect, one sees a potential for an opening to the instincts when he sings rounds with Hanne or learnedly dissects the notion of natural merits. And an erotic factor is apparent in phrases from the letter to Kretzschmar like "throw myself in the arms of music" (F, 173), "the promise and the vow to her" (F, 177), or "virginity is well, yet must to motherhood" (F, 182). But not until he makes a definite commitment by moving to Leipzig to study with Kretzschmar does something happen that causes Leverkühn to break out of his purely intellectual existence. His adventure with the prostitute awakens his sexuality, a drive which Nietzsche had identified as Dionysian and after *Birth* had increasingly seen as crucial in artistic creativity.[11] All of Zeitblom's anticipatory comments about his friend's nature are now becoming reality.

Adrian's second letter, written to Zeitblom himself, tells

the first part of his adventure with the prostitute and is a fine example of the two separate layers in Mann's response to Nietzsche. To portray his hero's mistaken entry into a brothel, he draws on selected details from the philosopher's biography in accordance with the montage technique. But because the incident also develops the issue of theory and the Dionysian which is so important for this segment of Adrian's life, it has been placed in a thematic structure with a more profound relationship to Nietzsche. Not simply the picture of an awkward sexual initiation, it dramatizes the shifting balance in Leverkühn's character as he chooses to become an artist. Thus Zeitblom is justified in calling this adventure "frightfully symbolic" (F, 197).

Some of this symbolism—and especially the description of the porter who leads Adrian astray—becomes fully comprehensible only when the devil appears before him in Italy. At this stage the emphasis falls on revealing the Dionysian sexual basis to art. When Adrian realizes that he is in a brothel, his first response is typical of his theoretical self. Though the madam greets him as "someone long expected" (F, 190), he is careful to hide what he calls his "affects" (F, 190†), a word Nietzsche often uses in speaking of instinctual man. Instead, he rushes to a piano on the other side of the room and plays "two or three chords . . . modulation from B major to C major" (F, 190), thus returning to the familiar world of musical technique. But this "friend" preserves the separation of realms only for a moment. Music and brothel unite when one of the prostitutes comes up to him and touches his cheek, with the very casualness of her gesture indicating the direct continuity that links the sexual to the artistic. Dionysus has appeared in still another guise.

Adrian again takes flight, but this moment has transformed him. He will eventually return to the prostitute, traveling all the way to Pressburg, in Hungary, to find her. After this experience, even if we disregard Zeitblom's reconstruction of their meeting as a mere hypothesis, the split in Adrian's nature is clearly at an end. For in his compositions

instinct now begins to take priority over theoretical awareness. Among the first of his pieces to be anything more than
a simple exercise is his setting for the Brentano lyric "O lieb
Mädel." Both word and music have grown out of his experience; the poem directly addresses a "dear lass," while his
technical virtuosity takes its point of departure in a "basic
figure" of notes which spells out his private name for the
prostitute (F, 206-207).

This work in turn prefigures much in his later achievement. Often he bases his compositions on literary material
which contains private allusions to his experience: his version
of *Love's Labour's Lost* gives special emphasis to the "faith-
less, wanton, dangerous" aspects of Rosaline (F, 288); his
accompaniment to a Blake poem shows its greatest power at
the lines, "But an honest joy / Does itself destroy / For a
harlot coy" (F, 350). Even in the *Apocalypsis* oratorio, despite
the richness of broader social implications in this first masterpiece, he achieves one of his most striking effects with the
whore of Babylon (F, 498). But the Brentano song is also
the fountainhead for his most original work as a composer.
Mann drew on Schönberg's twelve-tone system for Adrian's
most detailed descriptions of his mature aims, but this
method should be seen as an outgrowth of his initial experiments since it too relies on a "key word, whose elements
are to be found everywhere in the song, which it would like
to determine entirely" (F, 255). Then, in his second masterpiece, the *Lamentation of Doctor Faustus*, Adrian uses the same
basic figure he had devised after his visit to the prostitute (F,
648).

Probably the best way of gauging the growing importance
of the Dionysian in Adrian's character is to follow his changing attitude toward language. This problem came up in
Death in Venice, when Aschenbach's departure from a Doric
state could be seen in his musicalization of Tadzio's name
and manner of speaking; and it also appears elsewhere in
Mann's work. In *Doctor Faustus*, Zeitblom had already raised
the issue in his opening remarks, when he insisted on the

primacy in his friend of the inarticulate and the musical. But in the context of Leverkühn's developing creativity, it shows Mann's willingness to conflate different phases in Nietzsche's thought. Though present from the beginning, the sexual element in Dionysus was especially prominent at the end of his career, while Dionysian music was most important in *The Birth of Tragedy*.

Despite Zeitblom's remarks, Leverkühn's art initially has much that suggests he wants to join the characteristic media of Apollo and Dionysus. From seeing how Beethoven used words as he composed, he theorized that "music and speech . . . belonged together, they were at bottom one" (F, 217). Kretzschmar's lecture on Beissel, the self-taught German-American sectary who set already existing texts to music (F, 90-92), provided him with another model; and of course there was Wagner, with his "word-tone drama," who pursued a similar synthesis more systematically (F, 218). Throughout his career Adrian will compose with his eye on poems, legends, plays, and other literary material. At crucial points, however, the part that language takes diminishes. Thus, even as Leverkühn is theorizing about the oneness of word and music, he is composing a work in which Dante's poetry about the man with a light on his back yields to passages of "absolute music" (F, 217-218). An important innovation in his *Apocalypsis* oratorio tends to demote the word, for he uses the chorus to produce purely orchestral effects (F, 497). With the *Lamentation of Doctor Faustus* the retreat from language has become central. The work ends with a chorus fading into music, a deliberate reversal of what happens in the Ninth Symphony and thus a disavowal of Adrian's initial interest in Beethoven (F, 649).

His changing attitude toward words is also apparent in his life, where the shift can be traced back to the start of his musical training. From Kretzschmar's stutter in delivering his lectures the theme expands to Adrian's vision of a hell "never to be described and denounced in words" (F, 326), then on to his increasingly slurred and confused speech as a result of his disease. His breakdown at the end joins his involvement with music to a failure of language: striking a chord, he tries to sing but utters only an inarticulate wail (F, 667). It is appropriate that in several of these late scenes Adrian's foil has been the numismatist Dr. Kranich, a clear-spoken man who notably lacks any of Zeitblom's openness to the Dionysian and whose words are empty and ineffectual. Throughout the novel the tendency has been for Apollo and Dionysus to draw further apart. In both his life and his art the composer has progressively forfeited that fruitful interaction of language with the spirit of music which Nietzsche had found in tragedy.

□

These and similar glancing revelations of the increasing power of the Dionysian further confirm the decisive change resulting from Adrian's meeting with the prostitute. But Zeitblom's usual term for this realm of inarticulate instincts ranging from the sexual to the artistic has been the demonic. After a long subordination to other concerns, this word finally gets its proper force during Adrian's account of his interview with the devil. The scene is a crucial one. Placed at the center of *Doctor Faustus*, it has great imaginative power, because in it Mann has tied together so many of the diverse strands of his novel. The chapter is also the longest of Zeitblom's biographical documents, drawn from a period when the composer has already settled on his artistic mission and has traveled to Italy so as "to hold undisturbed conversations with my life, my fate" (F, 280). It is thus the most thorough and direct revelation in the whole novel of the innermost tendencies of his character. Furthermore, it is an especially graphic expression of Nietzsche's complex impact on Mann's imagination. An interview with the devil is traditionally Faustian, but the scene also echoes the philosopher's implicit dramatizations of the advent of some of his doctrines: the brief personification of nihilism in *The Will to Power* as "the uncanniest of guests" or the demon in *The Gay Science* which comes in a moment of solitude to whisper about eternal recurrence.[12] And, of course, the appearance of the devil is the most striking of the various transformations of Dionysus in *Doctor Faustus*. But the whole chapter abounds with images that the novelist has borrowed or invented to display his critical response to Nietzsche and his ideas.

What were Mann's aims in portraying a Protean devil who passes through three different shapes during his interview with Adrian? Undoubtedly this idea greatly enhanced the scene's atmosphere of mystery, but it also serves to sum up the stages of his hero's development. According to *The Story of a Novel*, Mann hit upon the basic donnée for this chapter relatively late, well after he had written the two chapters containing Adrian's letters (W:XI, 205). By returning to the issues of theory and sexual instinct raised in those letters while reversing chronological order, the devil's first two avatars embody the current priorities in Adrian's character. First the devil appears as a ruffian who later identifies himself as "Esmeralda's friend and pimp" (F, 311†). In this shape he casts light on a story left untold by Zeitblom, about how the composer had traced the prostitute to Pressburg after returning to the brothel and failing to find her. But the sexual element remains closely tied to the artistic; it is significant that the pimp understands the new level of achievement represented by the Brentano song and compliments Adrian for something "really ingeniously done and almost as though by inspiration" (F, 304). His second shape evokes Leverkühn's theoretical side. He is "a theoretician and critic, who himself composes, so far as thinking allows him" (F, 317), and who speaks of the perilous state of modern art. But by now the problem of intellectual refinement far in excess of creative impulse is no longer so direct a menace to Adrian. It affects several other characters whom he has come to know in Leipzig and Munich and who might be seen as versions of his former self. The critic's difficulties in composing parallel the situation of Leverkühn's friend Schildknapp, who has accompanied him to Italy and whose skill as a translator blocks his poetic talent; and the dimple on his cheek and his weak chin recall the appearance of Baptiste Spengler and Clarissa Rodde, both of them would-be artists.[13]

The chapter acquires new, religious dimensions with the devil's third avatar. Now he takes the form of Schleppfuss, the guest lecturer of Adrian's days as a theology student; and as he discusses the nature of hell, the forms of repentance, and the purchase of souls, we feel for the first time the full metaphysical weight of the Faust myth. Zeitblom's remarks about the demonic have finally been realized; the numerous uncanny elements in Adrian's early life have reached fruition. So the shift from pimp to critic to theologian has enacted in little the change of perspectives that the chapter as a whole has effected in *Doctor Faustus*. As in the novel, where the demonic supplants the Dionysian which had transformed the theoretical, the devil has steadily become a more literal presence.

Adrian's vision contains a number of striking images that express the ascendancy of instinct over theory. But their tenor is such that they give a wrenching twist to Nietzsche's attitude of heroic acceptance in taking a radically immanent view of existence. The pimp himself would be a first example. As a symbol for the primary sexual level of life he contrasts strikingly with the mythological grandeur of Dionysus. Vaguely criminal and jeering (we see the limitations in Zeitblom's imagined account of the rendezvous in Pressburg), he reduces instinctual life to a commercial transaction. Leverkühn's secretive encounter with a prostitute has replaced visions of a culture which glorified existence through a religious veneration of procreation and the mysteries of sexuality. We are far indeed from Nietzsche's and Lawrence's "triumphant Yes to life." Mann has continued the tendency, already apparent in his portrayal of Aschenbach, to imagine degraded versions of the Dionysian; the Neapolitan street singer in *Death in Venice* had also had the appearance of a pimp.

The link between this avatar of the devil and Leverkühn's brothel experience reinforces the ironic impact of the chapter. Just before writing it, Mann reread *Ecce Homo* (W:XI, 209); and the pimp is truer than anything in this autobiography to one of the philosopher's most direct experiences of the Dionysian as founded in sexuality. By replacing the mythbreaker's central myth with a problematic figure who yet has some reference to his life, Mann pointedly questions the whole outlook of aesthetic naturalism. Is it really possible, he asks, to live as Nietzsche preached when he himself could fall so far short of an integrated and richly self-sublimating life of the instincts?

Even more forceful and evocative as a revisionary image is Leverkühn's disease, which in Mann's handling becomes a brilliantly sardonic comment on the process of self-heightening. The devil as pimp informs him that the syphilis he got from the prostitute has spread to his brain, at last realizing a union of body and mind such as the one he had glimpsed when he interpreted natural merit in purely immanent terms. The pimp waxes eloquent in inventing terms for this self-refinement of instinct; it is a "metastasis upward," the effect of "metaveneric processes," a "general penetration" of the realm of theory by a force whose origin is ultimately sexual (F, 312). In short, the disease will end his inhibitions by returning artistic effort to its proper place among the faculties, where it is grounded in the instincts and develops out of them. For Mann, who greatly admired the passage in *Ecce Homo* which described the nature of artistic inspiration, a view of the creative process that stressed body rather than soul was characteristically Nietzschean.[14] But once again his presentation focuses on ambiguous and extreme elements. Inspiration through sexual disease makes it physiological in a more dubious sense than Nietzsche, ignorant of the root cause for his ailments, had allowed for. And when the devil identifies artistic creativity as "enthusiasm totally unvexed by criticism, lame thought, or the deathly control of reason" (F, 316), he goes beyond Nietzsche in the direction of the most ardent surrealists. For *Ecce Homo* does not endorse "demonic" forces of dark and unalloyed irrationality, but rather a continuum in which "the highest and lowest energies . . . well forth from one fount" (E:Z, 6).

But the most striking revaluation of aesthetic naturalism is associated with the technique that gives this chapter such imaginative power. Among the recurring motifs and incidents that now take on new meanings as they enter a more complex web of relationships is one of the most haunting images in all of Mann's work—the osmotic growths. As a boy Adrian had watched his father grow these crystals with their uncanny resemblance to life, both human and otherwise. Taking the shape of "mushrooms, phallic polyp-stalks, little trees, algae, half-formed limbs," they "so yearned after warmth and joy that they actually clung to the pane" of their aquarium as they turned toward the light which fell through it (F, 31). Now this image, as it coalesces with the meanings that the devil has given to syphilis, reveals itself to be an emblem for a totally naturalistic view of human existence. The disease has spread to Adrian's brain through the same osmotic pressure that caused the crystals to grow, and even his artistic works should be considered "osmotic growths" (F, 313, 323), since only his illness had made them possible.

Given Mann's admiration for a letter in which the philosopher spoke of his writings as "a strange growth" (W:IX, 708), it is possible that this very image as well as its intellectual tenor is Nietzschean. But, in Mann's development of the figure, it comes to express a nostalgia for transcendence within a materialistic universe. Zeitblom at least had felt that the crystals were a melancholy sight (F, 31), strange configurations of matter which turned toward the light but could not reach it due to the limitations of their element. And perhaps even Adrian has by now become uneasy with a philosophy of immanence, if his vision of the devil can be interpreted as a projection of his deepest impulses. The very presence of such a visitor serves to restore some contact with a world of transcendent values. It is this back-handed suggestion of a human need for transcendence, a need also conveyed by the yearning osmotic growths, that opens up a positive alternative to Nietzsche and thus constitutes the most fundamental revision of his ideas in this chapter.

Some direct allusions to Nietzschean ideas have a special structural relevance among the shifting perspectives of the interview. It is well known that the devil echoes Nietzsche's account in *Ecce Homo* of his exalted feelings when he wrote *Zarathustra*. Thus he asks, "Who knows today, who even knew in classical times, what inspiration is, what genuine, old, primeval enthusiasm . . . ?" (F, 316) or describes this mood of inspiration as "immediate, absolute, unquestioned, ravishing, where there is no choice, no tinkering, no possible improvement; where all is as a sacred mandate, a visitation received by the possessed one with faltering and stumbling step, with shudders of awe from head to foot, with tears of joy blinding his eyes" (F, 317). But Mann's placement of these echoes deserves comment as well.[15] Spoken as the devil changes shape from pimp to music critic, they invoke the doctrine of physiological inspiration also suggested by the sequence of the devil's avatars. A similar precision in adjusting allusion to imagery may be seen just before the critic turns into the theologian, where the devil's direct references to Nietzsche's aesthetic outlook will soon be dramatically undercut by a transformation which directly affirms the possibility of religious values. The phrase "in kühnem Rausch" (in audacious drunkenness) is a particularly rich one for the irrational and instinctual sources of creativity (F, 323†); it combines a telling syllable from Adrian's name with Nietzsche's usual term for Dionysian intoxication. The devil also rephrases one of Nietzsche's broadest definitions of the will to power, the one in *The Antichrist* referring to heightened feelings of power: "What uplifts you, what increases your feeling of force and power and mastery, to the devil with you, that is truth."[16] The speaker's identity lends irony to the shopworn interjection "to the devil with you"; while the last avatar, which appears immediately afterward, further undercuts this statement of Nietzschean principle by placing matters, at least temporarily, on a theological plane.

If we consider the background to this "quotation" from *The Antichrist*, we discover attitudes which provide a deeper insight into the working of Mann's imagination. The first two forms of the devil have evoked issues of instinct and theory raised by the early Nietzsche; his third form corresponds to the later writings which evaluate the role of Christianity in Western culture. Mann found much that was admirable in the early phase, while the final works—with *The Antichrist* being a special target—were largely repugnant to him. It is typical of this response that he should suggest, during the writing of *Doctor Faustus*, that Nietzsche's career might be interpreted as the decline and fall of a group of ideas which had been originally justified (W:IX, 685). Thus the chapter might be seen as shifting from a recapitulation of Adrian's development as an artist, presented in terms of ideas largely derived from *The Birth of Tragedy*, to the establishment of a perspective on his fate which reverses *The Antichrist*. This introduction of a religious perspective at the close of a Dionysian experience was already apparent in *Death in Venice*, where it had been a minor theme alongside the Platonic language in Aschenbach's rejection of art.

Another suggestive insight into the conception of this chapter occurs on a mythic plane. Mann was interested in Nietzsche's growing tendency to create mythological roles for himself in the period leading up to his insanity (W:IX, 707). It is not much of an imaginative leap to move from the philosopher's brief identification with the Antichrist to a Mephistopheles who has an easy familiarity with Nietzschean ideas. The result, again testifying to Mann's great skill at conflating material from various sources, is a remarkably thorough intermeshing of Nietzschean material with the devil's pact of the Faust myth. Once more, however, a major shift of meaning has taken place. The philosopher's mythic self-dramatization that envisions the end of Christianity has become a reassertion of Christianity's power to enforce some sense of absolute values.

Once the devil's actual appearance has driven home the

revaluation of the Dionysian in terms of the demonic, Adrian's life enters a new phase. On the whole his story is no longer tied so closely to Nietzschean themes, and yet Mann does continue a dialogue with the philosopher right up to the end of the novel. But before we inquire into the ultimate status of the religious myth that *Doctor Faustus* exploits so dramatically, we must consider another group of problems that have already become important. Even as the gradual unveiling of Leverkühn's inner self is proceeding to its culmination in chapter 25, Zeitblom has begun to explore the public side of culture in his role as mediator. His experiences raise two issues that are closely intertwined: the decadence of German society in the early twentieth century, and the connection of this historical situation with his friend's lonely creativity. These themes open up important new perspectives that will contribute to the final resolution of the novel.

BOURGEOIS HUMANISM AND AESTHETIC POLITICS: MANN'S DRAMA OF DECADENCE IN RELATION TO NIETZSCHE

During his interview with Adrian the devil distinguishes between two kinds of fatigue, "the small and the great, the private kind and that of the age" (F, 315). The decisive transition to this two-tiered handling of cultural questions has already occurred in chapter 23, which deals with Adrian's move to Munich. For a moment, as he lodges with the Rodde family and comes in contact with several groups of people interested in the arts, he enters a complex adult world which has many features typical of German and even of European modernity. But then he discovers Pfeiffering, the small village where he eventually settles down, isolating himself from his age in a milieu with an uncanny resemblance to his childhood home. As a result it is Zeitblom and not Leverkühn who becomes the main witness of Munich society as it enacts a Nietzschean drama of decadence. But whereas the philosopher identified science and later Christi-

anity as the cultural form whose progressive disintegration
has brought an entire epoch to an end, Mann focuses on an
entity he calls bourgeois humanism.

The claim that *Doctor Faustus* is the most German of
Mann's novels has confused discussion of his cultural themes.
Granted, the book does focus on twentieth-century German
history, and its subtitle does read "The Life of the German
Composer, Adrian Leverkühn." But it has wider dimensions: Zeitblom's Catholicism and his attachment to classical
antiquity, the German-American background of Adrian's
musical tutor, the English and French interests of his close
friends Schildknapp and Jeannette Scheurl, his own preference for foreign languages when he chooses texts to be set
to music. A novel that ends by contemplating its translation
into another language (F, 668) is highly self-conscious about
broader cultural contexts.

Even the narrowly German foreground attains a more universal significance through suggesting a general law of cultural crisis. Thus for Zeitblom the confused state of his country after World War I is not simply the result of defeat; it
represents the culmination of an entire epoch, "which included not only the nineteenth century but reached back to
the close of the Middle Ages . . . the epoch of bourgeois
humanism" (F, 468-469). As a result Germany is not an exception but a particularly instructive example of a process of
epochal change which concerns Europe as a whole. Only
because the victor nations tend to interpret the war as a "disturbance brought to a lucky conclusion," not as the "deep
and dividing historical incision" that it really was, do they
fail to perceive the larger pattern of events (F, 469). In taking
this attitude toward the German subject matter of *Doctor
Faustus*, Mann closely models himself on Nietzsche's stance
as a cultural critic. In *The Case of Wagner* the philosopher had
stressed the underlying European elements in Wagner—such
as his affinities with Flaubert—as well as the specifically German nature of his appeal. Only Mann's resistance to
Nietzsche's radical dismissal of the German in favor of the

European qualified his cordial admiration for this method of analysis (W:IX, 425-426). His counterassertion was "Germany and Europe at once" (W:IX, 329). This slogan emphasizes the wider, generally human relevance of characteristic national experience; it is this perspective that *Doctor Faustus* communicates so powerfully to foreign readers.

The phrase "bourgeois humanism" defines the sense of epoch that permeates *Doctor Faustus*. Coming to maturity in the early twentieth century, Mann's characters look back with nostalgia to the high point of the cultural form, the world that the devil calls scornfully the "bad, bourgeois nineteenth century" (F, 332). "An uncommonly pleasant age," remarks the young Adrian (F, 38), while Zeitblom instinctively resists the malicious joy with which the Kridwiss Circle greets its approaching end (F, 485-486).

But it is the epoch's point of origin that receives the most attention. Defined epigrammatically as the shift from cult to culture (F, 112, 324), it is located in the sixteenth-century borderland between the Middle Ages and the Renaissance where Mann sees a decisive transition from a religious to a secular world view. This moment of origins colors the very linguistic texture of the novel: witness the old-fashioned German that appears in the speech of Ehrenfried Kumpf who teaches Adrian some of his theology, in the prayers of the composer's young nephew Echo, and in the style of his own letters.* It also haunts Kaisersaschern, the town of his youth with its traces of "the hysteria of the waning Middle Ages"

---

* Mann's mocking parody of Luther's style in some of these passages indicates that he had come to share something of Nietzsche's view of him as a "calamity of a monk" who had led a reaction back to a medieval outlook. Mann thus rejects the modernizing pathos with which Deutschlin speaks of Luther during Adrian's years as a theology student (F, 158). But his countervailing image chosen from the families of Renaissance popes differs significantly from Nietzsche's. The philosopher had flaunted a preference for the Borgias; but in his early play *Fiorenza* the novelist had opposed the Luther-like Savonarola with the Medicis, probably in conscious reaction against the Cesare Borgia Nietzscheans he so despised at the time. Later, he develops an explicit contrast between Luther and Erasmus, whose distant spiritual descendant is the Catholic humanist Zeitblom.

(F, 52); and it helps determine the cultural attitudes to be found in several of his compositions. He can be drawn by both *Love's Labour's Lost*, on the threshold of the seventeenth century but mocking the humanists, and by the possibilities for a comic treatment of medieval piety offered by the *Gesta Romanorum*. The Faust legend itself epitomizes his situation of being suspended between two different epochs and drawn in contradictory directions by them. Theme of Leverkühn's last major work and mythical pattern for much of his life, it dates from the sixteenth century and mingles secular striving with the theme of damnation. Allusions such as these to the confused period before the establishment of the new age's premises serve a double purpose. They provide an analogue for the disintegration of cultural form in the present and set this modern world in a long temporal perspective going back to its origins.

Along with delimiting the epoch of bourgeois humanism, *Doctor Faustus* conveys a specific sense of the process of cultural change within the epoch. Gunilla Bergsten has already shown the almost encyclopedic thoroughness of the novel's allusions to key events in German intellectual history from Luther onward, and especially to religion and music.[17] But she has neglected Mann's patterning of this essayistic material so as to suggest an inverse relationship between cult and culture. It is the development of this relationship that explains the growth and then the decline of a humanistic age. Music becomes a cultural force when it separates from religion in the Renaissance; it traverses an ascending curve that peaks with Beethoven, but it continues to thrive in the rich variety of late nineteenth-century musicians, led by Wagner, whom Leverkühn studies during his apprenticeship. Only when Adrian's own generation comes to maturity does a crisis in musical creativity take place. Meanwhile the forces of cult have been declining into the trough of nineteenth-century religious liberalism, where they are "reduced to a function of the human" (F, 122). Then, during his theological studies, Adrian is introduced to their ambiguous reawakening, spearheaded by Schleppfuss's enthusiasm for the autos-da-fé of the "classical age of belief." Mann's presentation of modernity is thus characterized by a reversal of energies in cult and culture which recalls the situation Yeats had called, in his even more elaborate system of speculative cultural history, an interchange of the tinctures.[18]

This historical scheme implies an attitude toward the religious that differs markedly from the one that emerged during Adrian's interview with the devil. For Mann the forces that are undermining a golden age of humanism are religious in origin; from the desire to replace a stark naturalism with a sense for the transcendental, he shifts to revulsion at the excesses of cults and a preference for secular culture. These divided attitudes will be examined in more detail in the next section. For the moment, we need to consider how Mann moves from essayistic to fictive methods in presenting the cultural process when he turns to the present. On this general subject, Theodor Adorno has usefully commented that critics can sometimes pay too much attention to the novel's ideas at the expense of its specifically literary qualities.[19] This observation is especially telling, of course, because Mann drew so much of the discursive material in *Doctor Faustus* from Adorno.

With some scenes, a passing allusion serves to connect concrete details of setting or dramatic situation with some aspect of bourgeois humanism as it enters its period of crisis. For example, during Adrian's theological studies, the members of the Winfried Society go on long excursions into the surrounding countryside, where they enjoy roughing it and being close to nature. These outings are presented as brief relaxations of the reigning order, an escape from the "sphere of bourgeois comfort" (F, 155) or an interruption in lives which were soon "destined to return to bourgeois existence" (F, 169-170). Many topics in the students' discussions during these trips foreshadow the eventual breakdown of this bourgeois world when the Nazis rise to power. Adrian's first meeting with the prostitute shifts the emphasis from intellectual factors to social and economic ones. It occurs during the Leipzig fair, and Mann has his hero's letter mention the throngs "from all parts of Europe, and besides from Persia, Armenia, and other Asiatic lands" (F, 187). Indeed, the taxi driver who will guide him to the brothel begins speaking to him in snatches of French and English (F, 189), indicating that he has probably mistaken him for one of these pleasure seekers. The bourgeois city is evidently turning into a cosmopolitan metropolis, while the driver's total failure to understand Adrian's motives suggests the advent of a commercialism that replaces humanistic understanding with easy stereotypes.

With the story of the Rodde family, Mann relies extensively on conventional narrative to present his view of the cultural process. Part of the wider world introduced into *Doctor Faustus* after Adrian's move to Munich, this story focuses on the culminating period of bourgeois humanism, when the cultural form enters its crisis of dissolution. The background of the mother, wife of a senator in Bremen and closely resembling Mann's own mother, expresses his characteristic sense of the bourgeois. Based on the commercial and banking city-states of the late Middle Ages in Germany and Italy, it lies behind his choice of Lübeck, Hamburg, Venice, and Florence as settings in some of his major works. In *Reflections of an Apolitical Man* he had elevated this primarily central European definition, which stressed continuity and a "concrete" loyalty to native city, over the Western European conception.[20] There, the bourgeois was the heir to revolutions—the Puritan revolution in England and, of course, the French revolution in France—and considered himself, more abstractly, to be the citizen of a nation-state. For this version of the middle class Mann uses the French word *bourgeois*; for the other he reserves the German term *Bürger*. Despite the polemical intent of *Reflections*, he concedes that even in Germany, from at least the time of national unification, the "Bürger" has been steadily giving way before the "bourgeois." He interprets his first novel, *Buddenbrooks*, as the artistic expression of this historical process.

The Roddes' story maintains this perspective. Hence Mann does not intend a "symbolic" foreshadowing when he starts with experiences that come a generation before such dramatic events as the world war or the inflation. The crisis of the "Bürger" begins with the loss of a settled position in a native city. After Senator Rodde's death, the family discovers that they lack the money to maintain their standing in Bremen; seeking a new social identity, they move to Munich, a change that also suggests the emergence of a new Germany with the national horizons of a Western European state. But rather than evolving into "bourgeois," the family enters into an uneasy relationship with a world of art that has little in common with Adrian's lonely struggle for creative innovation. For them, the aesthetic becomes a measure of their inability to find a satisfactory new structure to their lives. Mrs. Rodde begins by responding warmly to the art world of Munich, even through she only gets to know it in the form of a "housebroken Bohemianism" (F, 261). But in the end she remains bound to the past. She gives a conventional bourgeois excuse for her active social life when she says that she needs to get her daughters established; and once she has fulfilled that obligation, she retires to the country where she lives among the relics of her Bremen furniture (F, 432).

For her daughters the pressures of finding a new role have intensified. For them, the collapse of the former order of the "Bürger" has been more extreme, while the artistic interests to which they devote themselves turn out to be morbid. They follow complementary paths to the discovery that neither world is a living alternative. Cut adrift, they move from decadence to suicidal nihilism and tragedy.

Clarissa begins with "a conscious, deliberate, and pronounced" rejection of her background and plunges into an acting career (F, 262). But she lacks real talent, and her most genuine artistic interests run toward death's heads and the macabre. At last she attempts to go back to her bourgeois roots and becomes engaged to an Alsatian businessman; then her theatrical life interferes when a former backstage lover causes the marriage to be broken off. After this collision between her two possible ways of life, her morbid tendencies come to the fore and she commits suicide. Inez's first step, on the other hand, is to try to win back "the old paternal, middle-class strictness and dignity" (F, 263); in marrying Helmut Institoris, she gains financial security, at least until the postwar inflation sharply reduces his fortune. But there is a suppressed aesthetic side to her character: she has written distinctly decadent poetry and chosen a husband with an arty veneer. This side breaks loose when she forms her scandalous liaison with the violinist Schwerdtfeger. When he betrays her, she too enters a void between two possible social roles and becomes decidedly suicidal before she murders him. She becomes a morphine addict, and welcomes the destructive effects of the drug for loosening the "unworthy chain and ignoble burden" of existence (F, 512).

Mann's portrayal of the Roddes, for all the independence it shows in choice of material, has the general outlines of a Nietzschean drama of decadence: it suggests an epoch entering the terminal stage where cultural form begins to disintegrate. The specific definition of this epoch in terms of bourgeois humanism derives mainly from Mann's own situation and experience. But his conception of humanism overlaps with Nietzsche's admiration for the Renaissance, his distrust of the Reformation, and his critique of religious transcendence. With his sense of the bourgeois, he joins the philosopher in dating Germany's decline from the founding of the unified national state. He comes closer to Nietzsche when he focuses on the incipient breakdown of cultural form as it manifests itself in a decadent artistry where a great deal of superficial activity masks a movement away from life-affirmation. The aesthetic, as the Roddes encounter it, reveals itself to be the expression of deathly instincts in people who have been unable to devise satisfactory responses to the passing of their way of life. But by shifting from Wagner to turn-of-the-century aestheticism in Munich, Mann has brought his own experiences to bear on the general issue of artistic movements and social mood.

In the concluding phase, where even decadent form is swept aside by suicidal nihilism, Mann hints at a parallel between the Rodde sisters and the last years of the Third Reich. He does so very delicately, having none of Tolstoy's ambitions to rival the historians in their own field; Zeitblom's excursions into the narrative present are a bare recital of events as they might appear to someone who lived through them. Moreover, the parallel does not extend to moral qualities but is limited to the psychology of nihilism; Zeitblom obviously respects both Inez and Clarissa, who were modelled on Mann's own two sisters.[21] Still, even though the women play "a very insignificant role in the general course of world history," he identifies both their fate and that of the Nazis as the "growth of catastrophe" (F, 397). As it too breaks loose from the cultural form of bourgeois humanism, a nihilistic Germany rages destructively against the world and finally brings destruction upon itself. In addition to this very broad parallel between different parts of his story, Mann sometimes becomes more specific in applying Nietzsche's thinking about nihilism to the Nazis. Right after World War II he called his prediction in *The Case of Wagner* of a classic age of war an "astonishingly prophetic anticipation" (W IX, 699). In the novel itself, in chapter 46, Zeitblom's account of Germany's "rapidly broadening catastrophe" refers to the Nazi leaders as "vowed to nothingness from the beginning" and specifies that "suicide is raging" among them (F, 636, 638).

□

Is Leverkühn's story intended to suggest the same broad historical parallels that we have seen in the Roddes? This question will eventually lead to a set of social themes whose relation to Nietzsche is much more intricate than the application of shared premises and attitudes to somewhat different problems. At first glance, however, it may be tempting to see Leverkühn as yet another representative figure. After all, Zeitblom's prayer at the end of the novel places the man and the age in apposition—"God be merciful to thy poor soul, my friend, my fatherland!" (F, 676)—and would seem to justify some sort of equation between the artist's tragic fate and the historical disasters of the Hitler era. Yet to identify the two in any rigid way, as has sometimes occurred in criticism of *Doctor Faustus*, would be a mistake. Though Mann certainly conceived of Leverkühn as a typical modernist, he was very aware of how problematic the linkage could be between complex works of art and the social and political issues of their age. In particular, he had learned a great deal from his varied and deeply divided responses over the years to the historical implications of Nietzsche's writings. Since *Doctor Faustus* draws so heavily on Nietzschean material, it is not surprising that traces of this ambivalent experience appear in the novel and often have a direct bearing on Mann's conception of Leverkühn.

Mann made at least four major attempts to define what image of society one gets from Nietzsche; again and again he was forced to admit that everything depends on the spirit in which he was read. We have seen in Chapter II his opposition at the turn of the century to the Nietzscheans who took the philosopher's admiration for the Italian Renaissance all too literally. Mann stressed the superficiality of these aesthetes, who seized upon a few striking phrases but disregarded the underlying concern for understanding the nature and destiny of man. This "ethical atmosphere"—as Mann, quoting Nietzsche, called it—showed the persistence in him of the North German, Protestant tradition into which he had been born (W:XII, 538-543). Later, during the First World War, he tried to make Nietzsche into a spokesman for his version of conservative nationalism. But he could not help feeling dissatisfied with his own one-sidedness: a full interpretation could not stop with piecing together fragmentary opinions but had to take into account the overarching impact of his style. Viewed in this way, Nietzsche had used "extremely Western methods"; essentially, therefore, he was a European figure and not a German nationalist (W:XII, 82-88).

After Mann renounced his conservatism in the 1920s, he came to grips with Oswald Spengler's prophecy of the fall of democracy and the rise of dictatorships. Spengler had acknowledged Nietzsche as a decisive influence upon his thinking. But Mann insists that he oversimplifies his master: his "frog cold" fatalism left out such key Nietzschean attitudes as his humanism, his tragic heroism that emphasized man's capacity for coping creatively with desperate situations, his awareness of irrational factors outside the ken of a narrow scientific determinism (W:X, 174). From Nietzsche's thinking one could develop a far more flexible and humane vision of society and history than was possible with Spengler's iron necessitarianism. Finally, after the Second World War and in the course of writing *Doctor Faustus*, Mann reconsidered the problem in "Nietzsche's Philosophy in the Light of Our Experience." Conceding the existence of ruthless statements all too similar to Nazi practice, he quotes others just as expressive of a socialist humanism, then suggests that Nietzsche's distress early in 1888 at the death of Friedrich III (the liberal "one hundred days" Kaiser) indicated a more abiding and ingrained allegiance. But basically Nietzsche was without conscious political commitments, a conclusion that Mann tempers with the insight that aloofness is itself a political stance (W:IX, 700-706, 708-709).

The specific questions addressed in these meditations find their way into *Doctor Faustus* along with the double perspective that plays off narrow and limiting versions of Nietzsche against broader possibilities. Thus we have seen how the proto-Fascistic intellectuals in the Kridwiss Circle both draw on the philosopher and distort him. A more detailed and prominent example would be the radical conservatism of Chaim Breisacher, whose mood of cultural crisis often recalls Nietzsche. He too has a general outlook which sees "in the whole history of culture nothing but a process of decline" (F, 371); he too deplores the petrifaction of religious myth into morality (F, 377) and praises Old Testament Jews for having an "effectively present national God" who was not abstract or transcendent (F, 374). But to take Nietzsche's historical sketches completely at face value is already a doubtful procedure, and Breisacher becomes laughable in his literalism when he misuses the philosophy of power. A cosmology that substituted dynamic forces for atoms is applied to the question of a national census, which he criticizes for its "mechanizing . . . dissolution by enumeration of the dynamic whole into similar individuals" (F, 376).[22]

In other scenes Leverkühn has the role of defending basic Nietzschean attitudes against overly limited interpretations. In the chapter describing the Winfried Society the theology students discuss ideas which show Nazi ideology at an earlier stage than with the Kridwiss Circle. The setting is near the philosopher's childhood home—Naumburg is explicitly mentioned (F, 154)—and characteristically Nietzschean topics are much in evidence. We hear talk of the "immediacy of life" (F, 158), of "herd existence" (160), of the "bipolar attitude" (168), of the interaction of depth and form (166), of the "psychology of drives" (167), of a critique of utilitarianism (162), and so forth. Yet, although many of these ideas become absorbed in the budding nationalism of Deutschlin and von Teutleben (both names evoke "Germanness"), Leverkühn's choice of a wider perspective is also Nietzschean. On several occasions, he refuses to accept their arguments for German uniqueness and chooses a European outlook instead. The same supranational attitude reappears at the beginning of World War I, when Adrian has confused but negative memories of the Winfried debates as Zeitblom delivers some elaborate patriotic arguments (F, 408-410). After the war he continues to keep his distance from proto-Fascistic and nationalistic ideas. What popularity his music has during the Weimar years comes from a "republican-minded public" (F, 516); in the Hitler period his work is consigned to obliv-

ion as "cultural Bolshevism" (F, 643; cf. 515). It is true that
at a moment of frustrated creativity he can fantasize to himself about "a war, a revolution" that might break his torpor
(F, 602), but in society his inclinations are moderate: thus he
discusses Bach with a social-democratic deputy at one of the
rare evening parties he still attends (F, 563).

Two other strands in Mann's response to Nietzsche's social significance emerge from the contrast between Leverkühn and several personalities from the mediocre art world
in Munich. Institoris, with his frantic admiration for the
Renaissance and with a daughter he has named Lucrezia, is
a turn-of-the-century Nietzschean. But when Leverkühn
himself goes to Italy, the underlying North German strain in
his character is decisive: he is visited by a Lutheran devil,
and the Dionysian south that was so important for Lawrence
and Gide has no effect on his sensibility. Adrian's friend,
who is actually named Spengler and is also a syphilitic artist,
provides another contrast. While the composer becomes creative as a result of his disease, somewhat in the manner of
Nietzsche who in *Ecce Homo* had attributed his intellectual
achievements to his illnesses, Spengler absorbs some of the
philosopher's more superficial characteristics. Calling himself a free spirit, he reads authors like the Abbé Galiani and
the Goncourt brothers (F, 310, 271). Though not totally un-
attractive, he is a failure as an artist—in the devil's words, a
"banal, tedious case, productive of nothing at all" (F, 310).

Zeitblom's prayer itself should be seen as the culmination
of Mann's practice of weaving his divided attitude about
Nietzsche's social role into the very fabric of his novel. Undoubtedly, as it raises the possibility of grace at the end of a
story about a devil's pact and damnation, it addresses religious concerns best treated in the next section. But, as a last
judgment on a character who functions in so many ways as
the philosopher's alter ego, the prayer also represents a rich
transformation of the conclusion Mann had reached again
and again in assessing Nietzsche. The spirit, finally, is more
important than the letter.

□

But the problem of Leverkühn's social role cannot be resolved simply by analyzing how Mann dramatized his various ambivalences about Nietzsche. We have not yet allowed
for one of the most strikingly original features of *Doctor
Faustus*, the attempt to give a detailed description of the artist-hero's work. If Leverkühn's hermetic isolation from the
world, or his explicit social sympathies, or the kind of audience to which he appeals do not parallel the rise of Hitlerism; if he steers clear of the negative possibilities embodied
in the Winfried Society and the Kridwiss Circle, and in
Breisacher and Spengler and Institoris, nevertheless there is
still one way in which he can be related to his age. It may be
that in itself the musical career that is placed so vividly before
the reader is somehow symptomatic of the German catastrophe.

In focusing on this question, Mann gave a vigorous twist
to Nietzsche's own thinking about art and society. *The Case
of Wagner*, with its premise of aesthetic politics, had taught
him that the best way of gauging the social implications of
art was to consider both the artist's general goals and his
specific techniques in handling his medium. But the twentieth century had alerted Mann to the dangers of authoritarianism, had shown him that nihilism could come in the guise
of dictatorial rigor as well as of anarchy. As a result, when
he depicts the achievement of this modernist composer, he
asks whether the Nietzschean ideal of a strict style having
the "rigorous logic" of classicism might not be as socially
problematic as Wagnerian formlessness. In the end, however, Mann's treatment of this theme as well coils back to
his root sense for the complexity of the relationship between
works of art or intellect and their historical context.

Leverkühn sums up his general aspirations for a new music
that will surpass the limitations of his age by using the slogans of rebarbarization and breakthrough. Kretzschmar's lectures had wakened his interest in the first notion: he comes
to deny that culture and barbarism are absolute opposites (F,

82); he admires music for having "elemental" qualities that permit it to return to earlier stages in its development (F, 86-87); he becomes fascinated with the example of Beissel, the self-taught composer who went back to the very origins of music (F, 94-95). As an adult he encounters the idea of break-through, which he calls the "one problem in the world" be-cause it means innovation in the grand style, the possibility of a qualitative, metamorphic change: "How can one burst the cocoon and become a butterfly?" (F, 410). The devil bluntly brings the two aims together when he predicts of Adrian: ". . . you will break through the epoch of culture and its cult and dare the barbaric, which is twice so because it comes after the humane, after all possible root-treatment and bourgeois refinement" (F, 324). These visions of a new art surpassing the categories of bourgeois humanism corre-spond to the primitivism and utopianism in confronting dec-adence that Mann had met in turn-of-the-century Nie-tzscheans. But these attitudes are no longer viewed as foolishly wishful dreams but as harbingers of sinister social forces. Zeitblom enlarges on the devil's words in his role as a mediator between private and public worlds. He calls Beis-sel an "archaic revolutionary" who exemplifies a German penchant for labeling as progress what is really a return to the past (F, 252); his digressions about his life under the Na-zis have already provided far more extreme instances of this trait, a rebarbarization in actual fact. Alternatively, at the be-ginning of World War I, Zeitblom identifies a wide-ranging transformation of German life as a breakthrough: a subordi-nation of cultural freedom to the demands of the state, the rise of a spirit of military socialism, the assumption of the status of a world power (F, 399-401).

Yet after pointing up these connections between Leverkühn's artistic goals and historical forces that lead toward Hitler, Mann reaffirms the distinction between the two realms. Zeitblom's speculations about the social meaning of rebar-barization and breakthrough occur in conversations with Adrian, but do not disturb his friend's artistic aspirations.

They seem to exist on a different plane, to have their own internal logic. In fact, Zeitblom discovers new implications for Adrian's slogans when he tries to interpret his two masterpieces. The charge that the *Apocalypse* oratorio is barbaric awakens "the most tormenting doubts" in him, with which he struggles at great length (F, 495-497; 499-501). Could the work be called barbaric because the aesthetic is closely allied with barbarism (a view that implicitly denies the self-heightening of aesthetic naturalism)? Or, more specifically, does barbarism mean a reliance on techniques from the earliest stages of music, like the glissando, the freedom in changing rhythm, or the borrowing from primitive rituals? Or, rather, could it refer to the oratorio's "streamlined" qualities, its loud-speaker effects, its use of jazz, its style of singing that imitates radio bulletins? Or, finally, could people be calling the work barbaric simply because of its apparent soullessness? After considering all these possible meanings for the term, Zeitblom at last decides that it has no real relevance to Leverkühn's work at all. Then, when he discusses the Faust *Lamentation*, he finds a breakthrough of an unexpected kind. In a transformation that has little to do with contemporary German history, Leverkühn's "calculating coldness" has become an "expressive resonance from the soul and a heartfelt revelation of the creaturely self" (F, 643). Adrian's half-mad confession enlarges on this implicit discrepancy between art and history: "But if someone invite the devil as guest, so as to get beyond this [i.e., the crisis of art] and come to the breakthrough, he burdens his soul and takes the guilt of the time on his own shoulders, so that he is damned" (F, 662). His work relates to its age not as a symptom but as a compensation; it gets its power from overcoming or purging those evils which the artist, as a representative man, has experienced in his personal life.

At the level of specific techniques are Adrian's preferences for polyphony and what he calls a strict style. These goals come to be associated with issues like the decline of rationality, a disregard for the rights of the individual, and the rise of dictatorship; indeed, it could be argued that Mann pays more attention to these social analogues than to the musical techniques themselves. Normally he draws a contrast between polyphony, which he usually associates with counterpoint, and the implications of harmony and melody. In part, this contrast relates back to the overarching polarity of Apollo and Dionysus. Zeitblom's tendency toward the "harmonic" is linked to his Apollinian rationality (F, 10), while Leverkühn's youthful admiration for a Dionysian naïveté and unconsciousness expresses itself in enthusiasm for the "old contrapuntal polyphonic culture" (F, 83). From another viewpoint polyphony becomes the appropriate style for an age of rising social disorder; thus Adrian can see harmonic music as a "lie" given "the total uncertainty, the problematic situation, and lack of harmony of our social conditions" (F, 241).

But the most important sociocultural analogue for this musical technique derives from Kretzschmar's distinction of "harmonic subjectivity, polyphonic objectivity" (F, 73). Harmony is linked to individualism, to "an ego painfully isolated in the absolute," while polyphony expresses "an abandonment of self" which leads to "the mythical, the collectively great" (F, 73, 74). These last phrases are ambiguous and acquire positive meanings later in the novel; but at first they point toward a sinister undermining of individual freedoms, such as occurs in Schleppfuss's lectures describing the religious authoritarianism of the Middle Ages. Adrian comes to praise "objective disciplining" over what he sees as "subjective demoralization" (F, 161); Zeitblom's defense of freedom he dismisses as a "political song" which overlooks the fact that "freedom is another word for subjectivity" (F, 253-254). The modern situation has brought a reversal: people now seek "shelter and security in the objective." Again it is Zeitblom who remains aware of the social dimension; he likens this reversal to a "dictatorship born out of revolution" which no longer deserves the name of freedom.

The ideal of a strict style raises the same issues as polyphony, but it also underlines Mann's polemical relationship to Nietzschean aesthetic politics. Strict style expresses Leverkühn's concern as an artist for a thorough organization of his material, a concern that leads to sweeping generalizations about the need for order which are highly questionable when extended to society. A particularly telling example would be Adrian's interest in Kretzschmar's lecture on Beissel, for this composer was also the strong-willed leader of a sectarian community. "Even a silly order is better than none at all" (F, 94), he declares of this man, who is called a "backwoods dictator" (F, 93) and whose music uses a rigid system of what he calls master and servant notes (F, 90). Mann's conception of Leverkühn's stylistic goals is thus the obverse of Nietzsche's analysis of stylistic decadence. Rather than the "anarchy of atoms" suitable to a democratic social order, he presents a polyphonic strict style linked to dictatorship. This revision may be traced to the later Mann's awareness of a broad affinity between some aspects of Nietzsche and twentieth-century Fascism. The "rigorous logic" of a classical style, which the philosopher saw as a cure for decadence, has become part of the problem.

Mann's exploration of aesthetic politics comes to a head in chapter 34. Chronicling Zeitblom's simultaneous involvement with the postwar intellectual scene and with his friend's composition of *Apocalypsis cum figuris*, this chapter brings the theme of art and society to a focus much as the interview with the devil did with Leverkühn's inner life. There is no need to show how Mann interweaves the topics of breakthrough and rebarbarization, of polyphony and the strict style, so as to produce a dramatic convergence of hitherto separate themes. But the imagery that enters the novel as a result of Leverkühn's immersion in the apocalyptic tradition does deserve mention, for it provides a set of concrete equivalents for these ideas. Underlying all four notions is the prospect of a radical redefinition of musical form and the birth of a new epoch; they propound a secular version of the end which is in rich accord with Leverkühn's choice of subject.

Moreover, the violence and primitive horror of the Book of Revelations is suitably barbaric, while Adrian's syncretistic approach that draws on other versions of apocalyptic myth recalls his stylistic goal of drawing many voices into an intense unity.

As this three-part chapter juxtaposes the artistic and social realms by moving from Adrian to Munich and back to Adrian, it allows Mann to clarify the distinction between them. The intellectuals in the Kridwiss Circle are part of the same historical current dramatized by the Roddes; as Zeitblom recognizes, their active sympathy for the fall of bourgeois humanism enables them to interpret the event and give it intellectual substance. But he insists that Adrian's oratorio, though it undeniably had "a peculiar correspondence" (F, 493) or even "coincided most precisely" (F, 494) with their ideas, exists "on a higher, more creative level" (F, 470). Mann has revised the very outlook of aesthetic politics. The artist does respond to the same cultural tendencies which find expression in history; as a result his works will often contain suggestive analogies with his social environment. But genuine creativity will also look beyond the limitations of its age, whether by understanding its problems in a richer sense or by glimpsing entirely different possibilities. No perfect equation between a great work of art and a given historical moment is possible. Leverkühn should be contrasted with Daniel zur Höhe, the mediocre artist who is totally possessed by his time. The creator of a Christus Imperator Maximus who exhorts military hordes to plunder the earth, he is the better spokesman for an age of dictatorship and war (F, 483). In this bizarre poet, we notice once again Mann's tendency to connect religion to an extreme authoritarianism in society.

Mann heightens this sense of art's relative independence from history in several less explicit ways. At one point Zeitblom mentions how movingly Adrian's music highlights Dante's parable "of the man who carries a light on his back at night, which does not light him but lights up the path of those coming after" (F, 217). On other occasions he remarks that neither his friend's works nor his own biography of him will have an audience until after the fall of the Nazis. We are reminded that art can be bigger than its age, that beyond expressing its own world it also addresses a future which may discover entirely new meanings in it. Or, we might consider one of the most striking ironies of *Doctor Faustus*: the extent to which the novel itself exemplifies Leverkühn's idea of a totally organized work of art. Except for the foreground of musical terminology, Zeitblom's descriptions of Adrian's compositions are directly applicable to a novel remarkable for its careful interweaving of motifs and its controlled development of themes.[23] This formal self-reflexiveness emphasizes the purely aesthetic features of the strict style, qualifying still further the correlations between Leverkühn's art and the politics of his time.

As the novel closes, the issue of polyphony undergoes a transformation like the one we have already noticed in the case of artistic breakthrough. It turns out to have a whole new set of social implications; the end of individuality may suggest the rise of tyranny, but it can also mean a renewed sense of community. It is hard to find anything dictatorial in the "genuine multiplicity of voices" that characterizes the polyphony of the *Apocalypse* oratorio (F, 494); we should remember the circumstances in which Adrian first learned about the technique—it was during the childhood idyll of singing rounds with the dairymaid Hanne and his friends (F, 43). This communal aspect to polyphony becomes paramount during his last performance. Adrian's animus against harmony is still in evidence, for he strikes a "strongly dissonant chord" just before his collapse (F, 667). But the social vision in this scene has shifted away from Adrian's audience, who live in a Germany about to accept Hitler and who let the vapid exclamations of the Kridwiss Circle speak for them. It focuses on a different possibility, absent in the *Apocalypse* chapter except when Zeitblom ventured a remark on "true community" (F, 488). In calling together his friends, Adrian has moved away from isolated individuality toward interpersonal awareness and sympathy, to what Zeitblom calls "creaturely togetherness" (F, 651), and Frau Schweige-still "human understanding" (F, 667).

For Mann, the dominant trait of Leverkühn's age is the disintegration of cultural form, and his artist-hero does not remain untouched by the ensuing problems. But Adrian's creative gift ultimately removes him from the drama of decadence that conditions the lives of so many other characters in *Doctor Faustus*; his works suggest richer possibilities than their limited and disabling attempts to escape. As a result, Zeitblom's prayer can not be read as a simple equation between the fates of his friend and his nation. Rather than following the premise of aesthetic politics and seeing Leverkühn as the representative artist of bourgeois humanism in decline, he is thinking about the state of his inner life. In this prayer that mercy be shown to Adrian's soul, he directs attention to the complex of religious themes that entered the novel with the appearance of the devil and tries to resolve them.

BETWEEN *Homo Dei* AND NIETZSCHE: THE RESOLUTION TO
Doctor Faustus

Shortly after Adrian's account of the interview with his uncanny visitor, Zeitblom reports a conversation in which the two friends discussed modern theories of the structure of the universe. Characteristically, the schoolteacher distrusts these visions of cosmic immensity and argues the merits of a "religiously tinged humanism" (F, 363). Leverkühn refers to this attitude toward man as *Homo Dei*, a phrase also used by Naphta in *The Magic Mountain*.[24] But Zeitblom stands far apart from this paradoxical Jesuit whose mystique of religious terrorism anticipated Schleppfuss. For him the phrase is an emblem for how the conflicting perspectives of private metaphysics and public social philosophy might be reconciled. With *Dei* he emphasizes an inner sense of belonging "with a decisive part of one's being to a spiritual world"; he greatly prefers this "feeling for the transcendental mystery of man" to a flattened view of him as a "purely biological being." Yet to combat the authoritarianism latent in cults he needs *Homo* as a social concept, because it stresses the immanent worth and dignity of the individual. As a humanist Zeitblom removes God from the transcendent heights by using formulas like "piety, reverence, spiritual decency, religious feeling are only . . . possible through limitation to the earthly and human" or "the reverence of man before himself is God." In *Doctor Faustus*, therefore, the term *Homo Dei* fuses (somewhat deceptively, since it is inconsistent on the precise status of the spiritual) the diverging attitudes toward the religious that emerge from the two-tiered structure we have examined in the previous sections.[25]

But the various facets of Zeitblom's credo are also crucial to the novel's later development. Both the transcendent side to human nature highlighted by *Dei* and the interpersonal awareness of a shared humanity that is emphasized by *Homo* will become central issues in Adrian's inner life. Yet Mann's treatment of these values can be profoundly ambivalent. Even as his hero's fate shows how vitally important they are, it also raises disturbing questions about their ultimate validity. A leading factor behind this refusal to make any simple commitment to the *Homo Dei* is Nietzsche, whose continued impact on Mann's imagination in the second half of *Doctor Faustus* is no less significant for being less overt.

Indeed, this impact is so strong that it infuses the thickening religious atmosphere of the novel. I have already mentioned the affinity between the theme of grace as announced in Zeitblom's final words and Mann's persistent dilemma of spirit versus letter in interpreting Nietzsche. The shortcomings of theory reappear in this new context in Adrian's concern with the problem of religious "speculation"; it is now a theological self-consciousness that prevents him from responding directly and spontaneously to his situation (e.g. F, 666). And the progression of his religious experience through the states of *attritio, contritio,* and hope beyond hopelessness closely mirrors Nietzsche's psychology of the tragic. First

Mann contrasts submission to a social form, or repentance by "churchly regulation," with the immediate confrontation that comes from "inner religious conversion" (F, 328). Then, out of this new openness to the fearsome in his situation comes the reawakening of the tonic emotions that is hope beyond hopelessness (F, 329, 651). But the focus has shifted in Mann's account from the philosopher's rigorously immanent view of the human condition to consciousness of sin. In the end, such drastic shifts in vocabulary and overall perspective override the glancing and somewhat fugitive similarities that connect some of the religious themes in the second half of the novel with Nietzsche.

The relationships involving extensive revision are more detailed. Especially striking are two instances in which Mann overturns values that Nietzsche characteristically associated with the Dionysian; they stand out because they continue the theme of a shift to the demonic. Thus one effect on Adrian of his interview with the devil is to replace an innocent acceptance of self with an attitude of guilt. His visitor mocks him for his "sweet innocence" (F, 312) in not realizing the spiritual consequences of his assignation with the prostitute; he has confirmed the demonic interpretation of sexuality advanced by Schleppfuss when he called "the act of procreation . . . the expression and vehicle of original sin" (F, 140-141). It is also revealing that later, when Leverkühn briefly seeks to escape the set of his personality, he should envision an art which he associates with the aim of "a new innocence" (F, 429). His experience of the demonic has encouraged in him that contrasting sense of ingrained evil which Nietzsche had analyzed as an aspect of the psychology of inadequacy.

But Mann emphasizes that the art that grows out of Adrian's religious questioning of human nature is the equal of one inspired by life-affirmation. In the *Apocalypse* oratorio and the Faust *Lamentation* he takes damnation as his subject, and yet the two works are masterpieces. The latter piece is also polemical in another sense; in taking back Beethoven's Ninth Symphony it replaces the "Ode to Joy" in Nietzsche's prime example of Dionysian art with a music whose strength comes from an "undisguised and untransfigured expression of suffering" (F, 321). These works that testify to genuine artistic capacity show that Mann has broken with Nietzsche's criticism of Christian art. Long before, he had opposed the aesthetic stance that "only people with strong brutal instincts can create great works" by invoking Michelangelo and Tolstoy: "I knew instead that works like 'The Last Judgment' . . . and the novel *Anna Karenina* had arisen from natures which were highly moralistic, open to suffering, and scrupulously Christian" (W:XII, 539). Mann's account of aesthetic naturalism seems to reflect the attitudes of Nietzscheans rather than of Nietzsche himself, and is therefore overly primitivistic. But in Leverkühn he has chosen to portray another such artist in whom great talent coexists with images of damnation and whose achievement does not depend on an unconditional affirmation of existence.

And yet, despite the growing importance of religious themes for understanding Adrian's character, they do not fully prevail. There is a fourth phase in the devil's transformations at the inverview; as he leaves, the theological avatar collapses and he reverts to the physiological and instinctual realm of the pimp. At this point Mann introduces his version of the bargain with Mephistopheles. The result is a carefully calculated anticlimax, which represents the most interesting and audacious of his conflations of Faustian and Nietzschean material. The values of the Faust myth had been dominant during the portrayal of Adrian's inner being as demonic rather than Dionysian, but now that the perspective of aesthetic naturalism has returned, the metaphysical drama of a devil's pact suddenly evaporates. In a world where the nature of the soul and the very existence of the devil are problematic, the apparatus of legend is unnecessary: "between us there needs no crosse way in the Spesser's Wood and no cercles. We are in league and business—with your blood you have affirmed it. . . . This my visit concerns only the confirmation thereof" (F, 331). The entry of the spirochetes into

Adrian's bloodstream has replaced the document signed in blood; the devil is not a supernatural agent but an afterthought who makes his appearance years after the onset of a biological process. In true Nietzschean fashion the emphasis has shifted from a spiritual explanation to a bodily phenomenon. It is easy to understand why some early critics of the novel spoke of a world without transcendence and of the secularization of the devil, even though these formulas oversimplify Mann's ambivalent attitude.[26]

The religious dimension can also be highly problematic elsewhere in *Doctor Faustus*. In the definition of the soul provided by Zeitblom and which Mann apparently endorses in *The Story of a Novel* (W:XI, 203-204), it is an entity with little objective reality. As a fiction whose purpose is to bridge an overly sharp split between mind and body, it has lost all specifically religious meaning; it has become "a mediating instance, strongly inspired with poetry, in which intellect and instinct interpenetrate each other and become reconciled in a certain illusory manner" (F, 197). To recall Yeats's line evoking a similar unity of being, where "The body is not bruised to pleasure soul,"[27] is to realize how far Mann has departed from the word's traditional implications. From being the term in a duality which pointed to the extreme of human transcendence, the soul has become the resolved balance among paired terms which are largely immanent. Zeitblom's *Homo Dei* is evidently so free-floating on the question of the spiritual that it can accommodate this drastic shift of meaning.

With Adrian, the problematic status of the soul is the occasion for intense anguish; the question stands at the very center of his two masterpieces. Thus Zeitblom emphasizes, in his defense of the *Apocalypse* oratorio, the presence of deeply felt passages which "are like a fervid prayer for a soul" (F, 501). For his Faust *Lamentation*, in turn, Leverkühn takes as the basis of his twelve-tone system the phrase "For I die as a good and a bad Christian" (F, 646). These words were spoken by the original Faust when the devil came to claim his part of the bargain; in evoking a theological version of the myth where a soul was actually at stake, they seek to counteract the return of the pimp.

But the best expression of Adrian's inner turmoil over man's spiritual nature is his fascination with the little mermaid in Andersen's fairy tale. Even the imagery he uses in discussing the story is relevant, for it recalls his earlier fascination with the uncanny shapes produced by the osmotic growths. Thus the mermaid's visit to the sea witch in a "wood of polyps" and her desire to gain human limbs (F, 457). And the story takes up as well the accompanying challenge of a totally immanent view of the human situation. In this case, Adrian's attitude seems at first to be one of acceptance. As he talks with Zeitblom during his illness before the composition of the *Apocalypse* oratorio, he denies that "mythological combinations of the human and the animal" are monstrous and gives the mermaid the status of a "perfectly natural phenomenon"; her longings for transcendence, in the form of both a life on land and an immortal soul, he dismisses as a "yearning for an hysterically overvalued upper world" (F, 457-458). At the scene of his breakdown, however, he reverses himself. In imagining her as Hyphialta, the demonic mistress of the Faust pact, he transfers her to a religious drama; and when he confesses to preferring her human shape, his statement amounts to a denial of her "natural" realm in favor of an "upper world" (F, 663-664). Adrian's changing perceptions of the mermaid grow out of the same search after spiritual depth to be found in his music—and yet there is the ironic qualification that his tormented speech might be nothing more than a symptom of his madness.

Paralleling this ambiguous attitude toward the soul is the uncertain mode of existence of Mann's devil. At the interview Adrian argues that his visitor is only an hallucination produced by his illness (F, 312-313), while elsewhere he can refer to his whole religious training as simply a "theological virus" (F, 472). This view of the devil as the projection of a diseased state of mind becomes especially striking when considered alongside the problem of decadence. The connection was a natural one for both Mann and Nietzsche, who often conceived of decadence through images of disease. Hence Adrian's growing fixation on the devil can at times suggest a basic failure of creative power. The rigid patterning of self and art that marks his relationship to the Faust story is far removed from the playfully flexible enactment of myth that Mann envisioned at the time of the Joseph novels.[28] More explicit is Zeitblom's telling comment that links what he calls a "quiet Satanism" with various kinds of arrested growth: "envelopment, the poison of isolation, provincial stagnation, neurotic entanglement" (F, 411). Each of his diagnoses hits home to Adrian in a number of ways, but the most obvious symptom of this encapsulation is the place he chooses for his mature work; it resembles his childhood home so closely that it is almost a repetition. Leverkühn himself will eventually relate his creativity to the demonic and decadent during his breakdown. He describes a children's choir that is the supposed source of his inspiration: "At times their hair was lifted as though from hot air. . . . Out of their nostrils curled sometimes little yellow worms, crawled down to their breasts and disappeared—" (F, 665). In this deluded fantasy an infernal breeze dissolves into a repulsive image of decay; as at the close of the interview, the supernatural has collapsed into the physiological.

□

At times, therefore, the thickening religious atmosphere of *Doctor Faustus* gives way to skepticism. Whether with explicit ideas or the tendencies of the imagery, whether through ironic undercutting or the veiled revelations provided by Adrian's art and his visionary experiences, Mann contrives to waken doubts along the lines of Nietzsche's critique of Christianity as a decadent falsification of a totally immanent universe. No less intricate is his presentation of the other value associated with *Homo Dei*, a shared consciousness of the dignity of man. In the previous section we noticed one

of its manifestations in the revaluation of Adrian's polyphony to allow for a renewed communal sense. But this shift
is only part of a larger thematic movement in *Doctor Faustus*
in which Leverkühn's cold aloofness and solitude yield before a tentative concern with relationship.

Adrian occasionally criticizes his isolation as an artist in
terms that recall the most extreme doctrines of the social
responsibility of art. Thus he condemns his music in his farewell speech because it made no contribution to his age; rather
than creating an aesthetic order, he should have labored to
produce "such an order among men which would again
make a living foundation for the beautiful work" (F, 662).
But this view does not do justice to his character or to the
place within it of his artistic gift. The shift of his religious
concerns from *attritio* to *contritio* suggests that his point of
departure cannot be a submission to social form but must be
a spontaneous fulfillment of the qualities of his own nature.
Zeitblom is therefore right to object to this desire for an art
which would be the "servant of the community" and "on
intimate terms with humanity" (F, 429). In testing the premise of aesthetic politics, Mann doubted whether art was totally determined by its immediate historical context; now he
questions whether the artist can deliberately choose to give
it social relevance of some specific kind. Instead, what relevance a work has will emerge in a "highly indirect way" as
the artist gives himself to his creative project (F, 429). It is
revealing that in spite of Leverkühn's discussions of a new
art his final piece, the *Lamentation*, achieves its larger meanings only by "starting out from the subjective" (F, 643).

The theme of relationship in *Doctor Faustus* takes in much
more than these episodic calls for a social conscience. Frau
Schweigestill's emphasis on human understanding and Zeitblom's on a creaturely togetherness point toward a communal vision which may be less grand but which goes much
deeper; the novel is primarily concerned with exploring the
psychological roots of the social impulse. At issue in the last
analysis is the condition of the devil's pact which Adrian,

with his eye on mythical models, noticed immediately: "I (in an exceeding cold draught): 'What? That is new. What signifies the *clausula?*' " (F, 331). To attain a proudly self-reliant creativity and an individualistic "feeling of your power" (F, 324), he must agree to terms more blighting than traditional hellfire and damnation. Leverkühn's intense sensation of cold throughout the interview corresponds to the injunction, "Thou maist not love" (F, 331). In focusing on this conflict, *Doctor Faustus* has dramatized the most intimate of Nietzsche's self-doubts about the kind of choices enforced by his philosophy; it also reverses the direction taken by D. H. Lawrence in the years following *Women in Love* when his concerns shifted from love to power. During the last quarter of the novel a major source of interest will be Adrian's struggle to reach the source of human fellow-feeling and thus evade the condition set by the devil.

This struggle helps explain the syncretism that creeps into Leverkühn's mythic self-identification. At times during his last years he seems to move away from Faust: he grows a beard that gives him a Christ-like appearance (F, 640), he stands before Zeitblom as if on a cross in his anguish at his nephew's illness (F, 632), and the visit of the impresario Fitelberg recalls the Satanic temptation of worldly power (F, 530). His *Lamentation of Doctor Faustus* also reflects this syncretism as he draws on motifs that irregularly merge with Christian myth and depart from it. This composition can reverse Gethsemane, imitate the Last Supper, and startlingly alter the motif of the temptation (F, 650). There are, of course, many possible meanings for this softening of the sharp outlines in the novel's mythic background. Undoubtedly it contributes to the general religious atmosphere, but it also supports the sense that Adrian's Faustian—and Nietzschean—quest for power may be giving way to an awareness of love encouraged by the example of Christ. Certainly the growth of this awareness has become an important theme in the foreground of the novel. Here Mann relies on simple storytelling to an unprecedented extent; because narrative can capture the ebb and flow of relationships so vividly, it is the suitable medium for involving the reader in this latest phase of Leverkühn's life. The complicated chain of events leading to the murder of the violinist Rudi Schwerdtfeger, the attentions of the enigmatic Frau von Tolna, and the tragic death of his nephew Nepomuk Schneidewein all collaborate to test Adrian's Nietzschean attitude of existential isolation.

At first, Rudi's story involves Leverkühn in his most serious effort to reach outward to others with his art. The violinist has a sociable personality and a naive delight at performing in public that are totally foreign to the composer's nature; after all, he had chosen his career in the full knowledge that he lacked "the desire for an exchange of love with the crowd" (F, 176). But in the years following the war the growing friendship—and perhaps even love—that he feels for Rudi brings a change. Adrian finally gives in to Schwerdtfeger's long-standing request for a bravura piece that would show off his talent to good advantage; this intensely private man even attends the first performance, though he declines to appear on stage before the audience. Yet the value of this new departure is questionable. It is apparently one of his weakest mature works; in it Zeitblom notices, though perhaps jealousy colors his perceptions, "a certain concentration of interest on the art of the performer" (F, 524) that recalls warnings in *The Case of Wagner* against the transformation of art into acting. Even when social awareness means nothing more than good-natured sociability, it suits poorly with Leverkühn's genius.

Later stages of Rudi's story turn from Adrian's art to the question of whether he is capable of love at all. On the surface, events would suggest a newly awakened warmth toward others which is then tragically frustrated. Somewhat like Nietzsche with Lou von Salomé and other women, Adrian is attracted to the theater designer Marie Godeau and after several relatively casual encounters resolves to marry her. He asks Rudi to be his spokesman, but the violinist ends up making a proposal of his own and is accepted; then, before the marriage can take place, Inez Institoris shoots him for having betrayed his love affair with her. For Adrian, who has lost both a friend and the expectation of a wife, the up-shot of his naively trusting openness to relationship has been deeper isolation.

This story does not satisfy Zeitblom, however, and the biographer advances another interpretation of his friend's motives in which love has no part. Annoyed by Schwerdt-feger's importunities and primarily concerned with preserv-ing his integrity as an artist, Leverkühn had foreseen the out-come of Rudi's flirtatiousness and Inez's jealousy when he first asked him for help in courting Marie Godeau. So certain is Zeitblom of the truth of this version that he departs from strict biography and in chapter 41 invents a whole scene in Adrian's life that bears it out. But he has little solid evidence. The only explicit confirmation from Leverkühn comes dur-ing his breakdown when he accuses himself of murder (F, 664); but such is his exacerbated mood of remorse and even his insanity at this moment that he has just made his fantastic confession to demoniality with the mermaid (F, 663). More-over, Zeitblom's explanation does not confront the crucial question of whether Adrian had merely pretended to a shy affection for Marie to serve the purposes of his scheme. As a result, Rudi's story leaves a final impression of conflicting possibilities. Zeitblom's emphasis on cold-hearted manipu-lation does not totally efface the sense of frustrated impulses toward love, and so there is deepening uncertainty as to the direction of the composer's innermost feelings.

Of course, this uncertainty is not new to *Doctor Faustus*, for the coolness with which Leverkühn responds to Zeit-blom's friendship had made it an issue long before. But, by the time Rudi's tragedy begins, the mysterious Frau von Tolna has entered Adrian's life; the result is a convergence of themes that gives an additional urgency to questions about his feelings toward others. It is not completely impossible that this woman might be the prostitute from whom he con-tracted syphilis. She is the widow of a dissipated Hungarian nobleman; she takes a doctor with her during her travels, a practice "which made one suspect that she was in delicate health"; she is very careful that Adrian should never catch sight of her (F, 518-520). Except for these tantalizing hints, Mann delights in placing the reader in a situation where further conjecture must fail due to unreliable data. Perhaps the scene in the brothel would suggest that the prostitute could never have become as cultured as Frau von Tolna so obviously is, yet it is also true that the woman first touched Adrian because of her interest in the music he was playing; whatever the case, the decisive point about the whole episode is that it is another of those creative reconstructions in which Zeitblom turns from biography to fiction (F, 198). On another level entirely, because they can hardly be ascribed to Zeitblom as Mann has characterized him, are some sly allusions in the text which encourage the reader to link the prostitute with Hungary. Included in the account of Adrian's visit to Pressburg is the seemingly irrelevant information that the town's name in Hungarian is Pozsony (F, 205), while Schleppfuss in his story of Heinz and Bärbel is curiously specific in mentioning that his hero's first experience of impotence came with a "slut, a Hungarian woman it was" (F, 144).

These uncertainties and mystifications about Frau von Tolna's real identity sharpen the reader's interest in whether Adrian is capable of love. If his hidden benefactress is really the woman in the brothel, then he has known at least one genuine relationship—and one that has been remarkably intense. Of course, this possibility is merely hypothetical, and there is the further difficulty of establishing what the nature of his feelings for the prostitute had been. The best indications come on his sister's wedding day, when he discusses love while walking with Zeitblom to the pond known as the Cow Trough; but even the schoolteacher admits that the only reason for taking these remarks as the fruit of personal experience was his feeling "that there was something strangely explicit" (F, 251) behind them. Leverkühn's ideas on this occasion also seem to Zeitblom to be humanistic rather than theological (F, 251), apparently because they affirm "the element of love within sensuality" by maintaining that "every sensual act means tenderness, is a give and take of desire, a happiness through making happy, a manifestation of love" (F, 250). These words suggest that the meeting with the prostitute did more than release Adrian's creativity; it also awakened his feeling for others and for human creatureliness in general. But for some reason the composer resists Zeitblom's interpretation of his outlook, preferring to call himself a psychologist because the term expresses "a neutral position" on humanity (F, 251). And his manner can indeed be extraordinarily distant when he speaks of love as "an entirely exceptional phenomenon" which consists of awakening "a desire for strange flesh" in flesh which "is normally inoffensive to itself only" (F, 250). Perhaps he really does know only the profound and melancholy isolation to which he reacts when the two friends reach the Cow Trough: " 'Cold,' said Adrian, motioning with his head; 'much too cold to bathe.—Cold,' he repeated a moment later, this time with a definite shiver, and turned away" (F, 259).[29]

These questions about Leverkühn's inner state come to a head in the poignant Echo interlude. Nepomuk Schneidewein, the late-born child of his sister's marriage, comes to the farm for a summer visit; and despite Adrian's usual reserve, he is obviously affected by his nephew's uncommon lovableness. These feelings, it would seem, are the answer to the tantalizing enigmas posed by Rudi Schwerdtfeger and Frau von Tolna. But then Echo dies cruelly and suddenly from meningitis. In his grief Adrian announces that "*it is not to be* . . . the good and noble, what we call the human" and promises as a suitable gesture that his next work will repudiate Beethoven's Ninth Symphony (F, 634). His first unambiguous commitment to love having ended in tragic frustration, he responds with an uncompromising affirmation of his previous state of solitude.

Yet even this agonizing moment does not finally resolve

the issue of Adrian's openness to humanity. When Zeitblom sees him the next day, he is quoting Prospero's last words to Ariel in what seems to be a mood of acceptance and reconciliation (F, 635). Equally significant are the schoolteacher's suppositions about his motives. Though Adrian confesses to being the source of demonic influences that caused the child's death, Zeitblom does not build up an elaborate theory proving his responsibility as he did with Rudi's shooting; rather, he immediately objects to his words as "absurd self-accusations in the presence of blind fate" (F, 633). For Leverkühn's biographer, the basis of his return to isolation is excessive sensitivity and not cold indifference. Given this psychological complexity, love might well have proved—as Adrian himself pointed out to the devil during the interview—to be "so elastic, so awkward a concept" (F, 331) that it could be doubted whether the devil's prohibition had actually held. Certainly when Leverkühn breaks through in the *Lamentation* to a "heartfelt revelation of the creaturely self" (F, 643) or when he shows that "the human remains" through the simple act of inviting friends and acquaintances to hear him play it (F, 651), he demonstrates a persistent openness to others that belies his promise to take back the Ninth Symphony.

Then comes the breakdown, which does cast Adrian back into an unalloyed state of isolation. An early emblem for this side of his temperament almost claims him as its own; in the early days of his madness he attempts to drown himself in an icy pond near Pfeiffering, confusing the spot with the Cow Trough which had once made him shudder (F, 672-673). And the long mystery of his feelings toward Zeitblom apparently comes to an end: on one occasion he gives his friend a look which "quickly resolved, to my great grief, in gloomy repugnance" (F, 672); while at another meeting, which echoes Rohde's and Deussen's memoirs of the insane Nietzsche (F, 675),[30] Adrian doesn't even recognize him. The final results of his hesitant striving for relationship have thus been highly problematic. Perhaps the intermingled attitudes of hope and doubt with which Mann has handled this theme have been captured most memorably by the ending to *The Magic Mountain*: "Out of this universal feast of death . . . may it be that love one day shall mount?"

Certainly Leverkühn's fate compels a similar question. Even as his story dramatizes human qualities which Nietzsche excluded from the main line of his thought, it also subjects them to major qualifications that suggest the philosopher's continuing hold on Mann. On several occasions the vehicle for the undercutting is a specific event recalling the loneliness of Nietzsche's own life. Much more important, however, is the general tendency of the stories tracing Adrian's attempts at relationship. Insofar as they leave the reader uncertain about his deepest motives and feelings, they encourage radical doubts about the efficacy of love and the possibility of a real connection with one's fellows. In the end, and despite the urgency with which Mann has explored an alternate image of man, he is incapable of ruling out a Nietzschean perspective on his hero's difficulties in overcoming isolation.

The ambivalences we have explored in this section come to the surface again in the last sentence of *Doctor Faustus*. Zeitblom's prayer might certainly be read as a reaffirmation of the values of *Homo Dei*. By addressing God, he reaches toward religious transcendence; while his anxious concern for his friend expresses interpersonal awareness. Yet given what has come before, his words could seem to be mere sentimental formulas clouding stark truths. After the moments of radical skepticism about the supernatural and the dual nature of man, does it necessarily mean anything to speak of God and the soul? And after our perplexity about Leverkühn's attitude toward others, how confident can we be in the primacy of merciful forbearance and understanding? Like the deceptive osmotic growths or the look-alike butterflies in Father Leverkühn's natural history book, Zeitblom's prayer could be assigned to mutually exclusive realms. *Doctor Faustus* has ended with words that register the continued impact of Nietzsche on Mann's sensibility at the same time that they voice the aspirations of *Homo Dei*.

This resolution recalls the moments in *Death in Venice* which undercut Nietzschean attitudes without finally excluding them. As with Aschenbach's heroism of weakness and his decision to condemn the artist, but now emphasizing other issues with the intricacy and gathering urgency possible only in a long novel, Mann is voicing his conflicting allegiances as an heir to Dionysus. Zeitblom's *Homo Dei*, ever more prominent since the entry of the devil into *Doctor Faustus*, represents a rival image of man—though ironically it is one that still parallels Nietzsche in certain very general ways. But the model that had influenced Mann for so long remains a powerful force in determining stories, images, dialogues, and the overall play of meanings in the text. As a result, the values of the *Homo Dei* challenge but do not fully supplant the disturbingly vivid sense of man's radical immanence and his existential isolation to be found in the philosopher's life and thought. Though as Adrian's story develops, it becomes less explicitly Nietzschean, it still testifies to Mann's close engagement with the brilliant and unsettling writer he had first read over fifty years before.

Conclusion

This book has followed an intellectual and artistic drama whose greatest interest lies in the multitude of issues it set in motion. To disentangle them and trace their ramifications has required a resolute empiricism, an insistence at every step on specificity and substance. Precise observations such as these are important, for if the recent turn toward theory in literary studies has raised the intellectual level of criticism, it has also undermined our respect for details. As Nabokov reminded us in a somewhat different connection, a "gradual accumulation of information" is valuable, for otherwise we slip into a state of abstraction, "surrounded by more or less ghostly objects."[1]

In this spirit, as we look back on this Nietzschean current in literary modernism, with all the swirls and eddies that mark the way from *The Birth of Tragedy* to *Doctor Faustus*, let us think first of its remarkable variety. It involves much more than the simple fact of Nietzsche's impact on writers, well known in spite of occasional attempts to minimize it. The really important element has been the many whats and hows of that impact, the great number of initiatives provided by Nietzsche, the multitude of strategies writers could follow in appropriating him, the wealth of instances that testify to his presence in works of great literary merit. Up to now much of this detail has been unappreciated—either not noticed at all, or when noticed not set in a sufficiently broad context.

On one level, then, the findings of this book must resist summary. I would justify this outcome by returning to my distinction in Chapter I between imitative and transformative influence. Imitative influence is essentially static, so that you keep finding the same thing as you go from one writer to the next. It is relatively easy to provide a capsule statement of what has taken place. But because transformative influence is dynamic, it presents the critic with a great number of trajectories whose most important quality is their individuality and difference. Thus the peculiar relevance of specific details in this study: they are not simply evidence in support of some general thesis, they are in a very real sense the thesis itself.

Nevertheless, few people will be as satisfied as Nabokov with an accumulation of precise observations. Nor is there any need to close with an attitude of total atomism, for this book has developed some general principles and critical positions that are worth drawing together and reflecting on. To begin with, though we have followed trajectories that move in many different directions, they do obey a few simple rules. Such scenes as Adrian's shifting visions of the devil, Birkin and Ursula's debate on star equilibrium, or old Gisors's and Lilly's discourses on power illustrate some of the varied ways of handling the problem of idea and image. At one point Nietzschean ideas have inspired new images, at another his images support new ideas, while elsewhere his ideas have evoked new thoughts. In other cases, when Lawrence distinguishes Gerald's nihilism from Gudrun's decadence, or Malraux uses Hemmelrich to push further in exploring *ressentiment*, or Mann ingeniously combats Nietzsche by substituting a cholera epidemic for Dionysus and the values of *Homo Dei* for aesthetic naturalism, we have responses to Nietzsche that move along the sliding scale from model to rival. Each of these examples, of course, is simply one particular manifestation of image and idea or model and rival; other examples might well differ greatly since they could be taken from anywhere else within the range of possibilities. Rather than accentuating any single classic case, these rules of influence cover a great variety of options. This method of conceptualizing Nietzsche's impact may not satisfy those who are more comfortable with hard-and-fast definitions. But it does provide some guidance within a dynamic situation; indeed, its flexibility would seem to be suited to the kinds of developments that took place.

Within this field of transformations and shifting emphases, a second and more stable constant has been Nietzsche's literary legacy itself. As shown in Chapter II, this legacy consists of a reasonably coherent set of psychological, cultural, and philosophical problems whose intrinsic interest is reinforced by Nietzsche's various literary initiatives. It is striking that a thinker who is so notorious for the number and diversity of his ideas should seem so consistent once he is viewed from the perspective of writers directly inspired by him. But this consistency becomes less surprising once it is seen to be a result of the distinctiveness and integrity of a Nietzschean current in literary modernism.

The notion of a literary legacy is especially interesting because it opens up a new way of thinking about the relation between thought and literature. Students have often turned to philosophical systems or ideologies to gain critical perspective on literature; or, conversely, they have tried to ascertain how literary issues fit into the general history of ideas. But this book has investigated a much more intimate relation, one in which a body of thought has a major, direct impact on ambitious creative projects. In such a case, the critic must do more than seek to understand a thinker's whole output as an entity in itself, and will find at times that philosophical or intellectual historical approaches do not mesh with his concerns. Other questions come to the fore, such as the meaning of a body of thought in light of the imaginative works it has nourished, the extent to which it follows literary strategies in pressing influential points, its potential for ambivalence and divergence, or the presence of connection and system among those parts that had an impact. This kind of analysis should result in new interpretations of the thinker's achievement. At this point the reader may object that Nietzsche's impact on writers is so exceptional that this model for relating thought to literature could apply to very few other cases. That could be true, though the problem needs more study. But at least the concept of a literary legacy does enlarge our repertory of models; it should also alert us to instances of direct literary appeal in other, less strikingly literary thinkers.

As for the way in which writers actually appropriate Nietzsche, this process could be grasped only after allowing for the intrinsic qualities of the work in which the Nietzschean material appears. Thus the unfolding tripartite structures of *The Immoralist* and *Death in Venice*, or the involuted chronology of the story line in *The Walnut Trees of the Altenburg* provides an essential basis for understanding the allusions and references in those stories. The major novels treated in this book are sufficiently complex for there to be several axes of interpretation along which the appropriation of Nietzsche takes place. In *Women in Love* Lawrence's fuller exploration of his material imagination coincides with a more traditional interest in the developing relationships of two couples. In *Man's Fate* Malraux is preoccupied with two levels of meaning, the cultural and the psychological, both of which result in richly nuanced and coherent stories. With *Doctor Faustus* appropriation occurs in three distinct thematic waves, often intermingled but reaching separate peaks as the novel progresses. To evaluate and interpret the way Nietzsche contributes to such ambitious creative projects, it was necessary to focus in turn on each of these artistic strategies.

In other words, the trajectories followed in this book move from one system to another. Beginning with a coherent set of issues in Nietzsche's writings, they end up being integrated into the complex aesthetic structures generated by major literary works. The remarkable fullness of this integration has several major consequences.

In general, it means that Nietzsche's impact on modernist writers can go very deep indeed, to a point where it intersects with the most basic imaginative conceptions. Though I am far from insisting that literature should rely on images to the exclusion of ideas, and would point to the occasions when Nietzsche's heirs respond to him discursively (as in

Birkin's sermonizing) or through some mixture of modes (as with the interplay of symptomatic discourse and vivid images in the account of Adrian's theoretical phase), still direct contact has gone furthest when it becomes directly presentational. Among Nietzsche's heirs, his insights could be so compelling that they inspire concrete enactment. Consider the route traveled by Mann from the discussion of a "Doric" art in the second chapter of *Death in Venice* to Aschenbach's vision of Tadzio against the backdrop of sun and sea, by Lawrence from his comments on the nihilism of Sue Bridehead to the network of images centering on crystallization and reflected light, by Malraux from his contemplation of disaggregation to the splendid suggestiveness and economy of his portrait of Ch'en, or by Mann again from the meandering reflections in his essay on Nietzsche to the enigmatic presence of the osmotic growths. Nietzsche has colored the outlook of these writers not simply on the intellectual level, important though it is for a full appreciation of their art. He remains a crucial factor even when it comes to the details of masterful literary invention.

More specifically, the discovery of such a close relationship between a thinker and some writers changes our attitude toward some major works in modern literature. At the level of isolated passages or episodes, the connection with Nietzsche makes it possible to develop more precise and detailed interpretations. Here I must refer the reader back to the various close readings of novels and stories, some of which cast new light on famous cruxes in the critical literature while others draw attention to previously neglected points. On a somewhat broader scale, these readings also illuminate major tendencies in entire works. Thus we have learned how an underlying engagement with *The Birth of Tragedy* accounts for the structure of two great short novels, or how Mann's themes of bourgeois humanism and the artist's place in society, as they are developed in *Doctor Faustus*, depend on Nietzsche's epochal thinking and on his attitude of aesthetic politics. Or, similarly, we have come to see Nietzsche's role in getting Lawrence to transform the love story into a thought-adventure, and to appreciate the priority of Nietzschean concerns over Marxist ones in *Man's Fate*, a novel so often stereotyped as a product of the social consciousness of the thirties. At all points, evaluation has accompanied analysis. Since the focus throughout has been on works of great literary ambition and merit, we have normally encountered Nietzsche's influence as it contributes to artistic successes. But there have been failures or problems—most notably Lawrence's disappointing course as a novelist after his major new work in *Women in Love*, but also Gide's glancing treatment of social issues in *The Immoralist*, the inconsistent attitudes toward transcendence to be found in *Doctor Faustus*, or Malraux's facile use of the walnut trees in the scene of the gas attack.

To move from single works to the shape of developing careers, the Nietzschean element has highlighted important continuities in the writers' imaginations. Thus Lawrence's novels after *Women in Love* exploit the technical discovery in "Mino" of an idea-image cluster that could at once give meaning and shape to a narrative situation, be tilted variously toward symbolism or argument, and embody a response to Nietzsche. In Malraux's fiction a great many characters and situations originate with brief comments in his early and heavily Nietzschean essayistic writings, while *The Walnut Trees of the Altenburg* sharpens and extends the concern in *Man's Fate* with dramatizing problems of life-psychology and cultural identity. With *Death in Venice*, written more than thirty years before *Doctor Faustus*, Mann masterfully anticipates the technique of successive avatars and especially the figure of the insolent pimp, makes a first move toward a religious evaluation of aesthetic naturalism, and introduces the strategy of severely questioning Nietzsche within a cross-cutting structure that does not finally eliminate the Nietzschean viewpoint.

Moreover, the Nietzschean phase in each of these careers suggests a distinctive way of responding to an influential predecessor. Some schema in the manner of Harold Bloom would be inappropriate, since even a single work will have examples of various stages in the shift from model to rival. Nonetheless, it is possible to identify three overall tendencies. Lawrence's sharp hostility toward Nietzsche does not exclude a great deal of unacknowledged acceptance; indeed, the hostility might be a factor in the high artistic level of his work at this point, since Lawrence's novels decline in quality once the confrontation slackens off. To some extent Gide's uneasiness about Nietzsche also attests to how critical distance can mask or even prepare the way for a far-reaching assimilation. Malraux, by contrast, freely acknowledges Nietzsche as a predecessor, though in limiting himself to vague generalities he perhaps reveals a final lack of candor. But as his novels explore problems like life-psychology or the quest for empire, Malraux's response moves closer to some of Nietzsche's basic attitudes. In this case, veneration has not prevented a growth of awareness. Finally, Mann is so self-conscious about influence that he can seem to build his career out of the tensions provoked by fascinating predecessors. When he seeks out ingenious symbolic or narrative equivalents for his acquiescence or doubt, ambivalence has become the motor for literary invention. It is clear that not only do these writers vary greatly in their attitudes toward Nietzsche, but that their attitudes have differing effects on their actual artistic practice. And there are undoubtedly other possibilities: Yeats's involvement with Nietzsche seems less crucial for any one phase of his work and less sharply focused in major poems.[2] So even when writers work with the same literary legacy, the critic must allow for their different and perhaps unique ways of integrating it into a developing artistic career.

Finally, in an even broader view, the works and careers may be taken as efforts to interpret and evaluate Nietzsche. They would then become outstanding examples of a fictive mode of response which has its own characteristic strengths as compared with other kinds of commentary. For writers whose best talents are engaged by novels and stories, this fictive mode provides a more flexible medium than discursive statements for voicing the full range of their attitudes toward Nietzsche. In the main, however, they do not conceive of their fiction as a place for deliberate critical judgments. Though the explicit references to Nietzsche at the beginning of *The Walnut Trees of the Altenburg* and at the end of *Aaron's Rod* are suggestive—they show that coming to terms with Nietzsche could indeed be a major aim of a piece of fiction—such explicitness is the exception. The process is normally more indirect. It takes place on the level of shifting attitudes and imaginative sympathies as those are rendered in images, characters, situations, and dialogue. Thus even in *Doctor Faustus* the calculated manipulation of Nietzschean "quotations" is relatively superficial when compared with Mann's underlying engagement with issues that had become a part of his own intellectual landscape. Precisely because it is literary, the fictive mode of interpreting Nietzsche is uniquely capable of registering these more subtle, even subconscious discriminations.

This way of viewing our subject joins the two systems treated in this book, the literary legacy passed on by Nietzsche and the artistic projects that draw on it. No recapitulation is needed here, since Chapter II has already outlined the writers' responses to the issues and methods that attracted attention. But, as a general point, my critical approach at this level has some affinities with recent Continental criticism. To the extent that it brings out Nietzsche's presence in certain modernist works, it is concerned with what the structuralists have called intertextuality, though it places special emphasis on coming to terms with a predecessor. Conversely, insofar as it shows how modernists interpret Nietzsche, it could be considered a variant on the German interest in literary reception, with the area of reception in this case being major literary projects.

Of course, the fictive interpretation of Nietzsche is partial. Though in the end many of the transformations and disagreements described in Chapter II serve to bring out the full significance of a Nietzschean position, there are also a number of major swerves and ambivalences on specific issues. In addition, one must allow for built-in biases of a much broader kind. For example, it is easy in fiction to apply Nietzschean psychology to problems of characterization, but often novelists have to handle his cultural speculations only with brief allusions. Because a dramatic clash of personalities is more memorable than a quick comment that establishes a significant frame of reference, the nature of fiction as a medium might give the impression that Nietzsche's psychological thinking is being taken more seriously than his culture criticism. An even more fundamental bias would be the natural tendency of a fictive mode to prefer those issues, as specified throughout Chapter II, which have already received some literary treatment from Nietzsche. But normally it can offer only an intuitive response to definitions and arguments that philosophers would want to subject to more methodical criticism. Another bias probably arises from the importance of human relationships in most fiction. As novelists Lawrence, Malraux, and Mann have to imagine people dealing with each other far more often and far more concretely than Nietzsche does in his writings. This requirement of their art may account for their emphasis on such themes of relationship as bipolar connection, communal feeling and dignity, or the capacity for love, themes that expand vastly on Nietzsche when not actually reversing him.

The list of divergences could be continued. But with a thinker who is so provocative and encyclopedic it would be no simple task to enumerate all the shifts or omissions by this group of modernists. At this point it would be more profitable for readers to compare their image of Nietzsche with the findings of this book, and draw their own conclusions. In emphasizing partiality, however, we should not forget these writers' accomplishments. In their responses to Nietzsche, they do succeed in uncovering new questions, meanings, and areas of achievement; they have made a contribution to the ongoing work of interpretation. Nor should it be forgotten that even as the need to explore and test Nietzschean problems enters into and shapes their fiction, that fiction can rank among the very best in the first half of the twentieth century for its speculative daring and its rewarding closeness of texture.

□

But what about the historical contexts of this intellectual and artistic drama? How does this episode in cultural life relate to the social and political developments of the time, what is its connection with literary modernism in general, and how may this literary response to Nietzsche be distinguished from the most recent interest in him? Some final comments on these points should help set this book's arguments in perspective.

To the extent that *Heirs to Dionysus* has defined and analyzed the workings of one complex system of thought in its relation to several literary systems, its main intent has been critical. But it has also had historical aims; after all, to trace a Nietzschean current in literary modernism means to show a pattern of development. However, this history has centered almost totally on high culture, and in addition views high culture as if it were a self-sufficient entity. This approach can be defended as the best way of capturing the writers' strong, even obsessive interest in Nietzsche. With Mann, Malraux, and Bely, he seems to have represented nothing less than their main initiation into intellectual life itself; and with Lawrence, Gide, and Yeats, he inspires a reorientation of outlook that is scarcely less important. Such an awakening of thought and sensibility is an obscure and profound experience, one that can be more important than the most shattering historical event. Nonetheless, many students of the late nineteenth and early twentieth centuries may want a more direct explanation for why I have advanced no general thesis involving social and political topics.

To be sure, this book has mentioned such leading issues of the period as individualism, the spread of urban industrialism, the impact of World War I, the rise of socialism and Fascism, or the growth of contacts with non-Western cultures. But they have been treated simply as one kind of tendency among the many consequences of Nietzsche's impact. These issues were all circumstances to be conceived by the writers, not factors conditioning their works. In a more ambitious explanation, these "encounters" with the historical milieu would be replaced by an understanding of the period itself. But such a project immediately raises difficulties. Not only is it better suited to a historian than to a critic, but it becomes especially problematic when we are dealing with a period whose shape and significance are still far from settled. If even World War I no longer seems to be a watershed in the same way as a generation ago, the critic who wants to argue a broad historical case must begin to feel overwhelmed by the shifting variables of his subject.

Modernist culture compounds these difficulties. A cultural movement centered on the sense of a break is not going to derive in any simple way from historical conditions. If modernism aims to surpass the past, its distinctive mood also requires some residual awareness of history: to feel that one is modern, one must have a strong sense of everything that once was. Even T. S. Eliot's endorsement of tradition, seemingly a sharp challenge to the mood of modernity, allows for this complex stance. He disowns tradition if it merely means "following the ways of the immediate generation before us in a blind or timid adherence to its successes." He prefers to see it as a simultaneous dismissal and acknowledgment of history, "a perception, not only of the pastness of the past but of its presence."[3] Works written with this double attitude will not yield a simple historical "message." We recall the complex relation of Leverkühn to his age.

In other words, modernist culture demands careful interpretation before it can usefully be related to its historical milieu. Thus the course followed in this book, which has focused on the inner dynamics of high culture because a firmer grasp on the details must come before any attempt at broader historical explanations. For a striking example of what can go wrong without such interpretive work, one need only turn to the strange blindness of many historians to the extraordinary range and diversity of Nietzsche's influence among the modernists. One often encounters assertions like the following on Nietzsche's relation to just one feature of the times: "It is quite irrelevant that he was also admired as a poet by people to whom Fascism was abhorrent: what counted was the doctrine spelled out at great length in *The Will to Power* and in the final half-mad pamphlets. . . ."[4] By now it should be apparent that this statement is misleading in every respect. The "poetic" interpretation of Nietzsche is far from irrelevant for understanding what he means, and the last works "spelled out" Fascistic doctrine only when they were read by "Nietzscheans." Moreover—as the crowning irony—his literary heirs could draw on elements of those very works to express their abhorrence of Fascism. We have seen that one outcome of Lawrence's model-rival struggle with the will to power is Somers' black rage at the Diggers and the ceremonial execution of Fascist plotters in *The Plumed Serpent*. More compellingly, Malraux's interest in dramatizing and elaborating on the inadequacy of pity as compared with the imperatives of life—a prominent issue in such final works as *Twilight of the Idols* and *The Antichrist*—underlies the passionate refusal of the German soldiers to accept the results of the gas attack, an attack which is presented as a natural consequence of Möllberg's proto-Fascistic outlook. For Mann, the Wagner pamphlet provides a point of departure for understanding the rise of the Nazis, and for all of his revisions of Nietzsche he does accept the psychology of suicidal nihilism as the key to understanding the age of war through which he lived.

I therefore welcome Carl Schorske's recent demonstration of a "post-holing" approach to the history and culture of this period. In *Fin-de-Siècle Vienna* he takes the position that his fellow historians have been "too long content to use the artifacts of high culture as mere illustrative reflections of political or social developments, or to relativize them to ideology." He recommends instead "the empirical pursuit of pluralities as a precondition to finding unitary patterns in culture."[5] This program for advancing our understanding of the modern period corresponds closely with my objectives. The Nietzschean current that runs through Gide, Mann, Lawrence, and Malraux is sufficiently complex to warrant detailed critical study on its own terms. But in its "encounters" with social and political issues, this current often moves in unexpected directions. These insights need to be taken into account as we seek to build up a more nuanced and satisfactory view of how modernist culture relates to the historical whole; they may even help illuminate the shape and significance of that history.

If we turn to the narrower historical context provided by developments within high culture, we come up against the issue raised and then postponed in the introduction—the question of Nietzsche's place within the modernist literary movement. Before suggesting an answer, I must concede that this book has examined just one of several meaningful currents leading from him to major modernist works. For example, my observations on Erich Heller's ideas in Chapter I depended in part on our having different frames of reference. I was concerned with Nietzsche's international impact (Mann being no exception, for we have seen that during World War I he was forced to acknowledge that Nietzsche was essentially international), but Heller focused on the responses of German-language writers. This distinction could be pursued further, with fuller attention to what actually goes on in the best German writing. It is also possible that Nietzsche inspired a specifically lyrical current among modernist poets, with qualities that differ significantly from the various "poetic" deployments of fictional imagery that have been analyzed in this book—Lawrence's material imagination, Malraux's psychological images, Mann's and Gide's concretizations of Nietzschean issues. In addition, the question of Nietzsche and modern drama remains an unexplored territory, both in general literary terms and as regards the special repercussions that *The Birth of Tragedy* could have on playwrights. Finally, it might be possible to step outside the ambivalences of the model-rival relation and locate a genuinely anti-Nietzschean current among literary modernists which would include figures like Joyce, Eliot, and perhaps Proust.

This is a large field for further research. Nonetheless, the writers we have studied in detail do provide an excellent vantage point for answering our question. In their creative work, after all, they move Nietzsche out of the intellectual background of the modernist movement and place him at the heart of major artistic projects. And they also point the way to broader cultural developments. By a happy coincidence, the amount of time and attention they devote to Nietzsche is roughly emblematic of their literary traditions. In England, the philosopher's impact has been brief and mixed when compared to the brilliant diversity, extending over many years, of both the French and German response.[6] More importantly, these writers have had a central role in the dissemination of Nietzschean viewpoints and concerns. The impetus of Mann on Lawrence, of Gide and then Lawrence on Malraux, and finally of Gide on the later Mann is simply the first step in a process that reaches out to literary culture as a whole. At least for certain periods and with at least some of the novels and stories we have considered, all four of these writers have stood very high in their respective literatures. They have therefore been in a position to influence the work of other writers, to change the taste of the literary audience, even to affect the aims of literary education.[7] In addition, they all succeeded in building reputations outside their own national traditions. It would be remarkable if their work were not open to fruitful generalization.

This book has described the five major traits of the Nietzsche that these writers made available to the emerging modernist sensibility in literature. His literary experiments make him at once accessible and appealing to writers: though incomplete, they provide striking illustrations of how the use of slogans and vivid phrases, the various aspects of narrative (especially character), the interplay of assertions (as shown in the aphoristic books), and most of all the resources of imagery can be mobilized to express complex intellectual positions. Four of these positions were influential in their own right. Nietzsche's polaristic dualisms dramatize his affirmation of intrinsic difference and conflict, his acceptance of process, and his preference for widely inclusive forms of unity. Psychological insight gains a new prominence when he probes and reassesses unconscious or irrational depths, when he investigates extreme states like tragic affirmation or nihilism, when he diagnoses the lesser of ills of decadence and *ressentiment,* or when he preaches the rewards of creativity. When he shows the emotional power of myth and its usefulness as an analytic tool, or when he joins apocalyptic attitudes with ambitious speculative concerns, Nietzsche brings both urgency and the awareness of long perspectives to the discussion of cultural issues. And, whether phrased as art drives or as power and "life," his aesthetic naturalism is a challenging philosophical outlook, at times inspiring and at times disquieting in giving such high value to creativity and art and in insisting so strenuously on the radical immanence of humanity.

As for the modernist sensibility itself, we saw in starting out that it is rooted in an overwhelming sense of a break with the recent past. This sense would certainly account for the sharpened commitment of modernist writers to their work; confronted with what they feel is a radical change in values and conditions, they assume the responsibility of representing it adequately. Hence the glorification of art and the artist, the intense concern with creativity, and the extraordinary experiments with literary forms and language. Basic to many of these experiments is the doctrine of the image, the conviction that art cannot simply portray or reflect the break but must find concrete, nondiscursive equivalents through which it may be presented or enacted in all its aspects and implications. This doctrine, in turn, assumes that the mind is peculiarly drawn to this way of generating meanings. It therefore furnishes one example of the dependence of literary modernism on psychological speculation. But psychology has many other uses, since it serves both to justify the widespread modernist premise that the self is primary and to provide a host of new insights into the suppressed, the ambivalent, the irrational, and the unexpectedly animating. Such a psychology turns against positivistic accounts of human nature and so contributes directly to the modernist break with the values of the recent past. Such a psychology also opens the way for the heightened awareness of myth among modernists. But myth is also a direct response to the mood of modernity, since it is capable of providing a long-term continuity to replace the one that was lost, of giving a better perspective from which to assess the significance of the loss, or of creating a sense for new cultural possibilities.

There are several possible objections to this definition of modernism. If it seems so broad as to cover writers from many other periods, it should be remembered that modernism has produced its own criticism, which by now has interpreted much of the past in its own image. Of course, there are many cases that cannot be disposed of so easily. Among some earlier writers these concerns are so prominent that they might fairly be seen as premodernists or as representatives of a perennial modernist temperament. It is also true that some of these issues have had an important role in other cultural movements, most notably romanticism and symbolism. But only some of them; this particular grouping of the factors and their distinctive tone as a whole do seem to mark a specific period. Finally, many accounts of this period give much less weight to the mood of modernity; and many prefer to specify just one factor instead of several, so that modernism is identified with specific innovations in technique, or with the preference for a psychological perspective, or with a self-reflexive concern for art, or with myth. The advantage of this definition is that it does give an immediate relevance to the term modernism, which otherwise tends to become an arbitrary tag. And because this definition joins a number of separate yet interrelated possibilities, it is flexible and broad enough to allow for many different routes to modernism. Depending on which elements are emphasized, it touches on the most striking achievements of writers as dissimilar as Woolf and Kafka, or Pound and Valéry, and registers the impact of modernist thinkers like Freud, Frazer, Bergson, and Jung.

Certainly this definition captures Nietzsche's impact on his modernist heirs, since almost every phrase recalls a leading theme in his literary legacy. Thus myth leads to his conceptions of cultural crisis, the doctrine of the image corresponds to the role of figurative language in his thought, the ambivalent can take the form of polaristic dualities, and so on. From this standpoint, it is not surprising that as their reputations spread, first Nietzsche and then his heirs should have been greeted as advocates of a new literary sensibility.

But such an absorption of Nietzsche into modernism is not in the end satisfactory. Despite the usefulness of all-encompassing definitions of literary and cultural periods, they depend on broad generalizations which can easily become stereotypes; it is important to preserve intermediate levels of generalization. Accordingly, this book has gone back to the complex process by which Nietzsche directly influenced literary modernists and has provided a more substantial and specific description of his role. He does not simply exemplify the various issues and strategies that cluster about the primary sense of the modern; he has his own distinctive approaches to them. As a result, and despite all the struggles of his heirs in coming to terms with him, he has helped inspire a characteristic array of literary experiments, dualistic conceptions, psychological and cultural interests, and philosophical attitudes. Thus, even as this book has given a critical account of this Nietzschean current, it has aimed to promote a less abstract and more discriminating sense for some of the possibilities of modernism.

One leading trait in this modernist Nietzsche may seem questionable, however. From the perspective of the contemporary Nietzsche revival, the proper rubric for his basic stance as a thinker would not be aesthetic naturalism, but a pure aestheticism that insists on illusion and revels in the free play of interpretation. Two influential American commentators on recent developments in French criticism have neatly captured this trend. Jonathan Culler cites Derrida on "Nietzschean affirmation, the joyful affirmation of the play of the world . . . the affirmation of a world of signs without guilt, truth, or origin, and proffered for active interpretation"; and Paul de Man, after a glance at Barthes and the "libération du signifiant," quotes Nietzsche himself: "The intellect, this master of deceit, feels itself freed from its habitual servitude when it is allowed to deceive without direct harm. Then it celebrates its own saturnalia."[8] This second passage comes from the early essay "On Truth and Lie in an Extra-Moral Sense" (1873), which first appeared in a posthumous collection of Nietzsche's unpublished writings and which I have had no occasion to mention until now. The reason is simple: the writers studied in this book choose aesthetic naturalism over the free play of aesthetic illusion. The best evidence is a set of crucial scenes in their major fiction.

The most instructive moments occur in Malraux, in the contrast of Clappique and Berger. When the former art dealer looks into his mirror and engages in an orgy of facial transformations, his actions revalue the free play of illusion; far from being affirmative, they simply testify to mythomania. Only with Berger's vision of the walnut trees anchored firmly in the earth does it become possible to accept multiplicity in one of its aspects, the great variety of cultures that make up human history. This grounding of the aesthetic also takes place in Lawrence, during Ursula's argument with Loerke and Gudrun about the nature of art. The sculptor places art in an absolute realm of its own, but Ursula objects and interprets his statue of Lady Godiva as a revelation of his basic orientation toward life. In the tradition of aesthetic naturalism, she is assuming that biological conditions and artistic execution are inseparable and must be seen as parts of a single process. Another telling instance would be Leverkühn's shift from parody to genuine creativity in his work as a composer. His own artistic impulses gradually take over from a playful but arid manipulation of elements drawn from his detailed knowledge of musical history; the catalyst for the change has been the touch of the prostitute, which brought sexuality into a sphere where previously signs had been freely combined and elaborated. For all the ambiguity surrounding this "demonic" awakening of instinct, the domain of parody was clearly not a viable alternative. Even in Gide's *The Immoralist*, which does not address this issue as directly, the problem of maintaining a naturalistic underpinning for the multiple configurations of the aesthetic makes itself felt. For example, the beauty that Michel discovers on returning to his Norman estate, where natural energies are shaped into an "ordered abundance," contrasts sharply with the attitudes of the poets he meets in Paris, who tend to see "life as a tiresome impediment to writing" (I, 410, 423).

This divergence between Nietzsche's modernist heirs and his more recent French interpreters serves as a useful reminder of the great wealth of insights scattered throughout his work. At times annoyingly perverse but more often bold, incisive, and extraordinarily stimulating, this thinker is larger than any single current of influence deriving from him. There is thus some justification for the post-humanist Nietzsche whose self-consciousness about language and philosophic rigor are currently being championed by the French. But there is also good reason for all the fascination with aesthetic naturalism described in this book. For writers who came of age in the aftermath of the late nineteenth-century debates about symbolism, naturalism, and art-for-art's-sake, Nietzsche's position was arresting. The outlook dimly anticipated in *The Birth of Tragedy*, proclaimed in *Thus Spoke Zarathustra*, and tersely formulated in *Twilight of the Idols* represents an ambitious alternative to the possibility identified long ago by Harry Levin in a pioneering survey of early twentieth-century writing. According to his account of the Irish literary movement, and especially of Joyce, the late nineteenth-century debates were to be resolved by innovative choices in artistic method and subject matter.[9] But for the Nietzschean current in literary modernism, these questions of craft can not be separated from the underlying assumptions and world views that conditioned them. At this level, Nietzsche's aesthetic naturalism offers a striking if also troubling synthesis, for by positing the artistry of instinct he succeeds in uniting the antagonistic claims of a symbolistic heightening of the literal, fidelity to nature, and the cult of art.

But whatever the historical context that has concerned us—whether the shift in Nietzsche's reputation, or his place in literary modernism, or the force of his ideas among the social and political issues of the modern period—we have had to refer back to the specifics of his influence on writers. So in the end the details remain the most important part of our story. Only through them do we get an adequate sense of all the challenges posed by Nietzsche's thought and way of writing. It is therefore best to close by recalling the hard intellectual and artistic struggle the details reveal. In Gide and Mann, in Lawrence and Malraux, and in what we have seen of Yeats and Bely the multiple shocks and uncertainties of direct contact have not yet given way to smooth cultural currency. The result of these pressures and polemics is a remarkable set of literary achievements, often of very high quality, and many penetrating insights into a fascinating and disturbing thinker. The Nietzsche thus appropriated and made into a central figure for the modernist sensibility is not the only possible Nietzsche. But this constellation of interconnected writers does represent a significant and dramatic episode in the life of the mind, especially as that life finds a voice in literature.

Chronology of Works, Writers, and Events

Unless otherwise indicated, dates of books are for the year of first publication. See David Thatcher's *Nietzsche in England*, p. x, for a useful chronology of French and English translations of Nietzsche's books.

1844   Nietzsche born.

1865   Yeats born.

1868   Nietzsche's first meeting with Wagner.

1869   Gide born. Nietzsche named professor of classical philology at the University of Basel in Switzerland.

1872   Nietzsche's *The Birth of Tragedy*, with a dedication to Wagner.

1875   Mann born.

1878   Nietzsche's *Human, All-Too-Human*, which he later interprets as marking his definitive break with Wagner.

1879   Nietzsche resigns his position at the University of Basel.

1880   Bely born.

1882   Nietzsche's *The Gay Science*, first four books. Friendship with Lou Salomé.

1883   Nietzsche writes "Night Song." *Thus Spoke Zarathustra*, the first two parts.

1884   Nietzsche's *Thus Spoke Zarathustra*, part III.

1885   Lawrence born. Nietzsche's *Thus Spoke Zarathustra*, part IV.

1886   Nietzsche's *Beyond Good and Evil*. "Attempt at a Self-Critique" added to a new edition of *The Birth of Tragedy*.

1887   The fifth book added to *The Gay Science*. Nietzsche's *On the Genealogy of Morals*.

1888   Nietzsche's sharpest critique of Wagner in *The Case of Wagner*. During this year he also writes *Twilight of the Idols*, *The Antichrist*, and *Ecce Homo*.

1889   Nietzsche's collapse. Publication of *Twilight of the Idols*.

1894   Mann's first contact with Nietzsche's work, perhaps as late as 1895.

1895   Publication of *The Antichrist*. Nietzsche's sister gets legal control of her brother's writings and later founds the Nietzsche Archives, with herself as director.

1897   Gide's *Fruits of the Earth*.

1899   Autumn: Bely's first enthusiasm for Nietzsche. December: Gide's review of Nietzsche.

1900   Nietzsche's death.

1901   Malraux born. Nietzsche's sister publishes *The Will to Power*, using 483 notes found among manuscripts from his last five years of work. Mann's *Buddenbrooks*.

1902   Publication of Gide's *The Immoralist*. Yeats begins reading Nietzsche.

1903   Publication of Mann's *Tonio Kröger* and *Tristan*.

1905   First publication of Mann's *Fiorenza*.

1906   Revised edition of Nietzsche's *The Will to Power*, consisting of the standard 1067 aphorisms.

1907   Bely's essay "Friedrich Nietzsche."

1908   Publication of Nietzsche's *Ecce Homo*. Lawrence begins discussing the will to power with friends.

1909   Gide's *Strait is the Gate*.

1910   Bely discusses Nietzsche in his essay "The Crisis of Consciousness."

1912   Summer: Mann's *Death in Venice*. November: Lawrence finishes *Sons and Lovers*.

1913   Bely's *Petersburg* begins to appear in *Sirin*, a modernist literary journal in Russia. March-April: Lawrence's first conception of *The Sisters*, later to become *The Rainbow* and *Women in Love*. July: Lawrence reviews *Death in Venice*.

1914	September: following the outbreak of World War I, Lawrence begins his "metaphysical" writings, "Study of Thomas Hardy" and "The Crown."
1915	February: the beginning of Lawrence's brief friendship with Bertrand Russell. September: publication of *The Rainbow*. October: Mann interrupts work on *The Magic Mountain* to start *Reflections of an Apolitical Man*.
1916	Lawrence's *Twilight in Italy*. Bely's *Petersburg* appears in book form. Lawrence hard at work on *Women in Love*.
1918	Spengler's *Decline of the West*.
1920	Publication of Lawrence's *Women in Love* in New York. Publication of Lawrence's *The Lost Girl*.
1921	June: Lawrence finishes *Aaron's Rod*.
1922	January: Mann writes Gide, and discusses his essay on Nietzsche. Spring: Malraux writes his first review of Gide. May-June: Lawrence writes *Kangaroo*. September: Lawrence arrives in New Mexico.
1923	Spring: Malraux's second review of Gide; Lawrence begins *The Plumed Serpent*. October: Malraux arrives in the Far East to begin his "Indochina Adventure."
1924	Mann's *The Magic Mountain*. Summer: Lawrence interrupts work on *The Plumed Serpent* to write *Saint Mawr*, "The Woman Who Rode Away," and "The Princess." September: Mann's critique of Spengler.
1925	Yeats's *A Vision*, first edition. February: Lawrence completes *The Plumed Serpent*. October: Lawrence returns to Europe. December: Malraux returns from Indochina.
1926	Malraux's *The Temptation of the West*. Gide's *The Counterfeiters* and *If It Die*. . . . Publication of *The Plumed Serpent*.
1927	Malraux's "Concerning a European Youth."
1928	Malraux's *The Conquerors*.
1929	Mann's review of Gide's *If It Die*. . . .

1930	Lawrence's death. Malraux's *The Royal Way.*
1932	January: Malraux's review of Lawrence in the *Nouvelle revue française.*
1933	January: *Man's Fate* starts to appear in monthly installments in the *Nouvelle revue française.*
1935	Death of Nietzsche's sister. Malraux's *Days of Wrath.*
1937	Malraux's *Man's Hope.*
1939	Mann's *Lotte in Weimar.*
1943	Swiss edition of Malraux's *The Walnut Trees of the Altenburg.* May: Mann begins *Doctor Faustus.*
1947	Publication of *Doctor Faustus.* Delivery of Mann's address, "Nietzsche's Philosophy in the Light of Our Experience."
1948	First French edition of Malraux's *The Walnut Trees of the Altenburg.*
1949	Mann's *The Story of a Novel.*
1951	Malraux's *The Voices of Silence*, with its comments on "the voice of the throat" in *Man's Fate.*
1967	Malraux's *Anti-Memoirs*, the first volume of his autobiography, reprints part of *Walnut Trees.*
1974	Malraux's *Lazarus*, part of the second volume of his autobiography, reprints part of *Walnut Trees.*

Notes

INTRODUCTION

[1] See Arthur O. Lovejoy's classic essay, "On the Discrimination of Romanticisms," in *Essays in the History of Ideas* (Baltimore: Johns Hopkins Press, 1948), pp. 228-253.

[2] "To Peter Gast," 30 October 1888, Letter 258, *Friedrich Nietzsche: Werke in drei Bänden*, edited by Karl Schlechta (Munich: Carl Hanser Verlag, 1966), vol. III, p. 1327.

[3] Monroe Spears, *Dionysus and the City: Modernism in Twentieth-Century Poetry* (New York: Oxford University Press, 1970), pp. 34, 35-37, 71-72.

[4] Conor Cruise O'Brien, *The Suspecting Glance* (London: Faber and Faber, 1972), pp. 9, 58-61, 63.

[5] For Mann's description of these discoveries, see Thomas Mann, "Freud and the Future," *Gesammelte Werke in zwölf Bänden* (n.p.: S. Fischer Verlag, 1960), vol. IX, p. 480, and *The Story of a Novel, Gesammelte Werke*, vol. XI, p. 214.

[6] Crane Brinton, *Nietzsche* (1941; rpt, with preface, epilogue, and bibliography, New York: Harper & Row, 1965), p. 257.

[7] Michel Foucault, *The Order of Things: An Archeology of the Human Sciences (Les Mots et les choses)* (New York: Vintage Books, 1973), especially pp. 263, 305-307, 342, 385.

[8] I have in mind such useful, but ultimately rather disappointing, surveys as Patrick Bridgwater, *Nietzsche in Anglosaxony: A Study of Nietzsche's Impact on English and American Literature* (Leicester, England: Leicester University Press, 1972); Geneviève Bianquis, *Nietzsche en France: L'Influence de Nietzsche sur la pensée française* (Paris: Félix Alcan, 1929) and Pierre Boudot, *Nietzsche et l'au-delà de la liberté: Nietzsche et les écrivains français de 1930 à 1960* (Paris: Aubier-Montaigne, 1970). David S. Thatcher's *Nietzsche in England 1890-1914: The Growth of a Reputation* (Toronto and Buffalo: University of Toronto Press, 1970) has a wealth of fresh information, but it too pays inadequate attention to imaginative work.

[9] T. S. Eliot as cited in F. O. Matthiessen, *The Achievement of T. S. Eliot: An Essay on the Nature of Poetry* (3rd ed.; New York: Oxford University Press, 1959), p. 99.

[10] Compare René Girard's contention about the relation of Stendhal's discursive writings to his novels: ". . . everything has to be gathered from the novels. The non-novelistic texts sometimes contribute details but they

should be handled with care." See *Deceit, Desire and the Novel: Self and Other in Literary Structure*, translated by Yvonne Freccero (Baltimore and London: Johns Hopkins Press, 1965), p. 114.

CHAPTER I

[1] Erich Heller, "The Importance of Nietzsche" in *The Artist's Journey into the Interior and Other Essays* (New York: Vintage Books, 1968), p. 174.

[2] Claudio Guillén, "The Aesthetics of Literary Influence" in *Literature as System: Essays toward the Theory of Literary History* (Princeton, N.J.: Princeton University Press, 1971), pp. 26-35.

[3] *Ibid.*, pp. 36, 39, 47, 36.

[4] Harold Bloom, *The Anxiety of Influence: A Theory of Poetry* (New York: Oxford University Press, 1973), p. 30.

[5] *Ibid.*, pp. 8, 49-52.

[6] Jurij Tynyanov, *Arkhaisty i Novatory (Archaists and Innovators)* (1929; rpt. Munich: Wilhelm Fink Verlag, 1967) and Boris Eikhenbaum, *Lev Tolstoy* (1928-1931; rpt. Munich: Wilhelm Fink Verlag, 1968). The essays available in English include Eikhenbaum's *The Young Tolstoy*, translation edited by Gary Kern (Ann Arbor, Mich.: Ardis, 1972) and Tynyanov's "Dostoevsky and Gogol': Toward a Theory of Parody," the first section of which may be found in *Dostoevsky and Gogol: Texts and Criticism*, edited by Priscilla Meyer and Stephen Rudy (Ann Arbor, Mich.: Ardis, 1979), pp. 101-117, and the second part in *Twentieth Century Russian Criticism*, edited by Victor Erlich (New Haven and London: Yale University Press, 1975), pp. 102-116. For a general survey of Russian formalist work in this area, and for further references, see Victor Erlich, "Literary Dynamics," chap. 14 in *Russian Formalism: History-Doctrine* (2nd ed. rev., The Hague: Mouton and Co., 1965), and particularly pp. 258-259, 262-263, and 267-268. For further comments on Tynyanov, see the tenth thesis of Hans Robert Jauß, "Literaturgeschichte als Provokation der Literaturwissenschaft" in *Literaturgeschichte als Provokation* (Frankfurt am Main: Suhrkamp, 1970), pp. 189-194.

[7] Harold Bloom, *Yeats* (New York: Oxford University Press, 1970), p. vii.

[8] Samuel Taylor Coleridge, *Biographia Literaria with his Aesthetic Essays*, edited by J. Shawcross (Oxford: Oxford University Press, 1907), especially pp. 62, 81, 195, and 202. Coleridge's remarks are notoriously elliptical, but nonetheless very suggestive about the creative process.

[9] Bloom, *Yeats*, and especially chaps. 2 through 6.

[10] See Frederick J. Hoffman, *Freudianism and the Literary Mind* (2nd ed., n.p.: Louisiana University Press, 1957), and John B. Vickery, *The Literary Impact of "The Golden Bough"* (Princeton, N.J.: Princeton University Press, 1973).

[11] Andrei Bely, *Na Rubezhe Dvukh Stoletij* (1930; rpt. Letchworth, Hertfordshire: Bradda Books, 1966), pp. 465, 466.

[12] "To Lady Gregory," ?26 September 1902, *The Letters of W. B. Yeats*, edited by Allan Wade (New York: Macmillan, 1955), p. 379 and "To John Quinn," 15 May 1903, *Letters of Yeats*, p. 403.

[13] William Butler Yeats, *A Vision* (1938; reissued with the author's final revisions, New York: Macmillan, 1956), pp. 126-129.

[14] E. T. (Jesse Chambers), *D. H. Lawrence: A Personal Record* with an introduction by J. Middleton Murry (New York: Knight Publications, 1936), p. 120.

[15] For further discussions of the problem of idea and image, but mostly as it relates to Nietzsche alone and the narrower "poetic" sense of image, see the collection of essays in *Nietzsche: Imagery and Thought*, edited by Malcolm Pasley (Berkeley and Los Angeles: University of California Press, 1978).

[16] Walter Kaufmann, *Basic Writings of Nietzsche* (New York: Modern Library, 1968), p. 761, n. 4, on a phrase from the critique of *Thus Spoke Zarathustra* in *Ecce Homo*.

[17] James Joyce, *Ulysses* (New York: Modern Library, 1934), pp. 416, 417. Joyce quotes the sentence in German, having taken it from "On Enjoying and Suffering the Passions," *Thus Spoke Zarathustra*, pt. I.

[18] Martin Heidegger, "Who is Nietzsche's Zarathustra?" *The New Nietzsche: Contemporary Styles of Interpretation*, edited with an introduction by David B. Allison (New York: Dell, 1977), p. 78. For a mythical interpretation of their significance, see David S. Thatcher, "Eagle and Serpent in *Zarathustra*," *Nietzsche-Studien* 6 (1977), pp. 240-260.

[19] For Nietzsche's dismissal of the novel, see his critique of Plato as a novelist in *The Birth of Tragedy*, sec. 14. Representative statements on Stendhal and Dostoevsky as psychological observers occur in "Why I Am So Clever," *Ecce Homo*, aph. 3, and in a parenthetical comment in the epilogue to *The Case of Wagner*.

[20] For an account of Bely's voluminous "philosophical" writings, see John Elsworth, "Bely's Theory of Symbolism," *Forum for Modern Language Studies*, vol. 11 (1975), pp. 305-333. Yeats expounded his system in *A Vision*, and Mann's main meditative work would be the *Reflections of an Apolitical Man*. Lawrence's "metaphysical" works would include "Study of Thomas Hardy" in *Phoenix: The Posthumous Papers of D. H. Lawrence*, edited with an Introduction by Edward D. McDonald (1936; reissued New York: Viking, 1968), pp. 398-516; "The Crown" in *Reflections on the Death of a Porcupine and Other Essays* (Bloomington, Ind.: Indiana University Press, 1963), pp. 1-100; and his essays on the unconscious collected in *Psychoanalysis and the Unconscious and Fantasia of the Unconscious* (1921, 1922; rpt. New York: Viking, 1960). I shall comment further on these works by Yeats, Mann, and Lawrence in the rest of this book.

[21] For a stimulating discussion of the larger, "fictive" sense of image as it contributes to Kierkegaard's thought and to the work of two figures influenced by him, see Edith Kern, *Existential Thought and Fictional Technique: Kierkegaard, Sartre, Beckett* (New Haven and London: Yale University Press,

1970). In *Six Existential Heroes: The Politics of Faith* (Cambridge, Mass.: Harvard University Press, 1973), Lucio Ruotolo does not address the issue of fictive strategies in existential thought, but does offer a wide-ranging discussion of its fictive repercussions, with a focus on problems of characterization.

On Plato, of course, the literature is vast. But in the modernist period Yeats's "Among School Children" includes several different instances of idea and image. In proposing "to alter Plato's parable" (st. 2), Yeats does what Joyce did in transforming Nietzsche's image; and when he characterizes nature in Plato as a "spume that plays / Upon a ghostly paradigm of things" (st. 6), he does what Gide did when he set out to find new and more vivid images for Nietzsche's thought.

[22] Bely, "Friedrich Nietzsche," *Arabeski* (1911; rpt. Munich: Wilhelm Fink Verlag, 1969), pp. 79, 81.

[23] W. Wolfgang Holdheim, "The Young Gide's Reaction to Nietzsche," *Publications of the Modern Language Association*, vol. 72 (1957), p. 539.

[24] See Brinton, "The Growth of a Reputation" and "Nietzsche and the Nazis," chaps. 7 and 8 in his *Nietzsche*, for a useful contemporary summary of what he calls the "tough" Nietzscheans; the book originally appeared in 1941. For a more recent discussion, consult the references to Nietzsche in Ernst Nolte, *Three Faces of Fascism: Action Française, Italian Fascism, National Socialism* (New York: New American Library, 1969). Nolte offers fascinating glimpses into how Nietzsche could be regarded as an ally by these movements, but unfortunately he buries in a footnote the crucial reservation that there was much more to Nietzsche.

[25] See especially Walter Kaufmann, "Editor's Introduction" in Friedrich Nietzsche, *The Will to Power*, translated by Walter Kaufmann and R. J. Hollingdale and edited, with commentary, by Walter Kaufmann (New York: Vintage Books, 1968), pp. xiii-xxiii. For a more detailed account of the role of Nietzsche's sister in building his reputation, see Kaufmann, "The Nietzsche Legend" and "Nietzsche's Life as Background of His Thought," in *Nietzsche: Philosopher, Psychologist, Antichrist* (1950; 3rd ed. rev. and enl., New York: Vintage Books, 1968), pp. 3-71.

CHAPTER II

[1] For an existentialist Nietzsche see, for example, Karl Jaspers, *Nietzsche: An Introduction to the Understanding of his Philosophical Activity*, translated by Charles F. Wallraff and Frederick J. Schmitz (Chicago: Henry Regnery, 1965). For a pragmatist Nietzsche see, for example, Hans Vaihinger, *The Philosophy of 'As if,'* translated by C. K. Ogden (New York: Harcourt Brace, 1924). For suggestions of a neo-Kantian Nietzsche see the comments of Arthur C. Danto, *Nietzsche as Philosopher* (New York: Macmillan, 1965), pp. 95-96, 221; among the literary heirs of Nietzsche considered in this book, Bely read him in the context of the resurgence of interest in Kant in

the early twentieth century. Nietzsche's philosophy is set against the thinking of Aristotle and Hegel by Walter Kaufmann in *Nietzsche: Philosopher, Psychologist, Antichrist*, p. 238. For a representative statement of the opposing view see the chapter on Nietzsche in Bertrand Russell, *A History of Western Philosophy* (New York: Simon and Schuster, 1945), pp. 760-773.

[2] I am referring to the ongoing publication of Nietzsche's complete writings in *Nietzsche Werke: Kritische Gesamtausgabe*, edited by Giorgio Colli and Mazzino Montinari (Berlin and New York: Walter de Gruyter).

[3] "Letter to Erwin Rohde," end of January and 15 February 1870, Letter 38, *Nietzsche: Werke*, ed. Schlechta, vol. III, p. 1021.

[4] Here and elsewhere I shall be following Walter Kaufmann in rendering Nietzsche's "apollinisch" as "Apollinian" rather than as "Apollonian," as is usually the case in English-language discussions of Nietzsche.

[5] Bernard Pautrat, *Versions de Soleil: Figures et système de Nietzsche* (Paris: Editions du Seuil, 1971), pp. 85, 84.

[6] Yeats, *A Vision*, pp. 72-73.

[7] "To Lady Gregory," ?26 September 1902, *Letters of Yeats*, ed. Wade, p. 379.

[8] Yeats, *A Vision*, p. 7. Compare this passage in Yeats with Nietzsche's account of his book in *Ecce Homo*, "Thus Spoke Zarathustra," aph. 1.

[9] Paul de Man, "Genesis and Genealogy in Nietzsche's *The Birth of Tragedy*," *Allegories of Reading* (New Haven and London: Yale University Press, 1979), p. 83.

[10] Compare Thomas Mann, *Der Zauberberg (The Magic Mountain)*, *Gesammelte Werke*, vol. III, pp. 678-681. This connection between Nietzsche and Mann is a commonplace in the critical literature. See, for example, Henry Hatfield, *Thomas Mann* (Norfolk, Ct.: New Directions, 1951), p. 79; or Eckhard Heftrich, *Zauberbergmusik: über Thomas Mann* (Frankfurt am Main: Klostermann, 1975), p. 274.

[11] Gilles Deleuze, *Nietzsche et la philosophie* (1962; rpt. Paris: Presses Universitaires de France, 1973), pp. 223, 224.

[12] D. H. Lawrence, *Kangaroo* (1923; rpt. New York: Viking, 1960), p. 286.

[13] Nietzsche's Dionysus is thus more flexible than most Western discourse about the East. Compare Edward Said's general comments on the Dionysus myth in *Orientalism* (New York: Pantheon, 1978), pp. 56-57. For a detailed account of how the communal element in the Dionysian developed in Austria, in a unique situation established before *The Case of Wagner*, so that Nietzsche could be assimilated to Wagner, see William J. McGrath, *Dionysian Art and Populist Politics* (New Haven and London: Yale University Press, 1974).

[14] Nietzsche himself chooses to emphasize these last two terms when he reviews the *Genealogy* in *Ecce Homo*, "On the Genealogy of Morals."

[15] Compare, for example, the discussion in *Beyond Good and Evil*, aph. 260, which was published in the previous year. For the way Nietzscheans

interpreted the "blond beast," see D. Brennecke, "Die blonde bestie. Vom Mißverständnis eines Schlagworts," *Nietzsche-Studien* 5 (1976), pp. 111-145.

[16] David Thatcher has argued for this connection in his chapter on Yeats in *Nietzsche in England*, where he reproduces Yeats's marginal notes in his edition of the *Genealogy*. See especially pp. 147, 151, 165.

[17] See Yeats's poem "The Phases of the Moon," line 35, in *A Vision*, p. 60.

[18] See Aristotle, *The Poetics*, Bekker 1448b2; and Sigmund Freud, *The Interpretation of Dreams*.

[19] See D. H. Lawrence, *Psychoanalysis and the Unconscious and Fantasia of the Unconscious*.

[20] Compare Kaufmann, *Basic Writings of Nietzsche*, p. 439; or Deleuze, *Nietzsche et la philosophie*, p. 99.

[21] "Letter to Franz Overbeck," 23 February 1887, Letter 211; and "Letter to Peter Gast," 7 March 1887, Letter 213, *Nietzsche: Werke*, ed. Schlechta, vol. III, pp. 1250, 1254. Nietzsche published the *Genealogy* in the following autumn. For a careful analysis of Nietzsche's first readings of Dostoevsky, see C. A. Miller, "Nietzsche's 'Discovery' of Dostoevsky," *Nietzsche-Studien* 2 (1973), pp. 202-257.

[22] See René Girard, "Superman in the Underground: Strategies of Madness—Nietzsche, Wagner, and Dostoevsky," *MLN*, vol. 91 (1976), pp. 1161-85 and especially pp. 1169-81, for a comparison of *ressentiment* and Dostoevskian psychology from the standpoint of his theory of mimetic desire. Girard argues for the superiority of Dostoevsky's psychological insight on the grounds that Nietzsche's philosophy of power is conditioned by his own feelings of inadequacy; in other words, he mistakenly limited the scope of his analysis of *ressentiment* so as to leave room for his own "ideological falsifications." The point is well taken as regards the superman, but its extension to other aspects of Nietzsche's thought needs further argument. After all, even Zarathustra tends to abandon the superman for eternal recurrence as *Thus Spoke Zarathustra* progresses. For another criticism of Nietzsche from a Dostoevskian perspective, followed by a lively discussion, see C. A. Miller, "Nietzsches 'Soteriopsychologie' im Spiegel von Dostoevskijs Auseinandersetzung mit dem europäischen Nihilismus," *Nietzsche-Studien* 7 (1978), pp. 130-157.

[23] For Nietzsche's definition of the core of *ressentiment*, see the opening paragraphs of the *Genealogy of Morals*, I, 10. For possibilities like rancor and malice, see the first paragraphs of *Genealogy*, II, 11; for the more passive cases of envy and suspiciousness, see *Genealogy*, III, 15. For a philosopher's comments on some of Nietzsche's basic concerns in analyzing inadequacy, see Joan Stambaugh, "Thoughts on Pity and Revenge," *Nietzsche-Studien* 1 (1972), pp. 27-35.

[24] Georg Lukács, "Der deutsche Naturalismus," *Schriften zur Literatursoziologie*, edited with an introduction by Peter Ludz (Neuwied and Berlin: Luchterhand, 1961), p. 456; and *Von Nietzsche zu Hitler, oder Der Irrational-*

ismus und die deutsche Politik (Frankfurt am Main and Hamburg: Fischer Bücherei, 1966), p. 54.

[25] This slogan from a speech of Malraux's in 1945 is reported by Horst Hina, *Nietzsche und Marx bei Malraux* (Tübingen: Max Niemeyer Verlag, 1970), p. 125.

[26] For "pessimism of strength" see the "Self-Critique to *The Birth of Tragedy*," sec. 1. For *amor fati*, see *The Gay Science*, aph. 276; *Nietzsche contra Wagner*, the epilogue, sec. 1; or *Ecce Homo*, "Why I Am So Clever," aph. 10. The saying "What does not kill me makes me stronger" appears in "Why I Am So Wise," aph. 2, and in *Twilight of the Idols*, "Maxims and Arrows," aph. 8.

[27] William Butler Yeats, *The Autobiography of William Butler Yeats* (1916, 1935; rpt. New York: Macmillan, 1965), p. 128.

[28] André Malraux, "Ménalque," *Le Disque vert*, Feb.-Mar.-Apr. 1923, p. 21.

[29] For the earlier statement, see "To A. W. McLeod," 6 October 1912, *The Collected Letters of D. H. Lawrence*, edited with an introduction by Harry T. Moore (New York: Viking, 1962), vol. I, p. 150. For the later statement see D. H. Lawrence, "Sun," *The Complete Short Stories of D. H. Lawrence*, in three volumes (New York: Viking, 1961), vol. II, p. 533.

[30] See Frank Kermode, *The Sense of an Ending: Studies in the Theory of Fiction* (New York: Oxford University Press, 1967), especially pp. 95-96.

[31] For "fundamental idea" see *Twilight of the Idols*, "Skirmishes of an Untimely Man," aph. 5; for "conjecture" see Zarathustra's remarks on the superman in *Thus Spoke Zarathustra*, pt. II, sec. 2.

[32] Nietzsche, "Wissenschaft und Weisheit im Kampfe," *Nietzsche: Werke*, ed. Schlechta, vol. III, p. 333.

[33] *Twilight of the Idols*, pt. IV. For a similar analysis of German philosophy, see also *The Antichrist*, aph. 10; and for one of science, see *On the Genealogy of Morals*, 3rd essay, aph. 25.

[34] On Rousseau and the French Revolution, see *The Will to Power*, aph. 94; *On the Genealogy of Morals*, 1st essay, aph. 16; or *Twilight of the Idols*, "Skirmishes of an Untimely Man," aph. 48. On egalitarianism, see *The Antichrist*, aph. 62. On socialism, see *The Will to Power*, aph. 765. On the state, see "On the New Idol," *Thus Spoke Zarathustra*, pt. I.

[35] For Mann's account of how Nietzsche's Wagner criticism affected him, see especially *Betrachtungen eines Unpolitischen (Reflections of an Apolitical Man)* in *Gesammelte Werke*, vol. XII, pp. 73-75. Bely discusses *The Case of Wagner*, giving special attention to the slogan "brutality, artificiality, decadence" in his article "Friedrich Nietzsche," *Arabeski*, p. 87. The essay was already translated into French in two different versions before 1900, first by Daniel Halévy and Robert Dreyfus in 1892 and then by Henri Albert in 1899. For Shaw's allusions to the Nietzsche-Wagner dispute, see George Bernard Shaw, *Man and Superman* (1903; rpt. *Nine Plays*, New York: Dodd, Mead, 1935), pp. 648, 649.

[36] Thus in the fourth section Nietzsche's analysis of Schopenhauer's influence on Wagner moves from the provisional insight that "the *nothing*, the Indian Circe beckons" to the famous epigrammatic conclusion: "Only the *philosopher of decadence* gave to the artist of decadence—*himself.*" In the first postscript a similar conceptual shift takes place in a single sentence: "He flatters every nihilistic (Buddhistic) instinct and disguises it in music; he flatters everything Christian, every religious expression of decadence."

[37] See Paul Bourget, "Charles Baudelaire, III: Théorie de la Décadence," *Essais de Psychologie Contemporaine* (1883; def. ed., Paris: Plon, ?1908), vol. I, p. 20. The closest echoes occur during Nietzsche's description of literary decadence: "The word becomes sovereign and leaps out of the sentence, the sentence reaches out and obscures the meaning of the page, the page gains life at the expense of the whole—the whole is no longer a whole." It is tempting to suppose that Bourget's influence is responsible for the essay's misleading emphasis on decadence at the expense of nihilism.

[38] On Schopenhauer's role in forming Wagner's outlook, see the passage quoted in n. 36, above. On Hegel's role see sec. 10: "Hegel is a *taste*.—And not merely a German but a European taste.—A taste Wagner comprehended—to which he felt equal—which he immortalized.—He merely applied it to music—he invented a style for himself charged with 'infinite meaning'—he became the *heir of Hegel*.—Music as 'idea.'—"

[39] Jacques Barzun, *Darwin, Marx, Wagner: Critique of a Heritage* (1941; rev. rpt. Garden City, N.Y.: Doubleday Anchor Books, 1958), p. 297; Peter Viereck, *Metapolitics: The Roots of the Nazi Mind* (1941; rev. rpt. New York: Capricorn Books, 1965), pp. xvii-xx.

[40] Compare Walter Benjamin's suggestive remark on the situation in the 1930s: "The logical result of Fascism is the introduction of aesthetics into political life." Walter Benjamin, "The Work of Art in the Age of Mechanical Reproduction," *Illuminations*, edited with an introduction by Hannah Arendt and translated by Harry Zohn (New York: Schocken Books, 1968), p. 241.

[41] Malraux's term is "désaggregation," which was the word chosen by Henri Albert in his translation of *The Case of Wagner* when he had to render Nietzsche's German word "Disgregation" in the phrase "disgregation of the will." The same word also appears, somewhat less prominently, in the closing sentences of *Twilight of the Idols*, "The Four Great Errors," aph. 2. Compare Frédéric Nietzsche, *Le Crépuscle des Idoles. Le Cas Wagner. Nietzsche contra Wagner. L'Antéchrist*, translated by Henri Albert (7th ed.; Paris: Mercure de France, 1908), pp. 32, 146.

[42] See Mann, *Betrachtungen eines Unpolitischen, Gesammelte Werke*, vol. XII, pp. 79, 538-541; and "Lebensabriss" ("A Sketch of My Life"), *Gesammelte Werke*, vol XI, pp. 109-110.

[43] André Gide, "Entry on 21 June 1930," *Journal: 1889-1939* (Paris: Bibliothèque de la Pléiade, 1951), p. 990.

[44] For the parallel situation in Yeats, see Thomas R. Whitaker, *Swan and Shadow: Yeats's Dialogue with History* (Chapel Hill, N.C.: University of

North Carolina Press, 1964). Whitaker concludes by quoting from one of Yeats's late letters: "I begin to see things double—doubled in history, world history, personal history" (p. 298).

[45] Stephen Donadio's recent book on the artistic will in Nietzsche and Henry James became available too late for me to take it into account in what follows. But his argument neatly complements the approach I have taken: he is concerned with an American writer who was almost exactly Nietzsche's contemporary but had no direct contact with his writings, whereas I deal with European writers a generation or two younger who were powerfully affected by his work at crucial points in their developing careers. Donadio is therefore concerned with parallel routes through the later nineteenth century, at the threshold of modernism; my interests lie in the actual flowering of Nietzsche's impact in modernist works in the first half of the twentieth century. It seems to me, however, that the focus on James somewhat obscures the naturalistic strain in Nietzsche's thinking about art. Also, Donadio is chiefly concerned with "aesthetic and general philosophical assumptions" (p. 47) rather than with literary enactment. See Stephen Donadio, *Nietzsche, Henry James, and the Artistic Will* (New York: Oxford University Press, 1978).

[46] Mann identifies the three passages while commenting on Nietzsche's account in *Ecce Homo* of the inspired state in which he wrote *Thus Spoke Zarathustra*: "The page is a stylistic masterpiece, linguistically a real tour-de-force, perhaps only to be compared with the wonderful analysis of the prelude to *The Meistersingers* in *Beyond Good and Evil* and to the Dionysian portrayal of the cosmos at the end of *The Will to Power*." See Mann, "Nietzsche's Philosophy in the Light of Our Experience," *Gesammelte Werke*, vol. IX, pp. 681-682.

[47] *Ibid.* Mann goes on to quote part of the passage that I analyze; but he emphasizes primitivism rather than naturalism, and irrationality instead of involuntary creativity: "he cannot help feeling [this mood of inspiration] as something atavistic, as a demonic reversion, belonging to other, 'stronger' conditions of humanity that were nearer the godly, and omitted from the psychic possibilities of our weakly rationalist age" (p. 682).

[48] This phrase derives from Henri Albert's translation of a passage in the first of the two aphorisms on the artist's psychology, where Nietzsche describes idealization in art as "ein ungeheures *Heraustreiben* der Hauptzüge." Albert renders the phrase as "une *formidable* érosion des traits principaux," which Gide's Édouard changes to "formidable érosion des contours." See Nietzsche, *Le Crépuscle des Idoles*, etc., transl. Henri Albert, p. 179; and André Gide, *Les Faux-Monnayeurs* in *Romans*, introduction by Maurice Nadeau with editorial apparatus by Yvonne Davet and Jean-Jacques Thierry (Paris: Bibliothèque de la Pléiade, 1958), p. 1080.

[49] Compare Nietzsche's parenthetical comment on nobility in a note from *The Will to Power*, where he makes his attitude toward the aristocracy clear:

"I am not speaking here of the little word 'von' or of the Almanach de Gotha: an aside to asses" (aph. 942).

[50] In the aphorism just before this one, Nietzsche had criticized Rousseau for popularizing this regressive naturalism, a *"Zurückgehn"* in contrast to the self-heightening of a *"Hinaufkommen."*

[51] The image of the tree thus has the same double potential, both emblematic and broadly suggestive, as Zarathustra's animals. See the discussion in Chapter I of Lawrence's and Heidegger's contrasting responses to eagle and snake.

[52] Nietzsche's phrase is *"will hinauf"* or "wants upward." The choice of verb points to the will to power, while the prepositional construction anticipates the emphasis on *"hinauf"* in the celebration of Goethe's relation to nature several years later.

[53] This appeal to the image of the tree has lent an unexpected concreteness to a common philosophical term. *"Grundform"* or "basic form" also suggests, literally, the ground.

[54] In *Le Côté de Guermantes* the narrator remembers his surprise at the sudden arrival of his friend Saint-Loup from Morocco, and then offers some reflections on friendship: "I find it hard to understand how men of some genius—for example, a Nietzsche—might be naive enough to ascribe to it a certain intellectual value. . . ." Marcel Proust, *Le Côté de Guermantes* in *À la Recherche du Temps Perdu*, edited by Pierre Clarac and André Ferré (Paris: Bibliothèque de la Pléiade, 1954), vol. II, p. 394.

[55] Compare Anke Bennholdt-Thomsen, *Nietzsches* Also Sprach Zarathustra *als literarisches Phänomen* (Frankfurt am Main: Athenäum Verlag, 1974), p. 112, n. 12.

[56] Yeats, *A Vision*, p. 128.

[57] See especially Karl Löwith, *Nietzsches Philosophie der Ewigen Wiederkunft des Gleichen* (1935; rev. ed. Stuttgart: Kohlhammer, 1956); Pierre Klossowski, *Nietzsche et le cercle vicieux* (Paris: Mercure de France, 1969); and Joan Stambaugh, *Nietzsche's Thought of Eternal Return* (Baltimore and London: Johns Hopkins Press, 1972).

[58] Thus Mann comments: "Dostoevsky, through the mouth of the devil, calls 'the most indecent boredom' what Nietzsche blesses with Dionysian affirmation . . . . I am inclined to hold 'eternal recurrence' for a fruit of his reading, an unconscious memory of Dostoevsky that has been given a euphoric coloring." Or Lawrence: "Nietzsche talks about the *Ewige Wiederkehr*. It is like Botticelli singing cycles. But each cycle is different. There is no real recurrence." Or, finally, Gide: "Nothing could be more gratuitous, more vain than such an hypothesis. It adds nothing to Nietzsche's system, and I can only take the kind of enthusiasm he felt for it as a sign of his approaching insanity." Mann, "Dostoevsky—With Measure" in *Gesammelte Werke*, vol. IX, p. 665; Lawrence, "Study of Thomas Hardy" in *Phoenix*, p. 461; Gide, *Journal: 1889-1939*, p. 1051.

[59] "To Peter Gast," 30 October 1888, Letter 258, *Nietzsche: Werke*, ed. Schlechta, vol. III, p. 1327.

CHAPTER III

[1] Yeats, *Autobiography*, p. 234. This anecdote does not appear in the first draft of the autobiography, which was written between late 1915 and early 1917. This draft has recently been published in William Butler Yeats, *Memoirs*, transcribed and edited by Denis Donoghue (New York: Macmillan, 1972).

[2] For the comments on Huxley and Tyndall, see *Autobiography*, pp. 77, 83, and so on; on Woodrow Wilson, *ibid.*, p. 194; on Shaw, *ibid.*, p. 195.

[3] *Ibid.*, p. 234.

[4] See Kenneth Burke, "Thomas Mann and André Gide," *The Idea of the Modern in Literature and the Arts*, edited with an Introduction and Commentary by Irving Howe (New York: Horizon Press, 1967), pp. 257-268 and especially p. 268; and Albert J. Guerard, *André Gide* (1951; rpt, New York: E. P. Dutton, 1963), especially pp. 113-117.

[5] On Nietzsche's role in *Death in Venice*, see especially Erich Heller, *The Ironic German: A Study of Thomas Mann* (Boston and Toronto: Little, Brown and Co., 1958), pp. 98-115; R. A. Nicholls, *Nietzsche in the Early Work of Thomas Mann* (Berkeley and Los Angeles: University of California Press, 1955), pp. 77-91; and Hans W. Nicklas, *Thomas Manns Novelle* Der Tod in Venedig: *Analyse des Motivzusammenhangs und der Erzählstruktur* (Marburg: N. G. Elwert, 1968), which is useful chiefly for its summary of German scholarship on *Death in Venice*. More ambitious in their discussions of the general significance of Nietzsche's philosophy for Mann's attitudes as a writer of fiction are Herbert Lehnert, *Thomas Mann-Fiktion, Mythos, Religion* (Stuttgart: Kohlhammer, 1965), especially pp. 25-35 on "the dynamic metaphysic"; and Heinz Peter Pütz, *Kunst und Künstlerexistenz bei Nietzsche und Thomas Mann: Zum Problem des Ästhetischen Perspektivismus in der Moderne* (Bonn: H. Bouvier, 1963). However, neither Lehnert nor Pütz brings these general insights to bear on a detailed reading of *Death in Venice*. On *The Immoralist*, see especially Renée Lang, *André Gide et la pensée allemande* (Paris: Egloff, 1949), pp. 81-120, 177-185. For a broader perspective that takes up the problem of Nietzsche's influence on Gide's theories of art and fiction without, however, attempting a detailed reading of *The Immoralist*, see W. Wolfgang Holdheim, *Theory and Practice of the Novel: A Study on André Gide* (Geneva: Librairie Droz, 1968) and especially pp. 45-51 and 58-65.

[6] Jean-Paul Sartre, *Search for a Method*, translated with an Introduction by Hazel E. Barnes (New York: Vintage Books, 1963), pp. 85-166 and especially the comments on studying Flaubert's *Madame Bovary* in the context of nineteenth-century French history, pp. 140-150.

[7] Mann's first great success was *Buddenbrooks*, which appeared in 1901, when Gide had already written most of *The Immoralist*. But even if Gide

could have learned about Mann by hearsay during the prewar period, there is no indication in his journal that he read anything by Mann until 28 October 1929. Mann's first encounter with Gide occurred in the early 1920s and will be discussed below. By that time Gide had become a dominant figure on the French literary scene; but before the war he had been neglected, making it difficult for Mann to have heard of him before he did. *The Immoralist*, in particular, originally appeared in an edition of only three hundred copies, and was not reprinted until 1917. On this last point, see the comments by Jean-Jacques Thierry in *Romans* (Pléiade edition), pp. 1512, 1536.

[8] Gide, *Journal: 1889-1939*, pp. 858-859.

[9] See especially Lang, *Gide et la pensée allemande*; and Holdheim, "The Young Gide's Reaction to Nietzsche."

[10] "Letter to André Gide," 21 January 1922, *Letters of Thomas Mann: 1889-1955*, selected and translated by Richard and Clara Winston (1970; abridged edition, New York: Vintage Books, 1975), p. 104. Mann's citation from Gide should be compared with Gide, *Prétextes*, p. 87.

[11] Nietzsche uses the term "immoralist" elsewhere in his late works, but in *Ecce Homo* he repeatedly calls attention to himself as "the first *immoralist*" ("The Untimely Ones," aph. 2; "Human, All-Too-Human," aph. 6; "Why I Am a Destiny," aph. 2). Eventually he emphasizes that "I have chosen the word *immoralist* as a symbol and badge of honor for myself" ("Why I Am a Destiny," aph. 6). He speaks of his scholarly career as something "into which I had got myself originally in ignorance and *youth* and in which I got stuck later on from inertia and so-called 'sense of duty' " ("Human, All-Too-Human," aph. 4). Of his illnesses he remarks: "This, in fact, is how that long period of sickness appears to me *now*: as it were, I discovered life anew, including myself" ("Why I Am So Wise," aph. 2). On the unconscious development of the true self, he says: "So many dangers that the instinct comes too soon to 'understand itself'—Meanwhile the organizing 'idea' that is destined to rule keeps growing deep down—it begins to command" ("Why I Am So Clever," aph. 9).

[12] Gide, *Journal: 1889-1939*, p. 1049.

[13] For these motifs, see *The Immoralist*, pp. 390, 392, 395, 407, and 405, respectively.

[14] Compare "he had grown up alone, without comrades" (V, 451) and "He had never had a son" (V, 456) with some details in his early response to Tadzio: "He was obviously in demand, sought after, admired" (V, 477) and "he was stirred by a paternal affection" (V, 479).

[15] See, for example, the opening sentences of the fourth chapter of *Death in Venice*, or the description of the sunrise (V, 495), or the evocation of the conflicting loves of Apollo and Zephyr for Hyacinth (V, 496).

[16] For "creative intercourse," see *Death in Venice*, p. 493; for "Rausch," see *Death in Venice*, pp. 490, 494 (twice).

[17] Lionel Trilling's influential account of the relation between *The Birth of*

Tragedy and *Death in Venice*, which has probably been taken more dogmatically than its author intended, overlooks this point, and in general neglects Mann's selectiveness in rendering Nietzsche's concept of the Dionysian. Trilling's reading of the story stresses the "witches' brew" aspect that emerges in Aschenbach's dream, though it is only a polar nullity and not the most striking passage in the third, declining phase of the action, and then makes it a key to understanding Nietzsche "on the orgiastic display of lust and cruelty." The result is an overly primitivistic view of the Dionysian, a view that fails to acknowledge the role of self-transformation among instinctual energies. Trilling has a much more acute grasp of the nuances in Nietzsche's historical thinking. See Lionel Trilling, "On the Teaching of Modern Literature" in *Beyond Culture: Essays on Literature and Learning* (New York: Viking, 1968), pp. 18-19, 21-23, and my remarks on his essay "The Sense of the Past" in Chapter VI. For a discussion of the American cultural situation in the sixties to which Trilling was responding, and for an account of how Nietzsche was absorbed into it, see Max L. Baeumer, "Das moderne Phänomen des Dionysischen und seine 'Entdeckung' durch Nietzsche," *Nietzsche-Studien* 6 (1977), pp. 123-153.

[18] Northrop Frye, *Anatomy of Criticism: Four Essays* (Princeton, N.J.: Princeton University Press, 1957), pp. 163-166.

[19] André Gide, *Si le Grain ne meurt . . .* in *Journal 1939-1949; Souvenirs* (Paris: Bibliothèque de la Pléiade, 1954), p. 607.

[20] Thus the young Malraux, in a review of Gide, complained gently that "you hide from us the death of Michel." See André Malraux, "Ménalque," p. 19.

[21] On Mann's use of Rohde in *Death in Venice*, see Lehnert, *Mann-Fiktion, Mythos, Religion*, p. 115.

[22] This interest seems to have been strongest around the turn of the century, when it formed a significant strand in Mann's suspicion of the artist. See, for example, "Letter to Heinrich Mann," 25 November 1900, *Mann's Letters: 1889-1955*, p. 16: "My Tolstoyism already predisposes me to feel that rhyme and rhythm are wicked."

CHAPTER IV

[1] For these episodes in Lawrence's growing interest in Nietzsche, see Chap. I, n. 14; D. H. Lawrence, *The Trespasser* (1912; rpt. London: Heinemann, 1955), pp. 25-26; and "Georgian Poetry: 1911-1912," *Phoenix*, p. 304.

[2] Compare above, Chap. II, sec. 4, "The Instinct of Life"; sec. 1, "Apollo and Dionysus"; and sec. 4, "The Will to Power and Aesthetic Naturalism."

[3] Lawrence, "The Crown" in *Reflections on the Death of a Porcupine*, p. 11.

[4] *Ibid.*, p. 88. Lawrence admits having made some revisions in the essays in "The Crown" in 1925, when they were first all published in *Reflections on the Death of a Porcupine* (see *Reflections*, p. ii). But this particular statement

dovetails so closely with *Twilight in Italy* (1916) that we can safely date it from the time of his association with Russell in 1915. For an account of Lawrence's use of the myth of Pan, both as it converges with his use of Dionysus and as it compares with Pan in the work of his contemporaries, see Patricia Merivale, *Pan the Goat-God: His Myth in Modern Times* (Cambridge, Mass.: Harvard University Press, 1969), and esp. pp. 194, 197, 220, 222, 227.

[5] Lawrence, *Twilight in Italy*, with an introduction by Richard Aldington (1916; rpt. London: William Heinemann, 1956), p. 73.

[6] *Ibid.*, p. 136. This allusion to Nietzsche's procreative Dionysus shows Lawrence's close knowledge of the second coda to *Twilight of the Idols* which is located, of course, just a few pages after Nietzsche's admiring comments on Goethe.

[7] Richard Aldington, *Portrait of a Genius But . . .* (1950; rpt. New York: Collier, 1961), p. 160.

[8] Lawrence, *Twilight in Italy*, p. 98.

[9] Thus, in "To Waldo Frank," 27 July 1917, *Collected Letters*, p. 519, Lawrence refers to *The Rainbow* as "a kind of working up to the dark sensual or Dionysic or Aphrodisic ecstasy."

[10] For the passage from the rejected first chapter, see Lawrence, *Phoenix II: Uncollected, Unpublished, and Other Prose Works by D. H. Lawrence*, edited by Warren Roberts and Harry T. Moore (New York: Viking, 1970), p. 94. For the judgments in the final version, which will be discussed in greater detail below, see *Women in Love*, pp. 64, 170, and 286.

[11] A recent and especially clear example of the tendency to view *Women in Love* as a culmination is Stephen J. Miko, *Toward Women in Love: The Emergence of a Lawrentian Aesthetic* (New Haven and London: Yale University Press, 1971). But this attitude has marked Lawrence criticism since F. R. Leavis's *D. H. Lawrence: Novelist* (1955; rpt. New York: Knopf, 1956) and may be found in books with such varied approaches as Eliseo Vivas, *D. H. Lawrence: Failure and Triumph of Art* (Evanston, Ill.: Northwestern University Press, 1960); Julian Moynahan, *The Deed of Life: The Novels and Tales of D. H. Lawrence* (Princeton, N.J.: Princeton University Press, 1963); and George H. Ford, *Double Measure: A Study of the Novels and Stories of D. H. Lawrence* (1965; rpt. New York: Norton, 1969).

There have been a number of book-length studies of Lawrence's North American years in themselves, but only Graham Hough—it seems to me— has succeeded in placing the early twenties within the sweep of his career as a whole, in *The Dark Sun: A Study of D. H. Lawrence* (New York: Capricorn Books, 1956). In prefaces to *The Plumed Serpent* and *The Later D. H. Lawrence* (New York: Knopf, 1952) that he wrote in the early 50s, William York Tindall also sketched in some broad continuities, and implied that *The Plumed Serpent*, "one of the great creations of our time," was superior to *Women in Love*, which he apparently felt was "a confusion of incompatibles." David Cavitch, in *D. H. Lawrence and the New World* (New York:

Oxford University Press, 1969), also argues for continuity but focuses on psychological questions rather than on Lawrence's artistic and intellectual development. Though Frank Kermode follows the customary division-lines in *D. H. Lawrence* (New York: Viking-Modern Masters, 1973), his interest in how Lawrence's "metaphysic" interacts with this fiction fixes on a crucial issue in the period from *Women in Love* to *The Plumed Serpent*.

There have been few studies of Lawrence and Nietzsche that go beyond compilations of the more obvious opinions and allusions. Even John Humma's lively "D. H. Lawrence as Friedrich Nietzsche" (*Philological Quarterly*, 53, [1974], pp. 110-120) concludes by discussing in greatest detail "The Border Line," a story he admits is "not a work . . . upon which Lawrence's *artistic* reputation will stand or fall." Eugene Goodheart's *The Utopian Vision of D. H. Lawrence* (Chicago: University of Chicago Press, 1963) comments perceptively on *The Birth of Tragedy* but not on the later Nietzsche. The works of fiction analyzed most carefully are *The Rainbow*, "The Fox," and "The Man Who Died," works which come before, alongside, or after Lawrence's most direct and intense confrontation with Nietzsche in the sequence of novels I shall be discussing.

12 Mark Kinkead-Weekes, "The Marble and the Statue," *Twentieth Century Interpretations of The Rainbow* (Englewood Cliffs, N.J.: Prentice-Hall, 1971), pp. 96-120 and especially pp. 97, 100.

13 Jean-Pierre Richard, *L'Univers imaginaire de Mallarmé* (Paris: Editions du Seuil, 1961).

14 *Women in Love*, pp. 127, 273, and 190, respectively.

15 The most striking of these lectures occur on pages 195-196, 439, and 487-488.

16 Lawrence, *Phoenix II*, p. 105. Compare Scott Sanders, *D. H. Lawrence: The World of the Five Major Novels* (New York: Viking, 1974), p. 126; see also Kinkead-Weekes, "Marble and Statue," p. 104.

17 Joseph Frank, "Spatial Form in Modern Literature," *The Widening Gyre: Crisis and Mastery in Modern Literature* (Bloomington, Ind. and London: Indiana University Press, 1968), pp. 3-60.

18 Nietzsche, *Thus Spoke Zarathustra*, "On the Gift-Giving Virtue," sec. 3; compare *Ecce Homo*, "Preface," sec. 4.

19 Lawrence, *Women in Love*, p. 281; compare pp. 227-228.

20 Lawrence, *Twilight in Italy*, p. 136.

21 This comment is quoted by Mark Schorer in *D. H. Lawrence* (New York: Dell, 1968), p. 10.

22 F. R. Leavis, *D. H. Lawrence: Novelist* (New York: Knopf, 1956), pp. 14-17.

23 Lawrence, *Sons and Lovers* (1913; rpt. New York: Viking, 1968), p. 407.

24 Lawrence, "The Risen Lord" from *Assorted Articles, Phoenix II*, p. 571.

25 Lawrence, "The Novel" in *Reflections on the Death of a Porcupine*, pp. 104, 111.

26 Lawrence, *Women in Love*, p. 354. Lawrence comments on this image

from *Thus Spoke Zarathustra* in a letter dated 19 February 1916 to S. S. Koteliansky: "I understand Nietzsche's child. But it isn't a child that will represent the third stage: not innocent unconsciousness: but the maximum of fearless adult unconsciousness, that has the courage to submit even to the unconsciousness of itself." It would seem that by the time he wrote the passage in *Women in Love* he had begun to retract this initial hostile reaction. See *The Quest for Rananim: D. H. Lawrence's Letters to S. S. Koteliansky, 1914 to 1930,* edited with an Introduction by George J. Zytaruk (Montreal and London: McGill-Queen's University Press, 1970), p. 70.

[27] This story is told in *The Rainbow*, chaps. 11 and 15-16.

[28] Perhaps the most extreme example of this approach would be Jeffrey Meyers, "D. H. Lawrence and Homosexuality," *D. H. Lawrence: Novelist, Poet, Prophet*, edited by Stephen Spender (New York: Harper & Row, 1973), pp. 135-146.

[29] Lawrence himself would later insist that he fell ill "the very day" that he finished the book (*Collected Letters*, p. 833). The nature and extent of his later revisions in June and October 1925 remain obscure pending L. D. Clark's critical edition of *The Plumed Serpent*. For an account of the difficulties, see L. D. Clark, "The Making of a Novel: The Search for the Definitive Text of D. H. Lawrence's *The Plumed Serpent*" in *Voices from the Southwest: A Gathering in Honor of Lawrence Clark Powell*, gathered by Donald C. Dickinson, W. David Laird, and Margaret F. Maxwell (Flagstaff, Az.: Northland Press, 1976), and especially pp. 124-127.

[30] Lawrence, *The Lost Girl* (1920; rpt. London: Heinemann, 1955), p. 124. It will be noticed that Lawrence is using the plumed serpent symbol well before his trip to Mexico, and that he has already given it considerable intellectual significance.

[31] For Mailer's comment, see Norman Mailer, *The Prisoner of Sex* (Boston and Toronto: Little, Brown and Co., 1971), p. 139; for Eliot's, see "London Letter, *Dial* 1922," *D. H. Lawrence: A Critical Anthology*, edited by H. Coombes (Harmondsworth, Eng. and Baltimore: Penguin, 1973), p. 147.

[32] See, for example, *Psychoanalysis and the Unconscious*, p. 44.

[33] See "To Peter Gast," 14 August 1881, Letter 146; and "To Peter Gast," 19 February 1883, Letter 173 in *Nietzsche: Werke*, ed. Schlechta, vol. III, pp. 1173, 1201. Eric Bentley first pointed out the Nietzschean element in the Mexican emblems in *The Plumed Serpent* in *A Century of Hero-Worship: A Study of the Idea of Heroism in Carlyle and Nietzsche, with Notes on Wagner, Spengler, Stefan George, and D. H. Lawrence* (1944; 2nd ed., Boston: Beacon Press, 1957), p. 223.

[34] Lawrence, "The Novel" in *Reflections on the Death of a Porcupine*, p. 118.

[35] E. M. Forster, *A Passage to India* (1924; rpt. London: Edward Arnold, 1978), p. 312. For a general account of the relations between Forster and Lawrence from Forster's perspective see Wilfred Stone, *The Cave and the Mountain: A Study of E. M. Forster* (Stanford, Cal.: Stanford University

Press, 1966), pp. 378-387. The character of Kurtz named earlier in this paragraph is, of course, from Conrad's *Heart of Darkness*.

[36] This description broadly echoes the conclusion to pt. I of *Thus Spoke Zarathustra*, where Zarathustra's disciples present him with a staff on whose handle is found a snake coiled around a golden sun. See "On the Gift-Giving Virtue," sec. 1.

[37] Simone de Beauvoir, *The Second Sex*, translated by H. M. Parshley (1952; rpt. New York: Bantam, 1961), pp. 208-209.

[38] Lawrence, *Kangaroo*, chaps. 9 and 12.

[39] Lawrence, *The Plumed Serpent*, pp. 42, 61, and 162 respectively.

[40] Leavis, *D. H. Lawrence*, p. 26.

[41] See Lawrence, "The Princess," *Complete Short Stories*, vol. II, pp. 511-512; and *Saint Mawr* and *The Man Who Died* (1925, 1928; rpt. New York: Vintage Books, n.d.), pp. 106-109, for the first two examples. For the second two, see "The Woman Who Rode Away," *Complete Short Stories*, vol. II, pp. 578-581; and *Saint Mawr*, pp. 154-159.

[42] Lawrence, *Saint Mawr*, pp. 69-70.

[43] Edgar Jaffe, husband of Frieda's sister Else (the woman to whom Lawrence dedicated *The Rainbow*), had been minister of finance in the *Räterepublik* for a few months in 1918-1919. Lawrence was in Italy from November 1919 to February 1922, except for short trips to Malta, Germany, and Austria; Italian socialist activity peaked with the occupation of the factories in September 1920, while Mussolini's march on Rome took place in October 1922. Lawrence first visited Mexico in April 1923 during the Obregón presidency which sought to consolidate the Mexican revolution which had begun in 1910. In February 1924 he made a brief visit to Germany, or shortly after Hitler's attempted *Putsch* in November 1923.

[44] For these references, see *The Plumed Serpent*, pp. 55-58, 339, and 112.

[45] Graham Hough, *The Dark Sun*, p. 157.

[46] *The Plumed Serpent*, p. 333. For other references, see pp. 339 and 271.

[47] Lawrence, *Saint Mawr*, p. 80.

[48] For the very different role that World War I played in the formation of Mussolini's attitudes, see Nolte, *Three Faces of Fascism*, p. 308.

[49] Lawrence, *Studies in Classic American Literature* (1923; rpt. New York: Viking, 1964), p. 51.

Chapter V

[1] Quoted by Joseph Hoffmann, *L'Humanisme de Malraux* (Paris: C. Klincksieck, 1963), pp. 21-22.

[2] Jean Lacouture, *André Malraux*, translated by Alan Sheridan (London: André Deutsch, 1975), p. 31.

[3] Clara Malraux, *Memoirs*, translated by Patrick O'Brian (New York: Farrar, Straus & Giroux, 1967), p. 159.

[4] Malraux, "Ménalque," p. 19.

[5] *Ibid.*, p. 21.

[6] Malraux, "Aspects d'André Gide," *Action*, mars-avril 1922, p. 20.

[7] Malraux, "Ménalque," p. 19.

[8] *Ibid.*, p. 20. It will be recalled from the discussion of *The Immoralist* in Chapter III that this "pirate's face" was recognizably Nietzsche's. Here, in germ, is Malraux's early—and reductive—response to themes of conquest and aggrandizement in the philosopher.

[9] Lacouture, *Malraux*, p. 301.

[10] See above, Chap. III. See also the discussion of Gide's influence as an interpreter of Nietzsche in the 1920s in Hina, *Nietzsche und Marx bei Malraux*, pp. 66–67.

[11] As we saw in Chap. II, n. 41, this term derives from Nietzsche's analysis of crisis and nihilism. Malraux uses it several times in his early writings as we shall see later in analyzing *The Temptation of the West*.

[12] This was the authoritative judgment of F. E. Dorenlot when she surveyed Malraux's whole intellectual development. "Up to now," she remarks, "every new book by Malraux took up the questions asked by the preceding ones. In fact, *The Temptation of the West*, in 1926, contains the essence of this thought." In the special case of Malraux's response to Nietzsche, the same assertion holds, though his understanding of certain problems and his ability to portray them in his fiction grow, producing major changes of emphasis. We shall be considering *Temptation* shortly, but the essays discussed so far also date from this period. See F. E. Dorenlot, *Malraux ou l'unité de pensée* (Paris: Gallimard, 1970), p. 9.

[13] Geoffrey H. Hartman, *André Malraux* (New York: Hilary House, 1960), p. 42.

[14] Gaëton Picon, "Man's Hope," *Yale French Studies*—"Passion and the Intellect: or André Malraux," no. 18 (Winter, 1957), p. 5.

[15] Two recent studies of Malraux's general relationship to Nietzsche have briefly considered the problem of how it affected his developing career as a novelist. Neither writer gives proper emphasis to *Man's Fate*, but I do prefer the trajectory sketched by Nicholas Hewitt, who calls *Walnut Trees* "his most authentically Nietzschean novel," over the one offered by Denis Boak, at least as it applies to Malraux, when he states that "the two most Nietzschean French novels are *The Immoralist* and *The Royal Way*". See Nicholas Hewitt, "Malraux et Nietzsche: un rapport qu'il faut nuancer," *La Revue des Lettres Modernes* (1975[2]), p. 151; and Denis Boak, "Malraux et Gide," *La Revue des Lettres Modernes* (1975[2]), p. 31.

I have already mentioned Horst Hina's book-length study, *Nietzsche und Marx bei Malraux*, which usefully complements the approach I shall be taking in this chapter. Hina gives a detailed account of Malraux's early interest in Nietzsche, and includes a wealth of important biographical and intellectual historical information. His book is essential for an understanding of Malraux's development in the 1920s. But though he is aware of the problem of "fictional equivalents," and agrees that *Man's Fate* is the high point of Nietzsche's (as well as Marx's) influence on Malraux, his analyses of the novels seem rather thin, especially when he moves beyond paraphrasable ideas. He offers no extended treatment of *Walnut Trees* at all. In addition, he tends to focus on social thought (on which he is very perceptive) at the expense of the cultural and psychological issues which I shall argue are at the heart of Malraux's appropriation of Nietzsche.

[16] See above Chap. II, sec. 3, under "Myth, Theory, and the Artistic Socrates." Blossom Douthat has also pointed out this convergence with *The Birth of Tragedy* in "Nietzschean Motifs in *Temptation of the Occident*," *Yale French Studies*, no. 18, p. 84.

[17] For the polemic with Massis, see Walter G. Langlois, *André Malraux: The Indochina Adventure* (New York: Praeger, 1966), p. 218. For background on the divergences between Spengler and Nietzsche to which Malraux (and Mann too, as discussed in Chapter VI) was responding see M. Ferrari Zumbini, "Untergänge und Morgenröten: Über Spengler und Nietzsche," *Nietzsche-Studien*, 5 (1976), pp. 194-254.

[18] For these anecdotes, see *Man's Fate*, pp. 297-298, 341, and 399.

[19] See Cecil Jenkins's comments on the possible historical basis for this episode in *La Condition humaine*, edited with an Introduction by Cecil Jenkins (London: University of London Press, 1968), p. 328.

[20] Horst Hina also argues that Nietzsche guided Malraux's response to Marx's ideas, but reaches different conclusions. Hina is more interested in Malraux's general outlook than in his priorities as he works out fictional conceptions. Thus he states: "By virtue of Nietzsche's influence in criticizing ideology, Malraux was able to vindicate the historical potential of Marxism within the novel" (*Nietzsche und Marx bei Malraux*, p. 172). For Hina, Nietzsche provides Malraux with an approach to Marx rather than with an underlying set of concerns into which Marxism itself is fitted.

[21] When the son in Bely's novel falls into a trance in front of a bomb that a terrorist group has entrusted to him, he meets an "age-old Turanian" and outlines a scheme of shifting cultural epochs in which Europe turns Asiatic. But his visitor corrects him, suggesting that the transformation has already taken place: " 'Not the destruction of Europe but its immutability. . . . / 'The Mongol cause. . . .' " A little later, the son has another vision in which the bomb destroys any sense of cultural form and his own identity as well: " 'What then is our chronology?' . . . 'The chronology, my dear boy, is— zero.' 'Oh! Oh! What then is "I am"?' 'A zero.' 'And zero?' 'A bomb.' " See Andrei Bely, *Petersburg*, translated, annotated, and introduced by Robert A. Maguire and John E. Malmstad (Bloomington, Ind. and London: Indiana University Press, 1978), pp. 166, 168. In an article several years earlier, Bely had linked the image of an exploding bomb and the idea of epochal cultural change with Nietzsche, saying "To stick dynamite under history itself in the name of absolute values not yet discovered by consciousness—that is the fearful conclusion of Nietzsche's lyricism and the drama of Ibsen." See

"Krizis soznanija i Genrik Ibsen," *Arabeski*, p. 174. Despite the emphasis on Ibsen in this comment, I would argue for the dominance of Nietzsche in Bely's imagination; after all *Ecce Homo*, "Why I Am a Destiny," aph. 1, begins with the statement "I am no man; I am dynamite."

[22] Lacouture, *André Malraux*, p. 438.

[23] Ferral's reflections should also be compared with Nietzsche's comment that "Hypocrisy has its place in the ages of strong belief," in *Twilight of the Idols*, "Skirmishes of an Untimely Man," aph. 18. Malraux will return to the subject of the Borgias in the preface to his next novel, *Le Temps du Mépris* (Paris: Gallimard, 1935), p. 11, where he argues that "concretely, 'the splendid wild beasts of the Renaissance' were always constrained to transform themselves into asses bearing religious relics, and the figure of Cesare Borgia loses its luster if one considers that the clearest part of his efficacy came from the prestige of the Church." Here Malraux has revised Nietzsche's own image so as to stress social factors over the assertiveness of the individual.

[24] Hina, *Nietzsche und Marx bei Malraux*, pp. 125-126. Malraux gave this speech on 9 June 1945, but the first Blum government was in power from June 1936 to June 1937.

[25] Malraux, *Les Voix du Silence* (Paris: Galérie de la Pléiade, 1951), p. 628.

[26] Malraux, "D. H. Lawrence et l'érotisme: À propos de 'l'Amant de Lady Chatterley,' " *La Nouvelle revue française*, janvier 1932, p. 136.

[27] *Ibid.*, p. 139.

[28] In a talk before the Modern Language Association, December 1974. He makes a similar claim in *Deceit, Desire and the Novel*, p. 186, n. 1, where he confronts Dostoevsky and Freud: "Dostoevsky's insight into the essence of desire is no less acute for being couched in a different language than the psychoanalyst's. Psychoanalysis is exclusively regressive, whereas the novel is both regressive and progressive."

[29] Thomas Jefferson Kline has drawn attention to this series of images, but doesn't carry his analysis beyond the erotic element to be found in them (actually in only one of them). See *André Malraux and the Metamorphosis of Death* (New York and London: Columbia University Press, 1973), p. 169, n. 2.

[30] See the convergence between the two concepts in *The Case of Wagner*, discussed in Chapter II, sec. 3, "Nihilism at the Door."

[31] In *The Birth of Tragedy* (sec. 19), Nietzsche had used the myth of Hercules and Omphale to sum up the character of the modern world; Malraux has developed the myth in a much different spirit.

[32] The scene itself appears on p. 344. Malraux stresses Ferral's feelings of revenge on pp. 339 and 341; his desire to defend himself comes out on p. 343. For a previous example of Valérie's malicious wit, see p. 267.

[33] *Thus Spoke Zarathustra*, pt. II, "On Self-Overcoming"; *Twilight of the Idols*, "Skirmishes of an Untimely Man," aph. 24. Compare also the discussions of the will to power and of tragic affirmation in Chapter II, above.

³⁴ See especially Hoffman, *L'Humanisme de Malraux*, p. 232; but compare also the tendency of W. M. Frohock's remarks, "The Power and the Glory," *Malraux: A Collection of Critical Essays*, edited by R.W.B. Lewis (Englewood Cliffs, N.J.: Prentice-Hall, 1964), pp. 39-40, 58.

³⁵ Cecil Jenkins, *La Condition humaine*, Introduction, pp. 17, 38.

³⁶ When compared with the success of *Man's Fate*, the reputation of *The Walnut Trees of the Altenburg* in English-speaking countries has been slight, largely because of Malraux's refusal to reprint the book. But it has figured prominently in two important studies of modern literature—Joseph Frank's *The Widening Gyre* and R.W.B. Lewis's *The Picaresque Saint: Representative Figures in Contemporary Fiction* (Philadelphia and New York: J. B. Lippincott, 1959). Lewis contends that *Walnut Trees* sums up the development of a whole generation of writers after Joyce, Eliot, and Proust. But I would hold that its Nietzschean inspiration makes it representative in another sense as well, so that it can be seen as a culmination of an alternative tendency within modernism that includes such figures as Gide, Yeats, and Lawrence who were active during the ascendancy of Lewis's first generation.

³⁷ Walter G. Langlois, "André Malraux, 1939-1942, d'après une correspondance inédite," *La Revue des Lettres Modernes* (1972), pp. 109, 115. Though there has never been an American translation of *Walnut Trees*, Langlois shows that an American editor, Robert Haas, had a major role in the novel's being written at all in the difficult conditions following France's defeat in 1940.

³⁸ *Walnut Trees*, p. 97. Compare Victor's comment on these remarks in the epilogue: "And from wasted day to wasted day I am increasingly obsessed by the mystery which does not oppose, as Walter stated, but which binds by a long-forgotten path the unformed part of my companions to the songs which hold up before the eternity of the night sky" (p. 250). Victor is asserting continuity over dichotomy.

³⁹ Malraux, *Antimémoires* (Paris: Gallimard, 1967), p. 15.

⁴⁰ Lucien Goldmann, *Pour une Sociologie du Roman* (n.p.: Gallimard-Collection Idées, 1964), pp. 255-256.

⁴¹ In reworking this description for his autobiography, Malraux omitted the last sentence, possibly because it was no longer needed for the gas attack later on. See *Antimémoires*, p. 36. Unfortunately, the revision also has the effect of flattening his presentation of life-psychology.

⁴² Another part of the uncle's commentary whose importance he fails to realize is his description of Nietzsche's appearance: "the photographs do not communicate the quality of his look: it was of a feminine sweetness, despite his mustaches of . . . a bogeyman" (A, 94). A fuller psychological awareness has seen through the mask of ruthless activism; this submerged discovery of the inadequacy of the "bogeyman" image should be compared with the "pirate's visage" that the young Malraux had admired in Gide's Ménalque.

⁴³ See his reactions to Thirard on p. 115, to Thirard on p. 118, and to Stieglitz on p. 122.

[44] Malraux, *Les Conquérants* in *Romans* (Paris: Bibliothèque de la Pléiade, 1964), pp. 139, 152.

[45] Joseph Frank, "André Malraux: The Image of Man," in *The Widening Gyre*, pp. 123 and 129, n. 8.

[46] I had these scenes in mind when, in analyzing Ferral in sec. 1, I spoke of Malraux's loss of confidence in the soldierly ideal. Berger learns that people who are capable of having an entire city shot with machine guns can indeed gain positions of command.

[47] For example Frank in *The Widening Gyre* speaks of "Berger's death by poison gas" (p. 123). But the son begins the next section by referring to the "rest of these 'encounters' of my father's" (A, 249), suggesting that his reminiscences will continue. And earlier he had given a vignette of his father as an older man: "When he became far-sighted, he had only to put on his glasses for his sharp harpooner's face to become that of an absent-minded wearied intellectual" (p. 49).

[48] *Walnut Trees*, pp. 221, 230, and 237.

[49] Malraux, *Antimémoires*, p. 18.

[50] The story makes up most of sec. 2 of the third part, which bears the title "The Temptation of the West."

CHAPTER VI

[1] Mann's wording is very difficult to render in English. In German, this passage runs as follows: "eben weil der euphorische Musiker an seine Stelle gesetzt ist, so daß es ihn nun nicht mehr geben darf." See Mann, *Gesammelte Werke*, vol. XI, p. 165.

[2] For a convenient summary of the facts, see Peter Pütz, "Thomas Mann und Nietzsche," in *Thomas Mann und die Tradition*, edited by Peter Pütz (Frankfurt am Main: Athenäum Verlag, 1971), pp. 225-227. See also Gunilla Bergsten, *Thomas Mann's Doctor Faustus: The Sources and Structure of the Novel*, translated by Krishna Winston (Chicago and London: University of Chicago Press, 1969), p. 59. Bergsten's book is an indispensable aid for students of *Doctor Faustus* since it draws together a great deal of the vast amount of research on the immediate sources for many details in the novel. However, the material she presents is susceptible to further interpretation, and she has little to say about what I shall be discussing shortly: the Nietzschean issues and assumptions that had become an ingrained part of Mann's intellectual and artistic life.

[3] Mann himself uses both of these terms, which have been discussed in detail by Herman Meyer, *Das Zitat in der Erzählkunst* (2nd ed. rev.; Stuttgart: Metzlersche Verlagsbuchhandlung, 1967); and by Bergsten in *Mann's Doctor Faustus*, especially pp. 10-14 and 99-114. An early example of this technique would be Mann's use of Rohde's book (see above, Chapter III) to fill out the details of Aschenbach's Dionysian dream.

⁴ Every English-speaking student of Thomas Mann must feel deeply indebted to Erich Heller. But this chapter proceeds along different lines from his well-known assertion about *Doctor Faustus*, that "There is no critical thought which the book does not think *about itself*" (*The Ironic German*, p. 277). Mann was not, and could not be expected to be, fully self-conscious about Nietzsche's impact on him.

Two German-language critics were especially helpful in orienting my thinking about Nietzsche's presence in *Doctor Faustus*. Herbert Lehnert's analysis of the emergence of a "dynamic metaphysic" that underlies Mann's "fictive structures" in his very earliest work encouraged me to expand this critical approach so as to include other deeply implanted preoccupations and later fiction. Peter Pütz has discussed *Doctor Faustus* itself in light of Mann's Nietzschean assumptions, and has shown how fruitful such an approach can be. But his study lacked an international frame of reference, and focused on the issue of artistic perspectivism and on a line of development coming out of *Tonio Kröger*. Pütz also lacked a sufficiently transformative conception of Mann's relation to Nietzsche, such as the one that Tynyanov shows between Dostoevsky and Gogol. It seemed to me that *Doctor Faustus* needed to be reconsidered on the basis of Nietzschean issues that roused a complex mixture of agreement and resistance in Mann, and with an emphasis on *Death in Venice* and other European writers. See Lehnert, "Die dynamische Metaphysik und die Ausbildung fiktiven Strukturen" in *Thomas Mann—Fiktion, Mythos, Religion*, pp. 9-98; and Heinz Peter Pütz, *Kunst und Künstlerexistenz bei Nietzsche und Thomas Mann*. For the fullest study of Mann's essay on Nietzsche, written during his work on *Doctor Faustus*, see Heftrich, "Nietzsche als Hamlet der Zeitenwende," in *Zauberbergmusik*, pp. 281-316.

⁵ Mann, *Betrachtungen eines Unpolitischen, Gesammelte Werke*, vol. XII, pp. 406-426. Compare Mann's phrases on p. 407—"Ich hörte Hans Pfitzners musikalische Legende 'Palestrina' dreimal bisher" and "es macht mich positiv, erlöst mich von der Polemik, und meinem Gefühl ist ein großer Gegenstand damit geboten, an den es sich dankbar schließen kann"—with these phrases from *The Case of Wagner*: "Ich hörte gestern—werden Sie es glauben—zum zwanzigsten Male *Bizets* Meisterstück," "Bizet macht mich fruchtbar. Alles Gute macht mich fruchtbar. Ich habe keine andre Dankbarkeit," and "Auch dies Werk erlöst; nicht Wagner allein ist ein 'Erlöser' " (CW, 1, 2).

⁶ Lionel Trilling, "The Sense of the Past," *The Liberal Imagination: Essays on Literature and Society* (1950; rpt. Garden City, N.Y.: Doubleday Anchor Books, 1953), p. 191.

⁷ In commenting on Zeitblom in *The Story of a Novel*, Mann stresses only one rather specialized aspect of this cultural role: "But, above all, the interposition of the narrator made it possible to tell the story on a dual plane of time, to weave together the events which shake the writer as he writes with those he is recounting" (pp. 164-165). Actually, the phenomenon of "dual planes" extends far beyond two levels of time.

[8] *Doktor Faustus*, p. 378. Elsewhere in the novel, Mann fails to develop this aspect of the Dionysian, as we shall see when we consider Leverkühn's isolation and coldness which is such an important theme until the last quarter of the novel. For some reason, the English translation has replaced the phrase I have quoted with "flashing eyes."

[9] In affirming human dignity by way of Apollo, Mann is apparently interpreting Nietzschean polarities in a very different spirit from Malraux, who is closer to the Dionysian when he speaks of dignity. But the word used by Zeitblom is "Menschenwürde"; often in Mann "Würde" has a strong element of self-esteem or sense of personal worth. It can therefore be derived from the Apollinian emphasis on aristocratic ranking and on the individual. But for Malraux, the value of dignity is closely connected with fraternal feelings, so that he stresses the rather different quality of awareness for the dignity of others. If we are to use the same English word in translating both writers, we should remember that in Mann it tends toward "dignified," and in Malraux toward "dignifying."

[10] *Doktor Faustus*, p. 132. Contrast this metaphor with the one Nietzsche uses in the "Chemistry of Concepts and Sensations," *Human, All-Too-Human*, discussed above in Chap. II, sec. 4, "The Will to Power and Aesthetic Naturalism." For a detailed analysis of Nietzsche's aphorism as a key to what I have called his aesthetic naturalism, see Peter Heller, "Chimie der Begriffe und Empfindungen," *Nietzsche-Studien* 1 (1972), pp. 210-233.

[11] Compare especially Chapter II, sec. 4, "Myths of Power."

[12] Compare Chap. II, sec. 3, "Nihilism at the Door," and sec. 4, "Myths of Power." Of course, Chapter 25 is also a reworking of the famous scene in *Brothers Karamazov* (bk. XI, chap. 9) where Ivan has an interview with the devil. Dostoevsky undoubtedly stands behind the thickening religious atmosphere of the novel and thus functions primarily as a counterweight to the Nietzschean impetus, even though Mann was concerned with drawing parallels between the two figures in the essay on Dostoevsky that he wrote while working on *Doctor Faustus*.

[13] *Doktor Faustus*, p. 317. Compare the descriptions of Spengler—"Blinking, a dimple in his cheek above the thick moustaches"—and of Clarissa—"proudly tilting her insufficient chin, with no hollow under the full lip"—on p. 271.

[14] For a fuller discussion of the passage from *Ecce Homo*, see Chap. II, sec. 4, "The Will to Power and Aesthetic Naturalism." For evidence that Mann paid close attention to this passage during the period that he wrote *Doctor Faustus*, see "Nietzsche's Philosophy in the Light of Our Experience," *Gesammelte Werke*, vol. IX, p. 682.

[15] Gunilla Bergsten has placed the passages in parallel in *Mann's Doctor Faustus*, pp. 61-62. But she does not interpret the structural significance of this "quotation" from Nietzsche, nor does she identify the allusion to *The Antichrist* discussed later in this paragraph. The allusions to *Ecce Homo* refer to the same description of artistic inspiration discussed in n. 14 above.

[16] *Doktor Faustus*, p. 242. Compare Chap. II, sec. 4, introductory.

[17] Bergsten, *Mann's Doctor Faustus*, pp. 135-163 and especially pp. 139-146.

[18] Yeats, *A Vision*, pp. 75, 89. He outlines his interpretation of cultural history on pp. 267-302.

[19] Theodor W. Adorno, "Zu einem Porträt Thomas Manns," *Die Neue Rundschau*, 1962 (vol. 73), p. 321. Though Adorno has images in a narrow sense in mind, I would like as usual to generalize image to mean fictional strategies in general.

[20] See especially *Betrachtungen eines Unpolitischen, Gesammelte Werke*, vol. XII, pp. 135-146.

[21] Carla Mann and Julia Mann-Löhr; see, for example, Mann, "A Sketch of My Life," *Gesammelte Werke*, vol. XI, pp. 119-122. For Zeitblom's tone of respect, see his comment on Clarissa's suicide, "so shattering to us all though at bottom we could hardly condemn it" (F, 504), and his confession of his feelings on learning that Inez had murdered Schwerdtfeger: "I felt definitely proud that in all her sunken state she found the strength, the furious energy to commit it" (F, 514).

[22] For Nietzsche's description of this cosmology, in a passage that Mann greatly admired, see Chapter II, sec. 4, introductory. Mann shows his appreciation for the full implications of this outlook in "Nietzsche's Philosophy," *Gesammelte Werke*, vol. IX, pp. 705-706.

[23] For a detailed analysis of the correspondence between Leverkühn's art and Mann's own, see Bergsten, *Mann's Doctor Faustus*, pp. 168-200.

[24] Mann, *The Magic Mountain* in *Gesammelte Werke*, vol. III, pp. 524 and 541 (for example).

[25] Herbert Lehnert touches on this complex of conflicting inclinations in *Thomas Mann—Fiktion, Mythos, Religion*, p. 203.

[26] I refer to Hans Egon Holthusen, *Die Welt ohne Transzendenz: eine Studie zu Thomas Manns* Dr. Faustus *und seinen Nebenschriften* (Hamburg: Ellerman, 1949), and to Erich Kahler, "Die Säkularisierung des Teufels: Thomas Manns Faust," *Die Neue Rundschau*, 1948 (vol. 59), pp. 185-202. Kahler's essay and excerpts from Holthusen are available in *Thomas Mann: A Collection of Critical Essays*, edited by Henry Hatfield (Englewood Cliffs, N.J.: Prentice-Hall, 1964), pp. 109-122 and 123-132.

[27] Yeats, "Among School Children," last stanza.

[28] See, for example, his comments in "Freud and the Future": "And is not the hero of this novel above all such a celebrant of life: Joseph himself, who with a charming sort of religious hocus-pocus enacts in his own person the Tammuz-Osiris myths . . . ? . . . This mystery becomes easy, playful, artistic, cheerful—yes, like the ruses of an illusionist or a con man—in Joseph." *Gesammelte Werke*, vol. IX, p. 498.

[29] Compare the icy coldness associated with the star-image in "On the Way of the Creator" and the doubts about love in "Night Song," as discussed in Chap. II, sec. 4, "Images of Power."

[30] Bergsten, *Mann's Doctor Faustus*, pp. 59-60.

Conclusion

[1] Vladimir Nabokov, *Strong Opinions* (New York: McGraw-Hill, 1973), pp. 10, 11.

[2] Thus my comments in Chap. II on the special version of the Apollinian in "The Statues" and on the limited validity of eternal recurrence as it is evoked in "Dialogue of Self and Soul." To these examples might be added the ambiguity of the tree and dance symbols in the last lines of "Among School Children": the turn of thought in the preceding stanza that prepares for this finale is so elliptical that it is difficult to tell whether Yeats intends an allusion to Nietzsche. Or, in "A Prayer for my Daughter," he endorses a more class-conscious version of nobility than is usual in Nietzsche.

A possible exception to this observation might be Yeats's interest in Nietzsche's presentation of formative moments in cultural history, an interest that becomes prominent at the time of *A Vision*. In Chap. II I suggested that this theme contributes to "Leda and the Swan" and "The Second Coming," while in Chap. VI I mentioned Yeats's concept of an "interchange of the tinctures." Further examples would be ambitious poems like "Meditations in Time of Civil War" and "Nineteen Hundred and Nineteen." Of course, Yeats's involvement with Nietzsche seems relatively minor or specialized only when it is compared to the responses of Lawrence, Malraux, and Mann.

[3] T. S. Eliot, *Selected Essays* (New York: Harcourt, Brace & World, 1950), p. 4.

[4] George Lichtheim, *Europe in the Twentieth Century* (New York: Praeger, 1972), p. 152.

[5] Carl E. Schorske, *Fin-de-Siècle Vienna* (New York: Knopf, 1980), and especially pp. xxi, xxii.

[6] Compare the place in English literature of the figures discussed by Thatcher in *Nietzsche in England* and by Bridgwater in *Nietzsche in Anglo-Saxony* with the standing in France and Germany of the writers and thinkers discussed by Bianquis in *Nietzsche en France*, Boudot in *Nietzsche et l'au-delà de la liberté*, or Heller in "The Importance of Nietzsche." Such prewar figures as George Moore, John Davidson, Havelock Ellis, and Arthur Symons simply do not hold up alongside Gide, Valéry, Malraux, Camus, and Bachelard or Rilke, Kafka, Mann, Musil, Heidegger, and Jaspers.

[7] Gide's extraordinary prestige in France during the 1920s has already been mentioned. Malraux became a leading voice of the thirties after winning the Prix Goncourt for *Man's Fate*, and later served as France's Minister of Culture. In England, F. R. Leavis has largely succeeded in transforming D. H. Lawrence into a major figure in the "great tradition" of the English novel. Mann is now established as a classic German author after having had his

books burned in public during the Hitler years; he has become the subject of a remarkable outpouring of dissertations, articles, and books.

[8] Jonathan Culler, *Structuralist Poetics: Structuralism, Linguistics, and the Study of Literature* (Ithaca, N.Y.: Cornell University Press, 1975), p. 247; and Paul de Man, "Rhetoric of Tropes," *Allegories of Reading,* p. 114.

[9] Harry Levin, *James Joyce: A Critical Introduction* (1941; revised and augmented, Norfolk, Ct.: New Directions, 1960), pp. 3-6, 17-20.

Index

AESTHETIC NATURALISM
(cont.)
procreation as the basis for
power and creativity, 124, 128,
141, 143, 356, and the references
to the procreative Dionysus in
"Dionysus and the Dionysian:
The Art Drive."
*The Artistic Self-Transformation
of Instinct*: 61, 62, 120, 120-121,
122, 123, 124, 127, 130, 132,
173, 177, 178, 179, 329, 330 n,
363, 382, 420-421, 436 n. 50; 447
n. 38; ambivalence on self-transformation—continuous art drives
or disembodied reason vs. raw
instinct, 49, 63, 64-66, 91 n, 97,
164, 167, 187, 188, 198, 202,
223, 237, 259, 262, 266, 275,
283, 291-292, 302, 313, 324, 347,
349, 351, 435 n. 47, 439 n. 17.
For narrower psychological
and moral issues associated with
Nietzsche's philosophic stance,
see "Psychologies of Creativity."
Aldington, Richard, 183.
Allison, David B., 429 n. 18.
Andersen, Hans Christian, 392.
APOLLO AND THE APOLLI-
NIAN, see Polarities.
Appropriation and Axes of Interpretation, 13, 147-148, 149, 155,
179, 206-207, 290, 293, 341, 344-
345, 367, 406; and Guillén on a
"textual function," 17, 149; as
related to Mann on "literary his-
torical interpretation," 152-153.
Aquinas, St. Thomas, 16, 26.
Archilochus, 46.
Aristophanes, 89.
Aristotle, 39, 63, 78.
Auerbach, Erich, 7-8.

Bach, Johann Sebastian, 379.
Bachelard, Gaston, 452 n. 6.

Baeumer, Max L., 439 n. 17.
Barrès, Maurice, 256.
Barthes, Roland, 420.
Barzun, Jacques, 105.
Baudelaire, Charles, 21, 103.
Beauvoir, Simone de, 239.
Beckett, Samuel, 429 n. 21.
Beethoven, Ludwig van, 55, 370;
the Ninth Symphony, 64, 359,
389, 399, 400.
Bely, Andrei, 13, 23-24, 26, 27,
29-30, 32, 33, 36, 37, 102, 412,
422, 429 n. 20, 433 n. 35; *Peters-
burg*, 24, 55-56, 266, 274, 445-
446 n. 21.
Benjamin, Walter, 434 n. 40.
Bennholdt-Thomsen, Anke, 436 n.
55.
Bentley, Eric, 442 n. 33.
Bergson, Henri, 419.
Bergsten, Gunilla, 370, 448 n. 2,
450 n. 15, 451 n. 23, 452 n. 30.
Bianquis, Geneviève, 427 n. 8, 452
n. 6.
Bizet, Georges, 449 n. 5; *Carmen*,
54, 103, 343.
Blake, William, 13, 44, 358.
Bloom, Harold, 17-18, 19, 21, 22,
34, 409.
Blum, Léon, 289, 446 n. 24.
Boak, Denis, 444 n. 15.
Bonaparte, Napoleon, 321.
Borgia Family, 112, 282, 369 n,
379, 446 n. 23.
Botticelli, Sandro, 436 n. 58.
Boudot, Pierre, 427 n. 8, 452 n. 6.
Bourget, Paul, 103, 434 n. 37.
Brennecke, D., 432 n. 15.
Brentano, Clemens, 358, 361.
Bridgwater, Patrick, 427 n. 8, 452
n. 6.
Brinton, Crane, 7, 430 n. 24.
Burke, Kenneth, 146.

Camus, Albert, 452 n. 6.

Library of Congress Cataloging in Publication Data

Foster, John Burt, 1945-
  Heirs to Dionysus.

  Includes bibliographical references and index.
    1. Literature, Modern—20th century—History and
criticism.   2. Modernism (Literature)   3. Nietzsche,
Friedrich Wilhelm, 1844-1900—Influence.   I. Title.
PN771.F59   809'.91   81-47127
ISBN 0-691-06480-6   AACR2